Information Technology and Law Series

Volume 39

The *Information Technology & Law Series* was an initiative of IT *e* R, the national programme for information Technology and Law, which was a research programme set up by the Dutch government and The Netherlands Organisation for Scientific Research (NWO) in The Hague. Since 1995 IT *e* R has published all of its research results in its own book series. In 2002 IT *e* R launched the present internationally orientated and English language *Information Technology & Law Series*. This well-established series deals with the implications of information technology for legal systems and institutions. Manuscripts and related correspondence can be sent to the Series' Editorial Office, which will also gladly provide more information concerning editorial standards and procedures.

Kostina Prifti · Esra Demir · Julia Krämer ·
Klaus Heine · Evert Stamhuis
Editors

Digital Governance

Confronting the Challenges Posed by Artificial Intelligence

ASSER PRESS

Springer

Editors
Kostina Prifti
Department of Law and Business
Erasmus School of Law
Rotterdam, The Netherlands

Esra Demir
Department of Law and Business
Erasmus School of Law
Rotterdam, The Netherlands

Julia Krämer
Department of Law and Business
Erasmus School of Law
Rotterdam, The Netherlands

Klaus Heine
Department of Law and Business
Erasmus School of Law
Rotterdam, The Netherlands

Evert Stamhuis
Department of Law and Business
Erasmus School of Law
Rotterdam, The Netherlands

ISSN 1570-2782 ISSN 2215-1966 (electronic)
Information Technology and Law Series
ISBN 978-94-6265-638-3 ISBN 978-94-6265-639-0 (eBook)
https://doi.org/10.1007/978-94-6265-639-0

This work was supported by Dutch Ministry of Education, Culture and Research, and Erasmus Graduate School.

Published by T.M.C. ASSER PRESS, The Hague, The Netherlands www.asserpress.nl
Produced and distributed for T.M.C. ASSER PRESS by Springer-Verlag Berlin Heidelberg

This T.M.C. ASSER PRESS imprint is published by the registered company Springer-Verlag GmbH, DE part of Springer Nature.
The registered company address is: Heidelberger Platz 3, 14197 Berlin, Germany

If disposing of this product, please recycle the paper.

Preface

In June 2023, Erasmus University Rotterdam played host to the inaugural conference on Law, AI, and Regulation (LAIR). 24 speakers from diverse institutions and disciplines tackled the challenges of regulating AI. Amidst the rich tapestry of discussions, a key insight emerged: the need for interconnected frameworks to navigate the complex landscape of AI regulation, a role which we believe the concept of 'Digital Governance' can discharge. It was this realisation that sparked the inspiration for this book.

Turning an idea into reality requires support, and we are indebted to many for their contribution along this journey. We extend our gratitude to the Sector plan for law '*Rebalancing of Public Interests in Private Relationships*' funded by the Dutch Ministry of Education, Culture and Research, the Jean Monet Centre of Excellence Digital Governance, and the Erasmus Graduate School of Law for their financial and organisational support.

We express our appreciation to all those who played a role in the planning and successful implementation of the LAIR conference. Namely, we are thankful to Koen Swinnen, Monika Glavina, Enrique Santamaria Echeverria, Shu Li, Alberto Quintavalla, Martien Schaub, Maria Campo Comba, Cheng Bian, Adrianus van Heusden, Michal Stambulski, Irem Akin, Anke van den Boomen, Daco Groeneveld, and Eva Jacobse. A special appreciation goes to Gillian Hadfield and Eduard Fosch-Villaronga for their keynote contributions.

We would also like to thank our reviewers. Their contribution is hidden under the quality of each book chapter. Finally, heartfelt gratitude extends to all the contributors of this edited book. Your passion and collaboration made our role as editors significantly easier and more pleasant.

Rotterdam, The Netherlands

Kostina Prifti
Esra Demir
Julia Krämer
Klaus Heine
Evert Stamhuis

Contents

Chapter 1
Governing the Digital: Artificial Intelligence, Disruption, and Governance

Esra Demir, Julia Krämer, Kostina Prifti, Klaus Heine, and Evert Stamhuis

Contents

Abstract The issues surrounding the governance of Artificial Intelligence (AI) have been discussed in numerous books, policy briefs, and papers. Some of the problems posed by AI are fundamentally new, others are simply new versions of existing challenges. What is certain is that AI is one of the most disruptive technologies in use today and that it brings opportunities and challenges in different areas and sectors. This book delves deeper into the framework of digital governance, in particular its regulatory patterns, to address the challenges posed by AI and explore ways for designing legal solutions. The chapter begins with information on AI as a disruptive technology, followed by information on digital governance as a framework for addressing the disruption posed by AI. After this background information, the chapter highlights the main theme of the book, including the novelty that this book brings

E. Demir (✉) · J. Krämer · K. Prifti · K. Heine · E. Stamhuis
Erasmus School of Law, Erasmus University Rotterdam, Burgemeester Oudlaan 50, 3062 PA Rotterdam, The Netherlands
e-mail: demir@law.eur.nl

J. Krämer
e-mail: j.k.kramer@law.eur.nl

K. Prifti
e-mail: prifti@law.eur.nl

K. Heine
e-mail: heine@law.eur.nl

E. Stamhuis
e-mail: stamhuis@law.eur.nl

K. Prifti et al. (eds.), *Digital Governance*, Information Technology and Law Series 39,
https://doi.org/10.1007/978-94-6265-639-0_1

to the literature, as well as the target audiences and readership. Finally, the chapter concludes with an overview of the chapters that this book contains.

Keywords Artificial Intelligence · Digital Technologies · Disruption · Governance · Innovation · Regulation

1.1 Artificial Intelligence as a Disruptive Technology

Throughout history, technology has presented both opportunities and challenges. In this respect, digital technologies make no exception: on the one hand, they are gaining importance in different areas and offer various opportunities; on the other hand, their applications harbour various risks.[1]

Among digital technologies, Artificial Intelligence (AI) has undergone rapid development in recent years and applications have emerged in various areas that have a significant impact on society.[2] There seems to be almost no area of human activity that is not potentially influenced by AI.[3] The applications of AI range across the automotive industry, defence, healthcare, energy management, banking, marketing, entertainment, education, justice, and public administration.[4] Although AI has a profound impact in society, there is no consensus on its definition and best practices.[5] In simple terms, AI refers to the development of machines that are capable of processing sophisticated (intelligent) information.[6] It can be understood as a generic term that encompasses sub-areas such as machine learning, deep learning, robotics, computer vision, neural networks, evolutionary computation, and natural language processing.[7]

The development, deployment, and use of AI technologies can serve many purposes and fulfil a multitude of desires. It introduces us to the next generation of data-driven practices that build on familiar processes of service delivery and value creation, but often also fundamentally innovate them. To name a few examples from different domains: the applications of AI technologies in healthcare can help to identify and reduce unnecessary costs, avoid or (at least) minimise diagnostic errors, analyse pathological findings, improve clinical decision support systems for medical diagnoses, and achieve the necessary (drug) discoveries in the treatment of diseases more effectively.[8] The application of AI technologies in the automotive sector can

---

[1] Gregorio and Dunn 2022, p. 473.

[2] Custers and Fosch-Villaronga, 2022, p. 10.

[3] Liu et al. 2020, p. 205.

[4] Girasa 2020, pp. 23–59.

[5] World Health Organization 2021, p.17.

[6] Dafoe 2018, p. 5.

[7] Girasa 2020, p. 13.

[8] Pesapane et al. 2018, p. 1; Oren et al. 2020, p. 486; Girasa 2020, pp. 24–28.

serve to minimise the risk of human error and reduce the number of road accidents, thus facilitating safer travel.[9] The application of AI technologies in the work environment can assist in increasing workplace and worker safety, especially in high-risk tasks, e.g. by developing software to increase information security and monitor high-risk behaviour to ensure consistent compliance with workplace safety regulations.[10] The application of AI technologies in eGovernment services can contribute to improve the processing of large amounts of data, create more efficient services and systems, reduce costs and realise economic savings, improve risk identification and monitoring, promote sustainability, and ensure accountability in decision-making systems.[11]

Not surprisingly, the numerous opportunities offered by AI technologies in various areas are also accompanied by various risks, as with any other technological development or invention.[12] The risks associated with AI technologies can arise during the development, deployment, and use of such technologies and can occur at the individual, group, or societal level.[13] These risks materialise as disadvantages, undesirable side effects, or unforeseen new applications.[14] For example, applications of AI technologies in healthcare can raise issues such as liability for misdiagnosis or treatment recommendations, limited clinical validity due to the inaccuracy of algorithms, and resistance to the adoption of such technologies due to the risk of inaccuracy and dependence on the technologies.[15] The application of AI technologies by public and private entities, especially government agencies, can lead to new tools for surveillance and control of individuals, as well as for strengthening authoritarian governments.[16] This could also raise fears that the datafication already taking place will become even more acute and irreversible through the use of AI, at a time when we are experiencing the loss of morality in public administration favoured by datafication. In addition, the applications of AI technologies can exacerbate existing privacy concerns in society, as AI relies on the processing of large amounts of personal data.[17] Additionally, AI applications may give rise to a number of issues pertaining to the interpretability of AI systems and the transparency of algorithmic decision-making (ADM). This is due to the opaque nature of ADMs, the potential for bias and therefore the risk of discrimination by ADMs, as well as the scepticism surrounding the decisions made by algorithms.[18]

[9] Kamran et al. 2022, p. 4212.

[10] Dafoe 2018, p. 9; Girasa 2020, pp. 34–35.

[11] Zuiderwijk et al. 2021, pp. 9–10.

[12] Girasa 2020, pp. 62–63.

[13] Floridi 2014, pp. 1–3; Mittelstadt et al. 2016, p. 2.

[14] Custers and Fosch-Villaronga, 2022, p. 10.

[15] Păvăloaia and Necula 2023, p. 30.

[16] Dafoe 2018, p. 9; Păvăloaia and Necula 2023, p. 33.

[17] Păvăloaia and Necula 2023, p. 32.

[18] Zuiderwijk et al. 2021, pp. 11–13; Păvăloaia and Necula 2023, p. 33; Surden 2019, pp. 1335–1337.

The opportunities and challenges presented by AI technologies can help to illustrate the disruption that AI can cause in various ways. The term 'disruptive technology' does not initially have a positive connotation; however, in recent literature it is essentially used to describe a technology that brings both opportunities and challenges.[19] AI technologies can lead to legal, ethical, and social disruption, i.e. their applications can disrupt many behaviours, practices, and institutions,[20] by mediating the social interactions, business transactions, and public and private decision-making systems in society.[21] Considering its disruptive effects, the question arises as to how these effects can be addressed and what kind of mechanisms can ensure that society will benefit from the technology while mitigating the risks associated with its development, deployment, and use. A focus on governance is crucial to confront the challenges posed by AI.

1.2 Governance of the Digital

To reap the benefits of digital technologies, particularly AI, and mitigate the associated risks, governance is a key concept. Despite a number of ideas and definitions for the concept of governance, a common definition remains elusive. It is admittedly vague and broad, difficult to operationalise and offers little guidance on the specific structures, processes, and actors involved.[22] From an analytical point of view, however, the use of this concept is valuable.[23] In general, the concept of governance refers to '*governance with and through networks*'.[24] Accordingly, it encompasses the interaction between a wide variety of actors. It is worth emphasising that the concept of governance is a different and broader concept than that of 'government', as it includes non-state actors.[25] Nevertheless, the use and understanding of the concept vary depending on the context.[26] Therefore, a contextualised definition and understanding of governance may prove more useful.

With the advances in technology, the need to tame technological developments[27] has given rise to the concept of digital governance. The role of digital governance is to create a comprehensive understanding of the actors and the mechanisms of how digital technologies are governed in order to reap the benefits and mitigate the associated risks. The concept of digital governance can therefore be defined as a

---

[19] Păvăloaia and Necula 2023, p. 6.

[20] Liu et al. 2020, p. 205.

[21] Mittelstadt et al. 2016, p. 1; Taeihagh 2021, p. 137.

[22] Bygrave 2015, p. 12; Hofmann et al. 2017, p. 1410.

[23] Hofmann et al. 2017, p. 1410.

[24] Rhodes 2007, p. 1246.

[25] Ibid.

[26] Bygrave 2015, p. 13.

[27] Moses 2007.

practice of establishing and implementing policies, procedures, and standards for the proper development, deployment, and use of digital technologies.[28]

Although there is much to be said about the concept of digital governance, from a legal perspective, it is important to emphasise its regulatory patterns. The digital governance framework may contain guidelines and recommendations that overlap with digital regulation.[29] This overlap relates to the regulatory patterns of digital governance, which refers to a system of laws that are developed and enforced by social or governmental institutions in order to regulate the behaviour of the relevant actors.[30] In other words, digital governance frameworks contain multiple regulatory patterns. The value of digital governance, therefore, is to offer a framework that connects regulatory pathways that may otherwise operate independently or clash when they address the same digital phenomenon. Focusing on digital governance, it may be possible to avoid or (at least) mitigate the disruptive effects of AI technologies resulting from their development, deployment, and use. Such an objective makes it possible to take certain norms and values into account when designing digital technologies and thus ensure appropriate protection for individuals, groups, and society as a whole.[31]

Legislative initiatives for the purpose of digital governance have become a key item on the regulatory agenda worldwide. Among other initiatives, the European Union (EU) is actively proposing and enacting new legislation to regulate the promotion of technological developments and the mitigation of risks associated with digital technologies.[32] These regulatory efforts have had a profound effect even beyond the EU, also known as the Brussels effect.[33] The Brussels effect refers to the EU's ability to influence the global market, among other things.[34]

In recent years, the EU positioned itself as a global leader in regulating digital technologies.[35] The European Commission has set the goal of following its own path towards digital transformation, i.e. developing, deploying, and using technologies that work for people and respect European values, creating a fair and competitive economy, and promoting an open, democratic, and sustainable society.[36] Within this context, the recent regulatory journey began with the General Data Protection Regulation (GDPR),[37] has continued with many ambitious new legislatives and proposals,

28 Floridi 2018, p. 3.

29 Ibid.

30 Ibid.

31 Custers and Fosch-Villaronga 2022, pp. 6, 10.

32 European Commission 2020, p. 6.

33 Bradford 2020, p. 8.

34 Roberts et al. 2021, p. 13.

35 Sharon and Gellert 2023, p. 8.

36 European Commission 2020, p. 5.

37 Regulation (EU) 2016/679 of the European Parliament and of the Council of 27 April 2016 on the protection of Natural Persons with regard to the Processing of Personal Data and on the Free Movement of Such Data, and repealing Directive 95/46/EC (General Data Protection Regulation) [2016] OJ 2016 L 119/1.

including the Data Governance Act (DGA),[38] the Digital Markets Act (DMA),[39] the Digital Services Act (DSA),[40] the Data Act (DA),[41] the Artificial Intelligence Act (AIA),[42] and the proposal on the European Health Data Space (EHDS)[43]. These legislative initiatives play a crucial role in the governance of the digital sphere. Within these initiatives, the AIA is of particular importance for this scientific collection as it specifically concerns the regulation of AI.

In April 2021, the European Commission proposed the regulation on AI, which aims to regulate AI by creating a harmonised legal framework in particular for the development, marketing, and use of AI in line with the values of the Union.[44] The publication of the proposal was widely publicised, and the proposal was intensively discussed over the following years. In light of the discussions, the Parliament reached a provisional agreement with the Council on the AIA on 9 December 2023 and the text of the AIA was endorsed by the Member States on 2 February 2024.[45] The agreed text was formally approved by the Parliament on 13 March 2024 and adopted by the Council on 21 May 2024. The AIA was published in the Official Journal of the European Union on 12 July 2024. On the twentieth day following that of its publication in the Official Journal of the European Union, i.e. 1 August 2024, the world's first comprehensive AI law came into force. The AIA will apply from 2 August 2026.[46]

In the context of AI, the concept of digital governance serves to understand and manage the scale, speed, and impact of AI technologies on society in order to realise the benefits and mitigate the associated risks.[47] In other words, it can be seen as an attempt to strike a delicate balance that leads to socially desirable outcomes that meet the legal, ethical, and social concerns of individuals and society. However, due to the high level of uncertainty and complexity of the AI landscape, digital governance

---

[38] Regulation (EU) 2022/868 of 30 May 2022 of the European Parliament and of the Council on European Data Governance (Data Governance Act) [2022] OJ L 152/1.

[39] Regulation (EU) 2022/1925 of 14 September 2022 of the European Parliament and of the Council on Contestable and Fair Markets in the Digital Sector (Digital Markets Act) [2022] OJ L 265/1.

[40] Regulation (EU) 2022/2065 of 19 October 2022 of the European Parliament and of the Council on a Single Market for Digital Services (Digital Services Act) [2022] OJ L 277/1.

[41] Regulation (EU) 2023/2854 of the European Parliament and of the Council of 13 December 2023 on harmonised rules on fair access to and use of data and amending Regulation (EU) 2017/2394 and Directive (EU) 2020/1828 (Data Act) [2023] OJ L 2023/2854.

[42] Regulation (EU) 2024/1689 of the European Parliament and of the Council of 13 June 2024 Laying Down Harmonised Rules on Artificial Intelligence and Amending Regulations (EC) No 300/2008, (EU) No 167/2013, (EU) No 168/2013, (EU) 2018/858, (EU) 2018/1139 and (EU) 2019/2144 and Directives 2014/90/EU, (EU) 2016/797 and (EU) 2020/1828 (Artificial Intelligence Act) [2024] OJ L 2024/1689.

[43] Proposal of the European Commission for a Regulation of the European Parliament and of the Council on the European Health Data Space (EHDS) [2022] COM/2022/197 final.

[44] AIA 2024, Recital 1.

[45] European Parliament 2023.

[46] AIA 2024, Article 113.

[47] Taeihagh 2021, pp. 138, 143.

mechanisms also face numerous challenges in developing and implementing effective measures to govern AI.

1.3 The Main Theme of the Book

This book contributes to the debate on digital governance by confronting the challenges posed by AI technologies. In this sense, the book focuses on existing and still unanswered open questions about the place and function of law and regulation for the governance of AI. These open questions relate to understanding the disruptive impact of AI in broader and specific contexts, exploring different forms of governance for AI, and utilising the framework of digital governance in the quest for legal solutions by incorporating interdisciplinary frameworks.

Divided into two parts, this book approaches the topic of AI and governance in a comprehensive and innovative way. The first part of the book presents a broad perspective on the disruptive impact of AI technologies which transform our lives in such a rapid and radical way. This part essentially aims to reflect on the various impacts of AI technologies covering a spectrum of different domains such as health, education, finance, and public administration. In this way, this section aims to inform the reader not only about the disruptive impacts of AI, but also to provide guidance on how these disruptive impacts may occur.

The second part of the book focuses on designing legal solutions for responding to the disruptive effects of AI using the framework of digital governance. This part aims to provide the reader with information on the development of context-specific digital governance remedies to address the challenges of AI. In this sense, this book not only highlights the problem and illustrates how AI can impact our lives, but also proposes solutions. These solutions are based on various regulatory frameworks. Some are based on the role of design and regulation by design, such as in Chap. 9 by Nouws and Dobbe. Others have examined a soft law approach, such as in Chap. 12 Vander Maelen and Griffin. Nonetheless, these various approaches are connected by a general theme of digital governance, that is, the understanding that particular regulatory solutions operate interrelatedly, as part of institutional and contextual structures. By looking at different contexts, identifying a range of problems, and designing context-specific solutions, this book stands out from many other available works.

In addition, this edited book is novel due to its topicality. During the preparation of this book, the Commission and the Parliament agreed on the text of the AIA. The latter has now been officially adopted. The chapters in this book have been prepared to provide up-to-date information in line with the official text of the AIA. As such, this book is one of the first publications to contain recent discussions on AI aligned with the official text of the AIA.

This book aims to contribute to the digital governance literature by approaching the challenges posed by AI from broad perspectives and for a broad range of audiences. This book is primarily directed at anyone interested in the field of law and technology. It provides an in-depth look at the disruption caused by AI technologies in different areas and outlines possible solutions through the framework of digital governance. The book contains a plethora of legal considerations on AI that may be instructive for legal scholars and practitioners, including academics, lawyers, judges, legal advisors, policy makers, and government officials, who are interested in the latest developments in AI governance, i.e. how these developments impact the legal field, what legal remedies are available to address these impacts, and how and to what extent these remedies can have a risk mitigating effect. Besides the legal domain, this book can also provide valuable insights to academics in other disciplines such as sociology, philosophy, science and technology studies, ethics, political science, and public administration, where knowledge of AI governance is essential. Given the rapid developments in the field of law and AI, it is becoming increasingly difficult to keep up with the changes in this area. Therefore, the book remains worth reading and consulting as a source for other people who want to gain an understanding on the topic of AI and governance.

Admittedly, the book is characterised by a Euro-centric approach, which is a limitation. This approach is mainly due to the affiliations of most of the authors, including the editors. Additionally, the EU is one of the first jurisdictions to take affirmative, decisive measures for the governance of AI. Nevertheless, we believe that the critical approach and constructive work that we provide in this book will turn out to be relevant, in various degrees, to other contexts.

1.4 The Structure of the Book

This book consists of two parts, with the chapters organised according to their respective content. The following subsections will provide a guidance on the introduction of each chapter accommodated by the two parts.

1.4.1 Part I: Disruptive Effects of AI

In Chap. 2, van Staalduinen examines the potential impact of AI systems on medical liability. The chapter provides a detailed exploration of EU product liability law, focusing particularly on its relevance to clinical decision support systems. These systems support decisions about patient care, for instance in analysing the risk for developing diseases, and are set to improve the general quality of healthcare. However, their integration may also leave injured patients without avenues for recourse. The chapter discusses to what extent EU product liability law applies to AI clinical decision support systems.

In Chap. 3, Mobilio explores how AI based technologies are finding their application in education settings, especially through the use of facial recognition technology. The chapter provides a detailed analysis on applicable provisions of the

GDPR through the lenses of the principle of proportionality and the principle of best interests of the child. Furthermore, the chapter highlights how the AIA relates to these existing provisions and its potential to heighten their baseline of protection.

In Chap. 4, Akar discusses Emotional Artificial Intelligence (EAI) by introducing the concept of emotional privacy. This chapter delves into the nature of emotions and their connection to privacy and explores various theories of privacy. The chapter emphasises the values that emotions represent, such as autonomy, intimacy, and self-esteem, and how these values relate to the concept of emotional privacy.

In Chap. 5, Muçi delves into Open Banking, which refers to the possibility of individuals and businesses to share payment account data with non-bank financial providers, particularly FinTech firms employing AI technology. The chapter delivers a doctrinal analysis of the Second Payment Services Directive (PSD2), GDPR, and the AIA, which reveals unexplored legal responsibilities of Open Banking actors that are crucial for mitigating risks associated with uncontrolled AI in finance, preserving financial stability, and maintaining consumer trust.

In Chap. 6, Wong-Toropainen problematises user control in the context of digital identity wallets. Using post-structural discourse analysis, the chapter discusses existing digital identity solutions and analyses the extent to which they give citizens control over their identity-related data. The chapter argues that the discourse around user control might have adverse effects on the protection of personal data and privacy.

In Chap. 7, Bastigkeit Ericstam explores the use of algorithmic management in traditional working relations. Automated decision-making in managerial decisions have the potential to violate workers' rights by an automated direction, automated evaluation, and automated discipline. The chapter argues that existing provisions in data protection law are underutilised in the protection of worker's rights and assesses how existing provisions in the GDPR are able to mitigate risks and enhance workers' rights by increased transparency.

1.4.2 Part II: Designing Legal Solutions for Digital Governance

In Chap. 8, Sumer, Gonzalez, Elbi, Jasserand, Czarnocki and Kindt, researchers from the Biometric Law Lab, analyse the potential impact of the AIA on the regulation of biometric data. This chapter examines the current legal landscape for biometric data and argues that the fragmentation of definitions leads to legal uncertainty. The chapter then discusses the role of the AIA in addressing the challenges posed by biometric law.

In Chap. 9, Nouws and Dobbe introduce a comprehensive framework to examine how AI applications influence the exercise of power in public administration and potential harms to citizens. By merging socio-legal perspectives on the Rule of Law with insights from system safety engineering, they address gaps in traditional legal thought and emphasise the socio-technical nature of AI systems. Through this approach, public organisations can identify and address potential hazards in AI systems, which may mitigate arbitrary exercises of power and safeguard citizen rights.

In Chap. 10, Görge, Haedecke, Schmitz, Borowski, Seeliger, and Poretschkin focus on the use of standards within AI technologies by examining how existing standards interact with the use of AI. The chapter presents findings from the 'AI Readiness of Standards' project and introduces a conceptual definition of AI readiness and a systematic approach to classify existing standards, laying the groundwork for automated analysis of AI readiness within the German standards framework.

In Chap. 11, Zweistra argues that the impact of AI adoption in the legal service sector is not fully grasped if only discovered in terms of risks. The sector of legal advice and conflict resolution as a service sector has to tackle existential questions as its production processes are inherently textual, thus informational. The chapter proposes a framework of reflexive techno-politics and existential-ethics to guide the appropriation of legal AI developments.

In Chap. 12, Griffin delves into the role assigned to codes of conducts within the Digital Services Act (DSA), which are also introduced in the AIA. In both DSA and AIA, codes of conduct may significantly influence the practical implementation of both pieces of legislation. The authors highlight various challenges that codes of conducts are facing, including their politicisation, potential repurposing and their instrumentalisation to promote EU interests on an international stage.

In Chap. 13, Costa dos Anjos explores algorithmic explainability through the lens of intellectual property and competition law. Algorithmic decision-making (ADM) plays a central role in the displaying of content within digital platforms and, in this context, raises significant concerns regarding transparency. The chapter explores the challenges posed by market dominance, perceived neutrality, and the legal opacity of algorithms, advocating for the implementation of a right to explanation within the EU to uphold accountability and fairness in ADM processes.

References

Bradford A (2020) The Brussels Effect' in The Brussels Effect: How the European Union Rules the World. NY: Oxford University Press, New York.

Bygrave L A (2015) Internet Governance by Contract. Oxford University Press, Oxford.

Custers B and Fosch-Villaronga E (2022) Humanizing Machines: Introduction and Overview. In: Custer B and Fosch-Villaronga E (eds) Law and Artificial Intelligence – Regulating AI and Applying AI in Legal Practice. Springer, the Netherlands.

Dafoe A (2018) AI Governance: A Research Agenda. Centre for the Governance of AI Future of Humanity Institute, University of Oxford.

de Gregorio G and Dunn P (2022) The European Risk-Based Approaches: Connecting Constitutional Dots in the Digital Age. Common Market Law Review, 59: 473–500. https://doi.org/10.54648/cola2022032.

European Commission (February 2020) Shaping Europe's Digital Future. https://doi.org/10.2759/48191. Accessed 11 January 2024.

European Parliament (2023) EU AI Act: First regulation on artificial intelligence. https://www.europarl.europa.eu/news/en/headlines/society/20230601STO93804/eu-ai-act-first-regulation-on-artificial-intelligence. Accessed 2 February 2024.
Floridi L (2014) Open Data, Data Protection, and Group Privacy. Philos. Technol., 27: 1–3. https://doi.org/10.1007/s13347-014-0157-8.
Floridi L (2018) Soft Ethics, the Governance of the Digital and the General Data Protection Regulation. Phil. Trans. R. Soc. A 376: 20180081: 1–11. https://doi.org/10.1007/s13347-018-0303-9.
Girasa R (2020) AI as a Disruptive Technology – Economic Transformation and Government Regulation. Palgrave Macmillan Cham, Springer Nature, Switzerland.
Hofmann J, Katzenbach C, and Gollatz K (2017) Between coordination and regulation: Finding the governance in Internet governance. New Media & Society, 19(9): 1406–1423. https://doi.org/10.1177/1461444816639975.
Kamran S S, Haleem A, Bahl S, Javaid M, Prakash C, and Budhhi D (2022) Artificial intelligence and advanced materials in automotive industry: Potential applications and perspectives. Materials Today: Proceedings, 62: 4207–4214. https://doi.org/10.1016/j.matpr.2022.04.727.
Liu H, Maas M, Danaher J, Scarcella L, Lexer M, and van Rompaey L (2020) Artificial Intelligence and Legal Disruption: A new model for analysis. Law, Innovation and Technology 12(2): 205–258. https://doi.org/10.1080/17579961.2020.1815402.
Mittelstadt B D, Allo P, Taddeo M, Wachter S, and Floridi L (2016) The ethics of algorithms: Mapping the debate. Big Data & Society: 1–21. https://doi.org/10.1177/2053951716679679.
Moses L B (2007) Recurring dilemmas: The law's race to keep up with technological change. University of Illinois Journal of Law, Technology, & Policy: 239.
Oren O, Gersh B J, and Bhatt D L (2020) Artificial intelligence in medical imaging: Switching from radiographic pathological data to clinically meaningful endpoints, Lancet Digital Health, 2: e486–e488. https://doi.org/10.1016/s2589-7500(20)30160-6.
Păvăloaia V and Necula S (2023) Artificial Intelligence as a Disruptive Technology—A Systematic Literature Review. Electronics 12(1102): 1–37. https://doi.org/10.3390/electronics12051102.
Pesapane F, Codari M, and Sardanelli F (2018) Artificial intelligence in medical imaging: Threat or opportunity? Radiologists again at the forefront of innovation in medicine. European Radiology Experimental, 2(35): 1–10. https://doi.org/10.1186/s41747-018-0061-6.
Proposal of the European Commission for a Regulation of the European Parliament and of the Council on the European Health Data Space (EHDS) [2022] COM/2022/197 final.
Regulation (EU) 2016/679 of the European Parliament and of the Council of 27 April 2016 on the Protection of Natural Persons with regard to the Processing of Personal Data and on the Free Movement of Such Data, and repealing Directive 95/46/EC (General Data Protection Regulation) [2016] OJ 2016 L 119/1.
Regulation (EU) 2022/868 of 30 May 2022 of the European Parliament and of the Council on European Data Governance (Data Governance Act) [2022] OJ L 152/1.
Regulation (EU) 2022/1925 of 14 September 2022 of the European Parliament and of the Council on contestable and fair markets in the digital sector (Digital Markets Act) [2022] OJ L 265/1.
Regulation (EU) 2022/2065 of 19 October 2022 of the European Parliament and of the Council on a Single Market for Digital Services (Digital Services Act) [2022] OJ L 277/1.
Regulation (EU) 2023/2854 of the European Parliament and of the Council of 13 December 2023 on harmonised rules on fair access to and use of data and amending Regulation (EU) 2017/2394 and Directive (EU) 2020/1828 (Data Act) [2023] OJ L 2023/2854.
Regulation (EU) 2024/1689 of the European Parliament and of the Council of 13 June 2024 Laying Down Harmonised Rules on Artificial Intelligence and Amending Regulations (EC) No 300/2008, (EU) No 167/2013, (EU) No 168/2013, (EU) 2018/858, (EU) 2018/1139 and (EU) 2019/2144 and Directives 2014/90/EU, (EU) 2016/797 and (EU) 2020/1828 (Artificial Intelligence Act) [2024] OJ L 2024/1689.
Rhodes R.A.W. (2007) Understanding Governance: Ten Years On. Organization Studies, 28(8): 1243–1264. https://doi.org/10.1177/0170840607076586.

Roberts H, Cowls J, Casolari F, Morley J, Taddeo M, and Floridi L (2021) Safeguarding European values with digital sovereignty: An analysis of statements and policies. Internet Policy Review 10(3): 1–26. https://doi.org/10.14763/2021.3.1575.

Sharon T, Gellert R (2023) Regulating Big Tech expansionism? Sphere transgressions and the limits of Europe's digital regulatory strategy. Information, Communication & Society. 1–18. https://doi.org/10.1080/1369118X.2023.2246526

Surden H (2019) Artificial Intelligence and Law: An Overview. Georgia State University Law Review 35(4): 1305–1337.

Taeihagh A (2021) Governance of artificial intelligence. Policy and Society, 40(2): 137–157. https://doi.org/10.1080/14494035.2021.1928377.

World Health Organization (Geneva, 2021) Ethics and governance of artificial intelligence for health: WHO guidance. https://www.who.int/publications/i/item/9789240029200. Accessed 11 January 2024.

Zuiderwijk A, Chen Y, Salem F (2021) Implications of the use of artificial intelligence in public governance: A systematic literature review and a research agenda. Government Information Quarterly, 38(3): 1–19. https://doi.org/10.1016/j.giq.2021.101577.

Part I
Disruptive Effects of AI

Chapter 2
European Product Liability for AI-based Clinical Decision Support Systems

Jan H. van Staalduinen

Contents

Abstract Clinical decision support systems (CDSSs) are computer systems that support medical professionals in the clinical decision-making process. If a decision that involved the use of a CDSS has detrimental effects, the patient might seek compensation for the damage incurred. Here, the involvement of a CDSS, particularly if it is AI-based, could give rise to liability questions. On the one hand, the liability of

This research was conducted as part of the ZonMW-funded project 'DECIDE-VerA' (grant no. 08540122120004)

J. H. van Staalduinen (✉)
Institute of Private law. Steenschuur 25, Leiden University, 2311ES Leiden, The Netherlands
e-mail: j.h.van.staalduinen@law.leidenuniv.nl

K. Prifti et al. (eds.), *Digital Governance*, Information Technology and Law Series 39,
https://doi.org/10.1007/978-94-6265-639-0_2

the medical professional, which often depends on medical standards, raises questions on the type of behaviour on which these standards will require, particularly for AI-based CDSSs. On the other hand, questions arise on the liability of the manufacturer of the system. Product liability regimes such as those in the US and the EU do not require the claimant to prove fault, but instead require a product defect. For these regimes, AI-based CDSSs challenge the notions of defect and causation. This chapter focuses on EU product liability law, analysing whether and how it applies to AI-CDSSs. The three main questions discussed are (i) whether AI-CDSSs could fall within the scope of this regime, (ii) how the term 'defect' should be construed with respect to AI-CDSSs, arguing for a novel interpretation of AI manufacturing defects, and (iii) whether and how a causal link between defect and damage could be established.

Keywords Product liability · Artificial Intelligence · Defect · Causal link · Medical liability · Clinical Decision Support Systems

2.1 Introduction

2.1.1 Clinical Decision Support Systems, AI, and Liability

As is shown throughout this book, Artificial Intelligence (AI) technology has promising applications in many different fields. Medical practice is certainly one of these. Advances in machine learning have made it possible for clinical decision support systems (CDSSs), traditionally based on pre-programmed rules,[1] to infer these rules autonomously from large collections of clinical data or past experience, allowing for more powerful and flexible systems.[2]

Given the view in medicine that AI should aid, rather than replace, human professionals, and the related aspiration to keep a 'human in the loop', CDSSs could play a significant role in the clinical AI landscape.[3] At the same time, the opaque nature of AI-based CDSSs (hereafter simply referred to as 'CDSSs') is troublesome. If CDSSs malfunction, e.g. by erroneously recommending an unsuitable drug for a particular patient, their opaque nature not only makes it hard for the clinician to assess the validity of the given advice, but it also complicates the matter of determining if someone is liable for ensuing harm.[4]

---

[1] Berner 2007, pp. 3–8.

[2] Berner 2007, pp. 6–8; Schönberger 2019, pp. 174–175; Zikmundová 2023, pp. 284–385; Zech 2023, pp. 193–194. One example is a recently proposed system that assists GPs by analysing a patient's risk of developing cardiovascular diseases, see Van Os et al. 2023.

[3] Schönberger 2019, p. 193; Selbst 2020, pp. 1318–1319; Braun et al. 2021; Rajpurkar et al. 2022; Čartolovni et al. 2022.

[4] Smith and Fotheringham 2022, p. 34; Duffourc and Gerke 2024, p. 6.

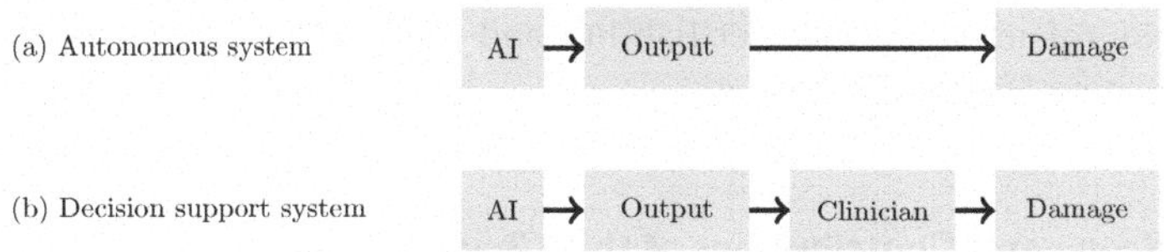

Fig. 2.1 Decision support systems can only cause damage indirectly

While this is true for AI systems in general, CDSSs pose specific challenges. In comparison to autonomous systems such as self-operating drug administration systems or self-driving cars, which directly impact their environment, CDSSs can only influence the environment through a human intermediary (see Fig. 2.1).[5] As for (strict) product liability of manufacturers,[6] the position of the clinician as an autonomous intermediary ('*novus actus interveniens*') creates difficulties in establishing a causal link.[7] However, the alternative, clinicians' medical liability,[8] is based on negligence and thus only applies in cases of substandard performance.[9] The reality is that clinicians do not always bear full legal responsibility for the devices they use.[10] As CDSSs become more powerful, negligence standards will evolve and might even effectively *require* clinicians to use these systems without being able to fully comprehend how they work—reducing a clinician's liability if it continues to be negligence-based.[11]

Although the general quality of healthcare might be improved with the widespread adoption of AI-based CDSSs, these observations show that their adoption may simultaneously leave injured patients without recourse.[12] Issues like these are referred to as 'liability gaps'.[13] This chapter's central objective is to analyse the aforementioned

[5] Cp. Wendehorst and Duller 2023, pp. 220–221.

[6] Smith and Fotheringham 2022, p. 50; Wagner 2022, p. 192 (although primarily on autonomous systems); Banja et al. 2022, p. 818.

[7] Smith and Fotheringham 2020, p. 145.

[8] As argued for by Selbst 2020, pp. 1319–1320 and 1322–1329. 'Clinicians' and other medical professionals will be used interchangeably throughout this chapter.

[9] Koch 2011, p. 628; Schönberger 2019, pp. 196–197; Zikmundová 2023, pp. 387–389; Buiten et al. 2023, para 3.2; Duffourc and Gerke 2023, p. 4; Duffourc and Gerke 2024, pp. 29–31.

[10] Cp. Smith 2021, p. 3; Smith and Fotheringham 2020; Smith and Fotheringham 2022, p. 49; Froomkin et al. 2019, pp. 61–62. This can differ between jurisdictions, as e.g. France (article 1142-1 Code de la santé publique) and The Netherlands (article 6:74 jo 6:77 Dutch Civil Code (DCC)) do have some form of strict liability for clinicians using (tangible) medical devices.

[11] Froomkin et al. 2019, pp. 61–63; Haftenberger 2023, pp. 263 and 265–267; Schneeberger et al. 2020, p. 219; Schönberger 2019, pp. 201–202; Kardasiadou 1998, p. 242. Cp. Selbst 2020, pp. 1338–1342.

[12] Cp. Schönberger 2019, pp. 185 and 199–202.

[13] Prifti et al. 2022; Buiten et al. 2023, para 3; Burton et al. 2020; Wendehorst 2023, p. 120; Borges 2023a, pp. 169–171; Duffourc and Gerke 2023. From a private law perspective, liability gaps might not be problematic *per se* ('the loss lies where it falls'). See e.g. Selbst 2020, p. 1363 and Zerilli 2022, pp. 500–502.

gaps as they relate to EU product liability and propose how they can be bridged through existing legal mechanisms.

2.1.1.1 Scope and Contributions of this Chapter

This chapter examines the circumstances under which EU product liability for CDSSs could be established, specifically examining the central requirements of *defect* and *causality*. The EU product liability framework is currently undergoing revision. To incorporate the latest developments, notably the view that software can be regarded as a product, this chapter is based on the 2022 European Commission revision proposal, referred to here as the draft Product Liability Directive (DPLD).[14] However, given that the DPLD retains many elements of the current Product Liability Directive (PLD),[15] this chapter will also draw from, and connect with, existing discussions.

Its contributions are threefold:

(i) it analyses the possibility of, and concludes in favour of, applying the DPLD to CDSSs;
(ii) it considers how the term 'defect' could be applied to CDSSs, proposing to adopt an 'intentional stance' while arguing that the current focus on design defects is problematic and that AI defects should instead be regarded as manufacturing defects; and
(iii) it analyses whether and under which circumstances it could be possible to establish a causal link between the output of a defective CDSS and subsequent damage, proposing the adoption of a rebuttable presumption based on normative standards.

2.1.1.2 Structure of this Chapter

This chapter is structured as follows. First, it provides an outline of the DPLD (Sect. 2.2). Then, it analyses whether the DPLD could apply to CDSSs (Sect. 2.3), concluding in the affirmative. In proceeding to analyse the substantive topics of the DPLD, the notion of defect is explored (Sect. 2.4), after which the requirement for a causal link is analysed, first by investigating whether it could at all be possible to establish a causal link with CDSS output under the DPLD (Sect. 2.5)—concluding in the affirmative—and then by investigating under which circumstances such a causal link could be established in fact (Sect. 2.6). The findings are summarised in Sect. 2.7.

[14] Proposal for a Directive on liability for defective products (2022/0302(COD), COM(2022) 495 final) (DPLD).

[15] Directive 85/374/EEC of 25 July 1985 concerning liability for defective products (Product Liability Directive, PLD).

2.2 Navigating the Draft Product Liability Directive

The DPLD is part of a larger package of legislative measures that also includes the Artificial Intelligence Act (AIA)[16] and the AI Liability Directive (AILD).[17] The new product liability directive retains much of the structure, vocabulary and underlying principles of the existing PLD. Like the PLD, the DPLD prescribes a no-fault liability for damage caused by defective products incurred by natural persons. 'No-fault' means that the claimant does not have to prove that the manufacturer was at fault. The claimant bears the burden of proving that the product was defective, that they suffered damage, and that there is a causal link between the defect and the damage.[18]

EU product liability hinges on the requirement of defectiveness. The standard for defectiveness is that a product 'does not provide the safety which the public at large is entitled to expect, taking all circumstances into account'.[19] This standard is referred to as the consumer expectation test.[20] The test is both normative and objective in nature, as it is based on the legitimate expectations of the general public and not on the subjective expectations of a particular individual.[21] In contrast to the product liability regime in the US,[22] there is no formal role for the so-called risk-utility test,[23] and no distinction is made between different types of defects, i.e. manufacturing defects, design defects and instruction/warning defects.[24] Nonetheless, these concepts do play a role in the reasoning of (Member State) courts and in (academic) literature.[25]

While the consumer expectation test takes all circumstances into account, the DPLD mentions eight circumstances explicitly, five of which are new. One of the new circumstances, '(c) the effect on the product of any ability to continue to learn after deployment', targets AI systems specifically. However, not all AI systems continue to learn after deployment. This is only true for 'online learning' systems, which continue to learn in real time through interactions with their surroundings or the user.[26] Many systems instead use 'offline learning', in which the system is trained

---

[16] Regulation (EU) 2024/1689 laying down harmonised rules on artificial intelligence (Artificial Intelligence Act).

[17] Proposal for a Directive on adapting non-contractual civil liability rules to artificial intelligence (2022/0303/COD, COM(2022) 496 final) (AI Liability Directive, AILD).

[18] Article 9 DPLD.

[19] Article 6-1 DPLD.

[20] Fairgrieve et al. 2016, pp. 50–61.

[21] Fairgrieve et al. 2016, p. 51, no 80; Verhoeven 2018, pp. 222–226.

[22] Duffourc and Gerke 2024, para II.A.1-3.

[23] The risk-utility test balances risks/costs and benefit of the product, i.e. an unsafe product could still be non-defective if it provides enough utility and alternative designs are either not available or prohibitively expensive.

[24] Fairgrieve et al. 2016, p. 53, no 82; High Court of Justice (UK), *A v National Blood Authority*, 26 March 2001, EWHC QB 446.

[25] Fairgrieve et al. 2016, pp. 51–53.

[26] Russell and Norvig 2021, pp. 702–704; Hacker 2023, p. 14; Wendehorst and Duller 2023, pp. 291–293.

and deployed iteratively.[27] Since this chapter aims to cover both online and offline learning systems, circumstance (c) will not be discussed any further, although it is a relevant and interesting addition.[28]

Another notable addition is circumstance (f), which establishes a relationship between product liability and product safety requirements. Previously, this link had been less clear.[29] It is important to note that compliance with relevant standards is not sufficient to avert liability.[30] After all, liability has a complementary role to safety standards, precisely because of its ability to 'regulate' uncertain risks that are hard to encapsulate in detailed *ex ante* rules.[31]

The DPLD includes several liability exemptions. The development risk defence, which was—although optional—already part of the PLD, shields the manufacturer from liability if the scientific and technical knowledge at the time the product was placed on the market or is out of the control of the manufacturer were such as not to allow for the discovery of the defect.[32]

2.3 Does the Scope of the DPLD Include CDSSs?

2.3.1 A Principal Question

In analysing the application of EU product liability law to CDSSs, the first question is whether the scope of the DPLD covers CDSS-induced damage at all. The DPLD does not explicitly declare these situations to be out of scope,[33] but some argue that the European Court of Justice's (ECJ) *Krone* judgment would exclude products that provide information.[34] The next section of this paragraph (Sect. 2.3.2) will discuss this case in detail, assert that this interpretation of the *Krone* judgment is too strict, and argue why these products could indeed fall within the scope of the DPLD.

---

27 Froomkin et al. 2019, pp. 60–61; Duffourc and Gerke 2023, p. 2.

28 See more extensively Hacker 2023, p. 14; Spindler 2023, p. 53; De Bruyne et al. 2023, p. 13.

29 Veldt 2020b, para 7.2.3.

30 Veldt 2020b, para 7.2.2; Spindler 2023, p. 95.

31 Veldt 2020a, para 3. See however Verhoeven 2018, pp. 99–104, who advocates equating product safety criteria with defectiveness; cp. Fairgrieve et al. 2016, pp. 100–103.

32 Article 6-1-c DPLD. See Stapleton 1994, pp. 49–52; Fairgrieve et al. 2016, pp. 75–79; Fairgrieve and Goldberg 2020, para 13.33–13.125; Borghetti 2023b, pp. 32–35. The defence tempers the no-fault character of EU product liability, in which Wendehorst describes it as 'mov[ing] it into the vicinity of fault liability', Wendehorst 2020, p. 158 (see also Howells 2020, pp. 92–93).

33 Other than the AILD, which does so in recital 15. See criticism by Hacker 2023, pp. 13–14 and Spindler 2023, pp. 76–77.

34 Borges 2023b, p. 39 (no. 49) and Borges 2022, p. 2652; opposed by Spindler 2023, p. 47. See earlier Triaille 1993, pp. 222–223.

There are other products, notably alarm systems, to which the DPLD applies, even though their main function is to provide output as a basis for a human decision. Section 2.3.3 analyses how these products compare to CDSSs. Section 2.3.4 concludes by clarifying that, while it is admittedly not clear whether all CDSS-induced damage could fall within the scope of the DPLD, a blanket rejection cannot hold either, paving the way for the substantive analysis in Sect. 2.4 onwards.

2.3.2 The Krone Case—Can Output Render a Product Defective?

On 31 December 2016, the Austrian newspaper *Kronen-Zeitung* published a column written by 'herbal medicine expert' 'Kräuterpfarrer Benedikt', who suggested to apply freshly grated horseradish to alleviate rheumatic pain and to leave it on the affected bodily area for two to five hours. As one reader found out after experiencing 'severe pain due to a toxic skin reaction', the advice should have read minutes instead of hours. She claimed compensation from the newspaper, which ultimately brought the ECJ to rule whether a newspaper containing incorrect health advice could qualify as a defective product.[35]

The ECJ concluded it could not. First, it expressed that the PLD only applies to products, not to services.[36] However, it then proceeded to analyse whether 'health advice which, by its nature, constitutes a service, can, when incorporated into a physical item—in this case, a printed newspaper—result, on account of the fact that it proved to be inaccurate, in the newspaper itself being defective in nature'.[37] Since in this case the service (provision of—incorrect—advice) was unrelated to the medium (the newspaper), it was not 'part of the inherent characteristics of the printed newspaper' and as such could not render the newspaper defective.[38]

What does this mean for CDSSs? The output of these systems would undoubtedly also qualify as a service, which means the output is not covered by the DPLD *per se*. However, as Haftenberger points out, the reasoning of the Court compels us to focus not on the output being a service, but on its potential to render the *system* defective.[39] If a CDSS itself qualifies as a product, as did the copy of the *Kronen-Zeitung*, its AI-mediated output is evidently more related to it than the health advice in the newspaper: the CDSS is not merely a carrier, but the source of the advice, since it is created or modified by the system.[40] Therefore, it is quite possible that

[35] ECJ, *Krone,* 1 June 2021, C-65/20, ECLI:EU:C:2021:471.

[36] ECJ, *Krone,* 1 June 2021, C-65/20, ECLI:EU:C:2021:471; Van der Putt and Westerdijk 2023, para 4.2; Veldt 2022, para 3; Wuyts 2014, pp. 5–7.

[37] ECJ, *Krone,* 1 June 2021, C-65/20, ECLI:EU:C:2021:471, para 32.

[38] ECJ, *Krone,* 1 June 2021, C-65/20, ECLI:EU:C:2021:471, para 36; see also Twigg-Flesner 2021.

[39] Haftenberger 2023, pp. 85–89.

[40] Wendehorst and Duller 2023, pp. 221–222; Haftenberger 2023, pp. 87–89; cp. Westerdijk 1995, pp. 242–243 and (in a different context) 208–210.

the output which is generated by these systems should be viewed as part of their 'inherent characteristics', implying that the DPLD could indeed apply to CDSSs.

2.3.3 Are CDSSs like Alarm Systems?

There is little doubt that the DPLD, like its predecessor, applies to alarm systems, even though their main function is also to provide information to a user. It is assumed here that a product failing to provide any signals is equally non-functioning as a product that provides incorrect signals, given that this is equivalent from a safety perspective.[41] Examples from literature and EU documents include medical smartwatch apps[42] and smoke detectors.[43] While alarm systems may intuitively seem different from CDSSs, the distinction is not easily justified using product liability rhetoric. This can be shown by analysing three arguments that might support this distinction: (i) the fact that CDSSs are used to provide services, (ii) the doctrine of the 'learned intermediary' and (iii) the exclusion of indirect risks in interpreting the term 'safety'.

The first proposition alludes to the notorious product-service dichotomy. The product liability directive applies to products, not to services, as the ECJ asserted in the *Dutrueux* case.[44] At the same time, it does apply to products being used for services, as noted in the *Veedfald* case.[45] This case law should be interpreted in line with the new directive. Under the new directive, software is clearly regarded as a product and not as a service (*Dutrueux*) and as such falls within the scope of the directive, even if it is used in the provision of services (*Veedfald*).[46] This renders the product-service discussion obsolete,[47] while raising the aforementioned question (Sect. 2.3.2) of whether information originating from AI software can indeed be inherent to it (*Krone*).

As for the second proposition, the learned intermediary docrine found in common law suggests that 'the manufacturer can discharge of [its] duty to warn by providing

[41] Compare recital 44 of Directive (EU) 2019/770 on certain aspects concerning contracts for the supply of digital content and digital services – although the perspective there is not that of safety risks, but of contractual performance.

[42] The DPLD impact assessment notes: '[S]oftware itself may also cause personal injury or property damage. For example, a medically-approved smartwatch app intended to send an alarm notification to the user or doctor when it recognises irregular heartbeats could defectively fail to do so, leading to injury, or a defective app or computer programs could cause a computer battery to overheat or explode', DPLD impact assessment, SWD(2022) 316 final, 28 September 2022.

[43] See AG Hogan in his Opinion for the Krone judgment, C-65/20, ECLI:EU:C:2021:298, para 28; Kardasiadou 1998, pp. 231–232 on medical warning systems.

[44] ECJ, *Dutrueux*, 21 December 2011, C-495/10, ECLI:EU:C:2011:869, para 18–39.

[45] ECJ, *Veedfald*, 10 May 2001, C-203/99, ECLI:EU:C:2001:258, para 12. See the dissenting Opinion, ECLI:EU:C:2001:697, para. 15.

[46] Cp. Liivak 2018, pp. 181–182; Rott 2020, p. 642.

[47] Even for 'software as a service' (SaaS), see Borghetti 2023a, p. 138.

the relevant information to a responsible intermediary',[48] i.e. the clinician. In medical situations, its (perceived but possibly overstated) effect is to block a product liability claim when a learned intermediary is involved, as it is the clinician's duty to correctly inform and warn the patient about risks (and possible defects), not the manufacturer's.[49] The status of this rule is debated.[50] In the absence of consensus, it could be argued that the existence of a learned intermediary, although it 'does not provide a complete or automatic defence for a producer',[51] precludes the application of the DPLD to CDSSs.[52] However, given the case law's narrow focus on the manufacturer's duty to warn, it seems likely that the rule is relevant solely from an information perspective, where for warning defects, the information in possession of the intermediary can influence the level of safety the consumer is entitled to expect. However, a product can be unsafe even if one considers both the knowledge of the patient and that of the intermediary clinician and therefore this rule would probably not preclude defective CDSSs as a matter of principle.

Considering the third proposition, it might be true that alarm signals should usually be heeded without much thought, whereas CDSS output might require more deliberation.[53] However, as described in Sect. 2.1.1, it is not implausible that clinicians (rightly) come to depend on CDSSs to interpret certain symptoms. A clinician should be able to have a certain level of trust in the fidelity of the output. As we know from the ECJ's *Boston* judgment, the public is entitled to expect a high level of safety from medical systems.[54] This would justify a broad interpretation of the term 'safety' which includes unsafe situations that indirectly result in damage.[55]

---

[48] Fairgrieve and Goldberg 2020, para 12.55. See for a US perspective Duffourc and Gerke 2024, p. 22.

[49] See e.g. Sullivan and Schweikart p. 162; Pasquale 2022, p. 205; Duffourc and Giovanniello 2023, pp. 222–223.

[50] Fairgrieve and Goldberg 2020, para 12.55.

[51] High Court of Justice (UK), *Wilkes v Depuy International Ltd*, 6 December 2016, EWHC QB 3096, para 108.

[52] In *Wilkes* at para 108, Hickinbottom J appears to place some emphasis on the agency of the intermediary in noting that it was the intermediary who '[had] chosen a particular prosthesis for a particular patient'.

[53] Wendehorst and Duller 2023, pp. 220–221. See also, although with regard to causation, Taeger 1995, pp. 206–209.

[54] At least where it can result in serious injury or death: ECJ, *Boston Scientific Medizintechnik*, 5 March 2015, C-503/13, ECLI:EU:C:2015:148; Fairgrieve et al. 2016, pp. 53–56; Verhoeven 2018, pp. 225–226; Triaille 1993, p. 221. However, this is not equal to *perfect* performance, see Kardasiadou 1998, pp. 174–175. Cp. Cayol 2021, p. 25.

[55] Wendehorst and Duller 2023, pp. 220–221; cp. Fairgrieve and Goldberg 2020, para 17.87: 'The general rule in English law as in the United States remains that he who creates a situation of danger must expect a third party carelessly (though not consciously) to activate its potential for harm.'

2.3.4 Conclusion

This section discussed whether the application of the DPLD to CDSSs should be ruled out as a matter of principle. A positive answer would end the discussion regarding CDSSs at this juncture. However, the view adopted here is that it is not that simple.

Given that software is considered a product under the DPLD, the question is no longer whether a CDSS would qualify as a product, but rather whether its output can render it defective. First, it was suggested that unlike the newspaper in the Krone case, a CDSS is not merely a medium for its advice but its source, and hence we should regard its output as 'inherent to it'. Second, it was suggested that it might be hard to distinguish between CDSSs and alarm systems, which do fall within the scope of the DPLD.

It does not seem unreasonable to conclude that the DPLD could apply to CDSSs. In the next sections, we will examine two specific DPLD requirements: defect (Sect. 2.4) and causation (Sects. 2.5 and 2.6).

2.4 AI Product Defects

2.4.1 Establishing a Defect

A product is defective if it does not provide the safety which the public at large is entitled to expect (the 'consumer expectations test'). Borghetti describes four 'usual' methods through which this is assessed (and explains why they are hard to apply to AI systems):[56] (i) *res ipsa loquitur*,[57] (ii) violations of relevant safety requirements,[58] (iii) risk-benefit analysis,[59] and (iv) product comparison.[60] These methods all have their specific drawbacks. To an extent, this is related to the open-ended nature of the consumer expectation test, limited by the development risk defence, which allows for a spectrum of possible defects that is hard to describe *ex ante*.[61] Specifically

[56] Borghetti 2019, pp. 67–68.

[57] Can be difficult to apply in medical cases, since the right treatment can still produce negative results. Holm et al. 2021, pp. 180–181; Zikmundová 2023, p. 390; Borges 2023a, pp. 183–184 and Wendehorst 2023, p. 108.

[58] See Hacker 2023, p. 16; Wendehorst 2023, pp. 112–114.

[59] Also Borghetti 2023a, p. 153; Wagner 2022, pp. 204–205; Santos Silva et al. 2021, pp. 127–131; Verhoeven 2018, pp. 119–131.

[60] Patti 2020, pp. 116–120; Holm et al. 2021, pp. 182–183; Borges 2021, pp. 35–37; Hacker 2023, pp. 15–16; Buiten et al. 2023, p. 16 on comparing AI and human performance; Verhoeven 2018, pp. 191–192.

[61] Veldt 2020a, para 3. Verhoeven 2018, pp. 99–104 advocates equating product safety criteria with defectiveness; cp. Fairgrieve et al. 2016, pp. 100–103.

for AI systems, they are hard to apply, given that these methods have been developed for traditional, mass-manufactured products.[62] They need to be adjusted to apply to AI systems.[63] The next paragraph offers a possible approach. Most of all, it provides a theoretical basis to counter the criticism that the *res ipsa loquitur* approach inappropriately takes AI output as the sole object of analysis.[64]

2.4.2 The Intentional Stance, or: Why AI Defects are Manufacturing Defects

One possible explanation for the abovementioned four methods being hard to apply to AI systems can be illustrated through Dennett's theory on 'stances'.[65] Traditionally, this chapter submits, products are judged through adopting a *design stance*, which means that their behaviour and associated level of safety are based on their intended function.[66] However, for AI systems, the *intentional stance* could sometimes be more appropriate. This stance assumes that AI systems possess internal (non-emotional) beliefs, desires, and the ability to respond and adapt to their environment. This more accurate view of AI systems may in fact correspond with how the general public regards AI systems.[67] Therefore, the adoption of the intentional stance can be seen as an interpretation of the consumer expectations test itself and thus permissible within the existing DPLD framework.

The intentional stance helps to conceptualise AI defects. Traditionally, since software production is seen as invulnerable to manufacturing defects, errors and bugs are approached as *design defects* (not to be confused with the unrelated design *stance*).[68] This focus on design defects is problematic, especially with AI, because it undermines the no-fault character of the DPLD by placing emphasis on its elements of negligence.[69]

For traditional software, the design defects-based approach might be reasonable given the idea that errors can in some way be traced back to a human who made a

[62] Cp. Froomkin et al. 2019, p. 80.

[63] Cp. Duffourc and Gerke 2024, pp. 56–57.

[64] Borges 2021, p. 35; Borges 2023b, p. 35 (no. 15). See also Froomkin et al. 2019, p. 66; Mazeau 2018, p. 8; Verhoeven 2018, p. 187; Borghetti 2023b, p. 34.

[65] Dennett 2017, p. 37.

[66] Dennett 2017, p. 37; Crilly et al. 2008, para 3.1–2 ; cp. Sartor 2009, pp. 257–260.

[67] See in a broader context Gröndahl 2008, pp. 89–92; Sartor 2009, pp. 260–263; Voulon 2010, pp. 30–35; Beckers and Teubner 2021, pp. 34–37. It is important to express that this does not entail an anthropomorphisation of AI: 'beliefs' and 'desires' as used here only refer to internally stored models of reality and objectives.

[68] Westerdijk 1995, pp. 223–224; Kardasiadou 1998, pp. 196–197; Ruesen 2017, para 2.2; Buiten et al. 2021, p. 54; Knetsch 2022, p. 111; Duffourc and Gerke 2023, p. 4.

[69] See e.g. Duffourc and Gerke 2023, p. 4; Werro et al. 2004, pp. 436–441; Wagner 2010, pp. 136–138 and 145; Giesen 2010, pp. 154–155; Patti 2020, pp. 116–120; Wendehorst and Duller 2023, pp. 272–273; Hacker 2023, pp. 29–30. Cp. Howells 2020, pp. 92–93.

design decision.[70] However, manufacturing AI software is different, since machine learning processes are not entirely within a programmer's control.[71] Manufacturing defects can be described either as 'a failure to screen out or eliminate something which is naturally within a product',[72] or as deviating from what the manufacturer intended to produce.[73] It is submitted here that similar to e.g. contaminated shellfish or a batch of horsemeat infected with a bacterium,[74] AI systems can autonomously develop manufacturing defects, namely when they learn statistical patterns from training data or develop behavioural patterns or model characteristics that defy safety expectations.[75] An AI system partly 'designs itself',[76] and where it fails, this is a manufacturing defect, not a design defect.

In essence, it comes down to this: typically, the goal of machine learning is to acquire an imperfect but representative model of (a part of) reality.[77] Adopting an intentional stance, it is the safety risk associated with these imperfections which should inform the consumer expectations test. If the imperfections in the trained model raise safety risks that exceed consumer expectations, it is fair to say the system contains a (manufacturing) defect. This has the advantage that the claimant can challenge the *result* of the machine learning process, instead of merely arguing that certain (procedural) design standards were not met.[78]

The approach proposed here should appeal to those who advocate a more manufacturer-focused liability scheme for medical AI systems,[79] as it places less emphasis on the manufacturer's level of care than a design defects-based perspective.[80] At the same time, it aligns with Borges' point that the incorrectness of the output should not, by itself, render an AI system defective.[81] EU product liability indeed does not require flawless output and therefore necessitates an evaluation of the AI system's (internal) properties—both 'AI model' and encompassing 'non-AI'

---

[70] Cp. Wendehorst 2020, p. 159.

[71] Tjong Tjin Tai 2022a, p. 117.

[72] Fairgrieve and Goldberg 2020, para 11.05.

[73] Kardasiadou 1998, pp. 170–171; Verhoeven 2018, pp. 132–136; Selbst 2020, p. 1323; Price et al. 2022, para III.A; Borghetti 2023b, p. 33.

[74] Examples borrowed from Fairgrieve and Goldberg 2020, p. 381 (n. 26) and Wuyts 2014, p. 32.

[75] Hacker 2023, p. 15 instead uses a wider definition of 'design defects', with which I respectfully disagree, given that the term 'design' implies a certain intent, although it is admittedly true that these defects, like design defects, affect the entire product 'series' (cp. Kardasiadou 1998, pp. 170–171; Fairgrieve and Goldberg 2020, para 11.05).

[76] Duffourc and Gerke 2024, p. 40: '[The] AI responded to vast amounts of data during the training process and, to some extent, *designed itself* using deep learning.' Cp. Patti 2020, pp. 108–110.

[77] Russell and Norvig 2021, pp. 651–656; Goodfellow et al. 2016, p. 8; cp. Tjong Tjin Tai 2022a, p. 117.

[78] Cp. Duffourc and Gerke 2023, p. 4; Duffourc and Giovanniello 2023, pp. 222–223. Similarly Liivak 2018, p. 183.

[79] See Sect. 2.1.1.

[80] Van Dam 2013, pp. 428; Fairgrieve et al. 2016, p. 53; See also Parasidis 2018, pp. 224–225. Cp. Froomkin et al. 2019, p. 80.

[81] Borges 2023b, p. 35 (no. 15). See also Froomkin et al. 2019, p. 66.

software—that brought it to produce the output.[82] However, it is worth noting that (internal) properties and (external) output are not disconnected, especially for less stochastic AI systems that operate in well-defined spheres of application. Hence, while output or behaviour should not form the *basis* for a defect, it can be a *strong indicator* for one.

It might not be an easy task for a claimant to prove such a defect. For some types of AI models, e.g. generative or reinforcement learning models, this approach is less realistic than for others, such as the GP's risk assessment model referenced in Sect. 2.1.1. At the same time, this should not prevent adopting this line of reasoning where it *is* possible. Additionally, it is not necessary to understand every aspect of the AI system in detail, since proving defectiveness does not require the highest possible technical precision.[83] A preliminary indication of a model's characteristics and built-in 'guard rails' could therefore be sufficient. Furthermore, the claimant might be aided by the new presumptions in article 9 of the DPLD (see Sect. 2.6.6), especially article 9-4 DPLD.

2.4.3 *The Development Risk Defence and XAI*

The development risk defence prevents the manufacturer from being liable for model characteristics they could not have discovered (article 10-1-e DPLD), for which the manufacturer bears the burden of proof.[84] The criterion for discoverability is objective and takes into account all scientific and technical knowledge available at the time of placing the product on the market, but also during the time in which it was within the manufacturer's control, regardless of whether the manufacturer was aware of it.[85] If we follow the line of reasoning outlined in the previous section, this mechanism could actually stimulate the manufacturer to keep up to date with 'explainable artificial intelligence' (XAI) techniques.[86] It requires the manufacturer to be able to argue in detail why the defence should apply, in other words: why the defect was indiscoverable, given the XAI methods available at the time—that is, if the courts set a sufficiently high bar for the substantiation of the defence.[87]

---

[82] Borges 2021, p. 35; Borges 2023b, p. 35 (no. 15).

[83] Rott 2020, pp. 655–656.

[84] ECJ, *Commission v United Kingdom*, 29 May 1997, C-300/95, ECLI:EU:C:1997:255, para 34; cp. Borges 2021, p. 37; this might be difficult to prove, see Triaille 1993, p. 221.

[85] Smith and Fotheringham 2022, p. 42; Patti 2020, pp. 115–116. Note, however, that the applicability of the development risk defence for manufacturing defects has been disputed, see Verhoeven 2018, pp. 277–280; Fairgrieve and Goldberg 2020, para 13.110–13.124; Borghetti 2023b, pp. 37–39. Compare in particular Knetsch 2021, pp. 175–177 on Cour de Cassation, 5 May 2021, No. 19-25102, ECLI:FR:CCASS:2021:C100330 with Chibanguza et al. 2022, p. 837 on Bundesgerichtshof (BGH), NJW 1995, 1094 and BGH, NJW 1995, 2162. See also Brun 2023, pp. 552–553.

[86] Russell and Norvig 2021, pp. 710–712.

[87] Cp. Borges 2021, p. 37; note that failing to comply with the prospective 'explainability requirements' in the AIA could also itself result in defectiveness through article 6-1-f DPLD.

2.5 Could a Causal Link Exist?

2.5.1 The Factual and the Normative Phase

If a CDSS is considered defective, the next question would be whether there is a causal link between the output resulting from this defect and the subsequent damage.[88] Some would argue that such a link is generally not possible. Taeger, for example, argued that the causal chain between CDSS output and damage is broken, since the intermediary—the clinician—ultimately bears the responsibility over the correctness of the medical decision.[89] However, from a legal point of view, clinicians are not strictly responsible for the devices they use.[90] Additionally, this view conflicts with the fact that clinicians are supposed to be influenced by the output of diagnostic systems.[91]

Under EU product liability law, the requirement of a causal link is a matter of national law.[92] The interpretation of this requirement differs between Member States. It is, however, common to distinguish two phases: (i) a 'factual' phase of testing for a *sine qua non* ('but for') link, and (ii) a subsequent 'normative' phase that eliminates some or all of the causes nominated in the first phase on normative grounds, e.g. because damages are too remote or result from the own fault of the party suffering damage.[93]

The first phase is of a factual nature. Most differences between Member States arise in the second, normative phase, where considerations such as 'foreseeability' and 'responsibility' come in.[94] In jurisdictions where the normative phase is more permissive,[95] the oft-cited AI liability hurdle of 'foreseeability' might pose a less difficult challenge.[96]

Hereafter, we focus on the first phase's challenge of establishing a *sine qua non* link between a CDSS defect and damage, as it can be encountered across all EU jurisdictions. The question of what would have happened in absence of the CDSS defect is hard to answer, since the occurrence of damage partly depends on the actions of the intermediary.[97] The next section (Sect. 2.5.2) will argue why there are

---

[88] A link between defect and output is also required.

[89] Taeger 1995, pp. 207–208; cp. Haftenberger 2023, p. 263.

[90] See n. 10 infra.

[91] Haftenberger 2023, p. 263.

[92] ECJ, *Sanofi Pasteur*, 21 June 2017, C-621/15, ECLI:EU:C:2017:484, para 18–43.

[93] Fairgrieve et al. 2016, p. 86; Fairgrieve and Goldberg 2020, p. 674.

[94] Fairgrieve et al. 2016, p. 86, although note that the standard of proof for the *sine qua non* link can differ across jurisdictions; Wuyts 2014, pp. 25–28; Verhoeven 2018, pp. 239–240 (BE); Van Dam 2020, pp. 533–561 (NL).

[95] This might be the case in jurisdictions where the 'theory of equivalence' plays a role, such as France (Brun 2023, para 237–248 and 249) and Belgium (Verhoeven 2018, pp. 239–240; Van Quickenborne 2007, pp. 13–43). See also Askeland 2016, p. 369 on Norway.

[96] See Selbst 2020, pp. 1344–1346, also for arguments why foreseeability might not be problematic.

[97] The importance of which seems to be underappreciated in Kardasiadou 1998, pp. 236–243.

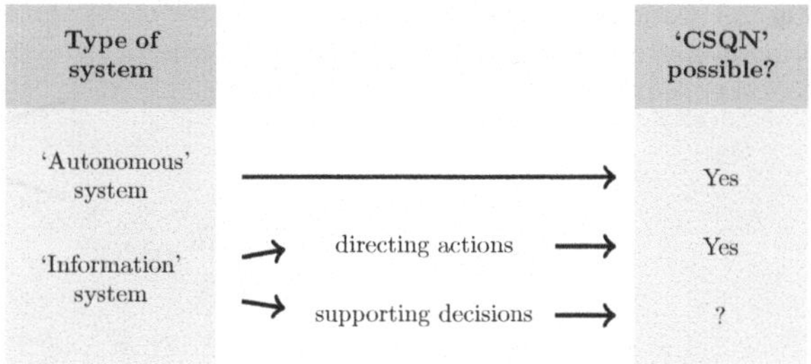

Fig. 2.2 Westerdijk's model separates directive and supportive information systems

no principal objections to the establishment of a *sine qua non* link, after which the following section (Sect. 2.6) will discuss several approaches for establishing a causal link in fact.

2.5.2 *Sine Qua Non Link: No Principal Objections*

A *sine qua non* link can be assumed if in the absence of the product defect the (same) damage would not have occurred.[98] Inevitably this theoretical exercise requires a certain appreciation of the expected actions of the intermediary: what would they have done if provided with the 'correct' output?

In 1995, Westerdijk described a model distinguishing between software-based information systems that *direct* the user towards certain decisions or actions (*beslissingssturend*), and systems that merely *support* the decision-making process of the user (*beslissingsondersteunend*).[99] For directive systems such as a pilot's flight instruments, a causal link, he argues, can exist both in the factual and normative sense between the output and the subsequent human action. This is not the case for supportive systems such as medical information systems, due to the larger role and autonomy of the intervening actor (see Fig. 2.2). In these situations, he argues, the requirements set by Dutch law for the normative phase are not met. While this distinction will be challenged in Sect. 2.6, accepting the possibility of a causal link for at least directive information systems would be a first step towards answering this section's main question.

Unfortunately, a search for case law in which EU product liability law is applied to such malfunctions did not return any instructive results. A case that nonetheless deserves mentioning is the Spanish Supreme Court's *Überlingen* judgment, in which it ruled that the (directive) Traffic alert and Collision Avoidance System (TCAS), which provides pilots with suggested route adjustments to avoid collisions, was defective, resulting in liability for the manufacturer under New Jersey/Arizona

[98] Fairgrieve et al. 2016, p. 86; Fairgrieve and Goldberg 2020, p. 684.

[99] Westerdijk 1995, pp. 242–243 and 270–271; Alheit 2001, pp. 205–208. Cp. Taeger 1995, p. 207.

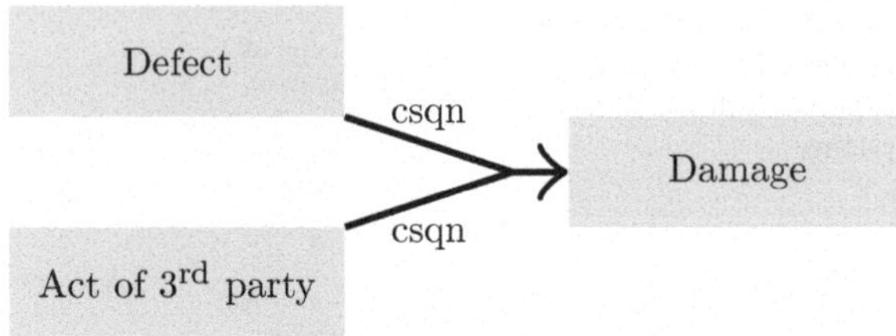

Fig. 2.3 Article 12-1 DPLD requires a sine qua non link for every cumulative cause

product liability law.[100] The Court did suggest, by way of *obiter dictum*, that this was an example of cumulative causation which, if Spanish law would have applied, would have seen the application of article 8-1 PLD (article 12-1 DPLD), suggesting that a causal link could be established.[101]

We can, however, use the examples discussed earlier in Sect. 2.3.3 to determine to the validity of both Westerdijk's and the Spanish Supreme Court's viewpoint. If it can be concluded that the alarm systems fall within the scope of the DPLD, this implies that it should be possible to establish causality for those systems. Based on the arguments provided in Sect. 2.3.3, this should arguably extend to (at least some) CDSSs. This section's question is therefore answered, tentatively, in the affirmative.

2.6 How to Establish a Causal Link in Fact

2.6.1 Introduction

The next question is how we can establish a causal link in fact. While Westerdijk's dichotomy provides a useful conceptual framework, its practical use is limited due to the lack of a clear test to distinguish between his two categories of systems, namely 'directive' and 'supportive' systems. After all, both directive and supportive systems provide information to the user upon which the user decides to act. In reality, these categories exist on a continuous spectrum. To separate them, we need to establish a suitable decision boundary. This section discusses several approaches.

First, it will discuss a rule in the directive (article 12-1 DPLD) that might seem to solve this problem and show why it does not (Sect. 2.6.2). Then, it analyses and criticises the approach taken by Haftenberger, who uses legitimate consumer expectations as a central concept to establish or reject a causal link (Sect. 2.6.3). As an alternative, the approach used under Dutch law in informed consent cases is described (Sect. 2.6.4), which is taken as a basis for a proposal for a rebuttable

[100] Spanish Supreme Court, *Überlingen*, 13 January 2015, STS 181/2015, ECLI:ES:TS:2015:181; discussed in Contissa 2017, para 7 and Schebesta 2017.

[101] Spanish Supreme Court, *Überlingen*, 13 January 2015, STS 181/2015, ECLI:ES:TS:2015:181, p. 46. See also Sect. 2.6.2 below.

presumption based on normative standards (Sect. 2.6.5), before briefly discussing the DPLD's article 9 presumptions (Sect. 2.6.6).

2.6.2 Article 12-1 DPLD (Cumulative Causation) Does Not Apply

While the DPLD does not provide a standard for causation, it does contain a rule on concurrent causes. According to article 12-1 DPLD, previously article 8-1 PLD, the liability of the manufacturer 'is not reduced when the damage is caused both by the defectiveness of a product and by an act or omission of a third party'. This rule applies to situations of cumulative causation, where the product defect and the actions of the third-party intermediary contributed independently and in parallel to the occurrence of the damage.[102] Through this rule, manufacturers cannot escape liability by claiming their product was only one of multiple contributing factors.[103]

However, to be able to successfully apply article 12-1, the *sine qua non* test with regard to the defective product must still be met (see Fig. 2.3).[104] Otherwise, the AI output cannot be said to have contributed to the damage, in which case it is not a—cumulative—cause of the damage. Article 12-1 DPLD is, therefore, not able to close this causality gap.[105]

2.6.3 The Consumer Expectation Test Does Not Apply

Haftenberger rightly states that the impact of human actions on the causal link between medical (software) product defects and damage is to be decided on a case-by-case basis.[106] As she also remarks, it could still be possible to propose a number of general rules through distinguishing certain categories of cases.

However, her categorisation focuses on the extent to which the user may rely on the output, given the legitimate safety expectations (as used in the consumer expectation test) regarding the software.[107] This could lead to an unjustified conflation of defectiveness and causality. Unlike defectiveness, establishing causality is currently

---

[102] Rolland 1990, pp. 220–221; Foerste and Graf von Westphalen 2012, para 51 (no. 10); Ehring and Taeger 2022, para 6 (no. 14–15); Lenz 2022, para 3 (no. 422); Ehring and Taeger 2022, para 6 (no. 15).

[103] This can be important when multiple software systems are used in conjunction to treat a patient.

[104] Van Empel and Ritsema 1991, p. 73; Foerste and Graf von Westphalen 2012, para 51 (no. 10); Kardasiadou 1998, p. 233.

[105] Similarly Kardasiadou 1998, p. 233, although Haftenberger 2023, p. 263 seems to disagree.

[106] Haftenberger 2023, p. 264.

[107] Haftenberger 2023, p. 264.

a matter of national law.[108] Applying the consumer expectation test for causation, therefore, has no basis. Aside from this formal criticism, there is also an objection of a substantive nature. In the first phase of causation (see Sect. 2.5.1), establishing a *sine qua non* link entails predicting the behaviour of the intermediary. This expected behaviour can indeed be influenced by (abstract) safety expectations, but other factors that are not related to the product, such as (abnormal) patient-specific circumstances, can also play a role. Such subtleties are lost when causation is viewed exclusively through the lens of legitimate safety expectations.[109]

2.6.4 Causality in Dutch Informed Consent Cases

The *sine qua non* test essentially inquires whether the intermediary would have chosen a different action if they were instead provided with the correct information.[110] An interesting parallel exists with a line of Dutch case law regarding informed consent.[111] In these cases, patients complain that their decision to agree to a certain treatment was based on incorrect information. If they had been given the correct information, they would purportedly not have agreed to this treatment, thus avoiding the harm they incurred. Unlike in several other jurisdictions, under Dutch law the patient bears the burden of proof with regard to the lack of consent and the causal link between it and the damage.[112]

For the causal link, the substantive *sine qua non* test requires patients to prove that, had they been given the correct information, they would have made a different decision. Dutch law has seen the development of a mostly objective test to answer the question: what would a 'reasonable patient' have decided, when given the correct information, under those circumstances? If this fictional reasonable patient would have been presented with the *correct* information, would they still have made the same decision? If so, the information cannot be said to have 'caused' the decision and thereby the damage. However, if a reasonable patient would have made a different decision when provided with the correct information, the court can assume the existence of a causal link between the (incorrect) information and the chosen treatment.[113]

---

[108] As discussed in Sect. 2.5.1.

[109] Although the patient-friendly way in which Haftenberger interprets these expectations could admittedly produce similar results, see Haftenberger 2023, pp. 265–267. See similarly Kardasiadou 1998, pp. 242–243. It may be true that consumer expectations also play a role in the 'second' phase of causation, but that depends on how this aspect is regulated in national law.

[110] Fairgrieve et al. 2016, p. 86; Fairgrieve and Goldberg 2020, p. 674.

[111] Dutch Supreme Court (HR), 23 November 2001, ECLI:NL:HR:2001:AB2737, NJ 2002/386, para 3.5.6; HR, 23 November 2001, ECLI:NL:HR:2001:AD3963, NJ 2002/387, para 3.5.5; HR, 23 April 2010, ECLI:NL:HR:2010:BL4882, JA 2010/97.

[112] Koch 2011, pp. 630–637; Wijne 2021b, para 25.4; Tjong Tjin Tai 2022b, para 453–454.

[113] De Tavernier 2010, para 2; Tjong Tjin Tai 2022b, para 454; Wijne 2021b, para 25.4; Wijne 2021a, pp. 665–670.

Let us consider a different context, that of liability arising out of misleading information in a prospectus. A similar question arises, specifically whether the claimant would have made the same investment decision if the information in the prospectus had been accurate. In a 2008 ruling, the Dutch Supreme Court concluded that in the absence of proof to the contrary, a causal link between the misleading prospectus and the subsequent investment decision can be presumed, in order to ensure effective protection under Directive 2003/71/EG (Prospectus Directive).[114] It considered that 'while it is, in principle, for the investor to prove the existence of a *sine qua non* link, this proof is problematic, given the fact that an investors will generally base investment decisions on a multitude of factors, while it will often not be possible to establish whether they actually received the misleading information, let alone that they were actually influenced by it'.[115]

2.6.5 Normative Standards as a Basis for a Rebuttable Presumption

There is a similarity between these lines of Dutch case law and establishing the DPLD's causal link for CDSS defects. The question is essentially the same: is it possible to establish a *sine qua non* link between the (incorrect) information provided to the decision-maker and the decision they have made?

Although it would go too far to adopt a general presumption of a causal link such as in the prospectus judgment, it would be appropriate to follow a similar approach as in the Dutch case law on informed consent. That approach entails that the question of what the *intermediary* (i.e. the decision-maker) would have done in fact can be approximated through answering the question of what normative expectations (the 'reasonable decision-maker') would require them to do in that specific situation.

Essentially, this boils down to the same test as for medical negligence. Unlike the test based on the product-related safety expectations (Sect. 2.6.3), this test allows the consideration of patient-specific circumstances. Expert reports can be used to answer the question what the intermediary should have done, similar to how courts approach the test for medical negligence. The established practice of using expert reports in medical liability cases makes this a viable approach for product liability related to specifically *clinical* decision support systems.

However, it is important to recognise that while what intermediaries *should* have done might be a reasonable estimation of what they *would* have done, these are not to be equated. The proposed approach can, therefore, not be accepted as a rule. It

---

[114] HR, *World Online*, 27 November 2009, ECLI:NL:HR:2009:BH2162, NJ 2014/201. See Pijls 2022, pp. 283–287 and Pijls 2023.

[115] HR, *World Online*, 27 November 2009, ECLI:NL:HR:2009:BH2162, NJ 2014/201, para 4.11.1–3.

can, however, play a role as a rebuttable presumption in the absence of superior information.[116]

Given the fact that causation is a matter of national law, the decision to adopt such a presumption is up to national courts and/or legislators.[117] Notably, this presumption would not change the fact that the claimant bears the burden of proving the causal link, since it is still up to them to show what a reasonable intermediary would have done, and is therefore not contradictory to article 9-1 DPLD.

2.6.6 The DPLD's Own Presumptions Regarding Causality (Article 9)

The DPLD itself contains, in article 9, several rebuttable presumptions alleviating the claimant's burden of proof. Given the provisional nature of the draft, this provision will only be described briefly here, referring to other works for a more in-depth discussion.[118]

Article 9 of the DPLD contains three 'alleviation mechanisms': (i) a presumption of defectiveness (article 9-2), (ii) a presumption of a causal link (article 9-3), and (iii) a presumption of both defectiveness and causal link for 'excessively difficult cases' (article 9-4). The presumption in article 9-3 applies when it has been established that the product is defective and the damage caused is of a kind typically consistent with the defect in question. The presumption in article 9-4 applies when the 'technical or scientific complexity' makes it excessively difficult for the claimant to prove defect, causal link or both.

The presumption in article 9-4 appears to target situations where the causal chain is obfuscated by the technical complexity of the product instead of the complexity within the causal chain itself (i.e. the presence of an intermediary), although it seems fit to resolve latter situations as well. It would therefore be valuable to observe how these rules evolve during the drafting process. However, it should be remembered that these presumptions are also *procedural* in nature. The importance of establishing a thorough understanding of the substantive aspects of causation, such as discussed in Sects. 2.6.2 and 2.6.3, should not be overlooked.

---

[116] See critically Kardasiadou 1998, p. 240.

[117] See also the presumptions in article 9 of the DPLD (Sect. 2.6.6).

[118] Hacker 2023, pp. 25–28; De Bruyne et al. 2023, para 3.5; Borges 2023b, para 4; Sormunen and Havu 2022, para III.2.b; Veldt 2023, para V; Borghetti 2023a, pp. 161–163; Spindler 2023, pp. 64–71; Zech 2023, pp. 198–199; Wagner 2022, pp. 217–218; Buiten et al. 2023, para 5.1.3.

2.7 Conclusions

This chapter focused on the application of EU product liability law to AI-based clinical decision support systems (CDSSs). The chapter claims that in some cases it should be possible to establish a causal link between incorrect information provided by the CDSS and damage caused by the intermediary acting on that information, and that the scope of the DPLD includes these situations.

Regarding the requirement of a product defect, this chapter argued for the adoption of the intentional stance in construing customer expectations for AI systems, rather than the more traditional design stance. A reinterpretation of the manufacturing defect allows us to retain the no-fault character of EU product liability, whereas design defects risk emphasising its elements of negligence.

With respect to establishing causality, this chapter argued that the *sine qua non* link between damage and CDSS output cannot be established through art 12-1 DPLD or through the consumer expectation test. Instead, this chapter proposed to adopt a rebuttable presumption in which the presence of a *sine qua non* link between output and damage is assumed in cases where a 'reasonable clinician' would have followed the system's advice.

References

Alheit K (2001) The applicability of the EU product liability directive to software. Comparative and International Law Journal of Southern Africa 34:188–209.

Askeland B (2016) Product Liability in Norway. In: Machnikowski P (ed) European Product Liability. Intersentia, Cambridge, pp 359–376.

Banja JD, Hollstein RD, Bruno MA (2022) When Artificial Intelligence Models Surpass Physician Performance: Medical Malpractice Liability in an Era of Advanced Artificial Intelligence. Journal of the American College of Radiology 19:816–820.

Beckers A, Teubner G (2021) Three Liability regimes for Artificial Intelligence: Algorithmic Actants, Hybrids, Crowds. Hart Publishing, Oxford.

Berner ES (2007) Clinical Decision Support Systems: Theory and Practice (Vol. 233). Springer Science+Business Media, New York.

Borges G (2021) AI systems and product liability. In: Proceedings of the Eighteenth International Conference on Artificial Intelligence and Law. Association for Computing Machinery, New York, pp 32–39.

Borges G (2022) Der Entwurf einer neuen Produkthaftungsrichtlinie [The Draft of a New Product Liability Directive]. Der Betrieb 45:2650–2654.

Borges G (2023a) Liability of the Operator of AI Systems De Lege Ferenda. In: Lohsse S, Schulze R, Staudenmayer D (eds) Liability for AI. Nomos Verlagsgesellschaft, Baden-Baden, pp 165–190.

Borges, G (2023b) The Manufacturer's Liability for AI Systems under Current and Future Law. Computer Law Review International 24:33–43.

Borghetti JS (2019) How can Artificial Intelligence be defective? In: Lohsse S, Schulze R, Staudenmayer D (eds) Liability for Artificial Intelligence and the Internet of Things. Nomos Verlagsgesellschaft, Baden-Baden, pp 63–76.

Borghetti JS (2023a) Adapting Product Liability to Digitalization: Trying Not to Put New Wine Into Old Wineskins. In: Lohsse S, Schulze R, Staudenmayer D (eds) Liability for AI. Nomos Verlagsgesellschaft, Baden-Baden, pp 129–164.

Borghetti JS (2023b) Taking EU Product Liability Law Seriously: How Can the Product Liability Directive Effectively Contribute to Consumer Protection? SSRN: https://ssrn.com/abstract=4502351.
Braun M, Hummel P, Beck S, Dabrock P (2021) Primer on an ethics of AI-based decision support systems in the clinic. Journal of Medical Ethics https://doi.org/10.1136/medethics-2019-105860.
Brun P (2023) Responsabilité civile extracontractuelle [Extra-contractual liability]. LexisNexis, Paris.
Buiten M, De Streel A, Peitz M (2021) EU liability rules for the age of Artificial Intelligence. CERRE, Bruxelles.
Buiten M, De Streel A, Peitz M (2023) The law and economics of AI liability. Computer Law & Security Review https://doi.org/10.1016/j.clsr.2023.105794.
Burton S, Habli I, Lawton T, McDermid J, Morgan P, Porter Z (2020) Mind the gaps: Assuring the safety of autonomous systems from an engineering, ethical, and legal perspective. Artificial Intelligence https://doi.org/10.1016/j.artint.2019/103201.
Čartolovni A, Tomičić A, Lazić Mosler E (2022) Ethical, legal, and social considerations of AI-based medical decision-support tools: A scoping review. International Journal of Medical Informatics https://doi.org/10.1016/j.ijmedinf.2022.104738.
Cayol A (2021) Le développement de l'IA dans le domaine de la santé: une révolution pour le droit de la responsabilité civile? [The development of AI in healthcare: a revolution for civil liability law?] Droit, Santé et Société 8:22–28.
Chibanguza K, Kuß C, Steege H (2022) Künstliche Intelligenz. Recht und Praxis automatisierter und autonomer Systeme [Artificial Intelligence. Law and Practice of automated and autonomous Systems]. Nomos Verlagsgesellschaft, Baden-Baden.
Contissa G (2017) Automation and Liability. An analysis in the context of socio-technical systems. I-lex Rivista di Scienze Giuridiche, Scienze Cognitive ed Intelligenza Artificiale 11:17–45.
Crilly N, Good D, Matravers D, Clarkson PJ (2008) Design as communication: exploring the validity and utility of relating intention to interpretation. Design Studies 29:425–457.
De Tavernier PCJ (2010) Over het bewijs van causaal verband met betrekking tot de geïnformeerde toestemming bij medische behandelingen [On the proof of causality regarding informed consent for medical treatments]. Maandblad voor Vermogensrecht 9:139–146.
De Bruyne J, Dheu O, Ducuing C (2023) The European Commission's approach to extra-contractual liability and AI—An evaluation of the AI liability directive and the revised product liability directive. Computer Law & Security Review https://doi.org/10.1016/j.clsr.2023.105894.
Dennett DC (2017) From Bacteria to Bach and Back: The Evolution of Minds. WW Norton & Company, New York.
Duffourc MN, Gerke S (2023) The proposed EU Directives for AI liability leave worrying gaps likely to impact medical AI. npj Digital Medicine https://doi.org/10.1038/s41746-023-00823-w.
Duffourc MN, Gerke S (2024) Decoding US Tort Liability in Healthcare's Black-Box Era: Lessons From the EU. Stanford Technology Law Review 27 (forthcoming).
Duffourc MN, Giovanniello DS (2023) The Autonomous AI Physician: Medical Ethics and Legal Liability. https://doi.org/10.1007/978-3-031-41264-6_11.
Ehring P, Taeger J (2022) Produkthaftungs- und Produktsicherheitsrecht [Product liability law and product safety law]. Nomos Verlagsgesellschaft, Baden-Baden.
Fairgrieve D, Goldberg RS (2020) Product Liability. Oxford University Press, Oxford.
Fairgrieve D, Howells G, Møgelvang-Hansen P, Straetmans G, Verhoeven D, Machnikowski P, Janssen AU, Schulze R (2016) Product Liability. In: Machnikowski P (ed) European Product Liability. Intersentia, Cambridge, pp 17–108.
Foerste U, Graf von Westphalen F (2012) Produkthaftungshandbuch. Verlag C.H. Beck, München.
Froomkin AM, Kerr I, Pineau J (2019) When AIs Outperform Doctors: Confronting the Challenges of a Tort-Induced Over-Reliance on Machine Learning. Arizona Law Review 61:33–99.
Giesen I (2010) The development of product liability in the Netherlands. In: Whittaker S (ed) The Development of Product Liability. Cambridge University Press, Cambridge, pp 152–191.
Goodfellow I, Bengio Y, Courville A (2016) Deep Learning. The MIT Press, Cambridge (MA).

Gröndahl HH (2008) Are Agency and Responsibility Still Solely Ascribable to Humans? The Case of Medical Decision Support Systems. In: Duquenoy P, George C, Kimppa K (eds) Ethical, Legal and Social Issues in Medical Informatics. IGI Global, Pennsylvania, pp 84–112.

Hacker P (2023) The European AI liability directives—Critique of a half-hearted approach and lessons for the future. Computer Law & Security Review https://doi.org/10.1016/j.clsr.2023.105871.

Haftenberger A (2023) Die Produkthaftung für künstlich intelligente Medizinprodukte [Product Liability for Artificially Intelligent Medical Devices]. Nomos Verlagsgesellschaft, Baden-Baden.

Holm S, Stanton C, Bartlett B (2021) A new argument for no-fault compensation in health care: the introduction of artificial intelligence systems. Health Care Analysis 29:171–188.

Howells G (2020) Safety Expectations as the Basis of Product Liability. In: Jansen A, Schulte-Nölke H (eds) Researches in European Private Law and Beyond—Contributions in Honour of Reiner Schulze's Seventieth Birthday. Nomos Verlagsgesellschaft, Baden-Baden, pp 91–106.

Kardasiadou Z (1998) Die Produkthaftung für fehlerhafte medizinische Expertensysteme [Product liability for defective medical expert systems]. Nomos Verlagsgesellschaft, Baden-Baden.

Knetsch J (2021) X. France. European Tort Law Yearbook 11:174–193.

Knetsch J (2022) Are Existing Tort Theories Ready for AI? A Continental European Perspective. In: DiMatteo LA, Poncibò C, Cannarsa M (eds) The Cambridge Handbook of Artificial Intelligence. Cambridge University Press, Cambridge, pp 99–115.

Koch BA (2011) Medical Liability in Europe: Comparative Analysis. In: Koch BA (ed) Medical liability in Europe: A comparison of selected jurisdictions. Walter de Gruyter, Berlin/Boston, pp 611–663.

Lenz T (2022) Produkthaftung [Product liability]. Verlag C.H. Beck, München.

Liivak T (2018) Liability of a manufacturer of fully autonomous and connected vehicles under the product liability directive. International Comparative Jurisprudence 4:178–189.

Mazeau L (2018) Intelligence artificielle et responsabilité civile: Le cas des logiciels d'aide à la décision en matière médicale [Artificial intelligence and civil liability: The case of medical decision support software]. Revue pratique de la prospective et de l'innovation 1:38–43.

Parasidis E (2018) Clinical Decision Support: Elements of a Sensible Legal Framework. Journal of Health Care Law and Policy 20:183–228.

Pasquale F (2022) Liability Standards for Medical Robotics and AI. In: DiMatteo LA, Poncibò C, Cannarsa M (eds) The Cambridge Handbook of Artificial Intelligence. Cambridge University Press, Cambridge, pp 200–212.

Patti FP (2020) Machine Learning and European Product Liability. In: Jansen A, Schulte-Nölke H (eds) Researches in European Private Law and Beyond—Contributions in Honour of Reiner Schulze's Seventieth Birthday. Nomos Verlagsgesellschaft, Baden-Baden, pp 107–124.

Pijls ACW (2022) Misleidende beursberichten. Kwesties van causaal verband en schade [Misleading stock market reports. Issues of causation and damages]. Wolters Kluwer, Deventer.

Pijls ACW (2023) Prospectus Liability and Causation. Journal of European Tort Law 14:189–205.

Prifti K, Stamhuis EF, Heine K (2022) Digging into the Accountability Gap: Operator's Civil Liability in Healthcare AI-systems. In: Custers BHM, Fosch-Villaronga E (eds) Law and Artificial Intelligence: Regulating AI and Applying AI in Legal Practice. T.M.C. Asser Press, The Hague, pp 279–295.

Rajpurkar P, Chen E, Banerjee O, Topol EJ (2022) AI in health and medicine. Nature medicine 28:31–38.

Rolland W (1990) Produkthaftungsrecht: Kommentar [Product liability law: Commentary]. Bundesanzeiger Verlagsgesellschaft, Köln.

Rott P (2020) Produkthaftung im Zeitalter der Digitalisierung [Product liability in the age of digitalisation]. In: Hentschel A, Hornung G, Jandt S (eds) Mensch—Technik—Umwelt: Verantwortung für eine sozialverträgliche Zukunft. Festschrift für Alexander Roßnagel zum 70. Geburtstag. Nomos, Baden-Baden, pp. 639–658.

Ruesen MRL (2017) Ongeschikte medische apps: wie is aansprakelijk? [Unfit medical apps: who is liable?] Computerrecht 34:67–72.
Russell SJ, Norvig P (2021) Artificial Intelligence : a modern approach. Pearson, Hoboken.
Santos Silva M, Fairgrieve D, Machnikowski P, Borghetti JS, Keirse ALM, Del Olmo P, Rajneri E, Schmon C, Ulfbeck V, Vallone V, Zech H (2021) Relevance of Risk-benefit for Assessing Defectiveness of a Product: A Comparative Study of Thirteen European Legal Systems. European Review of Private Law 29:91–132.
Sartor G (2009) Cognitive automata and the law: electronic contracting and the intentionality of software agents. Artificial intelligence and Law 17:253–290.
Schebesta H (2017) Risk Regulation Through Liability Allocation: Transnational Product Liability and the Role of Certification. Air and Space Law 42:107–136.
Schneeberger D, Stöger K, Holzinger A (2020) The European Legal Framework for Medical AI. https://doi.org/10.1007/978-3-030-57321-8_12.
Schönberger, D. (2019) Artificial intelligence in healthcare: a critical analysis of the legal and ethical implications. International Journal of Law and Information Technology 27:171–203.
Selbst AD (2020) Negligence and AI's human users. Boston University Law Review 100:1315–1376.
Smith H (2021) Clinical AI: opacity, accountability, responsibility and liability. AI & Society 36:535–545.
Smith H, Fotheringham K (2020) Artificial intelligence in clinical decision-making: Rethinking liability. Medical Law International 20:131–154.
Smith H, Fotheringham K (2022) Exploring remedies for defective artificial intelligence aids in clinical decision-making in post-Brexit England and Wales. Medical Law International 22:33–51.
Sormunen S, Havu K (2022) Harm Caused by (Intelligent) Medical Devices—Looking for a Level Playing Field and Consumer Trust? Helsinki Legal Studies Research Paper No. 76. https://doi.org/10.2139/ssrn.4307159.
Spindler G (2023) Different approaches for liability of Artificial Intelligence—Pros and Cons. In: Lohsse S, Schulze R, Staudenmayer D (eds) Liability for AI. Nomos Verlagsgesellschaft, Baden-Baden, pp 41–96.
Stapleton J (1994) Product Liability. Butterworths, London.
Sullivan HR, Schweikart SJ (2019) Are current tort liability doctrines adequate for addressing injury caused by AI? AMA journal of ethics 21:160–166.
Taeger J (1995) Ausservertragliche Haftung fur fehlerhafte Computerprogramme [Non-contractual liability for defective computer programs]. Mohr Siebeck, Tübingen.
Tjong Tjin Tai TFE (2022a) Mr. C. Assers handleiding tot de beoefening van het Nederlands Burgerlijk Recht. 7. Bijzondere overeenkomsten. Deel IV. Opdracht, incl. de geneeskundige behandelingsovereenkomst en de reisovereenkomst [Mr. C. Asser's Practical guide for the practice of Dutch Civil Law. 7. Particular Contracts. Part IV. Provision of services, including the medical treatment agreement and the travel agreement]. Wolters Kluwer, Deventer.
Tjong Tjin Tai TFE (2022b) Liability for AI Decision-Making. In: DiMatteo LA, Poncibò C, Cannarsa M (eds) The Cambridge Handbook of Artificial Intelligence. Cambridge University Press, Cambridge, pp 116–131.
Triaille, J-P (1993) The EEC Directive of July 25, 1985 on liability for defective products and its application to computer programs. Computer Law and Security Report, 5:214–226.
Twigg-Flesner C (2021) The Tale of the Grating Horseradish. Case Note on VI v KRONE-Verlag (Case C-65/20). Journal of European Consumer and Market Law 10:262–265.
Van Dam CC (2013) European tort law. Oxford University Press, Oxford.
Van Dam CC (2020) Aansprakelijkheidsrecht [Liability law]. Boomjuridisch, Den Haag.
Van Quickenborne M (2007) Oorzakelijk verband tussen onrechtmatige daad en schade [Causal link between tort and damage]. Kluwer, Mechelen.
Van Empel M, Ritsema HA (1991) Aansprakelijkheid voor producten [Liability for products]. Kluwer, Deventer.

Van Os HJA, Kanning JP, Bonten TN, Rakers MM, Putter H, Numans ME, Ruigrok YM, Groenwold RHH, Wermer MJH (2023) Cardiovascular Risk Prediction in Men and Women Aged Under 50 Years Using Routine Care Data. Journal of the American Heart Association https://doi.org/10.1161/JAHA.122.027011.

Van der Putt PG, Westerdijk RJJ (2023) AI en aansprakelijkheid: stappen naar een nieuw regime [AI and liability: steps toward a new regime]. Internetrecht 16:5–12.

Veldt GM (2020a) De betekenis van Europese productnormen voor privaatrechtelijke normstelling [The significance of European product standards for private law standards]. Rechtsgeleerd Magazijn Themis 82:30–45.

Veldt GM (2020b) Europese productnormen en privaatrechtelijke normstelling [European product standards and private law standardisation]. Wolters Kluwer, Deventer.

Veldt GM (2022) Het productbegrip bij productaansprakelijkheid aan de hand van drie arresten [The term product in product liability, three judgments] Tijdschrift voor Vergoeding Personenschade https://doi.org/10.5553/TVP/138820662022025001003.

Veldt GM (2023) The New Product Liability Proposal—Fit for the Digital Age or in Need of Shaping Up? Journal of European Consumer and Market Law 12:24–31.

Verhoeven D (2018) Productaansprakelijkheid en productveiligheid [Product liability and product safety]. Intersentia, Antwerpen.

Voulon MB (2010) Automatisch contracteren [Automatic contracting]. Leiden University Press, Leiden.

Wagner G (2010) The development of product liability in Germany. In: Whittaker S (ed) The Development of Product Liability. Cambridge University Press, Cambridge, pp 114–151.

Wagner G (2022) Liability Rules for the Digital Age—Aiming for the Brussels Effect. Journal of European Tort Law 13:191–243.

Wendehorst C (2020) Strict Liability for AI and other Emerging Technologies. Journal of European Tort Law 11:150-180

Wendehorst C (2023) Product Liability or Operator Liability for AI—What is the Best Way Forward? In: Lohsse S, Schulze R, Staudenmayer D (eds) Liability for AI. Nomos Verlagsgesellschaft, Baden-Baden, pp 99–128.

Wendehorst C, Duller Y (2023) Safety- and Liability-related Aspects of Software. In: Geistfeld MA, Karner E, Koch BA, Wendehorst C (eds) Civil Liability for Artificial Intelligence and Software. De Gruyter, Berlin/Boston, pp 185–318.

Werro F, Palmer VV, Hahn A-C (2004) Synthesis and survey of the cases and results. In: Werro F, Palmer VV (eds) The Boundaries of Strict Liability in European Tort Law. Carolina Academic Press, Durham, pp 378–462.

Westerdijk RJJ (1995) Productenaansprakelijkheid voor software [Product liability for software]. Kluwer, Deventer.

Wijne RP (2021a) Aansprakelijkheid voor zorggerelateerde schade [Liability for healthcare-related damages]. Boomjuridisch, Den Haag.

Wijne RP (2021b) De geneeskundige behangelingsovereenkomst [The medical treatment agreement]. Wolters Kluwer, Deventer.

Wuyts D (2014) The Product Liability Directive—More than two Decades of Defective Products in Europe. Journal of European Tort Law 5:1–34.

Zech H (2023) Liability for AI: Complexity problems. In: Lohsse S, Schulze R, Staudenmayer D (eds) Liability for AI. Nomos Verlagsgesellschaft, Baden-Baden, pp 193–200.

Zerilli J (2022) Book Review: We, The Robots: Regulating Artificial Intelligence and the Limits of Law by Simon Chesterman. Sydney Law Review 44:499–502.

Zikmundová K (2023) Artificial Intelligence and Medical Devices: Do We Need New Regulation? Časopis pro Právní Vědu a Praxi https://doi.org/10.5817/CPVP2023-2-5.

Chapter 3
When the Kids Aren't Alright: The Use of Facial Recognition Technologies at School

Giuseppe Mobilio

Contents

Abstract The use of artificial intelligence in the field of education has great potential. However, applications need to be approached with caution, as in the case of those for surveillance purposes and the use of biometrics. In particular, facial recognition technologies (FRTs) are highly controversial and problematic due to the ethical issues they raise, their intrusiveness on fundamental rights and the technical problems of accuracy. This Chapter looks at the specific use of FRTs on minors in schools as a paradigmatic case to address these concerns.

The analysis will provide a reasoned overview with selected use cases of the application of this AI-based technology in the school environment for different purposes. Considering the ethical implications for the development of children and adolescents, attention will be focused on the legislation applicable to this particular use of FRTs for the protection of children, namely data protection legislation. The legal regime will be assessed through the lens of the principle of proportionality and the principle of the best interests of the child in order to determine whether or not the data protection legislation fails to balance the protection of the fundamental rights and other interests of minors at stake with the actual benefits of the use of FRTs. The Chapter concludes with a look at the recent AIA and how the two pieces of legislation are expected to interact in this specific domain of application.

G. Mobilio (✉)
Department of Juridical Science, University of Florence, Pandette Street, 35, 50127 Florence, Italy
e-mail: giuseppe.mobilio@unifi.it

K. Prifti et al. (eds.), *Digital Governance*, Information Technology and Law Series 39,
https://doi.org/10.1007/978-94-6265-639-0_3

Keywords Education · Facial recognition · Surveillance · Schools · Proportionality · Best interests of the child · Data protection · AIA

3.1 Introduction

Artificial intelligence in education (AIED) is creating new opportunities for designing and developing learning environments.[1] Algorithmic technologies are transforming the educational landscape, by increasing understanding of students' needs, enhancing teaching performance and personalising learning experience.[2] As a consequence of these kinds of digital innovations, children are more and more 'datafied',[3] i.e. they are becoming objects of a multitude of monitoring devices that generate data about them. Biometrics is an advanced technique for monitoring students, as it allows the automatic recognition of individuals based on their biological and behavioural characteristics.[4] Among such biological characteristics, facial features deserve specific attention, as AI-based technology can exploit them for the purpose of recognising students, surveilling them, inferring information and, more generally, opening up a wide range of practical benefits for institutions and school communities.

Broadly speaking, facial recognition technologies (FRTs) work by automatically extracting facial features captured on a digital image of a face (so-called biometric template), and then comparing these data with previously analysed facial images already stored in a database (so-called watchlist). These databases contain large numbers of images with associated names and other personal information. FRTs are subtle instruments of surveillance, as they allow a child to be recognised from a distance, without contact, whether they are standing still or moving, and also without their awareness.[5] Moreover, FRTs can be easily deployed on a large scale around educational systems, because school infrastructures are already prepared to be equipped with these technologies, especially where extensive video monitoring and CCTVs have been widely implemented.[6] In addition, schools are institutions with relatively stable populations, and FRTs can leverage existing name-and-face photographic databases of school registers as watchlists to recognise children.[7]

However, good educational outcomes do not occur simply by virtue of the use of advanced technologies.[8] These innovations are going to affect the whole educational community, from schools to educators, parents and—above all—students.

---

[1] Hwang et al. 2020.

[2] Seldon and Abidoye 2018.

[3] Lupton and Williamson 2017.

[4] Jasserand 2015, pp. 68–70.

[5] Berle 2020, p. 5.

[6] Taylor 2013.

[7] Andrejevic and Selwyn 2020, p. 120.

[8] Castañeda and Selwyn 2018.

Careful consideration must be given to the pedagogical, ethical and legal implications deriving from the deployment of these surveillance means, which have not yet been fully addressed. This gap calls for an analysis of whether and how the regulatory framework provides for the protection of children's fundamental rights when dealing with much debated AI systems such as those deploying facial recognition.

This Chapter will focus on the use of FRTs in schools and their impact on students. Sect. 3.2 will describe the most widespread uses of these biometric technologies, mentioning some of the concerns that have been raised so far. In the light of this overview, Sect. 3.3 will analyse the resulting consequences at the ethical level. From Sect. 3.4 onwards the analysis will shift to the legal level and, in particular, will focus on the EU legal system. The objective is to delve into the regulatory response to these issues through data protection legislation, namely the EU General Data Protection Regulation (GDPR).[9] In particular, the protection of students' rights will be analysed through the lens of the principle of proportionality and the principle of the best interests of the child. In Sect. 3.5, the analysis will focus on the EU Artificial Intelligence Act (AIA),[10] to examine whether this regulation addresses the limitations of the existing legislation. In fact, the GDPR only regulates personal data processed by FRTs, with rules that have been directly enforced by courts and national supervisory authorities to ensure the protection of minors. By contrast, the AIA aims to directly regulate technologies such as facial recognition technology, but risks being less careful about the protection of minors. Section 3.6 will provide some brief concluding remarks.

3.2 The Applications of FRTs in the School Environment

In general FRTs can pursue three main objectives[11]: *verification*, when the biometric template extracted from the facial image is compared with an existing image (e.g., from the class register) of the individual child; *identification*, when the extracted biometric template is compared with a watchlist of many images (e.g., students of a class); *categorisation*, which is aimed not strictly at identifying a child, but rather at inferring several characteristics from the facial image (such as age or personality traits) and classifying the student into one or more categories. On the basis of these three objectives, it is possible to give an overview of the most widespread uses of FRTs in educational systems.

---

[9] Regulation (EU) 2016/679 of the European Parliament and of the Council of 27 April 2016 on the protection of natural persons with regard to the processing of personal data and on the free movement of such data, and repealing Directive 95/46/EC.

[10] Regulation (EU) 2024/1689 of the European Parliament and of the Council of 13 June 2024 laying down harmonised rules on artificial intelligence and amending Regulations (EC) No 300/2008, (EU) No 167/2013, (EU) No 168/2013, (EU) 2018/858, (EU) 2018/1139 and (EU) 2019/2144 and Directives 2014/90/EU, (EU) 2016/797 and (EU) 2020/1828 (Artificial Intelligence Act), in OJEU of 12.7.2024.

[11] Article 29 Data Protection Working Party 2012.

First, FRTs are used for *security control*, i.e. to secure access points, as an alternative to or in addition to locking or monitoring gates, or to monitor movements within school areas. These automated biometric systems make checks cheaper, faster, and possible on a large scale. By means of identification, FRTs will detect if there is someone on school grounds who is not supposed to be there and those people will be denied entry to particular classrooms or the school building. These systems have been used in the USA since the mid-2010s, particularly given the rise of school shootings.[12] In Russia as well, since 2020, thousands of schools have been testing a system named 'Orwell' to ensure children's safety.[13]

A similar application is for school *attendance* checks, where FRTs allow for saving time when it comes to this kind of routine activity. A significative example is offered by India, where in 2020 the Uttar Pradesh government started implementing such AI systems to tackle the issue of fraudulent attendance, both in regard to teachers' use of proxies and ghost students.[14] But more generally, as education switched online during the pandemic, many schools around the world have adopted attendance systems capable of recording online class participation.[15]

FRTs are also used for contactless lunch *payments*, with the aim of reducing administrative burdens for families and school institutions. By means of a combination of identification and verification, the system first confirms the pupil's identity and then accesses and deducts money from an online account, under the supervision of a catering staff member. In 2019, several schools in North Ayrshire, Scotland, launched a pilot project to enable schoolchildren to make payments of this kind.[16]

Another discussed use of FRTs, instead, is the assessment of student *engagement*. CCTVs installed in classrooms are embedded with facial recognition software, and the systems, through categorisation, are able to measure the level of involvement based on facial and nonverbal micro-expressions. The aim is to motivate students to stay focused and keep their minds from wandering and to personalise learning activities that consider students' emotions and moods, as well as to provide teachers with valuable feedback.[17] Schools in China have recently reported a massive use of FRTs in this way.[18]

In the face of this diversity of applications, many voices have been raised calling for caution. Not only in academia,[19] but also among regulators. For example, in October 2021, the UK Information Commissioner's Office (ICO) stepped in to probe into the use of FRTs in school lunch queues[20] and, in light of the investigation, North Ayrshire

[12] Harwell 2018.

[13] The Moscow Times 2020.

[14] Business Insider 2022.

[15] Kamil et al. 2023.

[16] Weale 2021.

[17] Bala 2020, p. 250.

[18] Connor 2018.

[19] Barrett 2020; Bala 2020; Andrejevic and Selwyn 2020; Berendt et al. 2020, p. 316.

[20] Information Commissioner's Office 2023.

Council paused the implementation of the above-described practices.[21] In the US, New York State adopted a law in 2020 placing a moratorium on the use of biometric surveillance in schools, although this law seems to have been circumvented.[22] The European Parliament has called for a ban on FRTs used for educational purposes.[23] Given these positions, a more in-depth analysis of some key concerns arising from the aforementioned uses of FRTs seems to be warranted.

3.3 Ethical Concerns

The need to consider the ethical issues arising from AIED has become increasingly urgent in recent years.[24] Many concerns stem from the view that children and young people are a vulnerable group who deserves special care and protection, especially when in contact with AI-based technologies, internet and social media. Minors' attitudes to privacy risks and their ability to protect themselves from surveillance intrusions are a very sensitive issue. However, a growing body of research demonstrates that children are not oblivious to the consequences of their behaviour as they interact with digital technologies and online environments.[25]

The use of FRTs in schools interferes with many ethical values that international guidelines and documents pose as requirements for the deployment of AI in education.[26] Furthermore, these technologies have a direct impact on the pedagogical context and the quality of education.[27]

In this respect, we need to consider the use of FRTs *within classrooms*, such as to assess student engagement. This deployment has many negative implications for students. Firstly, considering their *autonomy*, such surveillance narrows the definition of the 'acceptable student',[28] based on the (facial) characteristics that an ideal engaged student is supposed to meet through an automated assessment. Normal behaviours can be stigmatised, and those who fall outside that definition and do not fit within narrow standards of acceptability may be punished. Secondly, considering students' *agency*, this type of assessment pushes students to alter their behaviours in order to appear engaged or to 'game the system' by simply forcing themselves to change their facial appearance. The price of this is a curb on their individuality and chilling of their freedom of expression. Thirdly, considering students' *dignity*, there is a shift from active targeting to passive and generalised recognition, which leads to

[21] BBC News 2021.

[22] Miguel and Schwarz 2022.

[23] European Parliament 2021, para 45.

[24] Nguyen et al 2023; Holmes et al. 2021; Reiss 2021.

[25] Livingstone et al. 2019, pp. 21–22.

[26] UNESCO 2019; UNESCO 2021; European Commission 2022.

[27] Holmes et al. 2021.

[28] Galligan et al. 2020, pp. 43–46.

the dehumanisation of schools.[29] Assessment on the basis of schematic representations of facial features is a very reductive engagement with students. More in general, the attempt to detect emotions is largely unachievable given the technical and scientific failure to achieve such a result with certainty.[30] Although to a lesser extent, a similar impact on their dignity may result from attendance checks, where the use of biometric technologies risks objectifying the face of pupils and depersonalising the relationship between school institutions and students.[31]

Other implications arise from the use of FRTs *outside the classroom*, such as for security checks and monitoring of students within schools, or payment systems. Constant monitoring in school areas can have the same impact on students' autonomy, agency or dignity as it does within classrooms. In addition, considering students' *development*, careful attention must be paid to the longer-term individual and social impact of engaging with young people during a formative period. Indeed, the implementation of FRTs in schools will potentially normalise the experience of being under constant surveillance from an early age.[32] Moreover, considering students' *exercise of freedoms*, surveillance of children may have a profound effect on their privacy expectations in later life.[33]

3.4 The Answer of Data Protection Legislation

Given these ethical implications, there is a need to consider what the legal response should be. Currently, the regulation that protects children's fundamental rights against the use of FRTs in schools is data protection legislation.[34] While Directive 95/46/EC did not contain any child-specific provisions, Regulation 2016/679 (GDPR) declares that 'children merit specific protection with regard to their personal data, as they may be less aware of the risks, consequences and safeguards concerned and their rights in relation to the processing of personal data' (Recital 38). This statement is followed up with other specific provisions that regard FRTs.[35]

When applied to these biometric systems, the GDPR is deemed to protect different domains of the so-called 'institutional privacy' of children, in which personal data control is mediated by schools[36]: namely pupils' 'physical privacy', which is affected by technologies that track, monitor and broadcast children's live images, behaviour or locations; but also their 'informational privacy', which is at stake when children's

[29] Andrejevic and Selwyn 2020, p. 121.

[30] Barrett 2020.

[31] Nakar and Greenbaum 2017, p. 120.

[32] Galligan et al. 2020, pp. 38–42.

[33] Bala 2020, p. 250.

[34] Mobilio 2023.

[35] Lievens and Verdoodt 2018, pp. 270–278.

[36] Livingstone et al. 2019, pp. 13–14.

personal data are collected, stored or processed.[37] In addition, by protecting personal data, the GDPR indirectly provides protection for other rights, freedoms, interests and ethical values that are at stake when one is dealing with AIED, such as freedom of expression, freedom of assembly or the right to education.[38]

Considering all the ethical concerns discussed above in Sect. 3.3, the question is whether, and to what extent, this regulation achieves its objective of protection, given that we are talking about biometric technology, special subjects such as children, and a specific context such as schools. In order to attempt an answer, we need to consider that the use of FRTs in schools creates a conflict between interests that translates into the need to balance the protection of fundamental rights and other interests of minors with the achievement of different practical benefits, as seen in Sect. 3.2. In legal terms, the principle of proportionality and the principle of the best interests of the child come to the fore in this balancing assessment. The relationship between these two principles is complex and warrants a more in-depth analysis than can be carried out here.[39] For the purposes of this discussion, the two principles will be considered as complementary and will be used to examine whether the GDPR offers sufficient protection to students.

3.4.1 The Defence Based on the Principle of Proportionality

When considering the consequences of the use of FRTs in terms of the restriction of fundamental rights, the criterion for assessing the legitimacy of such use is the *principle of proportionality*.[40] In general, Article 52(1) of the Charter of Fundamental Rights of the European Union (CFREU) refers to the principle of proportionality as the criterion for striking the right balance between the objectives pursued by a particular measure and the sacrifice of rights. According to the Court of Justice of the EU (CJEU), the principle of proportionality requires that legal acts be appropriate for attaining the legitimate objectives pursued by the legislation at issue and do not exceed the limits of what is appropriate and necessary in order to achieve those objectives.[41] The Council of Europe has also laid down a similar provision with specific regard to children's rights in the digital environment.[42] However, the principle of proportionality is the criterion not only for assessing the legitimacy of a law that allows a limitation of fundamental rights, but also, according to the GDPR, for assessing *ex ante* the legitimacy of a measure in a specific situation, such as

[37] UNICEF 2018, p. 8.

[38] Simoncini and Longo 2021, p. 38.

[39] Committee on the Rights of the Child 2021, para 69.

[40] Barak 2012, p. 243; Dalla Corte 2022; Mobilio 2023.

[41] Ex multis, CJEU Judgement of 6 October 2020, Joined Cases C-293/12 and C-594/12, *Digital Rights Ireland Ltd v Minister for Communications, Marine and Natural Resources*, ECLI:EU:C:2020:791, para 46.

[42] Council of Europe 2018, para 38

the concrete use of FRTs. Therefore, the actual benefits of using FRTs must be balanced with the sacrifice of fundamental rights of students; hence, 'personal data should be processed only if the purpose of the processing could not reasonably be fulfilled by other means'.[43] The main tool for carrying out this balancing is the data protection impact assessment (DPIA),[44] which must include at least 'an assessment of the necessity and proportionality of the processing operations in relation to the purposes'.[45]

In this respect, the national data protection authorities have provided useful guidelines for better addressing whether the concrete use of FRTs in the school environment can be considered proportionate or not. The French Data Protection Authority (Commission nationale de l'informatique et des libertés—CNIL) reached a decision on FRTs installed at the entrances of two French high schools for security purposes, specifically to assist school officials in preventing intrusions and to reduce the time of checks; measures to which the students had previously consented. The CNIL ruled that such controls were in violation of the principle of proportionality, as there were much 'less invasive means' to achieve the same purpose in terms of privacy and individual freedoms, such as the use of badges.[46] The same conclusions were drawn by the Swedish Data Protection Authority (Integritetsskyddsmyndigheten—IMY) in a case where FRTs were used instead to monitor students' attendance. The use of these technologies was judged to be too 'intrusive' with regard to the personal integrity of students and excessive compared to what was necessary to monitor their attendance.[47] A similar disproportion can be seen in the different uses of FRTs for functions such as making payments (where, for example, prepaid cards can be used), and even more so where they are used to assess student engagement (rather than, for example, more educators).

In conclusion, to protect children's rights, data protection legislation, through the principle of proportionality, imposes strict conditions on the use of biometric surveillance that would be very difficult to meet.

3.4.2 The Best Interests of the Child, between Empowerment and Protection

A different criterion for balancing the interests at stake when using FRTs in schools is offered by the *principle of the best interests of the child*. This principle assists both regulators in adopting policies and general rules, and judges in making decisions in specific situations, by requiring an assessment appropriate to the specific context; under this principle, the special value of children is given priority over all other

[43] Recital 39 GDPR.

[44] Demetzou 2019.

[45] Article 35(7)(b) GDPR

[46] Commission nationale de l'informatique et des libertés 2019.

[47] Swedish Data Protection Authority 2019.

compelling interests.[48] At the same time, the principle has also been criticised for its breadth and open-ended, indeterminate nature, and for its exposure to cultural relativism.[49]

Many legal sources cite the principle of the best interests of the child and a large body of case law has helped to refine it: this principle was first affirmed by the UN Convention on the Rights of the Child (Article 3.1),[50] and then reaffirmed by the CFREU (Article 24).[51] At EU level, it has been developed in the context of regulation on the internal market and the Area of Freedom, Security and Justice, with a direct impact on family law cases.[52] But now it can be considered as a general principle to be taken into account when interpreting and assessing the legality of the relevant secondary legislation in order to ensure that the child's best interests are given primary consideration.[53]

Within this legal framework, the principle seeks to reconcile the dual objectives of ensuring the protection and welfare of children, on the one hand, and their autonomy and agency, on the other.[54] For its own part, the GDPR tries to address the so-called 'empowerment versus protection dilemma', that is, the need to empower children as digital users able to grasp the opportunities of playing, learning and communicating, while protecting them from privacy violations and harms.[55]

Thus, the analysis will now focus on the provisions of the GDPR that more directly address this dilemma vis-à-vis FRTs, namely the provisions related to the values of awareness (for empowerment) and inclusion (for protection). The aim is to examine whether this regulation adequately considers the best interests of the child in relation to both of these needs, thereby protecting students against the potential harms arising from FRTs.

---

[48] Eekelaar 1994; Freeman 1993.

[49] Alsto and Gilmour-Walsh 1996.

[50] States 'should have regard for all children's rights, including their rights to seek, receive and impart information, to be protected from harm and to have their views given due weight, and ensure transparency in the assessment of the best interests of the child and the criteria that have been applied' (Committee on the Rights of the Child 2021, para 13).

[51] Although there is no direct reference to it in the European Convention on Human Rights (ECHR), the European Court of Human Rights (ECtHR) largely uses it as a criterion for interpretation.

[52] Lamont 2021, pp. 694–703.

[53] CJEU Judgement of 6 June 2013, *MA et al. v. Secretary of State for the Home Department*, C-648/11, ECLI:EU:C:2013:367, para 57 ff.

[54] Verhellen 2015, pp. 50–52; McGlynn 2002, p. 397. According to the UNCRC, the former is reflected in the right to be heard (Article 12), while the second in the right to non-discrimination (Article 2) in relation to the right to education (Articles 28–29) (UN Committee on the Rights of the Child 2013, para 41–43).

[55] Macenaite 2017.

3.4.2.1 Learner Awareness

The GDPR protects the student's awareness and freedom to choose whether to be subject to FRTs in three main ways. The first one is related to the legal ground. Data processed by FRTs, such as biometric templates, are qualified as 'biometric data'[56]: consequently, the GDPR prohibits the processing of such data unless they are covered by one of the exceptions provided for in Article 9.

Should the use of FRTs fall within the institutional activities of the school, the processing could be considered, according to Article 9(2)(g)GDPR, necessary for reasons of '*substantial public interest*', as long as the use is regulated 'on the basis of Union or Member State law'. In this case, the use of such technologies does not require the student's permission. However, 'reasons of substantial public interest' is a very high standard to meet,[57] as the Swedish IMY also found in the aforementioned case that the school's monitoring did not fall within this case.

By contrast, when the use of FRTs does not fall under this exception, the legal ground is offered by the *explicit consent*[58] of students for the automated processing of their facial images in relation to the defined purposes.[59] In this way, greater awareness should be guaranteed. Indeed, the GDPR specifies that consent must be a freely given, specific, informed and unambiguous indication of the data subject's wishes.[60] However, in the case of students, the freedom of consent is generally undermined by an imbalance of power.[61] A decision of the Bulgarian Commission for Personal Data Protection (CPDP) in 2020 explicitly underlined this aspect.[62] When asked to rule on an access control system with FRTs and body temperature monitoring for COVID-19 installed by a school, the CPDP declared that the only basis for processing personal data that could apply is consent. However, it stressed that consent in a hierarchical relationship between a principal and a student is an inappropriate ground, because of doubts that it is not freely given. Consent will also not be free in cases where there are no alternatives to the use of FRTs that are easy to implement.[63]

The use of consent as a legal ground for data processing by public authorities is not totally excluded, as long as students are not denied education or services and can refuse the use of these technologies without any detriment.[64] However, there is still a risk that consent does not indicate actual awareness. FRTs, in fact, accentuate the crisis of the traditional principle of 'notice and consent': as it is well known, limited

---

[56] Article 4(1)(14) GDPR.

[57] Raposo 2022, p. 11.

[58] Article 9(2)(a) GDPR.

[59] No parental consent is strictly required, because the provisions of Article 8 GDPR regarding conditions for a child's consent applies only for information society services (as per Article. 4(25) GDPR, which refers to Directive EU 2015/1535), and therefore not for FRTs.

[60] Article 4(1)(11) GDPR.

[61] European Data Protection Board 2020, para 16–24.

[62] Bulgarian Commission for Personal Data Protection 2020.

[63] Consultative Committee of the Convention 108 2021, p. 7.

[64] European Data Protection Board 2020, para 20.

understanding, lack of available time, and information asymmetries are all elements that result in consent being given automatically, and without full awareness.[65]

The second way of ensuring student awareness is related to *information*. Regardless of whether or not they have actually given their consent, students have the right to receive certain information about the use of FRTs, as a corollary of the principle of transparency.[66] They must be able to exercise this right before recognition takes place, or in any case at the time facial images are collected, in order to avoid students being subjected to FRTs without their awareness. In particular, schools must make available various types of information about the use of FRTs, such as the legal basis, the purposes of the processing, the data retention period, the right to withdraw consent, and at least 'meaningful information about the logic involved, as well as the significance and the envisaged consequences of such processing for the data subject'.[67]

However, as the UK ICO emphasised in its opinion on the use of FRTs for payments, the provision of this type of information does not necessarily mean greater awareness; therefore, there is an issue of effectiveness here too. Technical terms may be unfamiliar not only to children, but also to parents. Hence, these individuals may benefit from an explicit explanation, in age-appropriate language, of how children's data will be collected, used, stored and retained.[68] This is the proper application of the GDPR, which states that information must be provided 'in a concise, transparent, intelligible and easily accessible form, using clear and plain language, in particular for any information addressed specifically to a child'.[69]

The third way of ensuring student awareness is related to *human supervision*. The intervention of a human being prevents machines from taking autonomous decisions that have a negative impact on people and provide him or her with a higher level of awareness.[70] According to the GDPR, students 'have the right not to be subject to a decision based solely on automated processing, including profiling, which produces legal effects concerning him or her or similarly significantly affects him or her'.[71]

Typically, the use of FRTs in schools does not involve a decision 'based solely on automated processing', because the intervention of a person, such as a school security official, or a teacher in the case of engagement assessment, is expected in any case. However, this supervision remains crucial because, from the educator's standpoints, machines could never replace human judgement, but at most support it,

[65] Custers et al. 2022, pp. 466–469.

[66] Article 5(1)(a) GDPR.

[67] Article 13 GDPR.

[68] Information Commissioner's Office 2023.

[69] Article 12(1) GDPR. See also Recital 58.

[70] European Commission 2019, p. 4.

[71] Article 22(1) GDPR. This regime does not apply where the legal ground – as mentioned above – is 'substantial public interest' (Article 22(2) GDPR), or 'explicit consent' (Article 22(3) GDPR). Nevertheless, invoking these exceptions should be avoided, as the same GDPR states in Recital 71 that such measures 'should not concern a child'.

since algorithms and AI systems lack self-reflection and social abilities.[72] At the same time, as far as students are concerned, exposure to purely automated surveillance would create a sense of resignation and internalisation of authority which could be detrimental to their educational process.[73]

However, the danger of uncritically relying on intelligent machines always lurks.[74] In this case there is a risk of overlooking the need for greater awareness on the part of both students and teachers. But more importantly, in the case of facial recognition errors—as will be clarified in the next Section—the consequence is that humans will be prompted to follow the machine's suggestions, which could lead to mistakes. This could be to the detriment of individual students or certain categories of students, leading to a misplaced focus of control on them or a negative evaluation of their engagement.

3.4.2.2 Equity and School Inclusiveness

The second need that the GDPR seeks to address, in accordance with the principle of the best interests of the child, is the protection of students, notwithstanding the other benefits that may arise from the use of FRTs. This need, in the perspective discussed here, is met through the construction of a more equitable and inclusive school.[75] Equity and inclusiveness in a school environment where algorithmic technologies are deployed depend mostly on how reliably the technologies operate, i.e. they should not produce harmful errors and should likewise not cause discrimination.[76]

The use of FRTs in schools is motivated by the assumption that they enable more efficient and equal supervision or assessments of pupils. However, there is a growing body of literature that directly correlates the accuracy of FRTs with the quality of the algorithmic training datasets, i.e. the absence of *bias*.[77] The more biased the datasets are—because they do not contain enough high-quality facial images of people of a certain gender, age or ethnic origin—the less accurate the recognition of the misrepresented people will be, leading to discrimination.[78]

Tests carried out on datasets and facial recognition algorithms show that recognition errors increase exponentially according to the age of the person they are trying to recognise.[79] From a technical point of view, it is clear that the images of young people generate a higher number of false negatives than those of adults, due to the rapid growth and changes in facial physiognomy that occur during their development. In this case, it is sufficient to compare a facial image taken in youth with images of

[72] Xu and Ouyang 2021.

[73] Andrejevic and Selwyn 2020, p. 123.

[74] Article 29 Data Protection Working Party 2017, p. 10.

[75] UNESCO 2019, para 22–24.

[76] Nguyen et al., 2023, pp. 4232–4233.

[77] Zuiderveen Borgesius 2018, p. 17.

[78] Leslie 2020.

[79] Grother et al. 2019, p. 2.

the same individual after only five years have passed and the accuracy of recognition will be compromised. In general, therefore, it has been demonstrated that the current state of technology makes the analysis of images of children under the age of thirteen less reliable.[80] This is why children need to be overrepresented in the construction of training datasets[81], while in the construction of watchlists facial images should be refreshed continuously.

The concern when it comes to minors is also linked to the fact that, more generally, black people and females are grossly underrepresented in training datasets.[82] As a result, FRTs will be less accurate for dark-skinned women than for light-skinned men of Caucasian origin, especially if the facial image is not captured under optimal conditions (lighting, posture, etc.).[83]

As a result, the inaccuracy of FRTs can undermine the hypothetical benefits of their use, paradoxically leading to less personalised education, less effective checks and less accessible services. Data protection legislation tackles bias and accuracy where it states that personal data, also when used to train FRTs or to create watchlists, should be 'accurate and, where necessary, kept up to date'; for this reason, schools wishing to employ FRTs must take every 'reasonable step' to ensure that 'personal data that are inaccurate, having regard to the purposes for which they are processed, are erased or rectified without delay'.[84] Accordingly, schools should implement appropriate 'technical and organisational measures' in order to prevent 'discriminatory effects'.[85] The UK ICO also stressed that 'to ascertain whether the algorithm is sufficiently accurate [the authority using FRTs] should seek information and assurances from the supplier about how the algorithm was trained (is the training data sufficiently representative?) and what kind of bias testing has been conducted'.[86]

However, this objective is not easily achievable, mainly because the search for bias or discrimination is not an explicitly mentioned justification for processing biometric data.[87] As a result, it may be difficult for someone other than the providers who develop FRTs to test a training dataset in search of bias, due to the lack of a legal ground. Furthermore, it will be difficult to replace or correct systems currently in use due to the widespread use of FRTs trained on non-representative data.[88]

---

[80] European Union Agency for Fundamental Rights 2018, p. 90.

[81] Han and Jain 2014.

[82] Cook et al. 2019; Merler et al. 2019.

[83] Buolamwini and Gebru, 2018.

[84] Article 5(1)(d) GDPR.

[85] Recital 71 GDPR.

[86] Information Commissioner's Office 2023.

[87] European Union Agency for Fundamental Rights 2022, p. 26.

[88] Hacker 2018, p. 1150.

3.5 FRTs in the New AIA

Data protection legislation offers different levels of protection against the use of FRTs in schools: more pronounced in the application of the proportionality principle, while it risks being less effective in meeting the best interests principle. However, the regulation of AI-based technologies is moving forward, as the EU institutions have just approved a new Regulation 'laying down harmonised rules on artificial intelligence' (so-called *AIA*).

The AIA reflects the EU's effort to develop a coordinated approach to the human and ethical implications of AI through a legal framework that addresses the risks associated with certain uses of AI. The aim is, on the one hand, to implement a trustworthy AI and, on the other, to foster the development of a Digital Single Market in the EU.[89]

The new regulation employs a risk-based approach,[90] distinguishing between "Prohibited AI practices", "high-risk AI systems" and AI systems associated with 'transparency obligations', each associated with different conditions. Therefore, we must first examine the conditions under which it will be possible to use FRTs in schools according to this regulation.

Within the first category, since Commission's proposal, the regulation bans 'the use of 'real-time' remote biometric identification systems in publicly accessible spaces for law enforcement purposes', except under specific conditions therein provided for.[91] However, the final version of the regulation also prohibits the scraping of facial images from the internet or CCTV and, more relevant here, the use of AI systems 'to infer emotions of a natural person in the areas of [...] education institutions'.

Within the second category of 'high risk' systems, the AIA distinguishes between 'Biometrics' and 'Education and vocational training'.[92] In the first case, the regulation considers: biometric identification of natural persons outside the prohibited uses; AI systems used for biometric categorisation, according to sensitive or protected attributes or characteristics based on the inference of those attributes or characteristics (evidently outside the school environment). In the second case, the regulation considers: AI systems used for determining access or admission or assigning natural persons to educational and vocational training institutions; AI systems used for evaluating learning outcomes; AI systems used for assessing the appropriate level of education that individual will receive or will be able to access; AI systems used for monitoring and detecting prohibited behaviour of students during tests. Significantly, the regulation does not consider as 'high-risk' AI systems intended to be used for 'biometric verification the sole purpose of which is to confirm that a specific natural

---

89 Laux et al. 2024.

90 De Gregorio and Dunn, 2022.

91 Article 5 AIA.

92 Annex III AIA. Article 26(10) also explicitly considers, with some exceptions, AI systems for post-remote biometric identification for law enforcement purposes to be 'high risk' and sets out further conditions for this specific use.

person is the person he or she claims to be'. The regime for 'high risk' systems is inspired by that of the New Legislative Framework and imposes numerous burdens on all value chain participants, especially providers before they can place technology on the market.[93] Providers must demonstrate compliance with such obligations by undergoing a 'conformity assessment' as an internal control check that, once passed, allows the CE mark to be affixed to high-risk AI systems.[94]

In the last category of AI systems, the regulation states that 'emotion recognition systems' and 'biometric categorisation systems' (which are also classified as high-risk) are also subject to 'transparency obligations', in the sense of an obligation to inform the persons exposed thereto.[95]

In sum, based on the examples in Sect. 3.2, the use of FRTs in schools is not generally prohibited,[96] while in others it is considered as 'high risk'.[97] FRTs are 'high risk' AI systems when they are used:

> to perform security checks in 'real time' (i.e., where the capturing of the biometric data, the comparison and the identification occur all instantaneously or without a significant delay)[98] and/or 'ex post' (i.e., where the biometric data have already been captured, and the comparison and identification occur only after a significant delay)[99], other than by law enforcement authorities; in relation to payments or attendance verification, if there is a 'live' identification coupled with verification; to assess student engagement, without inferring emotions, e.g. when analysing only facial micro-expressions (but it would be very hard to argue that there is no inference of emotion, such as satisfaction, in this case). In this case, schools must comply with 'transparency obligations'.

The new regulation will coexist with the current data protection legislation. However, we need to ask how the two pieces of regulation will coexist. In general, it has been observed that the AIA is to be implemented without prejudice to the EU data protection acquis, so that the applicability of the latter in its entirety will not in any way be affected by the AIA.[100] Nevertheless, there may be tensions between the two regulatory frameworks that affect the protection of fundamental rights, even if they are not explicit.

In some aspects, the two regulations are expressly related, such as for the processing of biometric data in the case of remote biometric identification for purposes other than law enforcement.[101] In other aspects, the two regulations do

---

[93] European Parliamentary Research Service 2021.

[94] Article 43 AIA.

[95] Article 50(3) AIA.

[96] Despite the Commission's proposal, categorisation or emotion recognition is now prohibited in schools; see Kind 2021.

[97] Kind 2021.

[98] Recital 8 AIA.

[99] Recital 8 AIA.

[100] Mazzini and Scalzo, 2023, p. 14.

[101] Recital 39 AIA.

not overlap and are in fact complementary. This is the case with the consent rules, which will continue to apply to allow the use of FRTs and the processing of personal and biometric data.

Moreover, through this complementarity, the AIA sometimes creates the conditions to facilitate the enforcement of the GDPR. This is the case of the rules on 'transparency and provision of information to deployers',[102] which impose on the provider (who develops FRTs) the obligation to provide the user or the deployer (in our case schools) with several items of information.[103] The information will allow the schools to better comply with their own obligation to provide information to the students who are subjected to FRTs, in accordance with the GDPR and the best interests principle. Another case is the risk management system, which must be applied throughout the entire lifecycle of a high-risk AI system.[104] The aim is to identify, analyse, mitigate or eliminate the most likely risks to fundamental rights, with specific consideration given to the impact on children.[105] This type of assessment could be a useful basis for subjecting FRTs to the proportionality test.

There are also cases in which the AIA and the GDPR do not overlap, but one limits the scope of the other. This is the case where the AIA directly regulates FRTs, imposing some conditions on their legitimate use and, consequently, setting limits on the application of the GDPR. We are referring to the prohibited uses set out in the regulation, as well as the many voices that have demanded an extension of the list of prohibited uses. The European Data Protection Board (EDPB) and the European Data Protection Supervisor (EDPS) have called for a general ban on any use of AI for automated recognition of human features in publicly accessible spaces and for categorising individuals into clusters according to any grounds for discrimination under Article 21 CFREU.[106] Civil society organisations[107] and academics[108] have also called for a ban on FRTs for non-law enforcement agencies, such as schools, given the evidence that they engage in mass biometric surveillance. The EU Parliament pushed (unsuccessfully) to include in the list of prohibited AI practices some uses of FRTs relevant here, such as 'real-time' remote biometric identification systems in publicly accessible spaces.[109] Here we see a shift in regulatory policy: from a general regulation of AI-based technologies to the regulation of a specific type of technology. It is the AIA in itself that balances the different freedoms and interests at stake, on the assumption that, in the case of FRTs and education or minors, there can be an absolute presumption of disproportionality and an excessive sacrifice of the child's

[102] Article 13 AIA.

[103] Such as the level of accuracy, robustness and cybersecurity; risks to fundamental rights; performance as regards the persons or groups of persons on which the system is intended to be used; relevant information in terms of the training, validation and testing data sets.

[104] Article 9(2) AIA.

[105] Article 9(8) AIA.

[106] EDPB and EDPS 2021.

[107] EDRi 2021.

[108] Smuha et al. 2021.

[109] European Parliament 2023.

interests. However, the legislator should be aware of the risk that the regulation may soon become obsolete, given the rapid development of biometric technologies in recent years.

Finally, we must consider the cases in which the AIA and GDPR overlap. Here the problem lies, first and foremost, in the difficulties of interpretation that arise from the possible lack of connection. Just think of the different definition of 'biometric data', which the GDPR defines as data resulting from (i) specific technical processing of (ii) personal data relating to the physical, physiological or behavioural characteristics, with the aim of (iii) uniquely identifying a person, while the AIA omits the purpose of identification.[110] However, such a lack of connection risks, above all, weakening the protection of students against FRTs. For example, there is an increase in protection where the AIA provides for the requirement of human oversight,[111] specifically where it states that two individuals must verify and confirm facial recognition matching, having been enabled by the measures adopted to correctly interpret the system's output and decide whether to disregard, override or reverse it: here the AIA establishes a framework that lends substance to the meaningful human involvement required by the GDPR,[112] again in accordance with the best interests principle.

In other parts of the regulation, the enhancement of the protection of fundamental rights risks being more apparent than effective, as in the case of data quality and bias. The AIA recognises that the technical inaccuracies of FRTs can lead to biased results and entail discriminatory effects due to the age of people.[113] Therefore, training, validation and testing data sets should be subject to appropriate data governance and management practices, to ensure that they are relevant, representative, free of errors and complete.[114] Datasets will consider the specific geographical, behavioural or functional setting within which FRTs will be used.[115] Bias monitoring, detection and correction will be separate justifications for the processing of sensitive categories of personal data as part of the measures taken to ensure compliance with the quality standards for 'high-risk' AI systems.[116]

Compared with the generic provisions of the GDPR, the requirements set forth by the AIA are more precise. However, we should not forget that the enforcement of the new rules is left up to providers, leaving them too much discretion in the assessment of 'adequacy'.[117] In addition, requirements such as 'error-free' or 'complete' can almost never be fully met in a large-scale AI training dataset without setting a qualitative threshold.[118] This threshold is particularly problematic if it is to be parametrised for minors, because of the difficulties outlined in Sect. 3.4.2.

---

110 Article 4(1)(14) GDPR and Article 3(1)(34) AIA.

111 Article 14(5) AIA.

112 Mazzini and Scalzo, 2023, p. 15.

113 Recital 32 AIA.

114 Article 10(3) AIA.

115 Article 10(4) AIA.

116 Article 10(5) AIA.

117 Smuha et al. 2021, p. 24.

118 Hacker 2021, p. 298.

The last example suggests that the AIA could include more specific provisions for minors—such as those found in the GDPR—consistently with Recital 48 of the regulation, which recalls children's rights according to Article 24 CFREU and the UN Convention on the Rights of the Child, 'both of which require consideration of the children's vulnerabilities and provision of such protection and care as necessary for their well-being'.

3.6 Conclusions

AI-based technologies are becoming increasingly widespread in education. FRTs, in particular, deserve special consideration. The many uses that these biometric technologies can find are accompanied by just as many significant concerns. This type of surveillance can have a direct impact both on the construction of the educational system and on the development of the school-age children. The protection of the fundamental rights of minors is supposed to be guaranteed by data protection legislation. The analysis has attempted to show how this legislation offers a very high threshold of protection, if the principle of proportionality is applied, in that it is designed to prevent the use of FRTs in schools for purposes that could well be achieved by other means. On the other hand, this legislation runs the risk of not really meeting the requirements underlying the principle of the best interests of the child, namely to ensure greater awareness among pupils and equity in the school system. In the light of these considerations, attention needs to be shifted to the AIA, to assess whether this regulation not only seeks to maintain the level of protection of personal data legislation, but also helps to remedy some of its limitations, in the event that FRTs find their way into schools. In the near future, therefore, it will be crucial to read the two regulations in an integrated way.

Funding The research is supported by the project 'SE.CO.R.E. TECH: Self- and Co-Regulation for Emerging Technologies: Towards a Technological Rule of Law', funded by the Italian Ministry for University and Research's (MUR's) 'Progetti di Ricerca di Rilevante Interesse Nazionale' (PRIN; Bando 2017—grant prot. no. 2017SW48EB).

References

Alston P, Gilmour-Walsh B (1996) The Best Interests of the Child Towards a synthesis of children's rights and cultural values. Innocenti Studies, https://www.unicef-irc.org/publications/pdf/is_best_interest_eng.pdf Accessed 30 January 2024.

Andrejevic M, Selwyn N (2020) Facial Recognition Technology in Schools: Critical Questions and Concerns. Learning, Media and Technology 2(45): 115–128, https://doi.org/10.1080/17439884.2020.1686014.

Article 29 Data Protection Working Party (2012) Opinion 02/2012 on facial recognition in online and mobile services, WP 192, https://ec.europa.eu/justice/article-29/documentation/opinion-recommendation/files/2012/wp192_en.pdf Accessed 30 January 2024.

Article 29 Data Protection Working Party (2017) Guidelines on Automated individual decision-making and Profiling for the purposes of Regulation 2016/679, WP 251, 3 October 2017, https://ec.europa.eu/newsroom/article29/redirection/document/49826 Accessed 30 January 2024.

Bala N (2020) The danger of facial recognition in our children's classrooms. Duke Law & Technology Review, 18: 249–267.

Barak A (2012) Proportionality: Constitutional rights and their limitations. Cambridge University Press, https://doi.org/10.1017/CBO9781139035293.

Barrett L (2020) Ban Facial Recognition Technologies For Children—And For Everyone Else. Boston University Journal of Science & Technology Law, 26(2): 223–285.

BBC News (2021) Schools pause facial recognition lunch plans, 25 October 2021, https://www.bbc.com/news/technology-59037346 Accessed 30 January 2024.

Berendt B, Littlejohn A, Blakemore M (2020) AI in education: learner choice and fundamental rights. Learning Media and Technology, 45(3): 312–324 https://doi.org/10.1080/17439884.2020.1786399.

Berle I (2020) Face Recognition Technology: Compulsory Visibility and Its Impact on Privacy and the Confidentiality of Personal Identifiable Images. Springer International Publishing, https://doi.org/10.1007/978-3-030-36887-6

Buolamwini J, Gebru T (2018) Gender shades: Intersectional accuracy disparities in commercial gender classification. Proceedings of the 1st Conference on Fairness, Accountability and Transparency, 81: 77–91. http://proceedings.mlr.press/v81/buolamwini18a.html Accessed 30 January 2024.

Business Insider (2022) Uttar Pradesh to start marking school attendance using facial recognition, 11 December 2022, https://www.businessinsider.in/india/news/uttar-pradesh-to-start-marking-school-attendance-using-facial-recognition/articleshow/96145648.cms Accessed 30 January 2024.

Castañeda L, Selwyn N (2018) More than tools? Making sense of the ongoing digitizations of higher education. International Journal of Educational Technology in Higher Education, 15(22): 1–10 https://doi.org/10.1186/s41239-018-0109-y.

Christakis T, Becuywe M, AI-Regulation Team (2021) Facial recognition in the draft European AI Regulation: Final report on the high-level workshop held on April 26, 2021. AI-Regulation.com, https://ai-regulation.com/facial-recognition-in-the-draft-european-ai-regulation-final-report-on-the-high-level-workshop-held-on-april-26-2021/ Accessed 30 January 2024.

Commission nationale de l'informatique et des libertés, Expérimentation de la reconnaissance faciale dans deux lycées: la CNIL précise sa position, 29 October 2019, https://www.cnil.fr/fr/experimentation-de-la-reconnaissance-faciale-dans-deux-lycees-la-cnil-precise-sa-position Accessed 30 January 2024.

Committee on the Rights of the Child (2021) General comment No. 25 (2021) on children's rights in relation to the digital environment, CRC/C/GC/25, 2 March 2021, https://www.ohchr.org/en/documents/general-comments-and-recommendations/general-comment-no-25-2021-childrens-rights-relation Accessed 30 January 2024.

Connor N (2018) Chinese school uses facial recognition to monitor student attention in class. The Telegraph, 17 May 2018, https://www.telegraph.co.uk/news/2018/05/17/chinese-school-uses-facial-recognition-monitor-student-attention/ Accessed 30 January 2024.

Consultative Committee of the Convention 108 (2021) Guidelines on facial recognition (T-PD(2020)03rev4), https://rm.coe.int/guidelines-on-facial-recognition/1680a134f3 Accessed 30 January 2024.

Cook C M, Howard J J, Sirotin Y B, Tipton J L, Vemury A R (2019) Demographic effects in facial recognition and their dependence on image acquisition: An evaluation of eleven commercial systems. IEEE Transactions on Biometrics, Behavior, and Identity Science, 1(1): 32–41 https://doi.org/10.1109/TBIOM.2019.2897801.

Council of Europe (2018) Guidelines to respect, protect and fulfil the rights of the child in the digital environment. Recommendation CM/Rec(2018)7 of the Committee of Ministers, https://rm.coe.int/guidelines-to-respect-protect-and-fulfil-the-rights-of-the-child-in-th/16808d881a Accessed 30 January 2024.

Custers B, Fosch-Villaronga E, van der Hof S, Schermer B, Sears A M, Tamò-Larrieux A (2022) The role of consent in an algorithmic society—Its evolution, scope, failings and re-conceptualization. In Kosta E, Leenes E (ed) Research Handbook on EU Data Protection Law. Edward Elgar, 455–473.

D Leslie (2020) Understanding bias in facial recognition technologies: an explainer. The Alan Turing Institute, https://doi.org/10.5281/ZENODO.4050457 Accessed 30 January 2024.

Dalla Corte L (2022) On proportionality in the data protection jurisprudence of the CJEU. International Data Privacy Law, 12(4): 259–275, https://doi.org/10.1093/idpl/ipac014.

De Gregorio G, Dunn P (2022) The European risk-based approaches: Connecting constitutional dots in the digital age. Common Market Law Review, 59(2): 473–500, https://doi.org/10.54648/COLA2022032.

Demetzou K (2019) Data Protection Impact Assessment: A tool for accountability and the unclarified concept of 'high risk' in the General Data Protection Regulation. Computer Law & Security Review, 35(6): 1–14, https://doi.org/10.1016/j.clsr.2019.105342.

EDRi (2021) EU's AI law needs major changes to prevent discrimination and mass surveillance, https://edri.org/our-work/eus-ai-law-needs-major-changes-to-prevent-discrimination-and-mass-surveillance/ Accessed 30 January 2024.

Eekelaar J (1994) The Interest of the Child and the Child's Wishes: The Role of Dynamic Self-determinism. International Journal of Law and the Family, 8: 42–61.

European Commission (2019) Communication "Building Trust in Human-Centric Artificial Intelligence", COM(2019) 168 final, 8 April 2019, https://ec.europa.eu/newsroom/dae/document.cfm?doc_id=58496 Accessed 30 January 2024.

European Commission (2022) Ethical guidelines on the use of artificial intelligence (AI) and data in teaching and learning for educators, https://op.europa.eu/en/publication-detail/-/publication/d81a0d54-5348-11ed-92ed-01aa75ed71a1/language-en Accessed 30 January 2024.

European Data Protection Board (2020) Guidelines 05/2020 on consent under Regulation 2016/679. Version 1.1, 4 May 2020, https://edpb.europa.eu/sites/default/files/files/file1/edpb_guidelines_202005_consent_en.pdf Accessed 30 January 2024.

European Data Protection Board, European Data Protection Supervisor (2021) EDPB-EDPS Joint Opinion 5/2021 on the proposal for a Regulation of the European Parliament and of the Council laying down harmonised rules on artificial intelligence (Artificial Intelligence Act), https://edpb.europa.eu/system/files/2021-06/edpb-edps_joint_opinion_ai_regulation_en.pdf Accessed 30 January 2024.

European Parliament (2021) Report on artificial intelligence in education, culture and the audiovisual sector (2020/2017(INI)), 19 April 2021, https://www.europarl.europa.eu/doceo/document/A-9-2021-0127_EN.html Accessed 30 January 2024.

European Parliament (2023) Amendments adopted by the European Parliament on 14 June 2023 on the proposal for a regulation of the European Parliament and of the Council on laying down harmonised rules on artificial intelligence (Artificial Intelligence Act) and amending certain Union legislative acts (COM(2021)0206 – C9-0146/2021 – 2021/0106(COD)). https://www.europarl.europa.eu/doceo/document/TA-9-2023-0236_EN.html Accessed 30 January 2024.

European Parliamentary Research Service (2021) Regulating facial recognition in the EU, PE 698.021, https://www.europarl.europa.eu/RegData/etudes/IDAN/2021/698021/EPRS_IDA(2021)698021_EN.pdf Accessed 30 January 2024.

European Union Agency for Fundamental Rights (2018) Under watchful eyes—biometrics, EU IT-systems and fundamental rights, https://fra.europa.eu/sites/default/files/fra_uploads/fra-2018-biometrics-fundamental-rights-eu_en.pdf Accessed 30 January 2024.

European Union Agency for Fundamental Rights (2022) Bias in algorithms—Artificial intelligence and discrimination, https://op.europa.eu/en/publication-detail/-/publication/c5bdd489-7cf4-11ed-9887-01aa75ed71a1 Accessed 30 January 2024.

Freeman M D A (1993) Laws, conventions and rights. Children & Society 7(1): 37–48.

Galligan C, Rosenfeld H, Kleinman M, Parthasarathy S (2020) Cameras in the Classroom. Facial Recognition Technology in Schools. University of Michigan Technology Assessment Project 2020, https://stpp.fordschool.umich.edu/sites/stpp/files/uploads/file-assets/cameras_in_the_classroom_full_report.pdf Accessed 30 January 2024.

Grother P, Ngan M, Hanaoka K (2019) Face recognition vendor test part 3: Demographic effects (NIST IR 8280; p. NIST IR 8280). National Institute of Standards and Technology, https://doi.org/10.6028/NIST.IR.8280 Accessed 30 January 2024.

Hacker P (2018) Teaching fairness to artificial intelligence: Existing and novel strategies against algorithmic discrimination under EU law. Common Market Law Review, 55(4): 1143–1185, https://doi.org/10.54648/COLA2018095.

Hacker P (2021) A legal framework for AI training data—from first principles to the Artificial Intelligence Act. Law, Innovation and Technology, 13(2): 257–301. https://doi.org/10.1080/17579961.2021.1977219

Han H, Jain A (2014) Age, gender and race estimation from unconstrained face images. MSU Technical Report (2014): MSU-CSE-14-5, http://biometrics.cse.msu.edu/Publications/Face/HanJain_UnconstrainedAgeGenderRaceEstimation_MSUTechReport2014.pdf Accessed 30 January 2024.

Harwell D (2018) Unproven Facial-Recognition Companies Target Schools, Promising an End to Shootings. The Washington Post, 7 June 2018, https://www.washingtonpost.com/business/economy/unproven-facial-recognition-companies-target-schools-promising-an-end-to-shootings/2018/06/07/1e9e6d52-68db-11e8-9e38-24e693b38637_story.html Accessed 30 January 2024.

Holmes W, Porayska-Pomsta K, Holstein K, Sutherland E, Baker T, Shum S B, Santos O C, Rodrigo M T, Cukurova M, Bittencourt I I, Koedinger K R (2021) Ethics of AI in education: Towards a community-wide framework. International Journal of Artificial Intelligence in Education: 1–23 https://doi.org/10.1007/s40593-021-00239-1.

Hwang G J, Xie H, Wah B W, Gašević D (2020) Vision, challenges, roles and research issues of Artificial Intelligence in Education. Computers and Education: Artificial Intelligence, 1, 100001: 1–5 https://doi.org/10.1016/j.caeai.2020.100001.

Information Commissioner's Office (2023) North Ayrshire Council's use of Facial Recognition Technology in its schools, 31 January 2023, https://ico.org.uk/media/action-weve-taken/4023847/ico-letter-to-nac-appendix.pdf Accessed 30 January 2024.

Jasserand C A (2015) Avoiding terminological confusion between the notions of 'biometrics' and 'biometric data': An investigation into the meanings of the terms from a European data protection and a scientific perspective. International Data Privacy Law, 6(1): 63–76, https://doi.org/10.1093/idpl/ipv020.

Kamil M H M, Zaini N, Mazalan L, Ahamad A H (2023) Online attendance system based on facial recognition with face mask detection. Multimedia Tools and Applications, 82: 34437–34457, https://doi.org/10.1007/s11042-023-14842-y.

Kind C (2021) Containing the canary in the AI coalmine—the EU's efforts to regulate biometrics. Ada Lovelace Institute, https://www.adalovelaceinstitute.org/blog/canary-ai-coalmine-eu-regulate-biometrics/ Accessed 30 January 2024.

Lamont R (2021) Art 24. In Peers S, Hervey, T K, Kenner J, Ward A (ed) The EU Charter of Fundamental Rights. A Commentary. Hart.

Laux J, Wachter S, Mittelstadt B (2024) Trustworthy artificial intelligence and the European Union AI act: On the conflation of trustworthiness and acceptability of risk. Regulation & Governance, 18(1): 3–32. https://doi.org/10.1111/rego.12512.

Lievens E, Verdoodt V (2018) Looking for Needles in a Haystack: Key Issues Affecting Children's Rights in the General Data Protection Regulation. Computer Law & Security Review 34: 269–278, https://doi.org/10.1016/j.clsr.2017.09.007.

Livingstone S, Stoilova M, Nandagiri R (2019) Children's data and privacy online: Growing up in a digital age. An evidence review. London: London School of Economics and Political Science, https://eprints.lse.ac.uk/101283/1/Livingstone_childrens_data_and_privacy_online_evidence_review_published.pdf Accessed 30 January 2024.

Lupton D, Williamson B (2017) The Datafied Child: The Dataveillance of Children and Implications for their Rights. New Media & Society 19(5): 780–794, https://doi.org/10.1177/146144481668632.

Macenaite M (2017) From universal towards child-specific protection of the right to privacy online: Dilemmas in the EU General Data Protection Regulation. New Media & Society, 19(5): 765–780, https://doi.org/10.1177/1461444816686327.

Mazzini G, Scalzo S (2023) The Proposal for the Artificial Intelligence Act: Considerations around Some Key Concepts, https://ssrn.com/abstract=4098809 Accessed 30 January 2024.

McGlynn C (2002) Rights for children: the potential impact of the European Union charter of fundamental rights. European Public Law 8(3): 387–400.

Merler M, Ratha N, Feris R S, Smith J R (2019). Diversity in faces. ArXiv:1901.10436, https://doi.org/10.48550/arXiv.1901.10436.

Miguel J, Schwarz D (2022) NY Is Ignoring The Ban On Facial Recognition In Schools. NYCLU, 28 June 2022, https://www.nyclu.org/en/news/ny-ignoring-ban-facial-recognition-schools Accessed 30 January 2024.

Mobilio G (2023) Your face is not new to me—Regulating the surveillance power of facial recognition technologies. Internet Policy Review, 12(1): 1–31, https://doi.org/10.14763/2023.1.1699.

Nakar S, Greenbaum D (2017) Now you see me. Now you still do: facial recognition technology and the growing lack of privacy. Boston University Journal of Science & Technology Law, 23(1): 88–123.

Nguyen A, Ngo H N,·Hong Y, Dang B, Nguyen B-P T (2023) Ethical principles for artificial intelligence in education. Education and Information Technologies, 28: 4221–4241 https://doi.org/10.1007/s10639-022-11316-w.

Raposo V L (2022) (Do not) remember my face: uses of facial recognition technology in light of the general data protection regulation. Information & Communications Technology Law: 1–19 https://doi.org/10.1080/13600834.2022.2054076.

Reiss M J (2021) The use of AI in education: Practicalities and ethical considerations. London Review of Education, 19(1): 1–14. https://doi.org/10.14324/LRE.19.1.05.

Seldon A, Abidoye O (2018). The fourth education revolution. Legend Press Ltd.

Simoncini A, Longo E (2021) Fundamental Rights and the Rule of Law in the Algorithmic Society. In Micklitz H-W, Pollicino O, Reichman A, Simoncini A, Sartor G, Gregorio G D (ed) Constitutional Challenges in the Algorithmic Society. Cambridge University Press, 27–41, https://doi.org/10.1017/9781108914857.003.

Smuha NA, Ahmed-Rengers E, Harkens A, Li W, MacLaren J, Piselli R, Yeung K (2021) How the EU Can Achieve Legally Trustworthy AI: A Response to the European Commission's Proposal for an Artificial Intelligence Act, https://doi.org/10.2139/ssrn.3899991.

Swedish Data Protection Authority, Supervision pursuant to the General Data Protection Regulation (EU) 2016/679—facial recognition used to monitor the attendance of students, 20 August 2019, https://www.imy.se/globalassets/dokument/beslut/facial-recognition-used-to-monitor-the-attendance-of-students.pdf Accessed 30 January 2024.

Taylor E (2013). Surveillance schools: Security, discipline and control in contemporary education. Palgrave Pivot.

The Moskow Times (2020) Russia to Install 'Orwell' Facial Recognition Tech in Every School—Vedomosti, 16 June 2020, https://www.themoscowtimes.com/2020/06/16/russia-to-install-orwell-facial-recognition-tech-in-every-school-vedomosti-a70585 Accessed 30 January 2024.

UN Committee on the Rights of the Child (2013) General comment no. 14 (2013) On the right of the child to have his or her best interests taken as a primary consideration (article 3, para. 1), CRC/

C/GC/14, 29 May 2013, https://www2.ohchr.org/english/bodies/crc/docs/gc/crc_c_gc_14_eng.pdf Accessed 30 January 2024.
UNESCO (2019) Beijing Consensus on artificial intelligence and education, https://unesdoc.unesco.org/ark:/48223/pf0000368303 Accessed 30 January 2024.
UNESCO (2021) AI and education: Guidance for policy-makers, https://unesdoc.unesco.org/ark:/48223/pf0000376709 Accessed 30 January 2024.
UNICEF (2018) Children's online privacy and freedom of expression: Industry toolkit, https://sites.unicef.org/csr/files/UNICEF_Childrens_Online_Privacy_and_Freedom_of_Expression (1).pdf Accessed 30 January 2024.
Verhellen E (2015) The Convention on the Rights of the Child Reflections from a historical, social policy and educational perspective. In Vandenhole W, Desmet E, Reynaert D, Lembrechts S (ed) Routledge International Handbook of Children's Rights Studies. Routledge, 43–59.
Weale S (2021) ICO to step in after schools use facial recognition to speed up lunch queue. The Guardian, 18 October 2021, https://www.theguardian.com/education/2021/oct/18/privacy-fears-as-schools-use-facial-recognition-to-speed-up-lunch-queue-ayrshire-technology-payments-uk Accessed 30 January 2024.
Xu W, Ouyang F (2021) A systematic review of AI role in the educational system based on a proposed conceptual framework. Education and Information Technologies, 27: 4195–4223, https://doi.org/10.1007/s10639-021-10774-y.
Zuiderveen Borgesius F (2018) Discrimination, artificial intelligence, and algorithmic decision-making. Council of Europe, https://rm.coe.int/discrimination-artificial-intelligence-and-algorithmic-decision-making/1680925d73 accessed 30 January 2024.

Giuseppe Mobilio is Assistant Professor at the University of Florence, where he is a researcher in Constitutional Law. He studied law at University of Florence (2009) and later obtained a P.h.D at University of Pisa (2014). His current research interests include biometric surveillance, the regulation of technology and the protection of fundamental rights. His previous work includes constitutional justice, dynamics of forms of governments, sources of law, territorial government and metropolitan authorities.

Chapter 4
Emotional Artificial Intelligence: Introducing the Concept of 'Emotional Privacy'

Emine Akar

Contents

Abstract Emotional Artificial Intelligence (EAI) represents a swiftly emerging category of technologies designed to sense, comprehend, and engage with human emotions. This unique technological landscape introduces distinct privacy risks that set it apart from other innovations. Given the substantial value of emotional data to both governmental and private sectors, there is an urgent need to recognise human emotions as a potentially private realm within the regulatory framework. To address this, I propose the adoption of the concept of 'emotional privacy'.

Nevertheless, both 'emotions' and 'privacy' are multifaceted concepts, lacking universally agreed-upon definitions. In this chapter, I aim to delve into the intricacies of emotions, seeking a deeper understanding of their nature and their connection with privacy. Additionally, I will explore various privacy theories to address the fundamental question of why emotional privacy is of paramount importance. This exploration will underscore the values that emotions encapsulate, including autonomy, intimacy, and self-hood, and how these values relate to the concept of emotional privacy.

Keywords Emotional Artificial Intelligence · Privacy · Emotional privacy · Surveillance · Autonomy · Intimacy · Self-hood

E. Akar (✉)
King's College London, Somerset House East Wing, King's College, London WC2R 2LS, UK
e-mail: emine.akar@kcl.ac.uk

K. Prifti et al. (eds.), *Digital Governance*, Information Technology and Law Series 39,
https://doi.org/10.1007/978-94-6265-639-0_4

4.1 Introduction

Your day begins at the ungodly hour of 7:30 a.m. Your body aches with fatigue, but the relentless demands of your job compel you to rise. You groggily reach for your smartphone, hoping for a sliver of solace in the news. Instead, the device bombards you with adorable dog videos, a misguided attempt to uplift your mood. A faint smile crosses your lips, though it does not penetrate the profound weariness within.

With low expectations, you shuffle towards the kitchen, only to find its shelves nearly barren. Having breakfast feels like an unreachable indulgence. The shower, at least, offers a brief respite. You search for the pink shirt that always garners compliments, but it is in the laundry. Instead, you have to settle for the black shirt, which never lets you shine.

You crawl into your car, but within minutes, its Aritificial Intelligence (AI) notices your sluggishness and desperate need for caffeine. In acquiescence, you pull over, surrendering your morning drive for a nondescript bus ride. Among the other passengers clutching their coffee cups, you blend in.

As the bus traverses the city's labyrinthine streets, you peruse the latest news, only to discover the shocking demise of the prime minister. A profound sense of disconnect washes over you, wondering how such a monumental event could escape your news feed. Yet, it hardly registers; in your homeland, such seismic shifts in leadership have become all too commonplace. You read all the articles to pass the time during the lengthy bus journey.

Upon arriving at your workplace, the prime minister's untimely demise dominates conversations. Your sardonic colleague can not resist a dig, teasing, 'Are you in mourning for your fallen leader?' He is well aware of your allegiance to the opposition. You offer no retort.

Talking to clients means you have to act like everything is okay, and you do, even though your voice sounds tired and dull. Understanding your emotional state, your boss empathetically sends you an email advising you to go home due to the shocking news. It is a surprise break, a chance to get away from the boredom of the day.

Embracing the opportunity, you embark on a shopping excursion, yearning to acquire a long-awaited pair of shoes. At the mall, a digital screen presents you with a menu of items to try on, eliminating the need for human interaction. Although you already knew exactly which shoes you needed, the AI system, sensing your apparent sadness, decided to make an unconventional suggestion. It recommended a different pair of shoes, slightly more expensive but remarkably appealing to your taste. Surprisingly, you found yourself drawn to these new shoes, their design and colour resonating with your mood. Despite the higher price tag, you decided to indulge in this unexpected choice.

After your shopping trip, you decide to pay a visit to your nephew. However, his mother informs you that his Emotional Artificial Intelligence (EAI) toy has detected that he has not laughed much today. Considering your fatigue, your choice of a black shirt, and the recent shocking news, the AI toy advises against any contact with him, fearing it might have a negative impact. Although you would like to disagree, you are aware of how much his parents rely on the emotional toy's recommendations, so you reluctantly concede.

As you wait at the bus stop on your way back home, a lingering sadness settles in because you could not visit your nephew. The frustration mounts as you reflect on how many times that seemingly well-intentioned but intrusive AI toy has thwarted your interactions with him. Your anger simmers beneath the surface until it erupts, and you kick a small tin nearby with surprising force.

The closed-circuit television (CCTV) system registers your outburst, prompting a concerned staff member to approach and inquire about your well-being. Realising the need to be truthful, you explain your frustration with the AI toy's interference, knowing that lying could also be detected by the vigilant surveillance system. Thankfully, the staff member shows understanding and lets you off without further consequences.

Upon finally reaching home, you are hit with a series of sneezes, realizing that your fatigue was due to catching a cold rather than lingering sadness.

The story presents a series of challenging aspects centered around the integration of EAI into daily life. One significant facet involves the personalised curation of news content on individuals' phones, determined by their facial expressions, thereby altering the timing and nature of the news displayed. Moreover, the story highlights the potential invasion of privacy as employers gain access to automated systems that extract and analyse emotional data, enabling them to make decisions affecting employees based on this information. Furthermore, the limitations of EAI become apparent in its struggle to comprehend sarcastic humour, leading to potential misinterpretations in interpersonal communication. Commercial exploitation emerges as a concern, with companies leveraging emotional states to recommend products, potentially prioritising profit over genuine consumer needs. Legal and ethical implications arise as insurance companies may attribute accidents to individuals based on data, potentially holding them accountable for conditions such as fatigue. Social dynamics are also affected, as individuals are compelled to justify their behaviors in public, fearing detection of falsehoods by EAI. Moreover, the story emphasises the impact on familial relationships, illustrating how EAI limitations hinder meaningful interactions, particularly with a nephew who is crucial for emotional development. Additionally, the unreliability of EAI is underscored by its misinterpretation of mood and behavior, mistaking illness for emotional states. Ultimately, the story portrays a dystopian reality where individuals' ability to authentically express emotions is stifled, replaced by interventions that discourage genuine emotional sharing and authenticity.

This fictional scenario underscores the imperative of developing robust safeguards against EAI hazards, emphasising the importance of *emotional privacy*. To address this, the chapter begins by defining EAI and exploring potential risks. The understanding of emotions follows, utilising the colour analogy for a pragmatic understanding. The focus is then on privacy which is seen as a pillar of the core values of autonomy, intimacy, and self-hood, and how emotions are aligned with these tenets. The narrative progresses into the development of *emotional privacy*, The section on emotional privacy aims to establish a connection by highlighting that emotions are intricately interwoven within the tapestry of social, cultural, and interpersonal contexts. Recognising its significance in preserving authentic human experiences amid evolving EAI technologies, the chapter concludes by acknowledging the multifaceted nature of emotions and privacy. In this chapter, I refrain from providing a definitive resolution to intricate inquiries about the essence of emotions or the precise delineation of privacy. Instead, I acknowledge the inherent complexity and subjectivity associated with these concepts, aiming to illuminate the connection between privacy and emotions through analogies and fundamental principles.

4.2 Emotional Artificial Intelligence (EAI)

EAI is a new and rapidly spreading technology that combines AI, biometrics data and machine learning.[1] Broadly, EAI is the 'ability of machines and devices to extract data of a person's emotional state by reading their facial expressions, body language, skin conductance level, eye movement, voice tone, respiration, and heart rate variability, as well as machine learning of images and words'.[2]

EAI is already used in different sectors and for different purposes. To give a few examples from the private sector: Honda uses biosensors to ascertain if drivers are stressed or sleepy, Grammarly deduces tone from words, Amazon's Halo bracelet claims to improve users' mood awareness using body temperature and voice recognition, Empath and Boston develop voice recognition to increase efficiency in call centres, and IBM, Unilever, and Softbank use EAI for hiring decisions.[3] As it is believed that word choice, body language, and facial expressions may predict job performance, EAI analyses these data during online assessments and video interviews.[4] Vibraimage measures a person's micro-movements to categorise their mental-emotional states.[5] In the public sector, EAI could be used by governments in security, law enforcement, risk detection, and decision-making.[6] Even in people's private lives EAI might be used, e.g., on romantic dates or in parent-child relationships, or elsewhere where bonds between people need to be established.[7] This growing industry is expected to reach US$37 billion by 2026.[8]

EAI is more than mere facial recognition: it aims to determine and analyse individuals' behaviour, emotional states, and even *hidden intentions*.[9] A danger of EAI is that it may contribute to growing the scale of analysis and predictive capacity of

---

[1] Mantello et al. 2021, p. 1.

[2] Ibid.; Mcstay 2020, p. 2.

[3] Mantello et al. 2021, p. 2.

[4] Richardson 2020, p. 81.

[5] Wright 2021, p. 13.

[6] Sedenberg and Chuang 2017, p. 7.

[7] Sedenberg and Chuang 2017, p. 8.

[8] Crawford 2021.

[9] Whittaker et al. 2018, p. 14.

machines beyond human limits in forming judgements about the emotional states of subjects.[10] Thus, EAI may lead to a quantitatively and qualitatively new levels of surveillance. This raises ethical problems,[11] since, as the European Data Protection Supervisor (EDPS) noted, '[t]urning the human face into another object for measurement and categorisation by automated processes controlled by powerful companies and governments touches the right to human dignity'.[12]

Understanding EAI's possible risks to emotional privacy requires capturing the importance and values of emotions. Therefore, it is important, to begin with the arguments on whether emotions can possibly be generalised and detected. EAI technologies are based on psychologist Paul Ekman's *Basic Emotion* theory from the 1960s, according to which there are seven basic universal emotions, namely happiness, sadness, anger, surprise, fear, disgust, and contempt.[13] According to him, emotions are static and universally consistent, exhibiting identical manifestations across all individuals and readily discernible through observable biological processes, irrespective of cultural influences.[14] Such a common belief that someone's facial movements indicate their emotional state has been even seen in a legal case: Supreme Court Justice Anthony Kennedy puts that *to know the heart and mind of the offender*.[15] This quotation highlights the potential application of EAI in the legal system, underscoring the critical need for accuracy in EAI technology.

However, some researchers criticise Ekman's view and disagree with the idea that emotions can be generalised.[16] For example, one study showed that of the nineteen different types of smiles, only six happen when people are *having a good time*.[17] Indeed, authors in psychology have argued that there is no direct link between emotions and face or body.[18] Furthermore, even leaving aside the fact that appearances/pretences of emotions can be simulated by people, there is an *epistemological gap* between 'how bodies feel and how subjects make sense of how they feel'[19] meaning that any physiognomic appearance is unlikely to be a reliable indicator of internal emotional states. In light of current applications of EAI technologies, this gap has not been considered properly (or, perhaps, at all). On the contrary, EAI over-simplifies the unique emotional experience by pigeon-holing and labelling it.

This over-simplification becomes even more problematic when the risk of EAI's assumption of interpretative authority is taken into account: Vibraimage's claim that EAIs 'know subjects better than subjects know themselves, by directly accessing

[10] Whittaker et al. 2018, p. 12.

[11] Crampton 2019, p. 55.

[12] Wiewiórowski 2019.

[13] Ekman 1992.

[14] Whittaker et al. 2018, p. 14; Ekman 1992.

[15] Riggins v Nevada, 504 US 127 (1992), para 144.

[16] Barrett 2006.

[17] Zaria 2017.

[18] Barrett 2012.

[19] White 2017, p. 177.

and revealing their unconscious'[20] can plausibly be seen as foreshadowing a world in which the public perception of what emotions we experience is determined by some EAI's assessment. This is consistent with the fact that, in the context of surveillance specifically, being monitored always entails the assigning of some identity through physical appearences.[21] Thus, while scientists continue to grapple with understanding emotions, there's a troubling trend towards more intrusive gathering of emotional data.[22]

Additionally, emotions, thoughts, and behaviours are intricately interconnected. How one thinks can influence emotions, how one feels can shape behaviour, and actions can, in turn, affect thought processes. If we introduce EAI into this dynamic, the mere awareness of surveillance can alter behaviour and subsequently impact feelings. This disruption may ultimately curtail one's capacity to experience emotions freely and authentically, with cascading effects on social relationships, as emotions are profoundly shaped by the social context in which they occur.

One might question the contrast between a psychologist, who excels at perceiving emotional expressions, and an EAI. Firstly, as AI systems, EAI can meticulously store vast amounts of data and exhibit unmatched speed in data interpretation and collection. Furthermore, they possess the capability to seamlessly transfer this data to other systems in real-time. In contrast, a psychologist's observations are typically confined to clinical settings. EAI, on the other hand, can amass emotional expressions data from diverse environments, including schools, shopping malls, public transportation, and even within the confines of one's home through smart devices. This extensive and continuous data collection allows EAI to provide a more comprehensive and holistic understanding of an individual's emotional states, transcending the limitations of traditional psychological assessment.

Some may argue that psychologists also influence emotional experiences. However, psychologists cannot be omnipresent, whereas EAI has the potential to infiltrate every aspect of life at any given time. This omnipresence amplifies the concerns regarding emotional privacy and the potential erosion of authentic emotional experiences in an increasingly interconnected world.

In recent years, significant strides have been made in establishing legal frameworks to govern EAI, with prominent examples including the enactment of the Artificial Intelligence Act (AIA) by the European Union (EU).[23] The AIA clearly defines and refers to the technologies that aim to identify or infer the emotions or intentions. According to AIA, employing AI systems to deduce the emotions of individuals within workplace and educational settings is prohibited, except when such systems

[20] Wright 2021, p. 15.

[21] Crampton 2019, p. 60.

[22] McStay and Urquhart 2019.

[23] European Parliament (2024) P9_TA(2024)0138 Artificial Intelligence Act European Parliament legislative resolution of 13 March 2024 on the proposal for a regulation of the European Parliament and of the Council on laying down harmonised rules on Artificial Intelligence (Artificial Intelligence Act) and amending certain Union Legislative Acts (COM(2021)0206 – C9-0146/2021 2021/0106(COD)). https://www.europarl.europa.eu/doceo/document/TA-9-2024-0138_EN.pdf. Accessed 21 August 2024.

are specifically intended for medical or safety purposes.[24] This consideration was made by the Commission based on the criteria of *reliability, specificity and generalisability*.[25] Regulating EAI systems based on reliability, specificity and generalisability is crucial for safeguarding fundamental rights, especially within the legal framework. Without adequate transparency and documentation, the exercise of procedural rights like the right to an effective remedy and a fair trial, as well as the presumption of innocence and the right of defense, could be compromised.[26] Providers and users have obligations to ensure that such systems are trained with high-quality data, meet performance standards, and are rigorously designed and tested. Failure to adhere to these standards could result in discriminatory or unjust outcomes, undermining fundamental rights such as free movement, non-discrimination, and privacy.[27]

The term "Emotional Recognition Systems (ERS)" is used in the context of the AIA instead of "Emotional Artificial Intelligence" (EAI). However, within the discussion of this chapter, the term 'EAI' will be utilized. Having said that, it is important to note that while these systems are often referred to as recognizing emotions, there are limitations to their ability to fully capture the complexity of human emotions. To address this limitation and to provide a more accurate representation of what these systems actually do, the term "Expression Recognition Systems" is suggested. Unlike the term "Emotional Recognition Systems" or "Emotional Artificial Intelligence", which implies an understanding of the underlying emotional state of an individual, "Expression Recognition Systems" focuses specifically on the recognition and interpretation of facial expressions, vocal tones, and other physiological cues that may indicate certain emotional states.[28]

By adopting the term "Expression Recognition Systems," the regulation can more accurately reflect the capabilities and limitations of these technologies, avoiding the implication of a deeper emotional understanding that may not be fully achievable with current AI systems. This terminology adjustment encourages a more nuanced understanding of the role and potential impact of emotion recognition technologies in various contexts.

Under the AIA, EAI, or ERS, is classified as a high-risk[29] category due to concerns regarding privacy infringement, accuracy issues, and potential manipulation leading to social control. [30] As a result, strict regulations are proposed, encompassing transparency, accuracy measures, human oversight, and limitations on data collection and usage. Notably, EAI is prohibited in workplaces and educational settings to protect

---

[24] Ibid., Article 5(1)(f).

[25] Ibid., Recital 44.

[26] Ibid., Recital 48.

[27] Ibid., Recital 60.

[28] Specifically, the next section will delve into the limitations of fully capturing emotions, providing context for the suggested terminology change to 'Expression Recognition Systems'.

[29] Ibid., Annex III 1(c).

[30] Ibid., Recital 28.

individuals' rights and privacy.[31] However, ambiguities arise in determining the applicability of these regulations, particularly in spaces like shopping malls, which serve as workplaces for some employees and leisure areas for visitors. In such settings, EAI may not be explicitly banned, leading to potential ethical concerns regarding its usage. Additionally, in sensitive areas like airports' passport control, where individuals may experience stress for various reasons, the enforcement of EAI regulations may be discriminatory or arbitrary. This inconsistency underscores the need for further clarification and refinement in the legislation to ensure comprehensive protection of individuals' rights across all settings.

On a global scale, the United Nations (UN) Human Rights Council has also adopted a Resolution titled The Right to Privacy in the Digital Age, which recognises emotional recognition technologies.[32] Moreover, EAI technologies in relation to children's emotional development has been clearly referred to in a UN Committee on the Rights of the Child comment on the Convention on the Rights of the Child in 2021.[33]

Such regulations show that there is an existing commitment to providing emotional privacy; however, there is still a lack of theoretical grounds for these provisions. The purpose of my study is to address the theoretical gap in the field by conceptualising the notion of *emotional privacy*.

4.3 Understanding Emotions

There is a lack of consensus among academics regarding the definition of emotions.[34] The challenge in defining emotions stems from methodological and disciplinary differences; for instance, philosophy, psychology, and neurology approach the study of emotions using distinct methodological tools.[35] Therefore, the term 'emotions'

---

[31] Ibid., Article 5(1)(f).

[32] UN Office of the High Commissioner for Human Rights, 15 September 2021, The right to privacy in the digital age, A/HRC/48/31, Article 28.

[33] UN Committee on the Rights of the Child, 2 March 2021, General comment No. 25 on children's rights in relation to the digital environment, Article 62, 68.

[34] Various theories have been proposed to explain how emotions are generated and experienced. Among these theories, three prominent ones stand out: the James-Lange theory, the Cannon-Bard theory, and the Two-Factor Theory (Schachter-Singer theory). Having said that, a leading psychology textbook tries to give an definition: "[i]n their basic form, emotions are specific and consistent responses to a significant internal or external event, which are brief in duration and consist of a particular pattern of physiological responses" Schacter 2019, p. 410. See also Scarantino (2012), p. 358.

[35] Crivelli and Fridlund 2019, p. 163. See also Vallverdú J 2016. Emotions: a Philosophical Introduction Coursera, Lecture 1, What is an emotion and why do we have them: Some definitions. https://www.coursera.org/learn/emotions Accessed 20 October 2023

may carry varying interpretations across different disciplines. Nevertheless, analogies can serve as a useful tool in comprehending emotions.[36] In this section, I aim to elucidate emotions by employing a colour analogy to highlight their resemblances.

In physics, colour is the visual perception of different wavelengths of light by the human eye. The sense/perception of colour is caused by the combination of reflected and/or transmitted wavelengths when light strikes an object, and this sense/perception has been generated in the receiver's brain.[37] In other words, colour is not an inherent property of an object.[38] Therefore, colour is a *sense/ perception* rather than a *being* in the reality. To be clear, I understand colour in two dimensions; first, as a feature of light in the physical world, and in this way, colour can be objectively determined by its wavelength and measured using scientific instruments. However, the second dimension is that the sense/perception of colour which is a response of our brain to different wavelengths of light and this sense/perception of colour is generated in the brain; the wavelengths of light are translated into colour and are named such as red, blue, and green in the brain thanks to the visual system.[39] The perception of colour in an individual's brain depends on how light reflected from objects interacts with the visual system. Since visual systems differ from individual to individual, the same visual stimulus may be perceived differently by different individuals.[40] Therefore, the sense/perception of colour is a subjective experience, and it is unique to each individual. The wavelength of light is objectively measured, but it cannot be perceived without brain-visual interaction. To have a sense or perception of colour, we do not only need the wavelength of light but also the visual system/brain of the receiver.[41] This generates the sense/perception of colour in the brain, and we name them blue, green, etc, and interpret them as calming, alarming, so on and give them a meaning in a context such as red meaning 'stop' when it appears in a traffic light.

Emotions are like colours. The feelings of happiness, sadness, anger, etc, do not exist in the physical world. Feelings are perceptions generated in the brain and explicitly expressed in the face and body, as a response to the physical world various stimuli.[42] In the same way as it is possible to measure the wavelength of the light objectively, it is also possible to measure individual's heart beats, body temperature, facial muscles' moves, and so on. Just as the perception of the colours generated in the brain uniquely as a response of the wavelength of the light, emotions are also responses to the physical world.[43] Furthermore, just as the perception of colour is influenced by factors such as brightness, saturation, or the object's surface, shape, roughness, and pose, the experience of emotions can be influenced by a range of

[36] Scarantino uses language anology: Scarantino 2017, p. 165.

[37] Nassau K 2024 Colour. https://www.britannica.com/science/color Accesssed 13 October 2023.

[38] The Physics Hypertexbook. https://physics.info/color/ Accessed 13 October 2023.

[39] Ibid.

[40] Ibid.

[41] Ibid.

[42] Schacter 2019, p. 410.

[43] Schacter 2019, p. 412.

internal and external factors, such as past experiences, social context, and physical sensations.

At this point, it is important to discuss the concept of *qualia* as it provides a deeper understanding of the subjective nature of experiences, including emotions. Qualia are often considered a core component of consciousness and are closely tied to subjective experience and self-awareness.[44] They refer to the subjective feeling of an experience, which cannot be fully captured or communicated through language or objective measurements. In this sense, qualia are unique to each individual.[45] For example, if two people look at a red apple, they might both agree that the apple is red. However, their experience of the colour red might be different in some subtle or indescribable way as the perception of colour is generated by an individual's brain uniquely.[46] This difference in experience is a result of differences in the individual's neural processing of sensory input, past experiences, and other factors that contribute to their unique perspective. Similarly, the experience of emotion involves a specific quality of subjective experience distinct from other kinds of physical sensations. This *experience* cannot be fully captured, understood, felt or experienced by anyone else. It is true that we can measure and detect brain activity and body changes via fMRI or other scanning techniques to understand changes associated with different mental states, but this is different from *experiencing* them. In this case, one may find it useful to describe this experience as a *feeling* rather than an *emotion*, as emotions have physical components such as neural activity, body temperature and other aspects. However, I believe a better explanation would be to regard emotions as, like colours, having different dimensions, where *feeling* corresponds to the second dimension of the colour analogy, which is that colour perception is a mental phenomenon; whereas the physical changes correspond to the first dimension of the colours which is the wavelength of the light.

In short, there is a complex interplay between objective physical properties and subjective experiences in both cases. It is true that both colours and emotions are based on physical processes, but they are also deeply personal and can differ greatly from person to person.

Based on this analogy, I propose that emotions have two phenomena: feeling and expression[47]. Brains produce feelings through stimulus from the environment and from within; expressions translate and transfer these feelings via bodily and facial changes. This distinction can be seen in the psychological literature as well. Kagan points that 'it is critical to distinguish between a feeling, which is a perception, and a semantic concept'.[48] Therefore, I suggest that in talking about emotions, we should encompass both feelings and expressions as they are both appearance of emotions, and neither cannot exclude the other one. As Boddice puts '[w]e translate

[44] Stanford Encyclopedia of Philosophy. https://plato.stanford.edu/entries/qualia/ Accessed 13 October 2023.

[45] Kanai and Tsuchiya 2012, p. R392.

[46] Ibid.

[47] Similarly Schacter 2019, pp. 410–411.

[48] Kagan 2007, p. 24.

emotions into verbiage imprecisely. Insofar as pain is an emotion ... we translate that experience imprecisely too. But imprecision ... tends only to heighten human efforts to enrich or deepen the confusion. As we translate bodily experience into words, grimaces and art—as we make metaphors of our inner experiences—we literally 'figure out' what we feel.'[49]

Emotions, with the feeling and expression aspects, are developed and change in the society; therefore, context emerges as a realm, influencing the nature of emotions. Contravening this consideration may us lead to miss an important aspect of emotional privacy. According to Boddice, our lives are influenced not only by our personal or recent experiences but also by the histories of our families and communities.[50] As beings who interpret biological conditions within cultural and historical contexts, we are interconnected with these broader narratives:'... therefore, that what we make of pain—how we translate states of suffering—is also dependent on time and place'.[51] Similarly, it has been suggested that '[f]eelings may be held in common, but they are described in different ways. In naming, in translating, we endow meaning. Even if emotions are, physiologically, changeable only over evolutionary time, what they mean changes far more rapidly than that'.[52] Our facial muscles evolve and change over a long evolutionary period, but the meaning of how we use facial muscles—in other words, facial expressions—depends on culture, which is constantly changing. Therefore, detecting expressions involves detecting information about the time and place as well. Hence, protecting emotional privacy requires protecting not only the facial/bodily appearance of emotions but also their information about the time, place, and context in which they are expressed and felt. Safeguarding emotional privacy, particularly in the era of advancing technologies like EAI, necessitates the development of a comprehensive privacy protection theory. Considering the collective nature of emotional experiences, this framework must address not only individual privacy concerns but also extend to group privacy.[53]

However, the limit and scope of this chapter prevent a detailed exploration of such a privacy protection theory. The intricacies involved require an in-depth discussion. Nonetheless, it is crucial to acknowledge that preserving emotional privacy presents a complex challenge that calls for creative solutions.

In the following section, I explore privacy as a pillar of fundamental values—autonomy, intimacy, and self-hood—establishing a foundational understanding to bridge the connection between *privacy* and *emotions* in our discussion on *emotional privacy*.

[49] Boddice 2014, p. 1.

[50] Ibid., p. 2.

[51] Ibid.

[52] Ibid.

[53] See Floridi 2017; Bloustein and Pallone 2017.

4.4 Privacy as a Pillar of Fundamental Values

In this section, I elucidate the indispensable role that privacy plays in our ability to exercise and nurture our autonomy, intimacy, and self-hood. I will argue that these fundamental values are pivotal for the cultivation of inner life, including our emotional life, and privacy serves as the necessary foundation for these functions to thrive. According to Schoeman, privacy nurtures more profound social and personal interactions, encompassing emotional experiences. It provides environments conducive to varied relationships and aspects of personal growth.[54] The primary goal of this section is to examine the reinterpretation of privacy through the lens of fundamental values. It aims to broaden the concept, extending its scope to encompass the complex domain of human emotions. This exploration sheds light on how emotional experiences flourish and evolve within the protected realm of privacy.

4.4.1 Autonomy

Autonomy refers to an individual's capacity to formulate plans and decisions for their life. This entails possessing a conceptualization of oneself as empowered to shape one's life according to personal goals and values. Without this self-perception of control and self-determination, one cannot effectively exercise autonomy.[55] Thus, the notion of an "autonomous self-concept" involves seeing oneself as a purposeful, self-determining, and responsible agent in charge of one's own actions and choices.[56] In other words, autonomy requires a self-concept because even when individual is free from the external interference, they also need to be aware that they are self-determining. According to Kupfer, privacy is an indispensable part and necessary condition of the development of an autonomous self because control over some of one's own information is a part of privacy. Privacy is also the ability to choose who can *experience* or *sense* us.'[57] The European Court of Human Rights (ECtHR) also sees autonomy as central to privacy. In Pretty v. the United Kingdom[58], the Court noted that 'the notion of personal autonomy is an important principle underlying the interpretation of its [the Article 8] guarantees'.

In the classical view, autonomy has been presented as a detachment from social and political life,[59] consequently, privacy has been seen as a shield protecting individual autonomy from social-political life. Indeed, according to Alan Westin '[v]iwed in terms of the relation of the individual to social participation, privacy is the voluntary

[54] Schoeman 1984, p. 416.
[55] Kupfer 1987, p. 82.
[56] Ibid.
[57] Ibid. p. 81.
[58] Pretty v United Kingdom, (App 2346/02), 29 April 2002, (2002) 35 EHRR 1, ECHR 2002-III.
[59] Mokrosinska 2018, p. 117.

and temporary withdrawal of a person from the general society'.[60] In this view, individual autonomy has been protected by creating a space in which individuals can build their lives freely from social and political pressure or they can make decisions freely without interference of state or society. Such understanding of autonomy assumes that there is a tension between privacy and society;[61] however, 'the separation between self and society ... does not exist'.[62]

Conceptualising privacy as *a right not to participate in collective life* might suggest that privacy has no social or political value; however, in Mokrosinska's view, privacy interests are socially embedded. In a parallel way, our autonomy-based interest in privacy serves social interests rather than merely individual interests. Privacy protects autonomy not by separating the self from society but by safeguarding social interactions that enable autonomy.

Mokrosinska explains this idea: '(1) autonomy is the ability to direct one's actions from within values and commitments central to one's identity, and (2) people's identities are constituted by a variety of social roles, relations and practices then (3) the exercise of autonomy cannot demand detachment from social life. Detachment from those social elements central to one's identity would alienate one from one's core commitments and, hence, undermine one's autonomy.'[63] I would suggest that we should also accept the following premises about emotions: (4) emotions are an indispensable element of social interactions, and (5) monitoring and analysis of one's emotions impedes one's social practices and performance of one's social roles and therefore impedes autonomy.[64] Indeed, the awareness of being watched can affect one's emotions, leading to changes in their behaviour within social situations. This is because when someone believes that they are being observed and that their emotions are being scrutinised, they may adjust their emotional responses accordingly.

In this logic of arguments, one creates their autonomous selves by engaging in social interactions such as family and intimate relations. These social relations and roles are an indispensable part of one's identity. Since autonomy is the ability to determine one's life and decisions, autonomy cannot be thought of without referring to the identity, and thus, one's social relations and social practices, which is the space individuals develop and exercises their autonomy. From this point, it is safe to assert that if privacy protects one's autonomy, then privacy protects social practices and relations as well. Such observation has been also made in the Niemietz [65] case, the ECtHR held that it is 'too restrictive to limit the notion [of privacy] to an 'inner

---

[60] Westin 1967, p. 7.

[61] Mokrosinska 2018, p. 118.

[62] Cohen 2012, p. 6.

[63] Mokrosinska 2018, pp. 121–122.

[64] Similarly, Fried puts that "[i]f we thought that our every word and deed were public, fear of disapproval or more tangible retaliation might keep us from doing or saying things which we would do or say..." Fried 1984, p. 210.

[65] Niemietz v Germany, (App 13710/88), 16 December 1992, Series A No 251-B, (1993) 16 EHRR 97.

circle' in which the individual may live his own personal life as he chooses…'.[66] Such limitation would exclude the 'opportunity of developing relationships with the outside world'.[67] The 'right to identity and personal development, and the right to establish and develop relationships with other human beings' fall within the scope of the private life.[68] Thus, in the Peck case,[69] the Court states that 'a zone of interaction of a person with others, even in a public context' may be considered 'private life'.[70] Understanding privacy in this expansive sense underscores its critical role in fostering both individual autonomy and rich social connections, thereby contributing to a more vibrant and fulfilling societal fabric.

4.4.2 Intimacy

Intimacy refers to a close and personal relationship between individuals, characterized by emotional connection, vulnerability, trust, and mutual understanding.[71] It involves sharing thoughts, feelings, and experiences with another person in a deeply meaningful way, often leading to a sense of closeness, belonging, and support.Our capacity to manage who may access us and information about us is closely related to our capacity to establish and sustain different kinds of forms of social relationships.[72] According to Rachels, privacy is necessary and important to maintain these various forms of social relationships. Rachels writes, 'our ability to control who has access to us, and who knows what about us, allows us to maintain the variety of relationships with other people that we want to have, it is, I think, one of the most important reasons why we value privacy'.[73]

Charles Fried argues that intimate relationships rely on privacy, akin to how combustion relies on oxygen.[74] He contends that respecting, loving, and trusting others, along with being the subjects of these emotions, constitutes a fundamental aspect of our identity as individuals among others.[75] Fried emphasises that human connections such as love, friendship, and trust are not merely abstract feelings; they encompass sets of behaviours and principles, shaping one's sense of self.[76] For instance, love entails willingly surrendering certain personal entitlements to the beloved, indicating a selfless and generous gesture. Fried posits that intimacy

---

[66] Ibid., para 29.

[67] Ibid.

[68] Ibid., para 57.

[69] Peck v United Kingdom, (App 44647/98), 28 January 2003, (2003) 36 EHRR 41, ECHR 2003-I.

[70] Ibid., para 57.

[71] Timmerman 1991, p. 21.

[72] Rachels 1975, p. 326.

[73] Ibid., p. 329.

[74] Fried 1984, p. 205.

[75] Ibid., p. 211.

[76] Fried 1984, p. 206.

between friends and partners involves sharing information exclusive to that relationship, information not disclosed to everyone, emphasising the right to withhold such details.[77] This possession of intimate knowledge necessitates security, mutual trust, and respect, which can only thrive in an environment where privacy is respected and maintained.

Besides, as no one has limitless emotional sources, it is necessary to have control over information in sharing with different levels of intimate relations; privacy gives us this control.[78] To be clearer, no one can smile all the time;[79] however, if we were aware of our emotions being watched and analysed, then, we would feel the pressure to display *positive* feelings such as happiness, gratitude, enthusiasm even while walking, sitting in a park, in a classroom; and this would be tiresome and fake.[80] We would waste our limited *happy face* resource in public rather than in intimate relations. We need to have control over when we share emotional sources and with whom. Related to using limited emotional resources, Schoeman points out that revealing the self without emotional attachment can be detrimental because revealing very intimate parts of oneself to someone who is not in one's intimate circle may deplete our limited emotional sources.[81] Therefore, Schoeman says that 'unbounded emotional involvement' between parties is not ideal for maintaining the different levels of relationships effectively with different people.[82]

Continuing the argument, given that the intimate relations of friendship and love are only revealed between friend and friend, lover and lover, it is safe to think that intimate relations account for being in a situation constituted of *two parts*: I and the other friend/ lover. When my emotions are surveilled, a *third party* who is not part of the friend/lover pair destroys the essential bipolarity of the relationship. Such ontological observation could be extended with Schoeman's statement: 'what makes things private is in large part their importance to our conceptions of ourselves and to our relationships with others'.[83] This means that something is private only if its

---

[77] Ibid., p. 207.

[78] Ibid., p. 211.

[79] A contemporary artist, Nicoletta Pazzaglia, raises questions about the 'happiness imperative' by using a wearable material-shaped 'bridle'. By wearing this device, the performer can "maximize the extension of [the] smile". The name of the device is "Smile-bridle". She says that "The bridle "forced smile" mimics a society in which to be happy constitutes the only normal: people must feel at fault because they experience sadness, anger or anxiety. Happiness is then another byproduct of individualism used for massive body surveillance and for silencing people, whilst ignoring major problematics that inform the actual status of happiness, such as income inequality, gender discrimination and racism." Nicoletta Pazzaglia, 'Smile-Bridle', <https://www.nikopazzaglia.com/performance-video-art> Accessed: 20 October 2023.

[80] Here, the Netflix series Black Mirror's episode 'Nosedive' provides an interesting example. This episode shows a world where people rate each other for every interaction they have, which impacts their socioeconomic status. In such a world, characters need to always be smiling, kind and inspiring to get high scores from other people.

[81] Schoeman 1984, pp. 404–405.

[82] Ibid., p. 408.

[83] Ibid., p. 406.

conception is important for us and for our friend/love pair. In light of the aforementioned scenario, EAI naturally assumes the role of the *third party* rather than the friend/lover, as its primary function is to gather and analyse this valuable information for commercial or governmental purposes. Consequently, while one is engaged in an intimate relationship, the presence of EAI erodes the fundamental essence of this dyadic connection.

According to Schoeman, rather than the content of information, that information's role in one's life *matters deeply to the revealer*; therefore, intimate information should be shared only with those who can appreciate the personal significance due to connectedness and involvement.[84] Schoeman defines such elimination as the term *selective disclosure*.[85] In contrast, for relations that do not share this level of connectedness, maintaining privacy necessitates the act of concealment. Thomas Nagel makes the same observation and describes this as *selective intimacy*. Selective intimacy in relationships allows for necessary personal exposure in the development of a fulfilling life. While not everything is shared with everyone, most people require someone with whom they can express thoughts and experiences not revealed to others.[86] In a similar way, Fried argues that revealing the very small aspect of one's personality, which one shares only with intimate relations, is also a violation of one's *integrity*.[87]

For a further argument in favour of the connection of intimacy-privacy, I appeal to Nagel's observations on what function intimacy can perform. Intimacy is crucial for cultivating a rich inner life, enabling exploration of private feelings outside solitude. It offers insights into the emotions of close associates, including their sentiments towards oneself. Intimacy provides a necessary backdrop for specific relationships and serves as a respite from the demands of public conduct, which, despite habit, can become burdensome.[88] The reading of the importance of intimacy in relation to improving one's inner life and exploring unpublic feelings sounds related to autonomy as well. Recalling the statement as touched upon briefly in the 'autonomy' section, privacy is 'an interest in breathing room...for self-flourishing' which is important for autonomy and *self-making*. Taken altogether, we can recognise how intertwined intimacy, autonomy, and privacy are.

4.4.3 Self-Hood

Self-hood or personhood is another important concept to discuss in terms of privacy. Reiman describes privacy as 'a ... social practice by means of which the social group recognises—and communicates to the individual—that his existence is his own. And

[84] Ibid., p. 407.

[85] Ibid., p. 406.

[86] Nagel 1998, p. 10.

[87] Fried 1984, p. 205.

[88] Nagel 1998, p. 20.

this is a precondition of personhood'.[89] According to Reiman, privacy is essential for personhood because being a person involves recognising the ability to shape one's destiny and having an exclusive moral right to do so. This acknowledgement is based on the belief that one's tangible reality morally belongs to oneself.[90]

Reiman goes even further and argues that not just personhood but even the notion of *self* is preconditioned by privacy. He contends that '*selves* are created in social interaction rather than flowering innately from inborn seeds… [and, therefore, that] privacy is necessary to the creation of *selves* out of human beings, since a self is at least in part a human being who regards his existence—his thoughts, his body, his actions—as his *own.*' [emphasise added][91] Fried too highlights that privacy plays an essential role to establish our self-hood, as he puts that '[t]o be deprived of this control [privacy] not only over what we do but over *who we are* is the ultimate assault on liberty, personality, and self-respect'. [emphasise added][92] Such an analysis is significant to show the link between self-hood and privacy. Privacy amounts to the acceptance of an individual's existence as something more than a material thing, like a table or bottle, but as something with a moral identity. Therefore, privacy is a prerequisite to be recognised as a self.

Reiman does not limit this argument to the physical body. Reiman extends this argument beyond the confines of the physical body. He asserts that merely having thoughts, images, daydreams, or memories exclusive to oneself does not automatically make them morally one's own. True ownership of these thoughts involves a social dimension. It encompasses the understanding that one can decide when and by whom their inner thoughts and experiences will be shared with someone other than themselves. Furthermore, it involves the entitlement to this control, ensuring that an individual cannot be compelled to disclose the contents of their consciousness, even when they choose to put those contents into writing. This moral claim to ownership of one's thoughts is established through the observance of the ritual of privacy: '[t]he contents of my consciousness become mine because they are treated according to the ritual of privacy'.[93]

Reiman's argument can be defended for emotions as well. If emotions are a part of my existence, then without the protection of privacy for emotions, it is not possible to think of this existence as mine. One may argue that in the public sphere emotions are displayed without our control. In other words, we may not be entitled to determine when and by whom our emotions are experienced *on a crowded street*. However, in Reiman's perspective, the right to privacy is about having control over who experiences one's body in significant places and the real possibility of seeking refuge in those places. It safeguards the capacity to engage in intimate relations, not by preserving a reserve of withheld information, but by facilitating the commitment

89 Reiman 1976, p. 39.

90 Ibid.

91 Ibid., p. 39

92 Fried 1984, p. 212.

93 Reiman 1976, p. 43.

inherent in caring. Consequently, the right to privacy safeguards an individual's interest in evolving, existing, and enduring as a person.[94]

4.5 The Concept of Emotional Privacy

In this part, I aim to bridge emotions and privacy by showing emotions are not isolated events but are deeply embedded in social, cultural, and interpersonal contexts. In other words, emotions are not confined to the boundaries of an individual's body or mind; but they extend into the realm of social interaction which matches the core values of privacy.

My analogy of depicting emotions as colours and highlighting the necessity of a social context for emotions to occur illustrates the idea that emotions are deeply intertwined with social interactions. Just as lightwaves require an object to interact with before they produce colours, emotions often require a social context or interpersonal relationships to manifest.

Emotions are not purely internal experiences but are influenced, triggered, and shaped by our interactions with others. In many cases, emotions arise in response to social situations, the actions of other individuals, or the dynamics of relationships. These social contexts provide the necessary conditions for emotions to emerge, much like how an object is needed for lightwaves to interact and create colours.

Moreover, my analogy also underscores the interconnectedness of emotions, biometric expressions, and feelings. Emotions involve not only the physiological and biological aspects (biometric expressions) but also the individual's internal, personal experience (feelings, qualia)[95]. However, both of these dimensions of emotions are profoundly influenced by the social context in which they occur.

While conventional wisdom often portrays emotions as deeply personal and internal experiences, a closer examination reveals that emotions are inherently social phenomena.[96] This essay argues that emotions require a social context to generate, emphasising the profound influence of interpersonal, institutional, and cultural factors on the causation and constitution of emotions.[97]

The influence of social context extends beyond individual emotions to encompass the dynamics of interpersonal relationships. Other people can act as both elicitors and influencers of emotions. Emotional reciprocity and feedback loops in interpersonal interactions can intensify emotional experiences, leading to mutual emotional escalation. Additionally, the expression of emotions can shape the interpretations of shared situations, further highlighting the interconnectedness of emotions within a social context.

---

[94] Ibid.

[95] Crivelli and Fridlund 2019, p. 170.

[96] Crivelli and Fridlund 2018, p. 397.

[97] Ibid., p. 183; Scarantino, 2018, pp. 1043, 1046.

The public expression of emotions also carries social meanings and evaluations, influencing how others perceive and respond to the individual experiencing the emotion. Moreover, the mere presence or imagined presence of an audience can impact the intensity of emotional expressions, emphasising the social dimension of emotions.

Furthermore, individuals often adopt emotional roles to communicate their identity and concerns, conforming to cultural scripts for making claims about their self-narratives. These roles are enacted in accordance with the cultural and social context, showcasing how emotions serve as communicative tools rather than purely cultural expressions.

In short, emotions are undeniably social in nature. They are shaped by interpersonal, institutional, and cultural factors, and they serve as communication tools that convey personal meaning and evaluations within a social context.[98] Understanding emotions requires a holistic approach that considers the interconnectedness of emotions, individuals, and their social environment. Emotions are not isolated experiences but are deeply embedded in the fabric of our social lives, influencing and being influenced by the world around us.

Bridging the analysis of emotions with privacy theories yields valuable insights into the concept of *emotional privacy*. Indeed, incorporating the analyses of privacy's core values, namely, autonomy, self-hood, and intimacy, into emotions' social nature can enhance our comprehends of emotional privacy. Overall, just as privacy theories emphasise the importance of autonomy, intimacy, and self-hood in the context of social interactions, emotions are intricately linked to these same principles. Both privacy and emotions require a social context for their development and expression, and they mutually influence and shape each other within the dynamics of human relationships and societal norms. Recognising this interconnectedness can lead to a deeper understanding of how individuals navigate their emotions and personal boundaries in a social world. In other words, recognising the interplay between emotions and privacy contributes to a more comprehensive understanding of the importance of *emotional privacy* in a connected world.

Emotional privacy is a unique facet of privacy often overlooked in existing legal frameworks. While traditional privacy laws focus on safeguarding personal data, emotional privacy introduces a layer of complexity. Emotions, being inherently personal yet shared experiences, extend beyond individual concerns to the collective, emphasising the need to protect emotional spaces within group interactions.

Privacy laws, although effective in safeguarding personal autonomy, may fall short in addressing the communal nature of emotions. This makes emotional privacy crucial for the protection of group dynamics, especially within communities like families, social circles, or cultural groups. Unfortunately, the chapter's limitations prevent a comprehensive exploration of emotional privacy's depth and breadth.

Recognising emotional privacy as integral to group dynamics underscores the necessity for a more expansive discussion within legal and ethical frameworks. This includes creating a conceptual space that explicitly addresses the preservation

[98] Crivelli and Fridlund 2018, p. 397.

of emotional privacy in interpersonal relationships, cultural contexts, and societal values. Unfortunately, despite advancements in privacy laws, including the recently passed AI Act, the focus tends to lean towards individual perspectives rather than the communal nature inherent in emotional privacy. Consequently, these regulations may fall short in adequately protecting the collective emotional dynamics within groups. Thus, to effectively safeguard emotions and emotional privacy, there is a pressing need to incorporate provisions for group privacy within regulatory frameworks.

4.6 Conclusion

At the outset, I introduced the complex facets of the story, shedding light on the challenging aspects it presents. I contended that in order to effectively grapple with the issues that have surfaced within this story, there is a compelling need to embrace and employ the concept of emotional privacy.

Indeed, the story underscores the complexity of the situation and ethical concerns surrounding the use of EAI. Emotions are multi-dimensional, encompassing both expression and the deeply personal realm of feeling. While EAI can excel in detecting and analysing expressions, it remains fundamentally limited in grasping the subjective experience of feeling, which is inherently unique to each individual. The primary issue lies in the terminology itself: *Emotional* Artificial Intelligence. EAI relies solely on biometric data and expressions to interpret and analyse emotional states, leaving the feeling aspect as an uncharted qualia, perpetually beyond its reach.

Moreover, as illustrated in the story, all expressions occur within specific contexts. Emotions are responses to the world, akin to how a surface must be struck by a lightwave to generate colour perception in the brain. Without context, emotions cannot be generated in the mind. Therefore, the concept of emotional privacy, aligned with broader privacy principles, should safeguard the integrity of one's emotions from EAI's interventions. This protection not only nurtures the ability to express feelings authentically but also fosters personal autonomy, self-hood, and meaningful intimate relationships.

In conclusion, in this chapter, I have not sought to definitively answer the complex questions surrounding the nature of emotions or the exact definition of privacy. Instead, it has acknowledged the inherent challenges in defining these concepts and drawn parallels between privacy and emotions by appealing the analogies and core values. Furthermore, it has emphasised the pressing issue of emotional privacy in the age of EAI and the need to conceptualise and protect it. The importance of emotional privacy becomes increasingly evident when considering the intricate interplay between individuals and society.[99] In this context, emotional privacy emerges not as a selfish endeavour but as a means of safeguarding the individual within the

[99] Philosophers like Dewey and privacy scholars like Simitis have highlighted the interconnectedness of individuals and their communities. (see Solove 2015, p. 79 from Dewey 1908, p. 268. Simitis 1987, p.709.)

larger societal tapestry. It is a vital element in preserving the autonomy, well-being, and dignity of individuals while contributing to the overall harmony and cohesion of society. As society grapples with the ever-changing terrain of technology and cultural norms, it becomes increasingly crucial to engage in deliberate discussions and take decisive actions aimed at safeguarding and advancing emotional privacy as an integral aspect of our collective human existence. Overall, from the position that emotional privacy is at least to some extent desirable, not least because 'you can uninstall apps on your phone, but you can't turn off your face',[100] I propose the necessity of thinking more about the concept of emotional privacy.

The story remains open-ended as the full extent of EAI's impact on our lives remains uncertain. Nevertheless, it is reasonable to speculate that it could evolve into a dystopian narrative characterized by a lack of regulations and the erosion of *emotional privacy*.

References

Barrett LF (2006) Are Emotions Natural Kinds? Perspect Psychol Sci 1:28–58. https://doi.org/10.1111/j.1745-6916.2006.00003.x.

Barrett LF (2012) Emotions Are Real. Emotion 12:413–429. https://doi.org/10.1037/a0027555.

Bloustein EJ, Pallone NJ (2017) Individual & Group Privacy. Routledge, London.

Boddice R (2014) Pain and emotion in modern history. Palgrave Macmillan, Basingstoke, Hampshire.

Cohen JE (2012) Privacy, Autonomy, and Information in Configuring The Networked Self : Law, Code, And The Play Of Everyday Practice. Yale University Press, New Haven.

Crampton JW (2019) Platform Biometrics. Surveillance & society 17:54–62. https://doi.org/10.24908/ss.v17i1/2.13111.

Crawford K (2021) Time to regulate AI that interprets human emotions. Nature (London) 592:167–167. https://doi.org/10.1038/d41586-021-00868-5.

Crivelli C, Fridlund AJ (2018) Facial Displays Are Tools for Social Influence. Trends in cognitive sciences 22:388–399.

Crivelli C, Fridlund AJ (2019) Inside-Out: From Basic Emotions Theory to the Behavioral Ecology View. Journal of nonverbal behavior 43:161–194.

Dewey 1859-1952 John (1908) Ethics, by John Dewey. Columbia University Press, 1908, New York (State).

Ekman P (1992) An Argument for Basic Emotions. Cognition Emotion 6:169–200. https://doi.org/10.1080/02699939208411068.

European Parliament (2024) P9_TA(2024)0138 Artificial Intelligence Act European Parliament legislative resolution of 13 March 2024 on the proposal for a regulation of the European Parliament and of the Council on laying down harmonised rules on Artificial Intelligence (Artificial Intelligence Act) and amending certain Union Legislative Acts (COM(2021)0206 – C9-0146/2021 2021/0106(COD)). https://www.europarl.europa.eu/doceo/document/TA-9-2024-0138_EN.pdf. Accessed 21 August 2024.

Floridi L (2017) Group Privacy: a Defence and an Interpretation. https://doi.org/10.1007/978-3-319-46608-8_5.

Fried C (1984) Privacy [a moral analysis]. In: Schoeman FD (ed) Philosophical Dimensions of Privacy: An Anthology. Cambridge University Press, Cambridge, pp. 203–222.

[100] Crampton 2019, p. 54, citing from Warnock 2015.

Kagan J (2007) What is emotion? : history, measures, and meanings. Yale University Press, New Haven, Conn.
Kanai R, Tsuchiya N (2012) Qualia. Current biology 22:R392–R396.
Kupfer J (1987) Privacy, Autonomy, and Self-Concept. American philosophical quarterly (Oxford) 24:81–89.
Mantello P, Ho M-T, Nguyen M-H, Vuong Q-H (2021) Bosses Without a Heart: Socio-demographic and Cross-cultural Determinants of Attitude Toward Emotional AI in the Workplace. AI & SOCIETY. https://doi.org/10.1007/s00146-021-01290-1.
McStay A (2020) Emotional AI, soft biometrics and the surveillance of emotional life: An unusual consensus on privacy. Big Data & Society 7:2053951720904386. https://doi.org/10.1177/2053951720904386.
McStay A, Urquhart L (2019) This Time with Feeling? Assessing EU Data Governance Implications of Out of Home Appraisal Based Emotional AI. First Monday 24:1–1. https://doi.org/10.5210/fm.v24i10.9457.
Mokrosinska D (2018) Privacy and Autonomy: On Some Misconceptions Concerning The Political Dimensions Of Privacy. Law and philosophy 37:117–143.
Nagel T (1998) Concealment and Exposure. Philos Public Aff 27:3–30. https://doi.org/10.1111/j.1088-4963.1998.tb00057.x.
Nassau K (2024) Colour <https://www.britannica.com/science/color> Accessed 13 October 2023.
Pazzaglia N (2021) Smile-Bridle <https://www.nikopazzaglia.com/performance-video-art> Accessed: 20 October 2023.
Rachels J (1975) Why Privacy is Important. Philosophy & public affairs 4:323–333.
Reiman JH (1976) Privacy, Intimacy, and Personhood. Philosophy & public affairs 6:26–44.
Richardson S (2020) Affective computing in the modern workplace. Business Information Review 37:78–85. https://doi.org/10.1177/0266382120930866.
Scarantino A (2012) How to Define Emotions Scientifically. Emotion Review 4:358–368.
Scarantino A (2017) How to Do Things with Emotional Expressions: The Theory of Affective Pragmatics. Psychological Inquiry, 28:165–185. https://doi.org/10.1080/1047840X.2017.1328951.
Scarantino A (2018) Emotional Expressions as Speech Act Analogs. Philosophy of science 85:1038–1053.
Schacter D et al (2019) Psychology. Macmillan Education, UK.
Schoeman F (1984) Privacy and intimate information. In: Schoeman FD (ed) Philosophical Dimensions of Privacy: An Anthology. Cambridge University Press, Cambridge, pp. 403–418.
Sedenberg E, Chuang J (2017) Smile for the Camera: Privacy and Policy Implications of Emotion AI.
Simitis S (1987) Reviewing Privacy in an Information Society. University of Pennsylvania law review 135:707–746.
Solove DJ (2015) The meaning and value of privacy. In: Roessler B, Mokrosinska D (eds) Social Dimensions of Privacy: Interdisciplinary Perspectives. Cambridge University Press, Cambridge, pp. 71–82.
Stanford Encyclopedia of Philosophy <https://plato.stanford.edu/entries/qualia/> Accessed 13 October 2023.
The Physics Hypertexbook <https://physics.info/color/> Accessed 13 October 2023.
Timmerman GM (1991) A concept analysis of intimacy. Issues in mental health nursing 12:19–30.
UN Office of the High Commissioner for Human Rights, 15 September 2021, The right to privacy in the digital age, A/HRC/48/31, <https://www.ohchr.org/en/documents/thematic-reports/ahrc4831-right-privacy-digital-age-report-united-nations-high> Accessed 15 February 2024.
UN Committee on the Rights of the Child, 2 March 2021, General comment No. 25 on children's rights in relation to the digital environment. <https://docstore.ohchr.org/SelfServices/FilesHandler.ashx?enc=6QkG1d%2FPPRiCAqhKb7yhsqIkirKQZLK2M58RF%2F5F0vEG%2BcAAx34gC78FwvnmZXGFUl9nJBDpKR1dfKekJxW2w9nNryRsgArkTJgKelqeZwK9WXzMkZRZd37nLN1bFc2t> Accessed 15 February 2024.

Vallverdú J (2016) Emotions: a Philosophical Introduction. Offered by Universitat Autònoma de Barcelona. Coursera, Lecture 1, "What is an emotion and why do we have them. Some definitions". https://www.coursera.org/learn/emotions, Accessed 20 October 2023.
Warnock J (2015) How Facial-Recognition Software Will Shape The Future of Email Marketing https://martech.org/facial-recognition-software-will-shape-future-email-marketing/ Accessed: 20 October 2023.
Westin AF (1967) Privacy and freedom / Alan F. Westin ; with a foreword by Louis Blom-Cooper. Bodley Head, London.
White D (2017) AFFECT: An Introduction. Cult Anthropol 32:175–180. https://doi.org/10.14506/ca32.2.01.
Whittaker M, Crawford K, Dobbe R, Genevieve F, Elizabeth K, Mathur V, West SM, Richardson R, Schultz J, Schwartz O (2018) AI Now Report 2018. AI Now Institute, New York University. https://ainowinstitute.org/AI_Now_2018_Report.pdf Accessed: 19 October 2023.
Wiewiórowski W (2019) Facial recognition: A solution in search of a problem? In: European Protection Supervisor. https://edps.europa.eu/press-publications/press-news/blog/facial-recognition-solution-search-problem_en. Accessed 19 October 2023.
Wright J (2021) Suspect AI: Vibraimage, Emotion Recognition Technology and Algorithmic Opacity. Science, technology & society (New Delhi, India). https://doi.org/10.1177/09717218211003411.
Zaria G (2017) There Are 19 Types of Smile But Only Six Are For Happiness. BBC Future. https://www.bbc.com/future/article/20170407-why-all-smiles-are-not-the-same Accessed 20 October 2023.

Table of Cases

Niemietz v Germany, (App 13710/88), 16 December 1992, Series A No 251-B, (1993) 16 EHRR 97.
Peck v United Kingdom, (App 44647/98), 28 January (2003) 36 EHRR 41, ECHR 2003-I.
Pretty v United Kingdom, (App 2346/02), 29 April 2002, (2002) 35 EHRR 1, ECHR 2002-III.
Riggins v Nevada, 504 US 127 (1992).

Emine Akar is a dedicated legal scholar specializing in the convergence of law, technology, and ethics. Her academic journey began with an LLM in General Public Law at Gazi University, Ankara, where her thesis on the legal status of child soldiers was later published as a book. She continued her education with an LLM in Public Law at University College London, earning an Outstanding Distinction for her thesis on recognizing Artificial Intelligence as legal persons. Ms. Akar also had the privilege of serving as a Visiting Researcher at the Digital Governance Centre, Erasmus School of Law.

In addition to her research pursuits, Ms. Akar is a Visiting Lecturer in Public Law at King's College London, where she contributes her expertise to the academic community. Currently pursuing her doctoral studies, her research focuses on the potential ramifications of Emotional Artificial Intelligence on privacy rights. Her doctoral studies are generously supported by the ESRC through the London Interdisciplinary Social Science Doctoral Training Partnership studentship.

Chapter 5
Open Banking in the EU: A Consumer Dystopia or Utopia?

Eugerta Muçi

Contents

Abstract Through 'Open Banking', enshrined in the Second Payment Services Directive (PSD2), individuals and businesses can make payment account data available beyond banks to other financial providers, who can offer them personalised products, lower prices, and innovative solutions. These other financial providers are FinTech companies that use artificial intelligence (AI) technology to offer services. A part of Open Banking data is also personal data, bringing into play the General Data Protection Regulation (GDPR). This chapter employs a doctrinal analysis to discuss how the PSD2, GDPR, and the Artificial Intelligence Act (AIA) interact in order to clarify the roles and legal responsibilities of the Open Banking actors, which is thus far not explored in academic literature, as the risks of uncontrolled AI in finance can be detrimental to financial stability and consumers' trust on the financial sector which is one of the foundations of its well-functioning.

E. Muçi (✉)
Erasmus University Rotterdam, Burg. Oudlaan 50, Rotterdam, The Netherlands
e-mail: muci@law.eur.nl

K. Prifti et al. (eds.), *Digital Governance*, Information Technology and Law Series 39,
https://doi.org/10.1007/978-94-6265-639-0_5

Keywords Open banking · AI · Payment Account Data · PSD2 · GDPR · Data protection · Data sharing

5.1 Introduction

In 2018, two forerunner legislative pieces entered into force in the European Union (EU), namely the Revised (or Second) Payment Services Directive (PSD2),[1] introducing Open Banking, and the General Data Protection Regulation (GDPR),[2] providing a landmark comprehensive personal data protection regime. PSD2 provisions introduce a data-sharing regime in payment services where customers (individuals and businesses)[3] can make their data available to other financial providers than their bank. As banks are obliged to make their consumer data available, this ecosystem is colloquially termed 'Open Banking'. When consumers are concerned, payment account data is also personal data within the meaning of the GDPR;[4] and applies, therefore, to the Open Banking ecosystem. The impact of the interaction between the PSD2 and the GDPR merits analysis, particularly concerning the legal protection of consumers.

However, Open Banking entails the use of personal data. Financial firms that leverage technology attention must ensure that such use is not detrimental to consumers and the economy when personal data are made available for use. Open Banking will increase the sharing and processing of data. To extract as much information as possible from this data,[5] financial service providers can and will use Artificial Intelligence (AI). The financial sector is one where the use of technology and AI is not new.[6] New is the generation of enormous amounts of data, catering to the possibility of discovering consumer behavioural patterns and enabling financial institutions to offer personalised products.[7] The financial sector is in the lead of

---

[1] Directive (EU) 2015/2366 of the European Parliament and of the Council of 25 November 2015 on payment services in the internal market, amending Directives 2002/65/EC, 2009/110/EC and 2012/36/EU and Regulation (EU) No 1093/2010, and repealing Directive 2007/64/EC [2015] OJ L 337/35 (PSD2).

[2] Regulation (EU) 2016/679 of the European Parliament and of the Council of 27 April 2016 on the protection of natural persons with regard to the processing of personal data and on the free movement of such data, and repealing Directive 95/46/EC (General Data Protection Regulation) [2016] OJ L 119/1 (GDPR).

[3] For clarity purposes, the term 'customer' encompasses businesses and individuals while 'consumer' encompasses only individuals. For this chapter, the terms 'customer', 'consumer', 'payment user' and 'account holder' are used interchangeably.

[4] Article 4(1) GDPR.

[5] See Scott Farrell who distinguishes between data and information. Information is a level higher than data, in Farrell 2023, p. 45.

[6] Buckley et al. 2024, p. 11 ff; Arner et al. 2016.

[7] Ibid.; Remolina 2019, p. 5.

using AI because, by its nature, it relies heavily on the gathering and use of data.[8] AI can be used in financial services for creditworthiness assessments; investment advice through robo-advisors; streamlining know-your-customer and customer due diligence processes leading to lower compliance costs; anti-money laundering and countering the financing of terrorism; optimisation of capital in peer-to-peer platforms and more.[9] On the other hand, using AI in finance can also pose consumer risks such as discrimination[10] and have implications for financial stability, for example, through algorithmic trading.[11] Data protection challenges could exacerbate those risks. Therefore, the combination of AI technology and finance within the recent Open Banking ecosystem merits attention.

Notably, there are two parts in the data chain, namely (i) availability and access of data and (ii) using data. The PSD2 and GDPR address the availability and access of consumer data but not how financial firms can subsequently process this consumer data. This is the other step in the chain to which other legislative acts are applicable. For example, suppose a financial institution with an Open Banking authorisation will grant loans and thus conduct a creditworthiness assessment by way of its authorisation. In this case, it needs to comply with the Consumer Credit Directive.[12] The applicable rules in this regard are several.[13] Still, this chapter will only focus on the Artificial Intelligence Act (AIA)[14] because it specifically addresses the use of AI, among other things, in the financial sector. The AIA is a legislative piece[15] that regulates one type of use of data, that is, through AI. As a means to clarify the legal responsibilities of Open Banking actors, an analysis of the three main applicable laws is necessary: the PSD2, the GDPR, and the AIA. The analysed research question is 'How are Open Banking consumers protected in light of the GDPR and the AIA?'. By answering the question, this chapter identifies a number of legal gaps that may lead to reduced consumer protection. The following second and third sections will analyse the PSD2 and the GDPR to clarify their interplay in Open Banking. The fourth section will explore the AIA and what using AI in financial services means for financial service providers and consumers. The analysis

[8] Rousseau 2019, p. 1 ff.

[9] Lee 2020, p. 731 ff.

[10] Zuiderven Borgesuis 2018, p. 15 ff. See for these types of discrimination in various scenarios, van Praag and Slooff 2020, p. 80 ff.

[11] Lee (n 9) 739 ff.

[12] Directive (EU) 2023/2225 of the European Parliament and of the Council of 18 October 2023 on credit agreements for consumers and repealing Directive 2008/48/EC OJ L 133/66.

[13] van Praag and Slooff 2020, p. 74 ff.

[14] Regulation (EU) 2024/1689 of the European Parliament and of the Council of 13 June 2024 laying down harmonised rules on artificial intelligence and amending Regulations (EC) No 300/2008, (EU) No 167/2013, (EU) No 168/2013, (EU) No 2018/858, (EU) 2018/1139 and (EU) 2019/2144 and Directives 2014/90/EU, (EU) 2016/797 and (EU) 2020/1828 (Artificial Intelligence Act [2024] OJ L 144/1 (AIA).

[15] On which the political agreement was reached in December 2023, European Parliament [2023]. https://www.europarl.europa.eu/news/en/press-room/20231206IPR15699/artificial-intelligence-act-deal-on-comprehensive-rules-for-trustworthy-ai Accessed 15 March 2024.

considers the recently published proposal amending the PSD2, split into a Directive (Third Payment Services Directive, PSD3)[16] and a Regulation (Payment Services Regulation, PSR).[17]

Open Banking, as a novel development in the combined area of European financial and data protection law, has attracted considerable attention in the academic literature, with various angles being taken in its analysis. A holistic and international approach has been adopted, analysing the approaches of the EU, US, Australia, and UK to Open Banking or ecosystems akin to it, including analyses of the opportunities and challenges of using AI and machine learning in finance; the technology at the basis of Open Banking; and how the latter has paved the path of EU to digitisation and datafication.[18] Other authors have discussed possible business models building upon Open Banking.[19] Moreover, the literature analyses the combination of PSD2 and GDPR in terms of legal bases for processing personal data and sensitive data, consenting to a combination of Open Banking data to other data and silent party data.[20] While some authors criticize the GDPR-PSD2 interplay as a poor coordination,[21] others regard it as the catalyst of Open Banking[22] empowering consumers to use their data to their advantage.[23] This chapter aims to contribute to the body of knowledge regarding applying personal data protection law and AI regulation in the Open Banking ecosystem.

5.2 Open Banking in the Second Payment Services Directive (PSD2): The Why and the What

The PSD2 is a revision of the Payment Services Directive, Directive 2007/64/EC,[24] and has been effective since 13 January 2018. The initial PSD framework effective since 2007 was challenged as, since then, the retail payments market has experienced significant technical innovation, with rapid growth in the number of electronic and mobile payments and the emergence of new types of payment services in the marketplace.[25] The new types of payment services, such as Open Banking services,

---

[16] European Commission 2023b.

[17] European Commission 2023c.

[18] Jeng 2022; de Pascalis 2022; Ferretti 2022a; van Praag 2022; Siciliani 2018; Vezzoso 2022; van Praag and Muçi 2023; Alexander 2019; Bramberger 2022; Zetzsche et al. 2020.

[19] Guibaud 2016; Nguyen and Megargel 2022.

[20] Ferretti 2022b.

[21] Ibid.

[22] De Pascalis 2022.

[23] Borgogno and Colangelo 2020a.

[24] Directive 2007/64/EC of the European Parliament and of the Council of 13 November 2007 on payment services in the internal market amending Directives 97/7/EC, 2002/65/EC, 2005/60/EC and 2006/48/EC and repealing Directive 97/5/EC, OJ L 319 (no longer in force).

[25] Recital 3 PSD2.

were not provided for by the PSD and operated, therefore, in a legal vacuum in the internal market.[26] These financial firms were accessing banking data through unsafe methods for end consumers like screen scraping,[27] which raised a series of issues, like consumer protection, security, liability, and data protection.[28] Moreover, as they were not licensed, these new financial providers were not supervised by any competent authority and did not follow PSD requirements.[29] In response to the above, the PSD2 brought a paradigm shift in payment services regulation[30] through several legislative amendments aiming at three core objectives: ensuring consumer protection, enhancing competition and levelling the playing field, and strengthening the European internal market for payment services.[31] There are three notable legislative additions introduced with the PSD2: the access to account rule, the inclusion of two new financial providers in the legal framework, and the strong customer authentication.

5.2.1 The Access to Account Rule

The PSD2 introduced an obligation on financial institutions that offer payment accounts (usually a bank[32]) to make available for free to other bank or licensed/authorised non-bank firms[33] (third party providers or TPPs) the payment account data of their customers when the latter request so. In other words, for the first time, consumers can make their payment account data available to a licensed firm of their choice other than their traditional financial service provider. This licensed firm can be another competitor bank or a start-up. Open Banking lies in two articles: Articles 66(1) and 67(1) PSD2, known as the 'access to account rule'. It facilitates[34] the porting of data from one institution to the other because (i) banks are obliged to make the data available if the consumer so requests and (ii) the third party providers can access this data for free. The first feature is a step forward from the

[26] European Commission 2023a, p. 25.

[27] Screen scraping involves asking bank customers to hand over their user ID and password for their bank's website or app, and then utilising these credentials to sign on to the bank, impersonating the user. This method is not safe in terms of privacy because the bank cannot confirm whether it is the consumer or the third party provider nor what and how much data is accessed, at Wolberg-Stok 2022.

[28] European Commission 2013, p. 26.

[29] Ibid.

[30] European Banking Authority 2022b, p. 1.

[31] European Commission [2017]. https://ec.europa.eu/commission/presscorner/detail/en/MEMO_17_4961 Accessed 15 March 2024.

[32] Formally termed as an Account Servicing Payment Service Provider (ASPSP), it is a payment service provider providing and maintaining a payment account for a payer, Article 4(17) PSD2.

[33] Non-bank firms are for example, FinTechs which refers to firms that bring technology-enabled innovation in financial services. See Arner et al. 2016, p. 1272.

[34] Largely because the data is accessed free of charge per Articles 66(5) and 67(4) PSD2.

GDPR because, in the latter, the data controller is not obliged to port the data if it is not technically feasible for them per Article 20(2), leading to a lack of practical effectiveness of GDPR data portability.[35] The PSD2 rule was, on the other hand, much more effective because of two reasons. First, it does not have the exception of technical feasibility.[36] Second, the EU supervisory body, the European Banking Authority (EBA), was active in PSD2 implementation through binding Regulatory Technical Standards[37] on, for example, technology standardisation, but also through non-binding methods such as guidelines; opinions; and question and answers[38] to ensure that the market would be interoperable and the data sharing would take place effectively.

Thecess-to-account rule was enacted primarily due to a lack of competition and innovation in the EU payment services sector.[39] Retail financial services, including payments, are characterised by a handful of incumbents controlling the client base, lock-in problems,[40] exclusivity of payment services linked to holding a bank account, and the costs for a new actor to enter the sector being too high.[41] The latter is especially true for FinTech start-ups, which lack the consumer base and brand recognition and have limited access to data about potential consumers.[42] Since existing financial institutions do not face enough competition, they lack strong incentives to lower prices, introduce new products, or generally make efforts to keep a consumer. To illustrate this point, the UK Competition and Markets Authority (CMA), in its investigation of the retail banking market, estimated that the UK consumer could gain an average of £92 annually from switching to one of the cheaper options available.[43] Moreover, some authors argue that competition law alone cannot tackle the issues mentioned

---

[35] Kuebler-Wachendorff et al. 2021.

[36] Except for that the payment account should be accessible online, but that is the case with payment accounts already, Articles 66(1) and 67(1) PSD2.

[37] Commission Delegated Regulation (EU) 2018/389 of 27 November 2017 supplementing Directive (EU) 2015/2366 of the European Parliament and of the Council with regard to regulatory technical standards for strong customer authentication and common and secure open standards of communication OJ L 69/23.

[38] These two instruments are formally non-binding but in practice are implemented by the market, following the comply-or-explain principles. See European Banking Authority. Payment Services and Electronic Money. https://euclid.eba.europa.eu/register/pir/search Accessed 15 March 2024.

[39] Recitals 29, 51, 52, 67 PSD2; European Banking Authority 2022a, b; The Netherlands Authority for Consumers and Markets (Autoriteit Consument & Markt) 2014.

[40] Lock in means that consumers do not easily switch providers because of administrative costs or due to inability to properly compare prices. See Borgogno and Colangelo 2020a, p. 146; Directive 2014/92/EU of the European Parliament and of the Council of 23 July 2014 on the comparability of fees related to payment accounts, payment account switching and access to payment accounts with basic features OJ L 257/214.

[41] Buckley et al. 2022, p. 61; Borgogno and Colangelo 2020b, pp. 576–583, 585–586; European Commission 2013, p. 38 ff.

[42] De la Mano and Padilla 2018, p. 496.

[43] UK Competition and Market Authority 2016, p. xi.

above in the sector.[44] A second driver is the contribution that Open Banking makes towards the EU digital transition as one of the pillars of the EU 'twin transition'.[45]

5.2.2 *Enlarging the Regulatory Scope: Two New Payment Service Providers*

The PSD2 brought into the regulatory scope two new payment services and two new payment service providers offering such services. Namely, Account Information Service Providers (AISPs) and Payment Information Service Providers (PISPs) (both under the name of third party providers), which are defined based on the services they provide, respectively, account information services and payment initiation services.[46] Bringing the services and the respective service providers that act as competitors of incumbent payment institutions into the regulatory scope reflects PSD2's explicit competition-enhancing objective.[47] Simultaneously, consumer protection is ensured by mandating their regulation, authorisation and supervision.[48] This is the case because third party providers need to fulfil certain conditions to obtain a license (PISPs)[49] and authorisation (AISPs);[50] and are supervised by competent authorities.[51] They are, therefore, subject to a clear legal regime and have to follow specific secure standards for data sharing.[52]

An account information service is an online service through which the consumer has an overview of all their payment accounts.[53] In other words, if a consumer has many bank accounts in different banks, an AISP in their app gives one general view of all these accounts.[54] The AISP provides this by going to the bank (named in the PSD2 ASPSP) after getting the consumer's consent and requesting the payment account data. After gathering such data from all the banks where the consumer has accounts, the AISP creates a consolidated view of them. This can facilitate account

[44] Borgogno and Colangelo 2020b.

[45] Van Praag 2024.

[46] Articles 4(18) and (19) PSD2.

[47] European Banking Authority 2022b, p. 1.

[48] Recital 29 PSD2.

[49] Article 11 PSD2.

[50] Article 11 PSD2.

[51] For example, in the Netherlands, the competent authority for supervising PISPs and AISPs is De Nederlandsche Bank (the Dutch Central Bank) at the European Banking Authority. Payment Institutions Register. https://euclid.eba.europa.eu/register/pir/search Accessed 15 March 2024.

[52] Commission Delegated Regulation (EU) 2018/389 of 27 November 2017 supplementing Directive (EU) 2015/2366 of the European Parliament and of the Council with regard to regulatory technical standards for strong customer authentication and common and secure open standards of communication OJ L 69/23.

[53] Article 4(16) PSD2. See also the definition in Article 3(21) PSR Proposal.

[54] Recital 28 PSD2.

management, providing a consolidated and transparent overview, and enhancing control over personal expenses.

A payment information service is a service whereby the consumer requests the PISP to initiate a payment from their account held at another payment service provider.[55] Concretely, the consumer wanting to buy a product online does not need to enter their card details but can request the merchant's PISP to make the payment for them. The PISP, after receiving the request, goes (virtually) to the bank and orders the latter on behalf of the account holder (consumer) to debit their payment account. This can be an alternative to large (and expensive) card schemes like Visa or Mastercard.[56] An advantage of PISPs is facilitating trade, as they assure the retailer that money is on its way,[57] and thus, the retailer can release the goods already without waiting for the funds to be in their bank account. This saves time while offering security.

To sum up simply, the landscape of EU Open Banking consists of three main actors: banks, third party providers and consumers. Unlike the other two, third party providers are newly introduced in the regulatory domain and consist of two types: AISPs and PISPs. The latter are not only included in the regulatory perimeter but also have obtained the right to access payment account data of the consumer which are usually kept by the bank. The bank is obliged to allow access to this data provided that the consumer has given permission. AISPs and PISPs use this data to develop and offer financial services to consumers.

5.2.3 Increased Security: Strong Customer Authentication

The third legislative addition is introducing detailed security requirements for the first time in EU payment services law to improve consumer protection and security in an increasingly digital era.[58] The crux of this addition is a requirement to apply two-factor strong customer authentication for initiating electronic payment transactions and accessing payment accounts online.[59] To provide access to their payment account to AISPs or PISPs, consumers have to authenticate themselves based on at least two of the three elements categorised as knowledge (some information that only the user knows, like a PIN or password), possession (something that only the user possesses, like a card or card reader), and inherence (some features of the user, like face or

---

[55] Article 4(15) PSD2. See also the definition on Article 3(20) PSR Proposal.

[56] Van Praag and Muçi 2023, p. 96.

[57] European Commission [2023]. https://ec.europa.eu/commission/presscorner/detail/en/SPEECH_23_1819 Accessed 15 March 2024.

[58] Article 97 PSD2.

[59] European Banking Authority 2022b, p. 1.

fingerprint identification).[60] Five years after its implementation, the data shows that this legislative addition effectively reduced fraud.[61]

5.3 Data Availability and Access: Data Protection in EU Open Banking

Following a bird's-eye view of the PSD2 services and how they use consumer data, it is evident that personal data is processed when the consumer concerned is an individual. The right to personal data protection is a fundamental right, provisioned for in EU primary law, Article 16(1) Treaty on the Functioning of the EU,[62] and Article 8(1) of the Charter of Fundamental Rights of the EU.[63] The relevant legal framework on personal data protection consists of the GDPR, the Data Protection Law Enforcement Directive[64] and Regulation 2018/1725.[65] Because of its comprehensiveness and relevance, and because it is considered the regulatory embodiment of the fundamental right to data protection,[66] this section will focus on the GDPR. The GDPR provides the framework for the protection of natural persons with regard to the processing of personal data.[67] In the following, the relation with the PSD2, the correct ground for processing personal data, clarification of PSD2 explicit consent, the responsible party for data minimisation, processing of silent party data, and the applicable law to the processing of special categories of personal data are examined.

5.3.1 The Relation between the PSD2 and the GDPR

To interpret the GDPR and the PSD2 in light of each other, their relationship must first be established. The question is whether the PSD2 prevails over the GDPR in case of conflicting provisions based on *lex specialis derogat legi generali*. Literature is

---

[60] Article 4(30) PSD2; Van Praag and Muçi 2023, p. 102.

[61] European Banking Authority 2022a, p. 19; European Banking Authority 2022b, pp. 2–3.

[62] Treaty on the Functioning of the European Union OJ C 326/13.

[63] Charter of Fundamental Rights of the European Union OJ C 326/391.

[64] Directive (EU) 2016/680 of the European Parliament and of the Council of 27 April 2016 on the protection of natural persons with regard to the processing of personal data by competent authorities for the purposes of the prevention, investigation, detection or prosecution of criminal offences or the execution of criminal penalties, and on the free movement of such data, and repealing Council Framework Decision 2008/977/JHA OJ L 119/89.

[65] Regulation (EU) 2018/1725 of the European Parliament and of the Council of 23 October 2018 on the protection of natural persons with regard to the processing of personal data by the Union institutions, bodies, offices and agencies and on the free movement of such data, and repealing Regulation (EC) No 45/2001 and Decision No 1247/2002/EC OJ L 295.

[66] Graef et al. 2020, p. 5.

[67] Article 1(1) GDPR.

divided in this respect. On the one hand, there is agreement that is principle is applicable given the sectorial nature of the PSD2.[68] On the other hand, the existence of this principle is disagreed upon, particularly in the context of PSD2 explicit consent versus GDPR explicit consent (see below Sect. 5.3.3), but also because recital 90 PSD2 states that the Directive should be implemented in accordance with data protection law.[69] A third opinion holds that the answer is non-conclusive because a distinction is made between GDPR portability and PSD2 data access.[70] According to them, continuous data access, such as that provided for by the access to account rule, was not envisioned in Article 20 GDPR, meaning they are two different regimes. In any case, it is agreed that the GDPR is a horizontal regulation that applies across sectors, while the PSD2 is a vertical legislation that applies only to payment services.[71] The predecessor of the European Data Protection Board (EDPB), Article 29 Working Party, considers the access to account rule a specific sectorial rule providing for portability but which does not override the general application of GDPR data portability.[72] This chapter argues that the PSD2 does not take precedence over the GDPR. The access to account rule and the right to data portability are similar in terms of putting the consumer in control of their data and enhancing competition,[73] However, an AISP has to observe both the PSD2 permission and the GDPR legal basis for processing personal data (see Sect. 5.3.3) as distinct requirements means. This shows that the PSD2 and the GDPR are two different legal regimes and have no hierarchical relation with each other. There are several intersections between the PSD2 and the GDPR. The following sections identify and analyse them to the benefit of legal certainty and clarity.

5.3.2 Grounds for Processing Personal Data

The six grounds for the processing of personal data in Article 6 GDPR are exhaustive.[74] With respect to Open Banking, both the bank and the third party providers process personal data; therefore, identifying the correct legal basis is relevant in these two instances. Regarding the AISPs and PISPs, there is no explicit legal provision regarding the legal basis. Still, the relevant possibilities are consent (Article

---

[68] Di Porto and Ghidini 2020, p. 312.

[69] Ferretti 2022a, p. 94. This provision is present in other legislative acts and proposals, too. See also Recitals 7, 8, 72, 102 Data Act, Regulation (EU) 2023/2854 of the European Parliament and of the Council of 13 December 2023 on harmonised rules on fair access to and use of data and amending Regulation (EU) 2017/2394 and Directive (EU) 2020/1828 (Data Act) OJ L, 22.12.2023; Recitals 10, 25 FIDA proposal, European Commission 2023d; Recital 97 PSR Proposal.

[70] Graef et al. 2020, p. 13.

[71] In the meaning that it is legislation that applies to a specific sector, Ferretti 2022b, p. 76.

[72] Article 29 Data Protection Working Party 2016, pp. 7–8.

[73] Graef et al. 2020. See, in a similar context, Open Finance, a wider data-sharing regime, Recital 5 FIDA Proposal.

[74] European Data Protection Board 2020a, p. 14.

6(1)(a)) and the necessity for the performance of a contract (Article 6(1)(b)).[75] Payment services are provided on a contractual basis between the payment service user (consumer) and the payment services provider (AISP/PISP).[76] The EDPB has stated that the primary legal basis for processing personal data to provide payment services, is laid out in Article 6(1)(b) GDPR.[77] For a PISP, it is clear that the performance of a contract is the legal basis for processing personal data because it offers services based on the payment initiation service contract with the consumer. For the AISP, however, the answer is slightly nuanced. Whether consent or performance of the contract is the proper legal basis depends on the type of service the AISP offers. AISPs offer two types of services: account information services to the consumer and account information services to non-AISP firms, the latter of which is an activity also known as PSD2-as-a-service.[78] According to it, AISPs gather consumer payment account or transaction data, consolidate it (arrive, for example, in a creditworthiness assessment), and then make it available to a non-AISP firm (a bank which gives out a loan) based on which the latter can offer (financial) services. In this case, the consumer obtains the service from the non-AISP firm (the loan from the bank).[79] Therefore, it is more sensible that the processing of personal data by the AISP itself is based on consent.

On the other hand, the legal basis for the ASPSP (bank) to provide access to the third party providers is clear, namely compliance with a legal obligation,[80] found in Articles 66 and 67 PSD2. As the EDPB explains, the legal obligation is imposed on the EU Member State, which should implement the Directive and formulate an obligation in national law for banks to make the data available.[81]

---

[75] Article 29 Data Protection Working Party 2016, p. 8.

[76] European Data Protection Board 2020a, p. 9. Also, see recital 87 PSD2 *'This Directive should concern only contractual obligations and responsibilities between the payment service user and the payment service provider. [...]'.*

European Data Protection Board 2020a, p. 14.

[77] Ibid.

[78] This service was not foreseen by the legislator when the PSD2 was drafted (Recital 28 PSD2). It is now provided for in the PSR Proposal in Article 3(21) and Recital 65.

[79] An example is Miet-Check. https://www.miet-check.de/ Accessed 15 March 2024. Miet-Check can be used by a landlord before accepting a potential tenant, to check the tenant's transaction data and come up with a creditworthiness assessment of him/her. This way, the landlord is able to know how likely the potential tenant is to pay the rent and/or pay it on time.

[80] Article 6(1)(c) GDPR.

[81] European Data Protection Board 2020a, p. 12.

5.3.3 *Clarifying the Confusion: GDPR Explicit Consent vs. PSD2 Customer Permission*

Explicit consent is a concept in the GDPR that relates to the processing of special categories of personal data. The processing of such data is, in principle, prohibited,[82] but it can be allowed under one of the exceptions listed exhaustively in Article 9(2) GDPR, one of them being explicit consent. The latter refers to the way consent is expressed, meaning that the data subject should give an express, written, and signed statement of consent for the specific processing purpose(s). Explicit consent cannot be inferred from potentially ambiguous statements or actions.[83] Financial data are not sensitive data per se, but if combined with other data, they can reveal sensitive aspects of one's life and, thus, merit higher protection.[84] Transaction data can relate to many aspects of people's lives as the payment account is a financial service we use daily.[85]

Explicit consent, as a term, is also mentioned in Articles 67(2)(a) and 94(2) PSD2, 84 applicable to AISPs and PISPs, respectively.[86] However, it is unclear whether the meaning of PSD2 explicit consent in these articles is the same as the GDPR explicit consent. The EDPB has explained that the notion of 'explicit consent' in the PSD2 does not have the same meaning as the GDPR explicit consent endorsed by the EBA[87] and the PSR proposal (Recital 69). The EDPB explains that PSD2 explicit consent is an additional requirement of a contractual nature.[88]

This chapter agrees that GDPR explicit consent and PSD2 explicit consent are two different notions for two reasons. The first reason is common to AISPs and PISPs, and the second is specific to each. Initially, for this analysis, a distinction must be drawn between the explicit consent in Article 67(2)(a) PSD2 (applicable to AISPs) and explicit consent in Article 94(2) PSD2 (applicable to PISPs). First, the grounds for processing personal data are provided exhaustively in Article 6(1) GDPR. Therefore, these two articles cannot constitute an additional ground. Second, regarding AISPs, Article 67(2)(a) PSD2 regards permission for the provision of service, and the consumer gives it through strong customer authentication (Article 97(4) PSD2). This permission differs from the GDPR explicit consent because obtaining explicit consent is a highly burdensome procedure. Therefore, through an *a contrario* interpretation, it would be much more difficult for AISPs to provide their services if they would need written and signed consent from the account holder every time

---

[82] Article 9(1) GDPR.

[83] European Data Protection Board 2020a, p. 13.

[84] Ferretti 2022b, p. 92.

[85] Commission Nationale Informatique & Libertés 2022, p. 11.

[86] Per Article 33(2) PSD2, Article 94(2) is not applicable to AISPs when they offer only account information service. A financial firm can offer other financial services in addition to account information service. For example, carry out creditworthiness assessments (the account information service) and grant consumer loans.

[87] European Banking Authority 2022b, p. 113.

[88] European Data Protection Board 2020a, pp. 13–15.

they have to access the payment account. This could render the primary purpose of PSD2 of enhancing competition ineffective. The second reason, specific to PISPs, regards Article 94(2) PSD2. This provision applies specifically to the processing of personal data, which means that the legislator intended a higher standard than the one for AISPs in Article 67(2)(a) PSD2. If GDPR explicit consent were intended, then that would lower the protection of the consumer because the PISP would apply explicit consent only when sensitive data are revealed. According to Article 94(2) PSD2 explicit consent, in the meaning of a higher threshold of obtaining confirmation, must always be obtained by the PISP. Additionally, the recent proposal for amending the PSD2 clarifies that Article 94(2) explicit consent is not GDPR explicit consent (Recital 69 PSR proposal).[89] The term 'explicit consent' suggests that the PISP must make clear to the consumer what data it is accessing, using, and retaining and obtain the necessary confirmation from the latter.[90] This confirmation is in addition to the strong customer authentication that the consumer has to carry out per Article 97(4) PSD2. In other words, regarding the PISP, the consumer must give two confirmations to enjoy a payment initiation service: first, permission through strong customer authentication to obtain a payment initiation service (Article 97(4) PSD2) and second, consent to PISP access, process, and retain of personal data (Article 94(2) PSD2). These two verifications must occur regardless of whether transaction data reveals sensitive data. To sum up, PSD2 explicit consent differs from GDPR explicit consent, not only because GDPR grounds for processing personal data are exhaustive, but also because (i) regarding AISPs, it would be too cumbersome for their business models and (ii) regarding PISP it would otherwise lower the consumer protection that the PSD2 intended to ensure.

5.3.4 Responsibility for Ensuring Data Minimisation

Data minimisation is a data protection principle that gains relevance in Open Banking. Third party providers access large amounts of data, some of which might not be necessary to provide their services.[91] Preventing them from processing more data than is necessary for the purposes for which the data is processed is essentially the principle of data minimisation, per Article 5(1)(c) GDPR. The data controller ensures data minimisation (Article 5(2) GDPR). Since the ASPSP (bank) and the third party provider (AISP and PISP) are both data controllers, the discussion is about which will

[89] The recital states that the object of Article 94(2) PSD2 is the permission to obtain access to those personal data, to process and store these personal data necessary for the purpose of providing the payment service. Although the PSR is not a binding law yet, it clarifies the legislator's stance regarding this discussion.

[90] European Data Protection Board 2020a, p. 15.

[91] Emanuel van Praag explains that a third party provider that carries out a creditworthiness assessment only needs to see the income and debits of an account holder. This third party provider does not need to know where the account holder goes shopping, member of which political party they are, their hobbies, etc. in van Praag 2022.

carry out this responsibility. The EDPB is of the opinion that third party providers are responsible for not using more data than necessary.[92]

In the PSD2, emphasis is given to the relationship between the AISP/PISP and the consumer, with the bank required to make that data available if the consumer ‘prefers’ so. Moreover, the bank cannot know which data to minimise because it is not aware of the contract between the third party provider and the consumer,[93] and does not have any role to play except for conducting strong customer authentication and making the data available to the AISP/PISP. Second, the bank is legally obliged to provide third party providers with the same information from the payment account that it is made to the payment account user.[94] In other words, whatever is visible to the consumer should also be equally visible to the third party provider. This does not leave space for the bank to filter or restrain any information; otherwise, it would be breaching this provision and thus risk fragmentation in how banks conduct their data minimisation obligations, posing difficulties to the operation of third party providers.

5.3.5 Silent Party Data

When providing Open Banking services, third party providers can access the personal data of data subjects other than the payment service user. For example, when an AISP analyses transactions, it can see to whom the consumer has transferred money in the last six months. The recipient’s account numbers and the amount of funds transferred are personal data, but they have not consented to this data being processed by the AISP. Hence, they are termed ‘silent parties’.[95] The legal basis for processing this type of personal data is not straightforward. Yet this is an important legal question because the processing of silent party data by the third party provider is inevitable due to how Open Banking services function.

The EDPB argues that this processing based on Article 6(1)(f) ‘legitimate interest’ is in principle allowed, whereby the third party provider has to process this data to provide the service to the payment service user.[96] But the provision includes a balance test, namely to the extent that the interests or fundamental rights and freedoms of the data subject that require protection of personal data are not overridden.[97] The EDPB suggests that to ensure the correct application thereof, third party providers should use technical measures to ensure silent party data are only processed for the purpose

---

[92] European Data Protection Board 2020a, p. 22.

[93] Per Articles 66(5) and 67(4) PSD2, a contractual relationship between the bank and the AISP/PISP is prohibited, Joint Payments Industry 2022, p. 2.

[94] Article 36(1)(a) Commission Delegated Regulation (EU) 2018/389 of 27 November 2017 supplementing Directive (EU) 2015/2366 of the European Parliament and of the Council with regard to regulatory technical standards for strong customer authentication and common and secure open standards of communication OJ L 69/23.

[95] European Data Protection Board 2020a, p. 16.

[96] Ibid; European Data Protection Board 2018, pp. 2–3.

[97] Article 6(1)(f) GDPR.

for which they were collected and, if feasible, employ encryption aimed at security and data minimisation.[98]

Because silent party data is necessary to provide account information or payment initiation services and the responsible entity for their processing is the AISP/PISP, it would be in the interest of consumers that the PSD2 explicitly provides the situation of silent party data processing. This can be in terms of its definition, safeguards that the third party provider should provide, and liability in case of data loss or misuse. Concerning silent party data, it is worth noting that the responsibility of the third party provider to ensure data minimisation is more crucial because the silent party is usually not aware of the processing taking place and, therefore, cannot protect him or herself.

5.3.6 Applicable Law to the Processing of Special Categories of Personal Data in Open Banking

Payment accounts contain vast amounts of data. Especially when combined with other data sets, transaction information in the payment account data can reveal sensitive information about individuals, such as behavioural preferences and vulnerabilities in all areas of life.[99] For example, repeated contributions to a political organisation may reveal political beliefs or payments to a hospital may contain information about health conditions. This category of data, therefore, warrants greater protection. To clarify the legal safeguards, a distinction must be drawn between different definitions of sensitive data in the GDPR and the PSD2.

The PSD2 talks of 'sensitive payment data', which can be used to carry out fraud, and excludes the name of the account owner and their account number (Article 4(32) PSD2). On the other hand, GDPR explains sensitive data from the aspect of the sensitivity of the information it can reveal (Article 9(1)).[100] The notion of the GDPR is broader than the PSD2 one because the latter is only linked to a specific consequence, namely, carrying out fraud in payment services. It is essentially about the security of the consumer's payment account.

The PSD2 does not provide rules for cases where an AISP accesses the consumer's sensitive data. For example, information about a trade union membership is not sensitive to payment data because it is not used to carry out fraud. This means that resorting to the general rules of the GDPR is necessary. In principle, the processing of sensitive data in the meaning of Article 9 GDPR is prohibited. Still, the processing

[98] European Data Protection Board 2020a, p. 16.

[99] EU Expert Group on European Financial Data Space 2022, p. 52 ff; Commission Nationale Informatique & Libertés 2022, p. 11.

[100] This article reads *'Processing of personal data revealing racial or ethnic origin, political opinions, religious or philosophical beliefs, or trade union membership, and the processing of genetic data, biometric data for the purpose of uniquely identifying a natural person, data concerning health or data concerning a natural person's sex life or sexual orientation shall be prohibited.'*

may be allowed in certain exceptional circumstances, which are exhaustively listed in Article 9(2). According to the EDPB, only explicit consent and substantial public interest are relevant out of all exceptions. If the third party provider cannot show one of these derogations, then they must implement technical measures to prevent the processing of sensitive data.[101] In my opinion, this will hardly be the case since obtaining explicit consent is too cumbersome and not attractive from a business perspective of the third party provider, because it is too costly. Secondly, falling into the substantial public interest exception is nearly impossible for the third party provider, considering the purely commercial services they offer.

It is also important to clarify that the processing of special categories of data of silent parties is not allowed. The reason is that the legal basis of legitimate interest is not an exception, and none of the other exceptions in Article 9(2) GDPR may allow such a processing. Unless, of course, the third party provider obtains the explicit consent of the silent data subject. However, if it does not carry out such a process, the silent party has no way of knowing that a third party provider is processing its sensitive data and, therefore, cannot challenge it. Thus, there are no precise mechanisms to enforce the prohibition of the processing of sensitive data of silent parties.

5.4 Data Use: Open Banking in the Context of Artificial Intelligence

After analysing the first part of the data chain, availability, and data access, this section delves into the second part, the use of the accessed data. The use of data in this chapter entails how Open Banking firms use payment account data to offer their services, mainly when using AI.

The financial services industry, especially retail banking, is a natural application area for AI, big data, and data analytics because of the amount of data gathered and processed.[102] While technological innovation in finance is not new, investment in technology and the pace of innovation have increased significantly in recent years.[103] The total value of AI spending in Europe in 2023 was estimated at USD 34.2 billion, with the banking sector accounting for the largest value of all investments.[104] AI is widely used by financial firms and regulators in the financial sector.[105] Financial

---

[101] European Data Protection Board 2020a, pp. 19, 20.

[102] Rousseau 2019, p. 4.

[103] European Banking Authority 2017, p. 41.

[104] The banking sector was also the leader in investments in AI worldwide in Statista Bergur Thormundsson [2023]. https://www.statista.com/statistics/1446052/worldwide-spending-on-ai-by-industry/ Accessed 15 March 2024.

[105] European Central Bank [2019] http://www.bankingsupervision.europa.eu/press/publications/newsletter/2019/html/ssm.nl190213_5.en.html Accessed 15 March 2024; De Nederlandsche Bank (The Dutch Central Bank) 2019, p 25 ff; Bundesanstalt für Finanzdienstleistungsaufsicht (The German Federal Financial Supervisory Authority) 2018.

firms use AI in all the stages of financial intermediation, including strategy setting,[106] compliance,[107] risk management,[108] and beyond.[109]

Open Banking especially is fit to benefit from AI because the data is shared through APIs,[110] which allows the accessing of large amounts of data.[111] In the Open Banking ecosystem, AISPs use AI to analyse the transaction data of the consumer and for subsequent advice on finances management, investment decisions, savings, or improve creditworthiness assessments for lenders to grant loans. One of the notable benefits of AI in Open Banking is increased access to finance for underserved consumer segments such as small businesses, young people, and marginalised groups,[112] as more data is available and technological methods to analyse it are advanced. For example, with enhanced data processing through AI, Open Banking firms can arrive at better credit scores than traditional methods,[113] thereby offering improved financing in terms of higher loans or lower interest rates.[114] Another example is lower insurance for consumers who usually have a higher premium.[115] People who pay higher life insurance premiums, for example, can show that their lifestyle has improved through transaction data and have their premiums lowered.

However, there are some accompanying challenges, most relevant of which relate to the transparency of the models used by AISPs to arrive at their decisions.[116] It needs to be clarified what premises the AISP uses to arrive at the final decision. Furthermore, it is a valid concern that the use of AI risks exacerbating existing societal biases and even contributing to financial exclusion.[117] Machine learning, which some define as a type of AI,[118] incentivises firms to gather as much data as possible. The common assumption is that the more data is used to train algorithms, the more

[106] Armour and Eidenmüller 2020, pp. 96–97.

[107] Bramberger 2010, pp. 690–693, 701–702.

[108] Aziz and Dowling 2019.

[109] Buckley et al. 2024, p. 97.

[110] APIs are a set of protocols which enable communication between computer applications, by setting out data available for retrieval and how it can be retrieved. They are deemed to be the most reliable technological foundation for open banking and are fundamental to the interoperability required for open banking to be effective in Farrell 2023, p. 11.

[111] Klarna Kosma [2023]. https://ecommerce-europe.eu/news-item/open-banking-in-the-age-of-ai/ Accessed 15 March 2024.

[112] EU Expert Group on European Financial Data Space 2022, p. 51 ff.

[113] Bruckner 2022, p. 75.

[114] Ibid 75 ff.

[115] Van Praag and Muçi 2023, p. 99.

[116] Other concerns accompanying the use of AI more broadly are job losses, in Buckley et al. 2024, p. 96. For example, the market share and role of credit bureaus have been eroded by technology firms in the European Parliament 2023, p. 23; Carrière-Swallow and Haksar 2022, p. 127.

[117] Recital 37 AIA; Buckley et al. 2024, p. 95 ff.

[118] Zuiderven Borgesuis 2018, p. 13.

accurate they become at predicting what they were trained to do.[119] This incentive, however, contradicts the legal obligation of AISPs[120] to ensure data minimisation. With no clear supervision and enforcement of data minimisation obligations, it is plausible that an AISP uses unnecessary information to deliver Open Banking services but is still valuable for their own AI model. Moreover, when the transaction data reveals sensitive information about a consumer, the AISP should have the infrastructure to stop its processing (see *supra*) unless they obtain GDPR explicit consent. Yet again, how this is supervised and enforced is more complex. Lastly, AI and algorithms could arrive at discriminatory decisions for consumers both when the algorithm is trained according to a human pattern of deciding, for example, on loan applications, and when certain data that can cause bias are anonymised or excluded from the given dataset (gender, age, or other). In the latter case, the algorithm can infer age or gender through other data such as buying behaviour. For example, people who frequently shop online at women's fashion stores drive cars better. The result remains the same: lower insurance premiums for women than men.[121]

The PSD2 does not provide specifically for cases where AI is used in the Open Banking ecosystem. Therefore, to analyse the safeguards for consumers, we turn to the general regime of the GDPR while referring to the AIA. First, the right to transparency is relevant. One of the rights of the data subject, the principle of and right to transparency, requires that any information and communication relating to the processing of personal data be easily accessible and easy to understand to make the data subject aware of the risks, rules, safeguards and their rights related to such processing of their personal data.[122] Open Banking firms ought to inform the consumer, for instance, in a privacy notice, about all stages of an AI decision-making process involving personal data.[123] This information must be concise, transparent, intelligible, and easily accessible.[124] However, this is difficult to achieve for two reasons; the first is the algorithms' complexity, which is akin to a 'black box'.[125] The complexity of the techniques and methods used is often to such an extent that data controllers find it hard to explain them. This lack of explainability is coupled with the lack of consumer ability to understand the information. Such difficulties risk leading to a lack of transparency towards the data subject and a loss of human autonomy for those working with algorithms.[126]

Second, rules on automated individual decision-making, such as profiling per Article 22 GDPR, are another safeguard for consumers when AI is used to analyse

---

[119] European Data Protection Board 2020c, p. 2.

[120] AISPs are more relevant in this aspect because they gather and analyse consumer transaction data. PISPs only access the payment account of the consumer to ensure that a certain amount of money is in the account.

[121] See for these types of discrimination in various scenarios, van Praag and Slooff 2020, p. 80 ff.

[122] Recital 39 GDPR.

[123] Articles 5(1)(a), 13, 14 GDPR.

[124] Recital 39 GDPR, Articles 5(1), 12-14 GDPR.

[125] European Data Protection Board 2020c, p. 3.

[126] ibid; Article 29 Data Protection Working Party 2018, p. 22 ff.

their financial data. Many AISPs carry out creditworthiness assessments, a type of profiling, and the consumer must be informed of its existence and consequences.[127] This automated processing type can significantly affect the consumer because a negative creditworthiness assessment leads to a refused loan application, leaving the consumer without the needed financing.[128] In light of this, consumers have the right not to be subject to a decision based solely on automated processing.[129]

Third, using or developing an algorithm can trigger the obligation to carry out a data protection impact assessment (DPIA), which is enshrined in Article 35 of the GDPR.[130] Accordingly, a DPIA should be carried out where a type of processing results in a high risk to the rights and freedoms of natural persons before the processing.[131] In Open Banking, such high risk is present when the AISP uses algorithms to conduct creditworthiness assessments based on which loan applications are decided. Put simply, a bank may deny a mortgage to a consumer based on the AISP's creditworthiness assessment (by way of algorithms) or an AISP itself may reject financing for a car or a business idea (if it is also authorised to give loans) based on such an analysis of the consumer data. In the second scenario, the AISP performs both the creditworthiness assessment and the decision to grant the loan. In this case, the AISP is a controller and thus obliged to carry out the DPIA per Article 35(3)(a) GDPR. However, there are many instances akin to the first scenario where the AISP carries out the creditworthiness assessment for separate lenders,[132] who ultimately decide to grant a loan. Regarding this scenario, the Court of Justice of the EU has ruled that the credit assessment for a separate lender also constitutes 'automated individual decision-making'.[133] Based on the same reasoning, the AISP is thus obliged to carry out the DPIA when it carries out a creditworthiness assessment for a separate lender. Moreover, this chapter argues that the AISP and the separate lender function in the capacity of joint controllers[134] and, therefore, must conduct the DPIA together. Both entities can be regarded as joint controllers because they pursue complementary purposes.[135] The processing would not be possible without both parties' participation.[136] In this case, the lending decision would not occur without the creditworthiness assessment. Therefore, the DPIA must be conducted

[127] Recital 60 GDPR.

[128] Recital 71 GDPR. See for more examples of automated decisions that could 'similarly significantly affect' data subjects, Article 29 Data Protection Working Party 2017a, p. 22 ff.

[129] Article 22(1) GDPR.

[130] Article 29 Data Protection Working Party 2017b; Kloza et al. 2017, p. 1.

[131] Article 35(3)(a) GDPR.

[132] This is a form of the PSD2-as-a-service business model.

[133] Court of Justice of the EU, *OQ v Land Hessen, intervener: SCHUFA Holding AG*, Judgment, 7 December 2023, C-634/21.

[134] See for the consequences of joint controllership, European Data Protection Board 2020b, p. 40 ff.

[135] Court of Justice of the EU, *Fashion ID GmbH & CoKG v Verbraucherzentrale NRW eV*, Judgment, 29 July 2019, C-40/17, paras 73-85.

[136] European Data Protection Board 2020b, p. 18.

by the lender and the AISP,[137] and each needs to define their respective obligations precisely.[138]

Fourth, the AIA is relevant because it provides *inter alia* EU harmonised rules on the use of AI systems.[139] AI systems are software developed with certain techniques and approaches and can generate outputs such as content, predictions, recommendations, or decisions for a given set of human-defined objectives.[140] AISPs use AI systems to analyse consumers' payment account data to deliver *inter alia* financial advice (recommendations) or creditworthiness assessments (predictions) regarding, for example, how likely the consumer is to pay the rent or repay a loan. The AIA provides that AI systems used to evaluate the credit score of natural persons are classified as high-risk AI systems.[141] AI systems used by small-scale providers to credit scores are exempted due to the limited impact and the available alternatives on the market.[142] Therefore, a large AISP company ought to know that its business model of carrying out creditworthiness assessments using AI must comply with Title III of the AIA.

The use of AI in the financial sector, particularly in the recently enacted Open Banking ecosystem, poses challenges that can be highly risky for natural persons. On the other hand, one ought to find the optimal balance between overregulating, which can inhibit innovation and consumer protection. The EDPB has concluded that the already extensive legal framework is sufficient to address the analysed concerns[143] in terms of rights for individuals, present obligations on firms, and room for supervision. Enforcement is thus key to ensuring that the use of AI in the EU Open Banking ecosystem is done safely and responsibly. No European regulatory nor supervisory body can solely address the issues above. They involve several areas of EU law and, therefore, require inter-disciplinary cooperation and coordination.[144]

---

[137] Article 29 Data Protection Working Party 2017b, pp. 7–8.

[138] Ibid.

[139] Article 1 AIA.

[140] Article 3(1) AIA.

[141] *'Because they determine those persons' access to financial resources or essential services such as housing, electricity, and telecommunication services'*, Recital 37 AIA.

[142] Recital 37 AIA.

[143] European Data Protection Board 2020c, p. 5.

[144] In addition, Buckley et al. recommend various measures to target the risks of AI in finance such as AI review committees; human involvement in the AI process; licensing requirement for AI use; AI insurance schemes; cybersecurity strategies; AI functions; limits and risks must be explainable to someone at a company, ideally someone at management level, in Buckley et al. 2024, p. 97 ff. See also the principles recommended by the Dutch Central Bank with regard to the use of AI in the financial sector, De Nederlandsche Bank (The Dutch Central Bank) 2019, p. 33 ff.

5.5 Conclusion

The Open Banking framework enshrined in the PSD2 has been ground-breaking in opening payment account data to other banks and licensed non-bank firms for the first time. The increased availability and use of data, including personal data, has brought GDPR into play. This chapter has identified and analysed several issues that emerge from the co-existence of PSD2 and GDPR. The analysis of the access to account rule versus data portability; the grounds for processing personal data in Open Banking services; the meaning of explicit consent in the PSD2; the responsible entity for ensuring data minimisation; the processing of silent party data and special categories of personal data are some of these issues. Finally, this chapter analysed the use of AI by Open Banking firms, the opportunities, risks, and respective legislative safeguards.

In conclusion, the intersections between Open Banking and personal data protection combined with the use of AI are numerous and remain, to a certain extent, vague to the detriment firstly of the individual consumer and secondly to achieving a competitive and safe market of Open Banking services. The potential of Open Banking is promising, but the need to pose the title question means that clarifications at the legislative level coupled with enhanced supervision and enforcement are necessary. The consumer utopia in Open Banking would then not be too far away.

References

Alexander K (2019) Principles of Banking Regulation. Cambridge University Press, Cambridge.

Armour J, Eidenmüller H (2020) Self-Driving Corporations?. Harvard Business Law Review 10(1): 87–116.

Arner D et al. (2016) The Evolution of FinTech: A New Post-Crisis Paradigm?. Georgetown Journal of International Law 47(4): 1271–1320.

Article 29 Data Protection Working Party (2016) Guidelines on the Right to Data Portability. Adopted on 13 December 2016. As last Revised and Adopted on 5 April 2017. https://ec.europa.eu/newsroom/document.cfm?doc_id=44099 Accessed 15 March 2024.

Article 29 Data Protection Working Party (2017a) Guidelines on Automated Individual Decision-Making and Profiling for the Purposes of Regulation 2016/679. Adopted on 3 October 2017. https://ec.europa.eu/newsroom/document.cfm?doc_id=47742 Accessed 15 March 2024.

Article 29 Data Protection Working Party (2017b) Guidelines on Data Protection Impact Assessment (DPIA) and Determining Whether Processing Is "Likely to Result in a High Risk" for the Purposes of Regulation 2016/679. Adopted on 4 April 2017. As last Revised and Adopted on 4 October 2017. https://ec.europa.eu/newsroom/article29/items/611236 Accessed 15 March 2024.

Article 29 Data Protection Working Party (2018) Guidelines on Transparency under Regulation 2016/679. Adopted on 29 November 2017. As last Revised and Adopted on 11 April 2018. https://ec.europa.eu/newsroom/article29/redirection/document/51025 Accessed 15 March 2024.

Aziz S, Dowling M (2019) Machine Learning and AI for Risk Management. In: Lynn T and others (eds) Disrupting Finance: FinTech and Strategy in the 21st Century. Palgrave, Cham, pp 33–50.

Borgogno O, Colangelo G (2020a) Consumer Inertia and Competition-Sensitive Data Governance: The Case of Open Banking. Journal of European Consumer and Market Law 9(4): 143–150.

Borgogno O, Colangelo G (2020b) Data, Innovation and Competition in Finance: The Case of the Access to Account Rule. European Business Law Review 31(4): 573–610.
Bramberger KA (2010) Technologies of Compliance: Risk and Regulation in a Digital Age. Texas Law Review 88(4): 669–739.
Bramberger M (2022) Open Banking: Repositioning of European Financial Institutions. Springer Fachmedien Wiesbaden, Enns.
Bruckner M A (2022) Artificial Intelligence and Machine Learning: The Opportunities and Challenges of Using Big Data. In: Jeng L (ed) Open Banking. Oxford University Press, New York.
Buckley R et al (2022) Australia's Data-Sharing Regime: Six Lessons for Europe. King's Law Journal 33(1): 61–91.
Buckley R et al (2024) FinTech: Finance, Technology and Regulation. Cambridge University Press, Cambridge.
Bundesanstalt für Finanzdienstleistungsaufsicht (The German Federal Financial Supervisory Authority) (2018) Big Data Meets Artificial Intelligence: Challenges and Implications for the Supervision and Regulation of Financial Services. https://www.bafin.de/SharedDocs/Downloads/EN/dl_bdai_studie_en.html?nn=19591082 Accessed 15 March 2024.
Carrière-Swallow C and Haksar V (2022) Open Banking and the Economics of Data. In: Jeng L (ed) Open Banking. Oxford University Press, New York.
Commission Nationale Informatique & Libertés (2022) When Trust Pays Off: Today's and Tomorrow's Means of Payment Facing the Challenge of Data Protection. https://www.cnil.fr/en/cnil-publishes-new-white-paper-payment-data-and-means-payment Accessed 15 March 2024.
De la Mano M, Padilla J (2018) Big Tech Banking. Journal of Competition Law & Economics 14(4): 494–526.
De Nederlandsche Bank (The Dutch Central Bank) (2019) General Principles for the Use of Artificial Intelligence in the Financial Sector. https://www.dnb.nl/media/voffsric/general-principles-for-the-use-of-artificial-intelligence-in-the-financial-sector.pdf Accessed 15 March 2024.
de Pascalis F (2022) The Journey to Open Finance: Learning from the Open Banking Movement. European Business Law Review 33(3): 397–420.
Di Porto F, Ghidini G (2020) "I Access Your Data, You Access Mine": Requiring Data Reciprocity in Payment Services. IIC-International Review of Intellectual Property and Competition Law 51(3): 307–329.
Directive 2007/64/EC of the European Parliament and of the Council of 13 November 2007 on payment services in the internal market amending Directives 97/7/EC, 2002/65/EC, 2005/60/EC and 2006/48/EC and repealing Directive 97/5/EC, OJ L 319 (no longer in force). https://eur-lex.europa.eu/legal-content/EN/TXT/?uri=celex%3A32007L0064 Accessed 15 March 2024.
EU Expert Group on European Financial Data Space (2022) Report on Open Finance. https://finance.ec.europa.eu/system/files/2022-10/2022-10-24-report-on-open-finance_en.pdf Accessed 15 March 2024.
European Banking Authority (2017) Discussion Paper on the EBA's Approach to Financial Technology (FinTech). EBA/DP/2017/02. https://www.eba.europa.eu/sites/default/files/documents/10180/1919160/7a1b9cda-10ad-4315-91ce-d798230ebd84/EBA%20Discussion%20Paper%20on%20Fintech%20%28EBA-DP-2017-02%29.pdf Accessed 15 March 2024.
European Banking Authority (2022a) Discussion Paper on the EBA's Preliminary Observations on Selected Payment Fraud Data under PSD2, as Reported by the Industry. EBA/DP/2022/01. https://www.eba.europa.eu/sites/default/files/document_library/Publications/Discussions/2022/Discussion%20Paper%20on%20the%20payment%20fraud%20data%20received%20under%20PSD2/1026061/Discussion%20Paper%20on%20the%20EBA%27s%20preliminary%20observations%20on%20selected%20payment%20fraud%20data%20under%20PSD2%20as%20reported%20by%20the%20industry.pdf Accessed 15 March 2024.

European Banking Authority (2022b) Opinion of the European Banking Authority on Its Technical Advice on the Review of Directive (EU) 2015/2366 on Payment Services in the Internal Market (PSD2). EBA/Op/2022/06. https://www.eba.europa.eu/sites/default/files/document_library/Publications/Opinions/2022/Opinion%20od%20PSD2%20review%20%28EBA-Op-2022-06%29/1036016/EBA%27s%20response%20to%20the%20Call%20for%20advice%20on%20the%20review%20of%20PSD2.pdf Accessed 15 March 2024.

European Commission (2013) Impact Assessment Accompanying the Document Proposal for a Directive of the European Parliament and of the Council on Payment Services in the Internal Market and Amending Directives 2002/65/EC, 2013/36/UE and 2009/110/EC and Repealing Directive 2007/64/EC and Proposal for a Regulation of the European Parliament and of the Council on Interchange Fees for Card-Based Payment Transactions SWD 288 Final. https://eur-lex.europa.eu/resource.html?uri=cellar:906ed6d3-f509-11e2-a22e-01aa75ed71a1.0001.04/DOC_1&format=PDF Accessed 15 March 2024.

European Commission (2017) Payment Services Directive (PSD2): Regulatory Technical Standards (RTS) Enabling Consumers to Benefit from Safer and More Innovative Electronic Payments. https://ec.europa.eu/commission/presscorner/detail/en/MEMO_17_4961 Accessed 15 March 2024.

European Commission (2021) Proposal for a Regulation of the European Parliament and of the Council Laying Down Harmonised Rules on Artificial Intelligence (Artificial Intelligence Act) and Amending Certain Union Legislative Acts COM/2021 206 final 2021. https://artificialintelligenceact.eu/wp-content/uploads/2024/01/AI-Act-FullText.pdf Accessed 15 March 2024.

European Commission (2023a) Impact Assessment Report Accompanying the Documents Proposal for a Regulation of the European Parliament and of the Council on Payment Services in the Internal Market and Amending Regulation (EU) No 1093/2010 and Proposal for a Directive of the European Parliament and of the Council on Payment Services and Electronic Money Services in the Internal Market Amending Directive 98/26/EC and Repealing Directives 2015/2366/EU and 2009/110/EC. https://eur-lex.europa.eu/LexUriServ/LexUriServ.do?uri=SWD:2023:0231:FIN:EN:PDF Accessed 15 March 2024.

European Commission (2023b) Proposal for a Directive of the European Parliament and of the Council on payment services and electronic money services in the Internal Market amending Directive 98/26/EC and repealing Directives 2015/2366/EU and 2009/110/EC (PSD3) COM/2023 366 final 2023. https://eur-lex.europa.eu/legal-content/EN/TXT/?uri=CELEX%3A52023PC0366 Accessed 15 March 2024.

European Commission (2023c) Proposal for a Regulation of the European Parliament and of the Council on payment services in the internal market and amending Regulation (EU) No 1093/2010 (PSR) COM/2023 367 final 2023. https://eur-lex.europa.eu/legal-content/EN/TXT/?uri=CELEX%3A52023PC0367 Accessed 15 March 2024.

European Commission (2023d) Proposal for a Regulation of the European Parliament and of the Council on a framework for Financial Data Access and amending Regulations (EU) No 1093/2010, (EU) No 1094/2010, (EU) No 1095/2010 and (EU) 2022/2554 (FIDA) COM/2023 360 final. https://eur-lex.europa.eu/legal-content/EN/TXT/?uri=CELEX%3A52023PC0360 Accessed 15 March 2024.

European Data Protection Board (2018) Letter to Sophie in 't Veld, Member of the European Parliament Regarding the Revised Payment Services Directive. https://edpb.europa.eu/sites/default/files/files/news/psd2_letter_en.pdf Accessed 15 March 2024.

European Data Protection Board (2020a) Guidelines 06/2020 on the Interplay of the Second Payment Services Directive and the GDPR. Version 2.0. Adopted on 15 December 2020. https://edpb.europa.eu/our-work-tools/our-documents/guidelines/guidelines-062020-interplay-second-payment-services_en Accessed 15 March 2024.

European Data Protection Board (2020b) Guidelines 07/2020 on the Concepts of Controller and Processor in the GDPR. Version 1.0. Adopted on 2 September 2020. https://edpb.europa.eu/sites/default/files/consultation/edpb_guidelines_202007_controllerprocessor_en.pdf Accessed 15 March 2024.

European Data Protection Board (2020c) Response to the MEP Sophie in 't Veld's Letter on Unfair Algorithms. https://edpb.europa.eu/our-work-tools/our-documents/letters/edpb-response-mep-sophie-int-velds-letter-unfair-algorithms_en Accessed 15 March 2024.

European Parliament (2023) Open Finance: What Can an Enabling Framework Look Like?. https://www.europarl.europa.eu/RegData/etudes/STUD/2023/754188/IPOL_STU(2023)754188_EN.pdf Accessed 15 March 2024.

Farrell S (2023) Banking on Data: Evaluating Open Banking and Data Rights in Banking Law. Wolters Kluwer, Alphen aan den Rijn.

Ferretti F (2022a) A Single European Data Space and Data Act for the Digital Single Market: On Datafication and the Viability of a PSD2-Like Access Regime for the Platform Economy. European Journal of Legal Studies 14(1): 173–218.

Ferretti F (2022b) Open Banking: Gordian Legal Knots in the Uncomfortable Cohabitation between the PSD2 and the GDPR. European Review of Private Law 1: 73–102.

Graef I et al (2020) Spill-Overs in Data Governance: Uncovering the Uneasy Relationship Between the GDPR's Right to Data Portability and EU Sector-Specific Data Access Regimes. Journal of European Consumer and Market Law 9(1): 3–16.

Guibaud S (2016) How to Develop a Profitable Customer-Focused Digital Banking Strategy: Open Banking Services and Developer-Friendly APIs. Journal of Digital Banking 1(1): 6–12.

Jeng L (2022) Open Banking. Oxford University Press, New York.

Joint Payments Industry (2022) Letter Regarding the Final EDPB Guidelines on the Interplay of the Second Payment Services Directive and the GDPR. https://www.ebf.eu/wp-content/uploads/2022/02/Joint-Payments-Industry-Letter-on-Final-EDPB-Guidelines-PSD2-GDPR-Interplay.pdf Accessed 15 March 2024.

Kloza D et al (2017) Data Protection Impact Assessments in the European Union: Complementing the New Legal Framework towards a More Robust Protection of Individuals. The Brussels Laboratory for Data Protection & Privacy Assessments. https://biblio.ugent.be/publication/8738562 Accessed 15 March 2024.

Kuebler-Wachendorff S et al (2021) The Right to Data Portability: Conception, Status Quo, and Future Directions. Informatik-Spektrum 44: 264–272.

Lee J (2020) Access to Finance for Artificial Intelligence Regulation in the Financial Services Industry. European Business Organization Law Review 21: 731–757.

Nguyen HHL, Megargel A (2022) Strategic Business Models under Open Banking: A Guideline for Incumbent Banks. Journal of Digital Banking 6(4): 366–380.

Remolina N (2019) Open Banking: Regulatory Challenges for a New Form of Financial Intermediation in a Data-Driven World. SMU Centre for AI & Data Governance Research Paper No. 2019/05. https://doi.org/10.2139/ssrn.3475019

Rousseau H-P (2019) GDPR, PSD2 and Open Banking Are Creating a New Dynamic in Personal Financial Services: A Note. Journal of Internet Banking and Commerce 24(1): 1–7.

Siciliani P (2018) The Disruption of Retail Banking: A Competition Analysis of the Implications for Financial Stability and Monetary Policy. Journal of Financial Regulation 4: 167–189.

The Netherlands Authority for Consumers and Markets (Autoriteit Consument & Markt) (2014) Barriers to Entry into the Dutch Retail Banking Sector. https://www.acm.nl/sites/default/files/old_publication/publicaties/13257_barriers-to-entry-into-the-dutch-retail-banking-sector.pdf Accessed 15 March 2024.

UK Competition and Market Authority (2016) Retail Banking Market Investigation. https://assets.publishing.service.gov.uk/media/57ac9667e5274a0f6c00007a/retail-banking-market-investigation-full-final-report.pdf Accessed 15 March 2024.

van Praag E (2022) The European Financial Data Space: Open Banking in Actie [The European Financial Data Space: Open Banking in Action]. Ondernemingsrecht 5(33): 1-14. Available at https://pure.eur.nl/ws/portalfiles/portal/53604286/Ondernemingsrecht_The_European_Financial_Data_Space_Open_Banking_in_actie.pdf Accessed 15 March 2024

van Praag E (2024) Voorwoord: De Kwetsbare Consument in de Digitale Transitie [Foreword: The Vulnerable Consumer in the Digital Transition]. Tijdschrift voor Financieel Recht 1(2). Available at https://denhollander.info/artikel/17969 Accessed 15 March 2024

van Praag E, Muçi E (2023) Open Finance in the EU: What Is Coming and Why Does It Matter. Journal of Financial Transformation 57: 94–107.

van Praag E, Slooff W (2020) Differentiatie of Discriminatie van Klanten van (Financiële) Ondernemingen. En Hoe Werkt Dat Bij Algoritmen? [Differentiation and Discrimination of Customers of (Financial) Enterprises. And How Does That Work with Algorithms?]. Ondernemingsrecht 14: 74–83.

Vezzoso S (2022) The Critical Journey from Open Banking to Open Finance. Available at SSRN at https://papers.ssrn.com/sol3/papers.cfm?abstract_id=4150255 Accessed 15 March 2024

Wolberg-Stok A (2022) Open Banking Ecosystem and Infrastructure: Banking on Openness. In: Jeng L (ed) Open Banking. Oxford University Press, New York.

Zetzsche D et al (2020) The Evolution and Future of Data-Driven Finance in the EU. Common Market Law Review 57: 331–360.

Zuiderven Borgesuis F (2018) Discrimination, Artificial Intelligence and Algorithmic Decision-Making. https://rm.coe.int/discrimination-artificial-intelligence-and-algorithmic-decision-making/1680925d73 Accessed 15 March 2024.

Legislation

Charter of Fundamental Rights of the European Union OJ C 326/391. https://eur-lex.europa.eu/legal-content/EN/TXT/?uri=celex%3A12012P%2FTXT Accessed 15 March 2024.

Commission Delegated Regulation (EU) 2018/389 of 27 November 2017 supplementing Directive (EU) 2015/2366 of the European Parliament and of the Council with regard to regulatory technical standards for strong customer authentication and common and secure open standards of communication OJ L 69/23. https://eur-lex.europa.eu/eli/reg_del/2018/389/oj Accessed 15 March 2024.

Commission Delegated Regulation (EU) 2022/2360 of August 3, 2022 amending the regulatory technical standards laid down in Delegated Regulation (EU) 2018/389 as regards the 90-day exemption for account access [2022] OJ L 312/1. https://eur-lex.europa.eu/legal-content/EN/TXT/?uri=CELEX%3A32022R2360 Accessed 15 March 2024.

Directive (EU) 2015/2366 of the European Parliament and of the Council of 25 November 2015 on payment services in the internal market, amending Directives 2002/65/EC, 2009/110/EC and 2012/36/EU and Regulation (EU) No 1093/2010, and repealing Directive 2007/64/EC [2015] OJ L 337/35. https://eur-lex.europa.eu/legal-content/EN/TXT/?uri=celex%3A32015L2366 Accessed 15 March 2024.

Directive (EU) 2016/680 of the European Parliament and of the Council of 27 April 2016 on the protection of natural persons with regard to the processing of personal data by competent authorities for the purposes of the prevention, investigation, detection or prosecution of criminal offences or the execution of criminal penalties, and on the free movement of such data, and repealing Council Framework Decision 2008/977/JHA OJ L 119/89. https://eur-lex.europa.eu/legal-content/EN/TXT/?uri=celex%3A32016L0680 Accessed 15 March 2024.

Directive (EU) 2023/2225 of the European Parliament and of the Council of 18 October 2023 on credit agreements for consumers and repealing Directive 2008/48/EC OJ L 30.10.2023. https://eur-lex.europa.eu/eli/dir/2023/2225/oj Accessed 15 March 2024.

Directive 2014/92/EU of the European Parliament and of the Council of 23 July 2014 on the comparability of fees related to payment accounts, payment account switching and access to payment accounts with basic features OJ L 257/214. https://eur-lex.europa.eu/legal-content/EN/TXT/?uri=celex%3A32014L0092 Accessed 15 March 2024.

Regulation (EU) 2016/679 of the European Parliament and of the Council of 27 April 2016 on the protection of natural persons with regard to the processing of personal data and on the free movement of such data, and repealing Directive 95/46/EC (General Data Protection Regulation) [2016] OJ L 119/1. https://eur-lex.europa.eu/eli/reg/2016/679/oj Accessed 15 March 2024.
Regulation (EU) 2018/1725 of the European Parliament and of the Council of 23 October 2018 on the protection of natural persons with regard to the processing of personal data by the Union institutions, bodies, offices and agencies and on the free movement of such data, and repealing Regulation (EC) No 45/2001 and Decision No 1247/2002/EC OJ L 295/39. https://eur-lex.europa.eu/eli/reg/2018/1725/oj Accessed 15 March 2024.
Regulation (EU) 2023/2854 of the European Parliament and of the Council of 13 December 2023 on harmonised rules on fair access to and use of data and amending Regulation (EU) 2017/2394 and Directive (EU) 2020/1828 (Data Act) OJ L, 22.12.2023. https://eur-lex.europa.eu/eli/reg/2023/2854 Accessed 15 March 2024.
Regulation (EU) 2024/1689 of the European Parliament and of the Council of 13 June 2024 laying down harmonised rules on artificial intelligence and amending Regulations (EC) No 300/2008, (EU) No 167/2013, (EU) No 168/2013, (EU) No 2018/858, (EU) 2018/1139 and (EU) 2019/2144 and Directives 2014/90/EU, (EU) 2016/797 and (EU) 2020/1828 (Artificial Intelligence Act [2024] OJ L 144/1. https://eur-lex.europa.eu/legal-content/EN/TXT/PDF/?uri=OJ:L_202401689 Accessed 15 March 2024.
Treaty on the Functioning of the European Union OJ C 326/47. https://eur-lex.europa.eu/LexUriServ/LexUriServ.do?uri=CELEX:12012E/TXT:en:PDF Accessed 15 March 2024.

Table of Cases

Court of Justice of the European Union, Fashion ID GmbH & CoKG v Verbraucherzentrale NRW eV, Judgment, 29 July 2019, C-40/17.
Court of Justice of the European Union, OQ v Land Hessen, intervener: SCHUFA Holding AG, Judgment, 7 December 2023, C-634/21.

Eugerta Muçi is a PhD Candidate in Open Finance at Erasmus School of Law, Erasmus University Rotterdam. Her research interests lie in how a safe and competitive infrastructure for Open Finance can be built in the EU. Eugerta has graduated summa cum laude from KU Leuven and the University of Zürich with a Double Degree Master in Law in European and Financial Law. Besides her PhD, she consults a global consultancy firm on financial law matters, specifically Open Finance. Eugerta is also a Member of the Albanian Bar Association.

Chapter 6
Problematising User Control in the Context of Digital Identity Wallets and European Digital Identity Framework

Sanna Wong-Toropainen

Contents

Abstract This chapter problematises user control in the context of the EU Commission proposal on the regulation for European Digital Identity Framework (EDIF). The proposed framework includes requirements for the European Digital Identity Wallet (EDIW), intended to give control to EU citizens over their identity-related data. The chapter puts forth an argument that while harmonisation of digital identity solutions is required at the EU level, the user control discourse is employed to justify technical choices that can adversely impact the protection of personal data and the right to privacy, such as the use of persistent identifiers that have a potential to enable tracking of users across databases. The chapter employs post-structural discourse analysis to examine the EDIF and related EU policy documents. The findings include that EU recognises individuals' lack of control in the digital environment due to unfair data collection practices by the digital gatekeepers but does not factor in the new challenges posed by artificial intelligence systems which increase the risks of surveillance and identity theft that also limit the benefits of user control achieved by EDIW.

S. Wong-Toropainen (✉)
University of Helsinki, P. Box 4, 00014 Helsinki, Finland
e-mail: sanna.wong-toropainen@helsinki.fi

K. Prifti et al. (eds.), *Digital Governance*, Information Technology and Law Series 39,
https://doi.org/10.1007/978-94-6265-639-0_6

Keywords Digital identity · Digital Identity Wallet · Data protection · User control · Artificial Intelligence · Problematisation · Discourse analysis

6.1 Digital Identity Wallets—User Empowerment at the Cost of Privacy?

In February 2024, the EU voted to adopt the regulation for the European Digital Identity Framework (EDIF)[1] that introduces a design framework for a mobile application called the European Digital Identity Wallet (EDIW). One of the main goals of the EDIW is to empower individuals to control their data by enabling selective sharing of identity-related attributes.[2] As such, the EDIF continues the same rhetoric on giving users control over their personal data as found in the General Data Protection Regulation (GDPR).[3] In the context of digital identity, however, there are concerns that the 'control ideology' is actually more harmful to users' privacy than it is helpful.[4]

The GPDR has been successful in giving users more rights in regard to their data, however it has also been criticised for placing the 'regulatory burden' on users, who might lack the capabilities to understand how their experience and interfaces are being manipulated with the help of algorithms and artificial intelligence (AI), leaving them vulnerable to unfair data collection, profiling, surveillance, etc.[5] Similarly, with the EDIW, there is a risk that a user control discourse is employed to justify technical choices which could adversely impact the protection of personal data and the right to privacy.

An example of the controversy related to the EDIW has been the question of persistent identifiers. Persistent identifiers are a string of numbers, such as social security numbers, that follow a user for a lifetime.[6] In Article 11(a) EDIF proposal, Member States were required to provide at least one unique identifier for situations when a wallet user accesses cross-border public services and identification is required

---

[1] European Parliament legislative resolution of 29 February 2024 on the proposal for a regulation of the European Parliament and of the Council amending Regulation (EU) No 910/2014 as regards establishing a framework for a European Digital Identity (COM(2021)0281—C9-0200/2021—2021/0136(COD)).

[2] EDIF Proposal 2024 (amended proposal), Article 5a.

[3] Regulation (EU) 2016/679 of the European Parliament and of the Council of 27 April 2016 on the protection of natural persons with regard to the processing of personal data and on the free movement of such data, and repealing Directive 95/46/EC (General Data Protection Regulation) (COM/2016/OJ L 119), Recital 7.

[4] Bietti 2020, p. 1.

[5] Ibid.

[6] EDIF Proposal 2024 (amended proposal), Article 11(a).

by law.[7] Academics and privacy activists warned against the use of persistent identifiers because they enable tracking across databases and the user cannot control when they are disclosed.[8] In the amended EDIF proposal, the wording thus changed to 'identity matching' and left out the specific mentioning of persistent identifiers.[9]

Against this background, the chapter problematises the user control discourse in the context of digital identity.[10] The purpose of the analysis is to understand the implicit predispositions regarding the user control discourse and possible unintended consequences. The chapter conducts a post-structural discourse analysis of the EDIF using the 'What is the Problem Represented' (WPR) methodology.[11] The method consists of six questions that help reverse engineering policy from a solution to a problem and reveal implicit assumptions and their effects. In Sect. 8.2, the chapter provides an overview of the EDIF. Section 8.3 presents the method and Sect. 8.4 reports on the analysis using the WPR methodology to examine the problem representation found in the EDIW. Section 8.5 discusses the results from the analysis, and lastly, Sect. 8.6 draws together the chapter's main conclusions.

6.2 The European Digital Identity Framework

The European Declaration on Digital Rights and Principles, signed in 2022, states that that every individual has the right to access digital technologies, products, and services.[12] The right to access includes, according to the declaration, a trusted digital identity, protecting against cyber threats like identity theft and manipulation. The European Union (EU) has set a goal that by 2030, 80% of EU citizens will have a government-verified digital identity solution to access both public and private digital services.[13] By 2026, each EU Member State should have either provided themselves with an EDIW or recognised a private EDIW solution that is offered to all citizens.[14]

Thus far, the only instrument regulating electronic identification in the EU has been the regulation (910/2014) on electronic identification and trust services for

---

[7] Proposal for a Regulation of the European Parliament and of the Conucil amending Regulation (EU) No 910/2014 as regards establishing a framework for a European Digital Identity (COM/2021/281 final), article 11(a).

[8] Fratini and Lo Tauro 2023; EDRI 2022a; Ortalda et al. 2021.

[9] EDIF Proposal 2024 (amended proposal), Article 11.

[10] Communication from the Commission to the European Parliament, the Council, the European Economic and Social Committee and the Committee of the Regions, A European strategy for data (COM/2022/66 Final).

[11] Bacchi 2009.

[12] European Declaration on Digital Rights and Principles for the Digital Decade (COM/2022/28 Final).

[13] Digital decade Communication from the Commission to the European Parliament, the Council, the European Economic and Social Committee and the Committee of the Regions: 2030 Digital Compass: the European way for the Digital Decade (COM/2021/118 final).

[14] EDIF Proposal 2024 (amended proposal), Article 5(a)(1).

electronic transactions in the internal market (eIDAS) adopted in 2014.[15] eIDAS concerns the mutual recognition of cross-border digital identification by the public authorities as well as trust services, including the Qualified Trust Service Providers and the creation of legal effects of e-signatures. The review of the eIDAS in 2020 resulted in a decision to amend the regulation and introduce a European Digital Identity Framework (EDIF) to overcome some of the failings of the eIDAS.[16]

The EDIF includes amendments to the eIDAS, such as provisions to establish the European Digital Identity Wallet (EDIW). While the EDIF does not define digital identity, Article 3(2) EDIF clarifies that 'electronic identification means' are immaterial and material units that contain personal identification data and is used to authenticate online and offline. The EDIW is later defined in Article 6a(7a) EDIF as an electronic identification means to store, manage and validate identity data and attributes securely, and to provide them to relying parties and other users. In other words, EDIW is a mobile application that enables the storage of identity-related attributes such as passports, driving licences and academic qualifications. The wallet is intended to be voluntary and free of charge for EU citizens.[17] Once passed, Member States are obliged either to provide a wallet or recognise a private solution that meets the requirements laid out in the regulation.[18] The EU will also adopt a EDIW Toolbox which includes a technical Architecture and Reference Framework for the wallet.[19]

In addition to EDIW, the EDIF expands the scope of the Trust Services which are electronic services that help different parties to conclude binding decisions online, such as enabling a company to conclude an e-commerce contract online that requires an electronic signature.[20] In the eIDAS regulation, the Trust services include the electronic signatures, electronic seals, and electronic time stamps. The new EDIF amendments expand the scope of the Trust Services to include electronic registered delivery services, electronic certificates for authentication, and electronic seals for electronic documents.[21] The proposal also introduces a new concept of 'Qualified Trust Services Providers' for technology providers that wish to certify as the highest assurance level providers in the EU for trust services.[22] Trust services have not been discussed in this chapter.

---

[15] Regulation (EU) No 910/2014 of the European Parliament and of the Council of 23 July 2014 on electronic identification and trust services for electronic transactions in the internal market and repealing Directive 1999/93/EC (COM/2021/OJ L 257).

[16] For example, only 15 out of 27 member states provided a cross-border eID under eIDAS to their citizens as stated in the Report from the commission to the European Parliament and the Council on the evaluation of Regulation (EU) No 910/2014 on electronic identification and trust services for electronic transactions in the internal market (eIDAS) (COM/2021/ 290 final).

[17] EDIF Proposal 2021, Article 6a(7a).

[18] EDIF Proposal 2021, Article 6a(2).

[19] EDIF Proposal 2021, Recital 36.

[20] EDIF Proposal 202, Article 3(16).

[21] eIDAS, Chapter III.

[22] EDIF Proposal 2024 (amended version), Recital 20.

6.3 Method: Problematisation of User Control

The main objective of this paper is to problematise the user control discourse in the context of EDIF. For this purpose, the chapter utilises the WPR, a post-structural discourse analysis developed by Carol Bacchi.[23] The analysis consists of six questions that are used to examine a policy (later referred to as the 'WPR questions'). WPR takes as its starting point the hypothesis that governmental practices produce problems, and rather than examining the solutions, the focus is on examining the representation of the problems as a counter-discursive activity.[24]

This method helps in questioning the assumptions and predispositions the policy is based on and whether they 'accurately' describe the existing situation. If the problem is based on assumptions that do not accurately depict reality, the solution offered in the policy can end up having adverse effects rather than reach the positive outcome envisaged.[25] While the method has been primarily used by sociologists and political theory scholars, it has also gained the interest of legal researchers studying technology regulation.[26]

In general, discourse analysis is a widely used method in legal research for studying linguistic tactics and problematising socio-political issues and events.[27] It is particularly well-suited to exposing trends and 'othering', in other words discriminatory effects of language and effects of laws. Thus, to examine the unintended consequences of the user control discourse in the context of EDIW critically, the WPR method provides a structured approach to step by step analyse a policy and effects. The WPR questions are[28]:

1. What is the 'problem' represented to be in a specific policy?
2. What presuppositions or assumptions underlie this representation of the 'problem'?
3. How has this representation of the 'problem' come about?
4. What is left as unproblematic in this problem representation, and where are the silences? Can the 'problem' be thought about differently?
5. What effects are produced by this representation of the problem?
6. How/where is this representation of the 'problem' produced, disseminated and defended. How could it be questioned, disrupted, and replaced?

The primary source used for the analysis is the proposal for the EDIF. To understand the evolution of the EU digital identity, the analysis also relies on the related

[23] Bacchi 2009, p. xii.

[24] Bacchi 2009 pp. xii, 8–9, 14.

[25] Bacchi and Goodwin 2019, p. 9.

[26] See e.g., Dent 2009; Koulu 2020; Padden and Öjehag-Pettersson 2021; Zimmermann 2022.

[27] Brown 1998.

[28] Bacchi 2009, p. 2.

preparatory documents like the evaluation study of the eIDAS regulation[29] and the impact assessment published by the EU Commission.[30]

6.4 Analysis

In this analysis, each WPR question is answered by analysing the EDIF and related documents.

6.4.1 Two Competing Problem Representations

The first WPR question is: What is the 'problem' represented to be in a specific policy? The purpose of the question is to identify the implied problem representations. The problem representations do not need to reflect the reality according to Bacchi and Goodwin, who believe that policies have a performative character and problem representations are deduced from the wording of a policy in the way they are presented.[31]

The starting point for the analysis at hand is Article 5a(1) EDIF, which guarantees that all EU citizens will have 'secure, trusted and seamless cross-border access to public and private services, while having full control over their data, each Member State shall provide at least one European Digital Identity Wallet'.[32]

Two problem representations are identified in this article. First, the article obliges each Member State to provide an EDIW to its citizens, implying that a lack of a government-provided digital identity is a problem. Recital 7 EDIF also specifies that currently Member States are offering diverging digital identity solutions, and in some cases, no solutions are available, hence harmonisation of electronic identifications is required at the EU level. In the Explanatory Memorandum to the EDIF it is also stated that the lack of digital identity causes inconvenience to individuals, and it is a risk that they will not be able to use online services while also maintaining their privacy.[33] The problem representation thus holds that it is a matter of state responsibility to ensure that each citizens has the possibility to electronically identify themselves.

Article 5a(1) EDIF holds also a second problem representation that is derived from the obligation that not only do Member States have to provide a secure and

---

[29] European Commission 2020.

[30] Commission staff working document impact assessment report Accompanying the document Proposal for a Regulation of the European Parliament and of the Council amending Regulation (EU) n° 910/2014 as regards establishing a framework for a European Digital Identity (COM/2021/124 final).

[31] Bacchi and Goodwin 2019, p. 30.

[32] EDIF Proposal 2024 (amended version), Article 5a.

[33] EDIF Proposal 2024 (amended proposal).

trustworthy digital identity, but they will also have to ensure that the application allows individuals to control their data. This is further specified in Recital 3 EDIF, which states the digital identity should be under citizen's 'sole control' and aid them to exercise their rights as well as to participate in the digital economy. The implicit problem representation here is that individuals lack control over their personal data and, consequently, their digital identity. The analysis will next reflect how these two problem representations are interlinked and their underlying competing interests.

6.4.2 Underlying Assumptions About the Market

The second WPR step is identifying presuppositions or assumptions that underlie problem representations.[34] For instance, Bacchi proposes examining the binaries, such as illegal/legal and key concepts that revolve around the problem representation.[35] This section begins by identifying binaries in the first problem representation, and in the second part, a key concept regarding the second problem representation is considered.

In the first problem representation, the predispositions relate to the digital market, where the EU appears to bid against the privately provided digital identities and government-provided identity solutions. The EU uses categories 'regulated' identity solutions versus 'unregulated' identity solutions.[36] The review of eIDAS showed that the current market for electronic identification within the EU is fragmented and the existing private digital identity solutions do not offer a high level of security. On top of that they are disconnected from a government-verified identity that makes digital identities more susceptible to fraud and identity theft.[37] In the impact assessment accompanying the EDIF proposal, the Commission calls out the US-based digital platforms and technology companies as unsafe and susceptible to precarious personal data collection, and as such, sees them as a risk to the privacy of EU citizens.

The European Commission's President Ursula von der Leyen illustrated the frustration poignantly in her State of Union speech in 2020, by stating that 'every time an App or website ask us to create a new digital identity or to easily log on via a big platform, we have no idea what really happens to our data in reality'.[38] In the impact assessment, the Commission also recognises that part of the problem is that individuals prefer to create a digital identity through a social media account.[39] This identity is not verified, nor does it require further authentication. For instance, Meta acts as the third-party identity provider, offering its users the option to use their Facebook

---

[34] Bacchi 2009, p. 5.

[35] Bacchi 2009, p. 7.

[36] Weigl et al. 2022, p. 76.

[37] EDIF Proposal 2021, Explanatory memorandum.

[38] Von der Leyen 2022.

[39] Vapen et al. 2016.

account to log into third-party services.[40] However, it is not always apparent to the users what information is shared with the third-party services. The EDIF proposal and related policy documents thus describe the market issues regarding the provision of digital identities and present the user-controlled digital identity as a solution to the market failure.

In the second problem representation, 'control' is thus identified as a key concept. While control is frequently mentioned in the EDIF proposal (26 times) and related policy documents as one of the policy objectives,[41] there is no clear definition of what it entails. This is not surprising since Anciaux et al. have made a claim that the concept of control is under-defined in law even when it is one of the main tenants in privacy and data protection laws.[42] For example, Graef et al. explain that the EU privacy and data protection framework has been built on the premise that privacy equals having control over one's personal data.[43] This premise is based on the work of US scholar, Allen Westin,[44] who described in 1967 that privacy is about one's ability to manage 'when, how and to what extent' information about them is shared with others. Today, US scholars Solove and Hartzog describe this approach as the Individual Control Model as it relies on individuals to make conscious choices about their data.[45]

In the EU, the GDPR, adopted in 2016, further entrenched the idea that privacy is about individual control over their data.[46] There is no definition of control in the GDPR either, but it gives an active role for individuals through consent mechanism and data subject rights.[47] Consent mechanisms refers to it being possible to process personal data lawfully, when the data subject has given their consent to it.[48] The data subject's rights include the right to access information and right to have human intervention when subjected to automated decision-making, among others.[49]

The Individual Control Model has nevertheless been criticised as to whether it is the best approach to uphold the right to private life and protection of personal data in the age of AI. Solove and Hartzog consider, for instance that individuals simply lack the ability to make informed choices online, due to the information asymmetry between users and technology providers and manipulation through technological design. They advocate instead for protection of societal values though governmental action and call this as the Societal Structure Model,[50] in which governments

---

40 Vapen et al. 2016.

41 EDIF Proposal 2024 (amended proposal).

42 Anciaux et al., 2021, p. 16.

43 Graef et al. 2023, p. 2.

44 Westin 1968.

45 Solove and Hartzog 2024, p. 6.

46 GPDR, Recital 71, Article 75.

47 GPDR, Article 13–23

48 GPDR, Article 6

49 GPDR, Articles 15–22.

50 Solove and Hartzog 2024, p. 7.

decide safe practices for individuals and place more requirements for companies on responsible data processing.[51]

The EDIF builds on the Individual Control Model, as it attempts empower individuals by giving them more control over their digital identity and personal data, through selective sharing of personal attributes and certificates. The EDIF also relies on the data subject rights found on the GDPR as properties of 'control', as shown by Article 6a(4) subsections that describe that the EDIW is a tool for exercising the right to data portability and the right to be forgotten. Also, when the EDIF introduces restrictions on the processing of personal data for the wallet providers, those restrictions can be circumvented with the user's consent.[52] The EU consequently relies on the assumption that the best way to uphold the individual privacy is to provide them control over their personal data as opposed to the Societal Structure Model.

6.4.3 Development of New AI Privacy Harms

The third WPR question is: How the representation of the 'problem' has come about? Bacchi sees that the question serves two purposes. First, to understand the specific developments and decisions that have led to the problem representation and second, to examine whether competing problem representation has existed.[53]

For the analysis, three essential developments are discussed. First, the COVID-19 pandemic has been an important development that contributed to the two problem representations. Above all, the pandemic showcased the importance of having a harmonised EU-level approach to digital identity when there was a sudden need to provide digital public services to EU citizens, regardless of the digital maturity of a Member State, and the need for remote identification for both public and private services.[54] During the pandemic in 2020, the EU Council recommended the development of the EDIF and declared at the same time that individuals should be empowered to control their online identity and data.[55]

Second, while the pandemic was one of the main drivers for the introduction of the EDIF and reinforced the user-control paradigm, the speedy introduction of the EDIF itself reveals a competing problem representation. Weigl *et al.* consider that the 'speedy' introduction of proposal for EDIF in 2021 presents an interesting case of 'policy punctuation', in a policy area in which the EU's legal competence has been

[51] Hirsch 2019, p. 462.

[52] EDIF proposal 2021, Article 6(a)(7).

[53] Bacchi 2009, p. 10.

[54] Commission staff working document impact assessment report Accompanying the document Proposal for a Regulation of the European Parliament and of the Council amending Regulation (EU) n° 910/2014 as regards establishing a framework for a European Digital Identity (COM/2021/124 final).

[55] Special meeting of the European Council (1 and 2 October 2020)—Conclusions (EUCO 12/20).

subject to interpretation.[56] They found that, during the Von der Leyen Commission mandate, there was a sudden urgency to create a European digital identity that would align with the Commission's digital priorities,[57] such as digital sovereignty and the Digital Single Market.[58]

Article 49 eIDAS required, that the regulation shall be reviewed before July 2020. However, before the eIDAS review, the European Digital Identity was not mentioned in any of the EU policy documents and the introduction of the EDIW came as an 'surprise', when the EU Commission brought the idea to light in 2020.[59] The Commission presented the European Digital Identity as one of the policy options to strengthen 'Europe's technical autonomy' in the in the Communication Shaping Europe's Digital Future.[60] Also the same year, the European Council called on the Commission to provide a proposal for 'European Digital Identification' by 2021.[61] This was considered as a mandate from the Member States.[62] Consequently, the eIDAS review turned into 'a revision' that introduced the EDIF.

According to Weigl *et al.*, this reveals the EU's motivation for pushing for digital constitutionalism and digital sovereignty'.[63] In other words, the policy aim may be to empower citizens in regard to their data but obliging Member States to build their own digital identity solutions is part of the aim to lessen the dependency on technology companies that most often originate from the United States.[64] As such, digital sovereignty provides a competing problem representation.

The third noteworthy development has been the increased use of AI that has impacted the provision of digital identities and the digital market at large. In the inception assessment of the EDIF proposal, the Commission considered that there are 'fundamental changes in the social context' regarding digital identities.[65] The changes include increased use of new technology like AI, biometrics, distributed ledger-based solutions and the Internet of Things.[66] Relatedly, in the study to support the impact assessment for the revision of the eIDAS in 2021, the Commission considered AI to be main factor to influence the digital identity markets and to drive the demand for technology that use AI or biometrics verify a claimed identity.[67]

[56] Weigl et al. 2022, p. 75.

[57] Weigl et al. 2022, p. 75.

[58] Weigl et al. 2022, p. 75.

[59] Communication from the Commission to the European Parliament, the Council, the European Economic and Social Committee and the Committee of the Regions Shaping Europe's digital Future (COM/2020/67 final).

[60] Communication from the Commission to the European Parliament, the Council, the European Economic and Social Committee and the Committee of the Regions Shaping Europe's digital Future (COM/2020/67 final).

[61] Special meeting of the European Council (1 and 2 October 2020)—Conclusions (EUCO 12/20).

[62] Weigl et al. 2022, p. 75.

[63] Weigl et al. 2022, p. 75.

[64] Floridi 2020, p. 369.

[65] European Commission 2020a.

[66] EDIF Proposal 2021, Explanatory Memorandum.

[67] European Commission 2020, p. 27.

The rapid adoption of the new technology has nevertheless brought concerns on what impact the AI systems will have on electronic identification, in which biometrics, for instance, is used to link an individual to a digital identity.[68] First of all, the linking is not infallible and mistakes can occur when AI is used.[69] Second, the use of AI by cyber criminals increases the risks of identity fraud, creation of new false digital identities and fraudulent transactions among others.[70] Third, the study to support the impact assessment of the revision of the eIDAS, found that when it comes to the development of biometrics for identity verification and authentication, there is not enough guidance at the EU level on how to process sensitive personal data to ensure high security.[71] The EU is expected to adopt the Artificial Intelligence Act (AIA) in 2024 which may bring some clarity by banning, for instance, the use of 'real-time' remote biometric identification systems in publicly accessible spaces for the purpose of law enforcement (unless for certain objectives).[72]

While the COVID-19 pandemic showcased the need for user-controlled digital identity solutions, the rapid adoption of AI poses new challenges as to how individuals can control those solutions, and as such providing another competing problem representation. The EDIF and related policy documents recognise that AI has the potential to bring about change, but the materials do not discuss the new AI privacy harms. Lee and others for instance have identified a taxonomy of new AI privacy harms, building on Solove's privacy taxonomy.[73] Their taxonomy includes new types of risks such as phrenology or physiognomy that refers to AI's capability to closely estimate sensitive personal attributes (e.g., sexual orientation, ethnicity) just from individuals' attributes like voice or image. Considering that EDIW will store government verified identity data, including biometrics and pictures, the new harms can come with severe consequences in the context of EDIF.

6.4.4 Relevance of Control in a Post-Algorithmic Era?

The fourth WPR question is what is left as unproblematic in this problem representation: Where are the silences; can the 'problem' be thought about differently? The fourth question invites a problematisation of the problem representation.[74] Bacchi proposes, considering the limits of the problem representation—in other words, what is not problematised—to identify the gaps and silences.

---

[68] Sullivan 2018, p. 724.

[69] Sullivan 2012, p. 224.

[70] Sullivan 2018, p. 729.

[71] European Commission 2020, p. 35.

[72] Proposal for a Regulation of the European Parliament and of the Council laying down harmonised rules on Artificial Intelligence (Artificial Intelligence Act) and amending certain Union legislative Acts (COM/2021/206 final), Article 5(1)(d).

[73] Lee et others 2023, pp. 8, 11.

[74] Bacchi 2009, p. 12.

Section 6.4.3. showcased that AI is producing new privacy harms that have not been addressed in the EDIF and related policy documents. They also remain silent on how the increased use of AI impacts an individual's ability to control their data. Control was identified as a key concept, regarding the problem representation in Sect. 6.4.2. Yet, the EU does not critically consider whether it is a suitable policy aim in the first place, and overlooks the critic put forth by privacy scholars.

Bietti, for example, criticises the Individual Control Model, because according to her data is relational and collectively construed.[75] According to her, an individual decision about data processing will impact other users' data and as consequence, the Individual Control Model does not work in the platform ecosystem. Likewise, Hartzog,[76] Herian,[77] Solove[78] and Reniers[79] are raising concerns about the individual capabilities of having control over their data and critically assess the fit between the technology design principles and the ability of laws to designate control effectively. An alternative tool for control is also proposed by Richards and Hartzog (among others) who consider that the responsibility should be with the data controllers, who should have a fiduciary duty towards the people whose personal data they process.[80]

Considering the growing criticism towards the Individual Control Model, Angel even proposes that privacy is undergoing a 'post-algorithmic turn' of which one consequence is that individual agency and digital self-determination are no longer seen as goals in themselves.[81] The term has been inspired and influenced by scholars such as Hildebrandt and De Vries,[82] Edwards and Veale,[83] Ajunwa[84] and Hartzog.[85] Coincidently, the AIA is showcasing a move towards a regulatory strategy that does not emphasise control. The AIA will provide a risk-based regulation that requires technology providers to consider the impact of the AI systems to on the fundamental rights, but it does not give new rights for individuals or emphasis user empowerment.[86] As such, AIA is closer to the Societal Structure Model that Individual Control Model.[87]

However, with the introduction of the EDIF, the regulatory burden becomes heavier for individuals who need to learn to make calculated choices regarding their personal data by acknowledging both rules in the GDPR and EDIF that may sound contradicting. Suppose the relying party accessing data on the EDIW is a public

---

75 Bietti 2023, p. 47.

76 Hartzog 2021.

77 Herian 2020.

78 Solove 2023a.

79 Renieris 2023.

80 Richards and Hartzog 2021.

81 Angel 2023, p. 2.

82 Hildebrandt and de Vries 2013.

83 Edwards and Veale 2017.

84 Ajunwa 2020.

85 Hartzog 2021.

86 Kamiski 2023.

87 Angel 2023, p. 2.

organisation that processes health data as one of its legal obligations. In that case, individuals do not have the right to request that their data be deleted, and they do not have the right to data portability.[88] Yet, the EDIF states that individuals should have the right to delete data, without clarifying that it only applies in certain cases.[89]

Also, in the case the relying party is a private organisation, the data subject's rights are not absolute. For instance, if the controller has anonymised the data accordingly, the GDPR no longer applies to the anonymised dataset, and the data does not need to be removed, as guided by the European Data Protection Board (EDPB).[90] Moreover, the rights need to be balanced against the rights and freedoms of others,[91] and the controller can consider the technical feasibility of deleting personal data.[92] In situations in which identification is not required, the controller is not even obliged to comply with most of the data subject rights, such as rights to access and deletion.[93] The actual control the EDIW can provide is thus limited by the contextual nature of data subject rights.

Thus, it can be questioned whether in the age of AI, the user-control paradigm is still relevant policy aim. Solove and Hartzog explicitly proclaim that 'although individual powerlessness is the right problem, the Individual Control Model is the wrong approach to address it'.[94] According to them, solutions that empower individuals regarding their personal data are not the answer, since individuals will continue to make choices that are to their detriment, regardless of the technology.[95] Considering this, it the EU seems push for the data empowerment of EU citizens at the cost of their privacy.

6.4.5 Effects: Risks of Surveillance and Deepfakes

The fifth WPR question is what effects are produced by this problem representation. Bacchi's analysis starts from the premise that inevitably, problem representations create difficulties and harm to individuals belonging to a specific social group while others may benefit.[96] As such, the WPR deviates from usual policy analysis and looks beyond the evidence-based approach. Here two interconnected and, at times, overlapping effects are discussed: discursive effect and lived effects.

Discursive effects examine how assumptions, discourses, and silences can impact individuals by 'closing off' particular options. To begin with, the EDIW can have a

---

[88] GPDR, Article 17.

[89] EDIF Proposal 2024 (amended proposal), Article 5(a)(5).

[90] EDPB 2021.

[91] GPDR, Recitals 73, 83, Articles 25 and 32.

[92] GPDR, Article 17(2).

[93] GPDR, Article 11.

[94] Solove and Hartzog 2024, p. 3.

[95] Solove and Hartzog 2024, pp. 3–5.

[96] Bacchi 2009, p. 15.

positive and negative effect on the society. In countries such as Finland, where 90% of individuals rely on bank services for strong authentication, being a bank customer can become a bottleneck to accessing digital public, and private services. Banks have diverging requirements on who they accept as their customers. A government-provided digital identity that is free to use can also work as a means of inclusion. Finland was preparing a new law to introduce a digital identity scheme that would have improved the current situation for migrants arriving to Finland and allowed them to have immediate access to digital identity and strong authentication. The law proposal was unexpectedly repealed when the new right-wing coalition came in during autumn 2023. The EDIF will, nevertheless, compel the Finnish government to continue working on providing a digital identity solution to Finnish citizens that is free to use and to ensure equal access to digital services.[97]

On the negative side, with the stringent link between the European Digital Identity and a government-verified identity, the effect is that certain groups of people will be 'closed off'. According to Recital 7 EDIF, the users of the digital identity wallets are 'Union citizens and other residents as defined by national law'. The requirements for citizenship and residency vary between countries, placing EU citizens on an unequal footing regarding access to the wallet.[98] It should be thus recognised that governments have an interest in controlling digital identity as part of their sovereignty and in the ability to control who gets to participate in society. In fact, Marion Ho-Dac warns that the main political agenda of the EDIF is to 'regain control over the identity of European citizens in the digital ecosystem'.[99]

As questions of digital identity become politicised, Fratini and Lo Tauro believe that the role of the state should be carefully thought through in providing digital identities, since too large of a role may bring a risk of mass surveillance of citizens' behaviour.[100] After the publication of the EDIF proposal in 2021, privacy activists indeed raised their concerns about the obligation for governments to use persistent identifiers as part of the minimum set of data that would be shared with a relying party.[101] In the proposal, Article 11a(2) required EU Member States to include a unique and persistent identifier in the minimum set of person identification data (defined in Article 12.4.(d)), when identification was is required by law. In adopted version, the heading of Article 11a was changed to 'cross-border identity matching' and in the article there is no requirement for persistent identifiers. Now Member States need to simply ensure 'unequivocal identity matching'.[102]

Another article that has raised concerns about government surveillance is Article 45 EDIF, introducing Qualified Website Authentication Certificates (QWAC). Put

---

[97] https://vm.fi/en/-/legislative-proposals-on-digital-identity-and-redesigning-the-system-of-personal-identity-codes-will-not-be-considered-during-this-parliamentary-session Accessed 29 February 2024.

[98] Sullivan and Stalla-Bourdillon 2015.

[99] Marion Ho-Dac 2022.

[100] Fratini and Lo Tauro 2023.

[101] EDIF Proposal 2021, Article 11a.

[102] EDIF Proposal 2024 (amended proposal), Article 11a.

briefly, the idea behind QWACs is to ensure that a website is not fraudulent for the user through certificates.[103] The technology providers are strongly against the introduction of QWAC, because it would require browsers to accept a new form of certificate to authenticate websites with lower security standards to what is already being provided.[104] On top of that, the article requires each EU Member State to form a certificate-issuing authority and according to the technology industry, this compromises the existing system, when 'an error of judgement or deliberate action by one Member State will affect citizens in all other Member States'.[105] The larger cybersecurity community has raised the alarm that the EDIF will eventually allow 'large-scale tracking of citizens based on government-issued identifiers'.[106] The AI exacerbates the risk by scale and ubiquity of personal data collected and what can be inferred from the data.[107]

Of course, the EDIW will be voluntary for individuals to use as stated in Article 5a(15) EDIF, and individuals can choose not to use the wallet.[108] The article moreover describes that individuals should be able to access public services regardless of the identification and authentication means, and that the EDIW cannot be the only means for login into a public service. Nevertheless, there is still a risk that the users will be subject to power imbalances, since in some situations they are required by law to identify themselves and if they do not want to use the EDIW, they will need to physically identify themselves.[109]

The European Data Protection Supervisor (EDPS), Wojciech Wiewiórowski is moreover concerned that strong identification is becoming the *conditio sine qua non* for the use of internet services and protests that it would be needed for all online interactions. He asserts that while in theory, strong authentication can make service more secure, in practice it could also be used to track users and profile them.[110] Similarly Member of the European Parliament, Patrick Breyer claims that 'overidentification can gradually erode our right to use digital services anonymously'.[111] With the increased use of artificial intelligence systems in authenticating users and profiling, privacy and data protection risks are accumulating, while also impacting the user's ability to control their personal data processing.

---

[103] EDIF Proposal 2024 (amended proposal), Article 45.

[104] https://blog.mozilla.org/netpolicy/files/2023/11/eIDAS-Industry-Letter.pdf Accessed 29 February 2024.

[105] https://blog.mozilla.org/netpolicy/files/2023/11/eIDAS-Industry-Letter.pdf Accessed 29 February 2024.

[106] https://eidas-open-letter.org and https://eidas-open-letter.org/statement-23-11-2023.pdf Accessed 29 February 2024.

[107] Lee et al. 2023, p. 8.

[108] EDIF Proposal 2024 (amended proposal), Article 5a(15).

[109] EDRI 2022b.

[110] EDPS 2023.

[111] https://www.patrick-breyer.de/en/eu-digital-identity-regulation-eidas-pirates-dont-support-blank-cheque-for-surveillance-of-citizens-online-2/ Accessed 29 February 2024.

Secondly, the lived effects include identity theft, which means that information related to a person's identity is used to transact online and make payments.[112] Identity theft can result in financial and psychological distress and especially the rise of 'deepfakes' put women at risk to experience defamation, intimidation and extortion.[113] Deepfake is a term referring to technology that can create fake images, audio and text using artificial intelligence and deep learning techniques to make for instance a video seem authentic.[114] Cybercriminals can bypass biometric identification checks using deepfakes and gain access to sensitive personal data in the EDIW.[115] Also, if EDIW is used to access online public services such as filing tax reports, a breach of digital identity can lead to a situation in which the identity thief can access the portal and change the account number to which tax returns are paid.[116]

Schroers and Tsormatzoudi have studied the liability of situations in which identity theft has occurred because of government mismanagement.[117] They concluded that it is difficult for individuals to seek redress for three reasons. First, once an identity theft happens, individuals have little means to 'investigate' why it happened, and second, to prove causation that it happened due to mismanagement of the public authority. Third, it is also difficult for individuals to prove the damage caused by the theft, as evidenced by the latest judgement from the Court of Justice of the European Union, which states that infringing against the GDPR alone is insufficient grounds for claiming damages; individuals will need to show that they have suffered material or non-material damages due to the violation.[118]

6.4.6 Proliferation of Empowerment Discourse

The sixth WPR question is how/where is this representation of the 'problem' produced, disseminated and defended and how could it be questioned, disrupted, and replaced. The sixth question examines how a problem representation reaches 'their target audience and achieve legitimacy'.[119]

The EU Commission refers to the coronavirus pandemic as a catalyst for the rapid digitalisation of online services. Hence the need for individuals to gain control over their digital identity and data.[120] However, the push for the user control narrative

[112] Schroers and Tsormatzoudi 2016, p. 8

[113] European Parliament 2021, p. 17.

[114] European Parliament 2021, p. 17.

[115] https://www.enisa.europa.eu/news/enisa-news/beware-of-digital-id-attacks-your-face-can-be-spoofed Accessed 31 January 2024.

[116] Schroers and Tsormatzoudi 2016, pp. 8, 9–11.

[117] Schroers and Tsormatzoudi 2016, pp. 12–14.

[118] C-300/21 *UI v Österreichische Post* [2020] ECLI:EU:C:2023:370, para 42.

[119] Bacchi 2009, p. 19.

[120] See e.g., Commission staff working document impact assessment report accompanying the document Proposal for a Regulation of the European Parliament and of the Council amending

can also be traced to a design research trend emphasising human-centricity. OpenID foundation explains that since 2003, scholars in information systems, the social sciences and development have argued for human-centric design and principles that have been developed by civil society and advocacy groups, such as the Human Technology Foundation (HTF) and Trust over IP Foundation.[121]

The EU Data Strategy also refers to civil society actors calling for the EU to 'give individuals the tools and means to decide at a granular level what is done with their data,' referencing the MyData movement.[122] Mydata is a civil society actor promoting the processing of personal data in a human-centric way.[123] The movement has been incremental in gaining the attention of the regulators to improve the standing of individuals in the data economy and furthering the user empowerment discourse, as evidenced by the reference in the EU strategy, however it has shied away from critically evaluating the effects of the empowerment discourse and avoided criticising the governmental actors. In contrast, EDRi, a network of non-governmental organisations defending rights and freedoms online has criticised the EDIF for leading the EU 'straight into surveillance capitalism'.[124]

The EU, thus somewhat naively, pushes for the user discourse. The naivety is visible from the push to oblige the gatekeepers to accept the European Digital Identity as a means of authentication. The Committee of the Region noted in their opinion on the EDIF that 'there are on the one hand, the major global social networks, which have a valid interest in getting their pseudonym accounts verified by a public institution. This would, however, undermine the freedom to use the internet and further drive users from its protected area into the dark web'.[125] In addition, from the targeted advertising perspective, the more verified accounts a gatekeeper has, the more it can show value for its corporate customers. Thus, the value of the data they have goes up. Taking as an example, when Elon Musk was in the process of buying Twitter, the question of the number of fake accounts almost halted the sale.[126]

Regulation (EU) n° 910/2014 as regards establishing a framework for a European Digital Identity (COM/2021/124 final).

[121] Garber and Haine 2023.

[122] Communication from the Commission to the European Parliament, the Council, the European Economic and Social Committee and the Committee of the Regions, A European strategy for data (COM/2020/66 final).

[123] Mydata 2023.

[124] EDRI 2022b.

[125] Opinion of the Committee of Regions—European Digital Identity (2022/ C 61/09).

[126] Feeley 2022.

6.5 Discussion

The analysis showed the growing importance of digital identity, and how it is becoming an increasingly politicised matter. The discourse analysis focused on two problem representations, where on the one hand, the EDIF proposal identifies that individual's control over their personal data is weakened due to the current market deficiencies caused by private digital identity providers. The gatekeepers are blamed for the untransparent processing of personal data they gain when individuals use their identity solutions. The problem representation thus showed that providing digital identity is a matter of state responsibility. On the other hand, the Commission emphasises the need to empower individuals to control their data, which places the responsibility on the individual behaviour and capabilities to make decisions in the digital environment. However, this is where they suffered from power imbalance vis-à-vis the platforms that processes their personal data in the first place.

The analysis uncovered the underlying predispositions and found the EDIF relies on the Individual Control Model; however, while scholars have repeatedly been critical that it is difficult for individuals to make conscious choices online, the EU still relies on the idea that the EDIW users would be capable of controlling their personal data. The silence may be caused by the fact that the EU is more focused on a competing problem representation on gaining digital sovereignty where it sees the capable individuals in control of their data as useful leverage in negotiating data processing terms with technology providers. As such, the control discourse appears performative at best.

Bacchi's methodological steps were useful in uncovering the silences in the EDIF and how the development of AI has not been comprehensively reflected in the EDIF and related policy documents. Hence, when it comes to the use of artificial intelligence and biometric authentication, the use of the rights should be clarified. The decentralised, user-controlled design of the EDIF is intended to minimise the cybersecurity threats for individuals, but the very design of the wallet may leave the user vulnerable to identity theft and surveillance, as shown with persistent identifiers and QWACs. Individuals use one wallet to access a number of private and public services that require strong authentication, if those actions can be linked with the help of AI, they may impose sensitive information about the user. To make matters worse, it is seemingly difficult to keep a wallet issuer, either a public or private provider liable for possible harm caused by the surveillance or mismanagement of data due to challenges in proving causation, among others.

6.6 Conclusion

The chapter provided a critical analysis of user control discourse in the context of digital identity. The EDIF and related policy documents have adopted the language of empowerment and user control familiar to the GDPR. It continues the trend to propagate the idea that individuals should control their personal data in the context of digital identity. However, how the EDIF will be able to give control to the users remains limited due to the contextual nature of data subject rights and increased use of AI that comes with new kinds of privacy harms. In this context, user control may not be the right tool to overcome the power asymmetry in the digital environment. In fact, scholars propose more government action to lessen the regulatory burden on individuals and shift it 'back' to the data controllers.

References

Ajunwa I (2020) The Paradox of Automation as Anti-Bias Intervention. Cardozo Law Review. 41:1671–1683 https://scholarship.law.unc.edu/cgi/viewcontent.cgi?article=1490&context=faculty_publications Accessed 29 February 2024

Anciaux N, Zolynski C, Chaudat S, Ladjel R (2021) Empowerment and 'Big Personal Data': From Portability to Personal Agency. Global Privacy Law Review. 2:1–30 https://kluwerlawonline.com/journalarticle/Global+Privacy+Law+Review/2.1/GPLR2021003 Accessed 29 February 2024

Angel M (2023) Privacy's Algorithmic Turn. Journal of Science & Technology 30 (Forthcoming) https://ssrn.com/abstract=4602315. Accessed 26 August 2024

Bacchi C, Goodwin S (2019) Post-structural Policy Analysis: A Guide to Practice. Palgrave Macmillan, London

Bacchi C (2009) Analysing Policy: What's the Problem Represented to Be? Pearson Education

Bietti E (2023) A Genealogy of Digital Platform Regulation. Geo. L. Tech. Rev. 1, Northeastern University School of Law Research Paper No. 450 https://doi.org/10.2139/ssrn.3859487 Accessed 29 February 2024

Bietti (2020) The Discourse of Control and Consent Over Data in EU Data Protection Law and Beyond. Aegis Paper Series. https://perma.cc/LV2Q-DX63 Accessed 29 February 2024

Breyer (2023) https://www.patrick-breyer.de/en/eu-digital-identity-regulation-eidas-pirates-dont-support-blank-cheque-for-surveillance-of-citizens-online-2/ Accessed 29 February 2024

Brown B (1998) Legal discourse. Routledge https://www.rep.routledge.com/articles/thematic/legal-discourse/v-1 Accessed 29 February 2024

Dent C (2009) Copyright, Governmentality and Problematisation: An Exploration. Griffith Law Review 18(1):129–150

EDPS (2023) "Where are we heading with digital identities?", Cybersecurity Standardisation Conference 2023 https://edps.europa.eu/system/files/2023-02/23-02-07_ww-enisa_en_2.pdf. Accessed 29 February 2024

EDPB (2021) Misunderstandings related to anonymization. European Data Protection Board https://edps.europa.eu/system/files/2021-04/21-04-27_aepd-edps_anonymisation_en_5.pdf Accessed 29 February 2024

EDRI (2022a) eIDAS Policy Paper. EDRI: https://epicenter.works/sites/default/files/eidas-policy_paper-ewedri_0.pdf Accessed 29 February 2024

EDRI (2022b) Orwell's Wallet: European electronic identity system leads us straight into surveillance capitalism. EDRI: https://edri.org/our-work/orwells-wallet-european-electronic-identity-system-leads-us-straight-into-surveillance-capitalism/ Accessed 31 January 2024

Edwards L., Veale M. (2017) Slave to the Algorithm? Why a 'Right to an Explanation' Is Probably Not the Remedy You Are Looking For, Duke Law & Technology Review 16:18–83 https://papers.ssrn.com/sol3/papers.cfm?abstract_id=2972855 Accessed 29 February 2024

European Commission (2020a) Study to support the IA for revision eIDAS regulation. European Commission. https://digital-strategy.ec.europa.eu/en/library/study-support-impact-assessment-revision-eidas-regulation Accessed 31 January 2024

European Commission (2020b) Inception Impact Assessment - Revision of the eIDAS Regulation – European Digital Identity (EUid). https://ec.europa.eu/info/law/better-regulation/have-your-say/initiatives/12528-EU-digital-ID-scheme-for-online-transactions-across-Europe_en Accessed 29 February 2024

European Parliament (2021) Tackling deepfakes in European policy. European Parliamentary Research Service. https://www.europarl.europa.eu/RegData/etudes/STUD/2021/690039/EPRS_STU(2021)690039_EN.pdf Accessed 29 February 2024

Feeley J (2022) Twitter must give Musk more data on bots in batter over deal. Bloomberg. https://www.bloomberg.com/news/articles/2022-08-25/twitter-must-give-more-data-on-bots-to-musk-in-battle-over-deal#xj4y7vzkg Accessed 29 February 2024

Fratini A, Lo Tauro G (2023) To Use or Not to Use the European Digital Identity Wallet: Data Protection issues in the ongoing legislative debate. EU Law Analysis. https://eulawanalysis.blogspot.com/2022/08/to-use-or-not-to-use-european-digital.html Accessed 29 February 2024

Floridi L (2020) The Fight for Digital Sovereignty: What It Is, and Why It Matters, Especially for the EU. Philosophy & Technology 33:369–378. https://doi.org/10.1007/s13347-020-00423-6 Accessed 29 February 2024

Graef I, Petročnik T, Tombal T (2023) Conceptualizing Autonomy in an Era of Collective Data Processing: From Theory to Practice. DISO 2:19. https://doi.org/10.1007/s44206-023-00045-3 Accessed 29 February 2024

Garber E, Haine M (2023) Human-Centric Digital Identity. OpenID Foundation. https://openid.net/wp-content/uploads/2023/09/Human-Centric_Digital_Identity_Final.pdf Accessed 29 February 2024

Herian R (2020) Blockchain, GDPR, and Fantasies of Data Sovereignty. Law, Innovation and Technology 12(1):156–174. https://doi.org/10.1080/17579961.2020.1727094 Accessed 29 February 2024

Hildebrandt M, de Vries K (2013) Privacy, Due Process and the Computational Turn at a glance. Pointers for the hurried reader. In Hildebrandt M, de Vries K (eds) Privacy, Due Process and The Computational Turn. Routledge, London, pp. 1–9.

Hirsch D (2019) From Individual Control to Social Protection: New Paradigms for Privacy Law in The Age of Predictive Analytics. Maryland Law Review 79:439-439. https://digitalcommons.law.umaryland.edu/mlr/vol79/iss2/4 Accessed 29 February 2024

Hartzog W (2021) What is Privacy? That's the Wrong Question. The University of Chicago Law Review 88(1):1677–1688. https://ssrn.com/abstract=3970890 Accessed 29 February 2024

Kamiski M (2023) The Developing Law of AI: A Turn to Risk Regulation. The Digital Social Contract: A Lawfare Paper Series https://www.lawfaremedia.org/article/the-developing-law-of-ai-regulation-a-turn-to-risk-regulation Accessed 31 January 2024

Koulu R (2020) Human control over automation: EU Policy and AI Ethics. European Journal of Legal Studies 12:1, 9–46. https://hdl.handle.net/1814/66992 Accessed 29 February 2024

Lee H, Yang Y J, von Davier T S, Forlizzi J, Das S (2023) Deepfakes, Phrenology, Surveillance and More! A Taxonomy of AI Privacy Harms. arXiv. https://arxiv.org/pdf/2310.07879.pdf Accessed 29 February 2024

Mantelero A (2022) Beyond Data. In: Beyond Data. Information Technology and Law Series 36 T.M.C. Asser Press, The Hague. https://doi.org/10.1007/978-94-6265-531-7_1 Accessed 29 February 2024

Marion Ho-Dac (2022) Towards a European Digital Identity Wallet? A Private International Law Perspective. https://eapil.org/2022/11/21/towards-a-european-digital-identity-wallet-a-private-international-law-perspective/ Accessed 29 February 2024

MyData (2023) How we operate. https://www.mydata.org/about/purposes-principles/ Accessed 29 February 2024

Ortalda A, Tsakalakis N, Jasmontaite L (2021) The European Commission Proposal Amending the eIDAS Regulation: A Personal Data Protection Perspective. Brussels Privacy Hub https://brusselsprivacyhub.eu/onewebmedia/Proposal%20to%20amend%20eIDAS.%20A%20personal%20data%20protection%20perspective_BPH_December%202021.pdf Accessed 29 February 2024

Padden M, Öjehag-Pettersson A (2021) Protected how? Problem representations of risk in the General Data Protection Regulation (GDPR). Critical Policy Studies 12(4):498–499. https://doi.org/10.1080/19460171.2021.1927776 Accessed 29 February 2024

Renieris E (2023) Beyond Data: Reclaiming Human Rights at the Dawn of the Metaverse. The MIT Press

Richards N, Hartzog W (2021) A Duty of Loyalty for Privacy Law. Washington University Law Review 99: 961–1021. https://doi.org/10.2139/ssrn.3642217 Accessed 29 February 2024

Schroers J, Tsormatzoudi P (2016) Identity-Theft Through E-Government Services—Government to Pay the Bill?. CiTiP Working Paper 27/2016 https://ssrn.com/abstract=2768877 Accessed 27 August 2024

Schwartz P, Treanor M (2000) The New Privacy, Michigan Law Review 101(6):2163–2184. https://repository.law.umich.edu/mlr/vol101/iss6/36 Accessed 29 February 2024

Solove D (2023a) The Limitations of Privacy Rights. Notre Dame Law Review 98:975–1036, GWU Legal Studies Research Paper No. 2022-30. https://ssrn.com/abstract=4024790 Accessed 29 February 2024

Solove D (2023b) Murky Consent: An Approach to the Fictions of Consent in Privacy Law. Boston University Law Review (Forthcoming), GWU Legal Studies Research Paper. No. 2023–2023 https://ssrn.com/abstract=4333743 Accessed 29 February 2024

Solove D, Hartzog W (2024) Kafka in the Age of AI and the Futility of Privacy as Control. Boston University Law Review 1021 (2024), GWU Legal Studies Research Paper No. 2024–31, GWU Law School Public Law Research Paper No. 2024-31, Boston University School of Law Research Paper No. 4685553. https://ssrn.com/abstract=4685553 Accessed 27 August 2024

Sullivan C (2018) Digital identity—From emergent legal concept to new reality. Computer Law & Security Review 34(4):723–731. https://www.sciencedirect.com/science/article/pii/S0267364918302024 Accessed 29 February 2024

Sullivan C (2012) Digital identity and mistake. International Journal of Law and Information Technology 20:223–241. https://papers.ssrn.com/sol3/papers.cfm?abstract_id=2379251 Accessed 29 February 2024

Sullivan C, Stalla-Bourdillon S (2015) Digital identity and French personality rights – a way forward in recognizing and protecting an individual's rights in his/her digital identity. Computer Law and Security Review. https://ssrn.com/abstract=2584427 Accessed 29 February 2024

Tsakalakis N, Stalla-Bourdillon S, O'Hara K (2016) What's in a name: the conflicting views of pseudonymisation under eIDAS and the General Data Protection Regulation. In: Hühnlein D, Roßnagel H, Schunck C and Talamo M (eds.) In Open Identity Summit 2016: October 13–14, 2016, Italy

Valtionvarainministeriö 2019. Sähköinen tunnistautuminen—Selvitys nykytilasta sekä kehittämistarpeista. Valtiovarainministeriön julkaisuja 2019:20.

Vapen A, Carlsson N, Mahanti A, Shahmehri N (2016) A look at the third-party management landscape. IEEE Internet Computing 20:2 https://ieeexplore.ieee.org/abstract/document/7420509 Accessed 29 February 2024

von der Leyen U (2020) State of the Union Address - Building the world we want to live in: A Union of Vitality in a World of Fragility. State of the Union. Address https://state-of-the-union.ec.europa.eu/system/files/2022-08/soteu_2020_en.pdf Accessed 29 February 2024

Weigl L, Amard A, Codagnone C, Fridgen G (2022) The EU's digital identity policy: tracing policy punctuations. 15th International Conference on Theory and Practice of Electronic Governance. https://doi.org/10.1145/3560107.3560121 Accessed 29 February 2024

Westin A (1968) Privacy and Freedom. Washington and Lee Law Review 25:166–170. https://scholarlycommons.law.wlu.edu/wlulr/vol25/iss1/20 Accessed 29 February 2024

Zimmermann P (2022) Governing by Protection: Studying the Problematization of Whistleblower Protection in the EU. Administrative Theory & Praxis 45(3):211–229. https://doi.org/10.1080/10841806.2022.2066381 Accessed 29 February 2024

Sanna Wong-Toropainen is a Ph.D. Researcher at the Legal Tech Lab, University of Helsinki. Her research is funded through the Trust-M research consortium, which aims to design trustworthy public digital services for migrants. Her research is focused on mapping the legal framework for digital identities and digital identity wallets as well as examining the data subject rights and user control.

Chapter 7
AI in the Workplace: Regulating Explainability and Consent in Algorithmic Management

Sonia Bastigkeit Ericstam

Contents

Abstract Automated systems are currently used to assign tasks, monitor employees, evaluate employee performance, and make managerial decisions. Thus, algorithms replace and augment traditional employer functions. Through the collection of vast amounts of data about employees and their performances, large portions of the managerial decision-making process can be automated. The protection of workers' rights in the deployment of automated systems in employer functions requires that workers understand that such systems are used and how they are used. From this perspective, the chapter analyses how explainability in automated decision-making and worker consent to the use of algorithmic management are addressed in the existing and proposed legal framework regulating algorithmic management. The chapter argues that, given the imbalance of power in the employment relationship, consent is not a suitable legal ground for automated decision-making in algorithmic management. Further, it argues that the potential for protection of workers' rights found in the General Data Protection Regulation is underutilised. This potential has been clarified by the recently issued judgment SCHUFA Holding (Scoring), where

S. B. Ericstam (✉)
Faculty of Law, Stockholm University, Universitetsvägen 10 C, 106 91, Stockholm, Sweden
e-mail: sonia.bastigkeit-ericstam@juridicum.su.se

K. Prifti et al. (eds.), *Digital Governance*, Information Technology and Law Series 39,
https://doi.org/10.1007/978-94-6265-639-0_7

the European Court of Justice provided some guidance on the scope of the prohibition of automated decision-making under Article 22 GDPR. Consequently, pending the entry into force of rules promoting explainability in the Artificial Intelligence Act and Platform Directive, the GDPR can be used to achieve greater understanding of automation used in algorithmic management.

Keywords Algorithms · Algorithmic management · Labour law · Explainability · Consent · Future of work · Workers' rights · Article 22 GDPR · SCHUFA Holding (Scoring)

7.1 New Technology and Old Questions in the Employment Relationship

'Are you sure you want to go offline? Demand is very high in your area. Make more money, don't stop now!' This is an example of a message showing up in the app when an Uber driver is about to log off.[1] The message is illustrative of new ways to direct persons performing work through the use of technologies. The use of artificial intelligence[2] (AI) in the work context has been discussed from the perspective of the impact of automation on the existence of jobs.[3] The focus of this chapter, however, is on the effects of automation on the jobs that remain. The development of AI and its use in working life brings with it the hope for objectively taken managerial decisions, increased efficiency, and safer working conditions. However, as the cost of data collection and processing is falling, privacy rights of workers may be threatened as employers are now able to use technology to monitor and control what is happening in the workplace to a degree that was unimaginable in the past.[4]

Automated systems[5] are currently used to assign tasks, monitor employees, evaluate employee performance, and make managerial decisions.[6] These practices, where algorithms are used to replace or augment traditional employer functions, are inherent to the business models of digital labour platforms and are to a growing extent

[1] Rosenblat and Stark 2016, p. 3769.

[2] Here defined as the application of a class of statistical methods and algorithms usually subsumed under the generic term of 'machine learning' to potentially very large and often heterogenous sets of data ('big data'). See Sect. 7.3.1 for further elaboration on the use of the term AI.

[3] The most well-known example perhaps being Frey and Osborne, who predicted that 47% of white-collar workers in the United States were at risk of being replaced by robots. Frey and Osborne 2017, p. 265. For a more recent discussion, see Hui et al. 2023 on the effects of generative AI such as ChatGPT on the labour market.

[4] Adams-Prassl 2022, p. 233.

[5] For the sake of convenience, the terms 'automated systems' and 'algorithms' are used interchangeably throughout the chapter. The term algorithm is defined in Sect. 7.2.

[6] See Adams-Prassl 2019, p. 124. For an account of the effects of generative AI in the field of human resource, see Budhwar et al. 2023.

becoming present in the ‘regular’ economy.[7] Through the collection of vast amounts of data about employees and their performance, this form of management can be used to automate large portions of the managerial decision-making process.[8] One central question is how the rights of workers can be safeguarded when new digital technology with disruptive potential for both working conditions and the power dynamic between the worker and the employer is introduced.

Explainability is one of the fundamental values emphasised by the High-Level Expert Group on Artificial Intelligence (HLEIG).[9] According to the HLEIG guidelines on trustworthy AI, explainability concerns not only the technical process of the AI system, but also the decisions made by humans in the implementation of the system.[10] When applying the concept of explainability to algorithmic management, this chapter assumes that for workers to be able to protect their rights, they must be aware of the existence of algorithmic management and understand why the particular outcome was reached in the automated decision.[11] As algorithms are dependent on the processing of personal data, the rules in the General Data Protection Regulation (GDPR)[12] are applicable to algorithmic management. Whereas not mentioned in the HLEIG guidelines on trustworthy AI, in the GDPR, consent to data processing is a central concept.[13] In the spring of 2024, two legal frameworks that will impact algorithmic management were adopted by the European Union (EU). These legal

---

[7] The term ‘regular’ (applied to the economy or the labour market) is used in its sense of ‘typical’, ‘standard’, ‘customary’ and ‘conventional’, in contrast to the more recently emerging platform economy, jobs and work setting. The proposed Platform Directive (see Sect. 7.4.2) defines in its Article 2(1) a digital labour platform as a natural or legal person providing a commercial service meeting the requirements of being provided at a distance through electronic means, at the request of a recipient of the service, involving as a necessary and essential component, the organisation of work performed by individuals, irrespective of whether that work is performed online or in a certain location.

[8] Adams-Prassl 2022, p. 239.

[9] Independent High-Level Expert Group on Artificial Intelligence 2019, p. 37.

[10] Independent High-Level Expert Group on Artificial Intelligence 2019, p. 18. The HLEIG defines a set of questions that can be posed in the implementation of the AI systems to assess the levels of explainability. Examples of questions include: To what extent can the decisions and outcome of the AI systems be understood? To what degree do the AI decisions influence the decision-making process in the organization? Why was the particular system deployed? Was the simplest and most interpretable model possible for the application in question chosen? Independent High-Level Expert Group on Artificial Intelligence 2019, p. 29.

[11] This assumption is based on the arguments made by Wachter et.al. 2018, at p. 844, who propose that algorithmic decisions should provide the person subject to the decision with information about what the decisive factors for the decision were and what factors would have needed to be different in order for the decision to lead to another outcome. See similar argument made by de Fine Licht and de Fine Licht 2020, at p. 924.

[12] Regulation (EU) 2016/679 of the European Parliament and of the Council on the protection of natural persons with regard to the processing of personal data and on the free movement of such data and repealing Directive 95/46/EC.

[13] In Article 6 GDPR, the first legal ground of processing of personal data is that the data subject has given consent to the processing of his or her personal data.

frameworks are the omnibus regulation on Artificial Intelligence[14] (AIA) and the Platform Directive,[15] containing sector-specific legislation. This chapter discusses how explainability and consent in the context of algorithmic management are to be understood from a worker perspective and how far the existing and proposed legal framework at the EU level reach in the protection of workers' rights.

Rather than providing clear-cut answers, this chapter aims to identify and reflect on questions that need to be addressed in the ongoing discussion on workers' rights in an era of rapid digitalisation of the workplace. Nevertheless, the chapter argues that the potential for protection of workers' rights found in the GDPR is underutilised. Section 7.2 provides an introduction to algorithmic management and includes examples of different uses of such management and the contexts in which they occur. Section 7.3 describes automated decision-making as the central element of algorithmic management and discusses legal developments in the interpretation of Article 22 GDPR, which includes a prohibition of fully automated decisions. Section 7.4 explores the legal framework governing explainability in automated decision-making. After having analysed the legal framework governing automated decision-making, Section 7.5 analyses the concept of worker consent to algorithmic management. Section 7.6 offers a discussion on the concept of explainability in algorithmic management and on how the takeaways from the development in relation to Article 22 GDPR can be applied to algorithmic management. Section 7.7 closes the chapter with conclusions.

7.2 Algorithmic Management

Technological development has gradually impacted the way the workforce can be managed.[16] However, the first use of the term 'algorithmic management' in the employment context appears to have been in 2015. It was then defined as the use of 'software algorithms that assume managerial functions and surrounding institutional devices that support algorithms in practice'.[17] An algorithm is a set of instructions carrying out commands.[18] Algorithms can also be described as processes or sets

[14] 2024/1689 REGULATION (EU) 2024/1689 OF THE EUROPEAN PARLIAMENT AND OF THE COUNCIL of 13 June 2024 laying down harmonised rules on artificial intelligence and amending Regulations (EC) No 300/2008, (EU) No 167/2013, (EU) No 168/2013, (EU) 2018/858, (EU) 2018/1139 and (EU) 2019/2144 and Directives 2014/90/EU, (EU) 2016/797 and (EU) 2020/1828 (Artificial Intelligence Act).

[15] Improving working conditions in platform work, European Parliament legislative resolution of 24 April 2024 on the proposal for a directive of the European Parliament and the Council on improving conditions in platform work (COM(2021)0762 – C9-0454/2021/0414(COD)). https://www.europarl.europa.eu/doceo/document/TA-9-2024-0330_EN.pdf (Accessed 22nd August 2024).

[16] For an interesting discussion on the relationship between scientific management (Taylorism) and algorithmic management, see Baiocco et al. 2022, pp. 9–10.

[17] Lee et al. 2015, p. 1603.

[18] Dignum 2019, p. 3.

of rules that can be followed in calculation or other forms of problem-solving.[19] Through algorithmic management, a given workforce can be managed remotely using technological tools and methods. Characteristic of this form of management is that real-time responsiveness to data informs management decisions. The common denominator for the systems used is that they rely on data collection and surveillance to enable automated or semi-automated decision-making.[20] The cycle of algorithmic management can be distinguished into three phases: (i) data collection, manipulation, and training, (ii) definition of parameters and metrics to be used and machine learning loops, and (iii) the final decision.[21]

In the employment relationship, the employer's collection of the personal data of its employees is legitimate where the employer has a contractual or legitimate interest in its processing. The employer's rights to exercise authority and control over its workforce or to direct the enterprise and plan the work can be considered legitimate interests.[22] The employees are, in their capacity of individuals, data subjects when the information processed is related to them as identified or identifiable natural persons.[23] Furthermore, data from a collective of workers may be used as training data regarding the group to inform managerial decision-making.[24] In order for the data to be used as a ground for management decisions, the employer must make use of tools to process and analyse what has been captured in the data. This is enabled by machine learning, in that probabilistic analyses of large datasets can be pursued, where sophisticated statistical modelling is used to recognise patterns or correlations in the data.[25] Such datasets can be collected as employers are able to track their employees over time through devices such as smartphones, desktops, tablets, vehicles, and wearables. An example of a new way in which data are collected is the use of techniques capturing the digital activities of employees, such as keystroke logs and screenshots. It is also possible for employers to collect data on activities such as phone calls, emails, and other forms of digital communication. Even if information about the material contents of the communications cannot be gathered, so-called 'metadata' regarding the frequency of communication can be collected and used.[26] Through automated rating mechanisms and incentive-based 'nudging' mechanisms, large groups of workforces can be managed in ways that can avoid the appearance

---

[19] OED Online (2021) Algorithm. OED Online. Oxford: Oxford University Press. Algorithm noun—Definition, pictures, pronunciation and usage notes | Oxford Advanced Learner's Dictionary at OxfordLearnersDictionaries.com, https://www.oxfordlearnersdictionaries.com/definition/english/algorithm. Accessed 31 January 2024.

[20] Mateescu and Nguyen 2019, p. 3.

[21] Baiocco et al. 2022, p. 29. See also Tambe et al., who discuss the use of AI in human resources through what they call the 'AI life cycle', consisting of the phases operations, data generation, machine learning, and decision-making, Tambe et al. 2019, p. 21.

[22] Hendrickx 2019, p. 159.

[23] See definition of personal data in Article 4 (1) GDPR.

[24] Dagnino and Armaroli 2019, p. 174.

[25] Adams-Prassl 2019, p. 139; see also Polson and Scott 2018.

[26] Adams-Prassl 2022, p. 236.

of traditional employer control.[27] Examples of this nudging mechanism are found both in blue-collar and white-collar jobs. Whereas the first category of workers may experience nudging in the form of messages urging them to continue accepting rides, the latter group may experience it through suggestions from productivity assistants integrated in a computer system used on a daily basis.[28] These new ways of directing work are examples of how algorithmic management can differ materially from traditional management where the latter entails instructions from the employer that must be followed at risk of sanctions.[29]

Algorithmic management can be divided into three forms of automated managerial functions: direction, evaluation, and discipline of workers. Direction involves deciding what sort of work should be performed and when it should be performed. Evaluation entails reviewing the work performed by workers to assess their performance and identify individuals that do not meet the set standards. Discipline involves decisions on reprimands and rewards of workers.[30] Set forth below are examples of how these functions can be automated. These examples provide the contextual foundation necessary for the analysis of the legal framework in the subsequent sections of the chapter.

7.2.1 Automated Direction

With the use of algorithms, allocation of tasks can be pursued through devices such as smartphones and computers. Examples are predominantly found in ride-hailing platform work, where workers receive trip requests that must be accepted within a limited timeframe. After accepting a task, the worker is provided with the details necessary to complete the trip.[31] From the same sector, there are also examples of how workers are logged out from the app if they do not accept a task.[32] In general, in the platform work context, whereas it is technically possible for a worker to decide not to accept a work task, information asymmetries—such as the worker not being

[27] Adams-Prassl 2022, p. 239.

[28] Rosenblat and Stark 2016, p. 3768; see as an example of an email assistant www.microsoft.com/en-us/cortana/ (Accessed 31 January 2024).

[29] In accordance with the so-called managerial prerogative, see Rönnmar (2006). When management is taking the form of suggestions rather than commands, the dynamic in the employment relationship is diffused, with a potential consequence that the worker will experience increased stress as the expectations on her becomes unclear. Examples from platform companies Uber and Deliveroo show how nudges in the form of notifications and badges are used to make drivers work longer shifts and perform the work faster. See Schreiber. N (2017, April 2) How Uber Uses Psychological Tricks to Push Its Drivers' Button. The New York Times. https://www.nytimes.com/interactive/2017/04/02/technology/uber-drivers-psychological-tricks.html and O'Byrne, E. (2019, February 20) Slave to the Algorithm? What it's really like to be a Deliveroo rider. The Irish Examiner. https://www.irishexaminer.com/lifestyle/arid-30905680.html (both links accessed on 31 January 2024).

[30] Kellogg et al. 2020, pp. 367–368.

[31] Rosenblat and Stark 2016, p. 3762.

[32] Bloodworth 2018, p. 225.

provided with full information about the details of a particular task before accepting it—limit the freedom to accept or decline a task.

Algorithms are also used in work allocation in the regular economy. Scheduling can be performed based on algorithmically calculated customer demands. Algorithmic work allocation is used in factories in planning the production to allow for real-time adjustments to be made.[33] Consulting firms provide examples of how algorithms are used to make assessments of how much time it should take to finish certain tasks.[34] Examples of algorithmic direction in the regular economy also include algorithmic management through the use of hand-held devices communicating the time that workers need in order to finish a work task, such as unpacking and sorting products in warehouses.[35]

7.2.2 Automated Evaluation

A central tool for performance evaluation in algorithmic management involves ratings made by customers. From ride-hailing platform work, there are examples showing that passenger rating is the most fundamental metric used in worker performance assessment.[36] Rates of work acceptance are also used in this respect. Examples of other metrics used by platform companies are the number of shifts taken in evenings, hours performed on a weekly basis, no-shows, and late log-in percentage. As such, digital tools enable new management systems for remotely monitoring and evaluating workers. Algorithms are also used within delivery platform work to estimate predicted time for finishing a delivery. If a task is not finished within the predicted timeframe, the worker will receive a message from the platform.[37]

In the regular economy, for instance in warehouse work and at consulting firms, team leaders are notified when algorithmically calculated timeframes for the completion of tasks are not met.[38] At call centres, algorithmic voice evaluation can assess a worker's speed and tone of voice.[39] The hand-held tools and wearables used in warehouses to allocate and distribute work can also be used to document whether workers meet productivity goals.[40]

---

[33] Briône 2017, p. 17.

[34] Schweyer 2018, p. 9.

[35] Wood 2021, p. 3.

[36] Rosenblat and Stark 2016, p. 3772.

[37] Ibid. Wood 2021, pp. 5–6.

[38] Wood 2021, pp. 6–7.

[39] Briône 2020, p. 13.

[40] Delfanti, 2021, p. 42.

7.2.3 Automated Discipline

In the platform economy there are examples of how persons performing ride-hailing work have their accounts deactivated if their customer ratings fail to meet certain levels.[41] This form of sanction is also seen in other areas of platform work, such as delivery work. In some cases, low customer ratings do not entail deactivation, but result in work being automatically filtered from those workers affected.[42]

In the regular economy, there are examples of augmented disciplinary operations. Productivity metrics used in warehouses can inform the disciplinary actions of human supervisors. As the algorithmically produced metrics are trusted by the human management, the role of a human manager can in certain situations be described as 'executing decisions based on data analytics'.[43] The challenging task of defining what constitutes an automated decision will be explored in the section below.

7.3 Automated Decision-Making

In order to discuss potential risks related to algorithmic management and potential legal remedies of these risks, one first needs to contextualise in what ways automated decision-making differs from human decision-making. In 1951, this was done through distinguishing between what 'Men Are Better At' on the one hand and what 'Machines are Better At' on the other hand. As examples, humans were considered to perform better at improvising, whereas machines were thought to excel at repetitive and routine tasks.[44] However, no matter how trustworthy they are in pursuing repetitive tasks and notwithstanding their abilities to make decisions quickly and process large amounts of data, algorithms fail when facing the slightest variations in a task or context.[45] Algorithms rely on proxies in their decision-making.[46] The risk that these proxies are incorrect, or hard to detect, necessitates caution—especially as humans tend to believe that algorithms have mathematical objectivity.[47]

As seen above in Section 7.2, the fundamental aspect of algorithmic management is automation of the decision-making process. A distinction can be made between conditional automation, high automation, and full automation in algorithmic management.[48] In the first category, direction, evaluation, and discipline are sometimes automated. However, there is an expectation of appropriate responses to requests to intervene. In the second category, direction, evaluation, and discipline are always

[41] Rosenblat and Stark 2016, p. 3774.

[42] Wood 2021, pp. 8–9.

[43] Briken and Taylor 2018, p. 453.

[44] Fitts 1951, pp.10–11; Crootof et al. 2022, p. 460.

[45] Crootof et al. p. 464.

[46] O'Neil 2016, pp. 20–21.

[47] Ajunwa 2020, p. 1686.

[48] Wood 2021, p. 12.

automated and there is no need for human managers to intervene. In the final category (which can be described as hypothetical), direction, evaluation, and discipline are always automated and there is no possibility for human managers to intervene.[49] Seeing that most systems used in algorithmic management today require a human manager to respond to the system on request and since the human manager can choose whether or not to abide by the algorithm's decision, algorithmic management can be described as most often being conditional.[50]

As algorithms operate on data, regulations on data protection constitute a relevant starting point when investigating the legal framework governing this new form of management practice. In Europe, Article 22 GDPR includes a prohibition against fully automated decision-making.[51] However, the article is ambiguous in its wording. It includes in its first point the prerequisite that in order for a decision to be covered by the scope of the prohibition, the decision needs to be *based solely on* automated processing.[52] In its guidelines, the predecessor of the European Data Protection Board, the Article 29 Working Party (Article 29 WP), has commented that this prohibition cannot be circumvented by the fabrication of human involvement. The Article 29 WP states that the oversight carried out by the human must be not merely a 'token gesture' but must be meaningful, meaning that the person who is involved in the decision-making should have the authority and competence to change it.[53] However, an assessment of what should be considered meaningful human involvement might be difficult, not least in situations where the decision-making procedure has several stages. In those situations, the question is where the critical point of the decision-making should be placed.[54]

To illustrate the problem of locating a decision in the context of algorithmic management, one can imagine a situation where a human manager is choosing which employees to promote. In the selection process, the manager applies an automated system where an algorithm sorts employees based on performance scores. The manager will, as a basis for her promotion decision, be served a ranking of employees suggested for promotion (group A) and employees who are not considered deserving of promotion (group B). If we imagine that the manager has historically had no reason to question the validity of the algorithmic performance evaluation tools used,

[49] Ibid.

[50] Ibid.

[51] Whether Article 22 GDPR entails a right that needs to be invoked by the data subject or a prohibition has been debated, see for example Mendoza and Bygrave 2017, Veale and Edwards 2018, and Pehrsson 2018. However, as will be seen below in this section, through the Judgment in Case C-634/21 OQ v. Land Hesse, Joined party: SCHUFA Holding AG (Scoring) issued 7 December 2023, this debate is settled, as the CJEU clarifies that Article 22 GDPR entails a prohibition. It should be noted that Article 22 GDPR includes several exceptions. The exception based on consent from the data subject will be discussed in Sect. 7.5.

[52] Article 22(1) GDPR.

[53] Article 29 Working Party 2018, p. 21. This document is produced by the 'Article 29 Working Party', a group established under the Data Protection Directive 1995. However, the guidance has been endorsed by its successor, the European Data Protection Board.

[54] Binns and Veale 2021, p. 319.

it can at least be questioned whether the decision of the manager to carry through the promotion of employees sorted in group A will be anything more than a mere 'rubber stamping' operation, where it is questionable whether her human involvement is meaningful. Depending on where the critical point for the decision is placed (in the assortment made by the algorithm or when the manager makes the decision based on the algorithmically produced proposal) and depending on to what extent one considers the human involvement meaningful, the decision could be deemed to be either solely based on automated processing or not solely based on automated processing.

In order to be prohibited, the decision also needs to have 'legal effects' on the data subject or must affect the data subject 'similarly significantly'.[55] What is required for an effect to be *legal* or *similarly significant* has also been an open question, as the GDPR does not define those concepts. According to Article 29 WP, the effects covered by Article 22 GDPR are only '*serious impactful effects*'.[56] The Article 29 WP defines *legal* effects as affecting a person's legal rights, such as their exercise of freedoms, or effects affecting a person's legal status or contractual rights.[57] As for effects *similarly significant*, the Article 29 WP states that they must have the potential to significantly affect the circumstances, behaviour, or choices of the individuals concerned, have a prolonged or permanent impact on the data subjects, or lead to the exclusion or discrimination of individuals.[58] Regarding decisions that do not have legal effects, the Article 29 WP acknowledges the difficulty in defining in a precise way how *significant* should be interpreted. However, in the guidelines, it mentions decisions affecting financial circumstances, access to health services, employment opportunities, or access to education as examples that meet the threshold.[59]

Recently, a plethora of cases on the interpretation of what constitutes prohibited automated decision-making in accordance with Article 22 GDPR has emerged from courts and data protection authorities in EU member states.[60] Some of the most interesting cases with regard to algorithmic management are from the Netherlands, where drivers performing work for ride-hailing platforms made claims regarding individual data processed in the app they used in performing work. In the rulings from the Appellate Court in Amsterdam, assessments were made regarding what constitutes fully automated decision-making under Article 22 GDPR, as well as what constitutes decisions meeting the qualifying conditions of necessary effects on the drivers.[61] In the case against the ride-hailing platform company Ola Cabs, a function imposing a fine on a driver after a ride was automatically determined as 'invalid' was

---

[55] Article 22(1) GDPR.

[56] Article 29 Working Party 2018, p. 21.

[57] Ibid.

[58] Article 29 Working Party 2018, p. 22.

[59] Ibid.

[60] See, for instance, the collection of cases in Barros Vale and Zanfir-Fortuna 2022.

[61] Gerechtshof Amsterdam Appellants v. Uber B.V. 4 April 2023, 200.295.742/01, Gerechtshof Amsterdam Appellants v. Uber B.V. 4 April 2023, 200.295.747/01, and Gerechtshof Amsterdam Appellants v. Ola Netherlands B.V. 4 April 2023, 200.295.806/01.

one of the functions in the app that were examined in the light of Article 22 GDPR. This function was considered to have sufficiently serious effects on the driver as to be prohibited under the GDPR.[62] The rulings indicate that the onus of showing that the condition of having necessary effects is met in the automated decision-making process is placed on the individual data subjects.[63]

In December 2023, the European Court of Justice (CJEU) issued a judgment on the interpretation of Article 22 GDPR in SCHUFA Holding (Scoring).[64] The judgment regards a request for a preliminary ruling from a German District Court. To begin with, the CJEU clarifies that Article 22 GDPR establishes a general prohibition—in other words, that the data subject does not need to actively invoke the right not to be subject to automated decision-making.[65] The CJEU notes that Article 22 GDPR does not include any formal requirements for a decision to be at hand—the focus is rather on the effect that it has on the data subject.[66] The German case related to an individual who was denied credit from a credit institution. The credit institution had decided to deny the individual the credit based on an automatically generated credit score constituting a creditworthiness assessment. The credit institution received the credit score from a third-party credit information agency.[67] The CJEU states that the establishment of the credit value meets the threshold of producing legal effects concerning the data subject or affect her 'similarly significantly', given that an insufficient credit value in almost all cases would lead to a refusal of the credit applied for.[68] The CJEU emphasises that in a situation where an automatically established value based on data relating to an individual is transmitted from a data controller to a third-party controller, and the latter, in accordance with consistent practice, draws strongly on the automatically established value in making a decision, that decision is to be considered solely automated, even if a human formally makes the ultimate decision (in this case, whether to grant the individual the loan).[69]

The CJEU notes that a restrictive interpretation that would consider the automated credit score as a preparatory act and not a decision would risk creating a lacuna in legal protection for the data subject. According to the CJEU, such interpretation would entail that the prohibition in Article 22 GDPR could be circumvented.[70] Furthermore, the CJEU states that unless the decision is placed where the automated credit score is generated, the data subject would not be able to assert her information rights in accordance with Article 15(1)(h) GDPR, as it is the credit information agency and

---

[62] Gerechtshof Amsterdam Appellants v. Ola Netherlands B.V. 4 April 2023, 200.295.806/01, paras 3.35–3.45.

[63] Bygrave 2021, p. 100.

[64] Case C-634/21 OQ v. Land Hesse, Joined party: SCHUFA Holding AG (Scoring) Judgment of the Court (First Chamber) issued 7 December 2023.

[65] N. 64 para 52.

[66] N. 64 para 46.

[67] N. 64 paras 14–15.

[68] N. 64 paras 48–50.

[69] N. 64 para 62.

[70] N. 64 para 61.

not the credit institute who has that information.[71] The ruling entails legal guidance on how automated decision-making is to be interpreted in accordance with Article 22 GDPR. The next section will look into the legal framework on information rights in relation to automated decision-making.

7.4 Explainability in Algorithmic Management

At the heart of the discussion on the need for explainability in automated decisions is the concept of algorithmic opacity. This form of opacity can be described as entailing inherent challenges in understanding the way the algorithm operates to reach a particular output.[72] The individual who is subject to an automated decision rarely has the technical knowledge necessary to understand why the result was generated from the inputs.[73] Algorithmic programs are sometimes described as 'black boxes', meaning that they will make predictions and decisions in a way similar to human decision-making, but without being able to communicate the grounds for the outcome of the decision-making process.[74] Moreover, the individual subject to the automated decision might be unaware of what inputs are used in the algorithm.[75] Finally, algorithmic opacity can be a result of a strategy used by the data controller to hide particular forms of conduct in the decision-making process behind a veil of technical inscrutability.[76] Below, the legal response to algorithmic opacity in the context of algorithmic management will be discussed.

7.4.1 The GDPR

Articles 13–15 GDPR contain rules on information rights for individuals subject to automated decision-making. According to those articles, the individual data subject has the right to know of the existence of automated decision-making and to get 'meaningful information about the logic involved, as well as the significance and the envisaged consequences of such processing for the data subject'.[77] Furthermore, Article 22 GDPR contains an obligation for the data controller to implement measures to safeguard the rights of the data subject to 'express his or her point of view and to

[71] N. 64 para 63.

[72] Burrell 2016, p. 1.

[73] Ibid.

[74] Bathaeea 2018, pp. 893–894.

[75] Burrell 2016, p. 1.

[76] Pasquale 2015, p. 163.

[77] See Articles 13(2)(f), 14(2)(g), and 15(1)(h) GDPR.

contest the decision' under certain circumstances.[78] In addition, in the (non-binding) preamble of the GDPR, it is stated that a data subject who is subject to automated decision-making has the right to an explanation of the decision.[79]

The contents of the information rights in the GDPR regarding automated decision-making have been debated. On the one hand, the fact that the right to an explanation of an automated decision, found in the preamble, did not make it to a legally binding article has been suggested to show that the GDPR does not entail a right to explanation.[80] Furthermore, the wording of the rights in Articles 13–15 GDPR has been assessed as including only a right to information *ex ante*, not a right to explanation *ex post* of automated decisions.[81] Furthermore, contrasting rights, such as the property rights of the owner of the data processing systems, have been defined as obstacles for the data subject to get information regarding the functioning of the automated systems used in the data processing.[82] On the other hand, it has been argued that the right to contestation found in Article 22 GDPR must implicitly entail a right to explanation of the decision, as the appeal right would be hollow without it.[83] In its guidelines on automated individual decision-making, the Article 29 WP states that for a data subject to be able to challenge a decision or express their views on it, they must fully understand how the decision was made and on what grounds.[84]

Above, Sect. 7.3 has elaborated on the scope of Article 22 GDPR. Importantly, even in cases where the qualifying requirements of that article are not met, other information rights in the GDPR apply regarding the data processed.[85] It follows from Article 5(1)(a) GDPR that personal data shall be processed in a transparent manner in relation to the data subject and Article 6 GDPR spells out the legal bases for processing of data.

In SCHUFA Holding (Scoring), the CJEU does not elaborate on the extent of the information rights under Article 15(1)(h) GDPR. However, in the Opinion of Advocate General Pikamäe delivered in the case before the Judgment, some guidance is provided on the scope of those information rights.[86] According to the Advocate General, Article 15(1)(h) GDPR should be interpreted to mean that the credit information agency must provide the calculation method used to establish the credit score, given that there are no conflicting interests worthy of protection. After acknowledging that protection of trade secrets or intellectual property would in principle

[78] Article 22(3) GDPR. These circumstances are when the decision is 'necessary for entering into, or performance of, a contract between the data subject and a data controller' Article 22(2)(a) GDPR or 'is based on the data subject's explicit consent' Article 22(2)(c) GDPR.

[79] Recital 71 GDPR.

[80] Pehrsson 2018, p. 26.

[81] Wachter et al. 2017, p. 96.

[82] Wachter et al. 2018, p. 843.

[83] Brkan 2019, p. 106; Mendoza and Bygrave 2017, pp. 16–17.

[84] Article 29 Working Party 2018, p. 27.

[85] Barros Vale and Zanfir-Fortuna 2022, p. 13.

[86] Case C-634/21 OQ v. Land Hesse, Joined party: SCHUFA Holding AG (Scoring), proposal for decision by Advocate General Pikamäe 16 March 2023.

constitute a legitimate reason for the agency to refuse to provide the individual with the algorithm used to calculate the score, the Advocate General concluded that such protection can never justify an absolute refusal to provide information, as there are appropriate means of communication combining aid for understanding and guaranteeing a degree of confidentiality. Furthermore, the Advocate General stated that the wording in Article 12 GDPR, entailing that information shall be provided in a 'concise, transparent, intelligible and easily accessible form, using clear and plain language', excludes the alternative that the agency should be obliged to provide the algorithm as such. The Advocate General proposed that the agency should be obliged to provide the individual data subject with explanations sufficiently detailed that the individual could challenge the decision. According to the Advocate General, this would mean information about the method used to calculate the credit score and the reasons for the result, notably information on factors considered and their respective weight at an aggregate level.[87]

7.4.2 The Platform Directive

The Platform Directive, based on an initiative taken by the European Commission to regulate the working conditions in platform work, constitutes the first EU rules on algorithmic management.[88] Whereas the term explainability is not explicitly used in the Platform Directive, the concept of providing for understandable functioning of the automated systems used in algorithmic management is addressed. The rules establish obligations for digital labour platforms to inform affected workers and their representatives about the existence of automated systems used with the purpose of monitoring workers as well as automated systems used to make or support decisions affecting working conditions in a significant way. According to the Directive, information regarding the functioning of the automated systems used shall be presented in a transparent, intelligible, and easily accessible form, using clear and plain language.[89] The transparency rules entail that not only the categories of data and actions handled by an automated system, but also the aim of the monitoring, how the system will achieve it, and details on the functioning and mode of operation of features that affect the employment relationship, need to be provided by the platform.[90] The Platform Directive also includes a prohibition on automated decisions

---

[87] N. 86, paras 53–58.

[88] Another explicit aim of the Platform Directive is to address misclassification of persons performing work. In order to do so, the Directive introduces a presumption of an employment relationship for persons performing work for a platform.

[89] Article 9 Platform Directive includes rules on transparency on and use of automated monitoring and decision-making systems, Article 13 Platform Directive includes rules on information and consultation.

[90] Article 9(1)(a) Platform Directive.

having an impact on the health and safety of a worker, on a contractual relationship or on disciplinary decisions of equivalent detriment.[91]

The Platform Directive entails a right to human review of decisions significantly affecting working conditions. In this regard, member states are responsible for making sure that workers encompassed by the Platform Directive have a right to receive explanations from the platforms for any decisions made or supported by automated systems that significantly affect the working conditions of the workers.[92] Furthermore, the Platform Directive entails proposal that member states require platforms to ensure human resources for effective oversight of the impact of individual decisions made or supported by automated systems. The person who has the function of carrying out an impact assessment and of overseeing and reviewing decisions made or supported by automated systems, must have the requisite competence, including the possibility of intervening against and reverting those decisions.[93]

7.4.3 The AIA

The AIA entails harmonised rules on the development, placement on the market, and use of AI systems in the EU. The AIA is without prejudice to the GDPR. The AIA does not provide legal bases for the processing of personal data.[94] In the AIA, an AI system is defined as a 'machine-based system designed to operate with varying levels of autonomy and that may exhibit adaptiveness after deployment and that, for explicit or implicit objectives, infers, from the input it receives, how to generate outputs such as predictions, content, recommendations, or decisions, that can influence physical or virtual environments'.[95] The regulation applies a risk-based approach. Uses of AI that are considered to entail significant risks to the health and safety or fundamental rights of persons are considered 'high-risk' and therefore require certain safeguards. Algorithmic management fits into the definition of AI used in the AIA and is defined as high-risk, involving AI systems that are 'intended to be used to make decisions affecting terms of the work-related relationships, promotion and termination of work-related relationships, to allocate tasks based on individual behaviour or personal traits or characteristics and to monitor and evaluate performance and behaviour of persons in such relationships'.[96] The justification for defining AI systems used in employment

---

[91] Article 10(5) Platform Directive..

[92] Article 11 Platform Directive includes rules on human review of decisions significantly affecting working conditions.

[93] Article 10 Platform Directive includes rules on human oversight of automated systems.

[94] Recital 10 AIA.

[95] Article 3(1) AIA.

[96] Annex III Para 1(4)(b) AIA.

and worker management as high-risk is that they impact future career prospects and livelihoods, as well as data protection and privacy rights.[97]

The AIA includes provisions requiring a certain degree of transparency in AI systems deployed in high-risk uses. These requirements in the AIA mean that the provider of the system must ensure certain safeguards: that there is a risk management system in place (Article 9), that appropriate data governance and practices for training, validation, and testing of models and datasets are in place (Article 10), that sufficient technical documentation is available (Article 11), that record-keeping is sufficient (Article 12), that transparent system design and instructions for use are ensured (Article 13), and that the systems used have sufficient levels of accuracy, robustness, and cybersecurity (Article 15). Furthermore, there is a requirement of human oversight (Article 14), which can be translated into human intermediaries functioning as interpreters of the algorithms. The aim of the human oversight is improving transparency in the operations of the system.[98] However, in the case of AI systems applied in the employment context, whether or not the requirements on safeguards are met is subject to self-assessment.[99]

The central article when it comes to explainability is Article 13 AIA, fleshing out requirements on what information shall be provided to users of high-risk AI systems. Among those requirements are information on the level of accuracy, robustness and cybersecurity of the system, any known foreseeable circumstance which might lead to risks to the health and safety or fundamental rights of workers, the performance of the system as regards the persons or groups of persons on which the system is intended to be used, and—when appropriate—the specifications for the input data or any other relevant information in terms of training, validation, and testing datasets used, taking the intended use of the AI system into account.[100]

In the explanatory memorandum of the AIA, the opaque nature of AI is explicitly mentioned as an aspect of the use of AI jeopardising fundamental rights.[101] It is stated that in order to address the opacity that makes it difficult for natural persons to comprehend AI systems, transparency is required—to the extent that users of AI systems should be able to interpret the outputs of the systems. Such systems should be designed and developed so it is possible for natural persons to oversee their functioning and the natural persons to whom human oversight has been assigned should have the competence, training, and authority necessary to meet those requirements. It is also stated that human oversight could include built-in operational constraints that cannot be overridden by the system itself.[102]

---

[97] In recital 57 AIA, 'workers' rights' are mentioned explicitly, as well as the acknowledgement that 'AI systems used to monitor the performance and behaviour of these persons may also undermine the essence of their fundamental rights to data protection and privacy'.

[98] Enqvist 2023, p. 523.

[99] Article 43 AIA includes rules on conformity assessment.

[100] Furthermore, Article 13(3)(b)(iv) AIA entails an obligation to provide information regarding the degree to which the AI system can provide an explanation for the decisions it makes.

[101] Section 3.5 Fundamental rights in the Explanatory Memorandum of the AIA.

[102] Recital 72 AIA.

The obligations on human oversight included in Article 14 AIA are mainly addressed to the providers[103] of the AI system.[104] It does not follow from Article 14 AIA who, at the user's end of a particular AI system, should perform the oversight.[105] Thus, users of AI systems have quite broad discretion when it comes to how they implement and pursue human oversight. However, the deployer[106] must make sure that the natural person to whom human oversight has been assigned fulfil the preconditions necessary in order to meet the requirements of efficient human oversight.[107]

EU member states shall be able to regulate the use of AI in the employment relationship in order to strengthen the rights of workers.[108] Deployers who are employers shall, prior to putting a high-risk AI system into service or use, inform worker representatives and affected workers that they will be subject to the system.[109] Finally, the AIA includes a provision entailing that persons subject to decisions producing legal or similarly significant effects, considering to adversely impact the health, safety and fundamental rights, taken by the deployer on the basis of the output from an high-risk system shall have the right to request an explanation of the decision.[110]

---

[103] The term 'provider' is defined as 'a natural or legal person, public authority, agency or other body that develops an AI system or a general-purpose AI model or that has an AI system or a general-purpose AI model developed and places them on the market or puts the system into service under its own name or trademark, whether for payment or free of charge' see Article 3(3).

[104] It follows from Article 16 AIA that providers of AI systems are responsible for ensuring that the systems are compliant with the requirements in Chap. 2, in which Article 14 AIA is found.

[105] This has been pointed out by Enqvist 2023, p. 529.

[106] The term 'deployer' encompasses a 'natural or legal person, public authority, agency or other body using an AI system under its authority except where the AI system is used in the course of a personal non-professional activity' see Article 3(4) AIA. According to Article 25 AIA the deployer is considered a provider, and as a consequence take on the responsibilities of the provider, under certain circumstances.

[107] Article 26(2) AIA. Article 26 AIA entails the obligations of the deployers of high-risk AI systems.

[108] Article 2(11) AIA.

[109] Article 26(7) AIA entails that the information shall be provided in accordance with rules and procedures laid down in Union and national law and practice on information of workers and their representatives.

[110] Article 86 AIA entails a right for the 'affected person' to request a 'clear and meaningful' explanation. According to Article 86(3) AIA, the article shall only apply to the extent that the right to explanation is not otherwise provided for under Union legislation.

7.5 Worker Consent to the Use of Algorithmic Management

The potential risks associated with algorithmic management[111] and the rules aiming at mitigating these risks[112] give rise to questions in relation to the concept of worker consent. The first question relates to the freedom of the employer to make decisions related to its business. The use of algorithms in management functions and issues relating to explainability of automated managerial decisions do not arise in a vacuum. In accordance with the managerial prerogative, entailing a right to lead and direct work, the possibilities for the employer to decide over its operations are large. Unless the initiative of the employer is in violation of applicable law, workers—as individuals or as a collective—have very limited possibilities to impact the decisions that the employer makes regarding its operations.[113] Against this background, the prohibition of automated decision-making in Article 22 GDPR can be considered an infringement of the managerial prerogative, as it can be interpreted as entailing a limitation on the freedom of the employer to decide what methods to use when executing its right to lead and direct work. The exception from the prohibition of automated decision-making in the form of worker consent[114] can therefore be considered a novelty in the employment relationship.

The second question relates to the concept of consent from the perspective of the worker. In order to analyse consent as a legal basis for automated decision-making, one must acknowledge the existence of a power imbalance between the employer and the employee. This imbalance, where the employer is the stronger party—combined with the opacity of the algorithmic systems applied—may create a risk that the data subject has neither the adequate information and understanding of the functioning of the automated decision-making needed for informed consent nor the ability to consent freely.[115] Consent is listed as the first legal basis for processing of data in the GDPR.[116] However, in the preamble to the GDPR, the limitations of consent as a legal basis for processing of data are emphasised in a statement that a clear imbalance between the data subject and the controller means that consent should not be considered a valid legal basis.[117] In their guidelines on how the concept of consent in the GDPR shall be interpreted, the Article 29 WP states that the imbalance

[111] In Recital 57 AIA, privacy rights of workers are mentioned as being at risk when AI is used in managerial functions. Furthermore, in the explanatory memorandum of the Platform Directive, it is stated that workers who are 'subject to algorithmic management lack understanding on how algorithms influence of determine certain managerial decisions and that such understanding is paramount given that those decisions impact the income and working conditions for affected workers'.

[112] See above Sects. 7.4.2 and 7.4.3.

[113] Rönnmar 2006, pp. 61–63.

[114] Article 22(2)(c) GDPR.

[115] Abraha 2023, p. 184.

[116] Article 6(1)(a) GDPR. Consent is defined in Article 4(11) GDPR as 'any freely given, specific, informed and unambiguous indication of the data subject's wishes by which he or she, by a statement or by a clear affirmative action, signifies agreement to the processing of personal data relating to him or her'. Article 7 GDPR describes the conditions for consent.

[117] Recital 43 GDPR.

of power between the employer and the employee makes it unlikely that a data subject who is an employee can deny the employer consent to data processing and not fear or experience detrimental effects as a consequence of this refusal. According to the Article 29 WP, it is unlikely that the employee's consent is freely given. Therefore, the Article 29 WP concludes, in most cases where the employer processes employee data, consent cannot and should not be the legal basis.[118] Furthermore, consent as a legal basis for data processing requires that the data subject understands what she consents to.[119] Consent must also be possible to withdraw at any time in order to be a legal basis for data processing.[120]

While the concept of consent as legal ground for automated decision-making might, at first glance, appear to be an important protective tool for the data subject, it is of questionable relevance in the employment relationship due to the imbalance of power present. It is also challenging to imagine how a manager would be able to use this form of legal ground for automated decision-making as the worker must be able to withdraw consent at any time. A further reason why consent is a weak ground for algorithmic management is the opaque nature of algorithmic decision-making in general. Until complete explainability regarding the functioning of automated systems can be achieved, consent to being subject to it cannot be considered completely informed.

According to the GDPR, when an automated decision is based on consent, the data controller shall implement safeguards entailing at minimum rights for the data subject to human intervention on the part of the controller, to express their point of view, and, lastly, to contest the decision.[121] These specific safeguards equate to a right for the data subject to 'humanise' the decision.[122] How this humanisation of the decision shall be achieved is a matter that leads to further questions, as the same difficulties are present in assessing what level of human intervention should be required as in the question of how to define decisions as based 'solely' on automated processing.[123]

7.6 Discussion

As a starting point, it is useful to reflect on to what extent the use of algorithmic management entails novelties. In other words: does automation of managerial functions lead to significantly new consequences for workers or is it rather a case of

[118] Article 29 Working Party 2017, p. 8. According to the Article 29 WP, employee consent to data processing can only be considered as freely given when the employee will not suffer any adverse consequences depending on whether they give consent.

[119] Article 29 Working Party 2017, p. 13.

[120] Article 7(3) GDPR.

[121] Article 22 (3) GDPR.

[122] Brkan 2019, p. 107.

[123] See discussion in Sect. 7.3.

'old wine in new bottles'?[124] This is a question that may not easily find a definitive answer. Suffice it to say, perhaps, that the potential of algorithmic opacity and granular data collection necessitates caution. One complicating aspect when crafting a legal response to the potential harms of AI is that we do not know what AI will look like in the future. This uncertainty means that regulation will have to keep pace with technological developments or must be flexible enough to encompass risks associated with future AI traits.

The discussion on the concept of explainability in relation to the use of algorithmic management hinges on the aim of maintaining human welfare in the application of AI. This entails respect for fundamental rights such as human dignity and workers' rights in workplaces where automation is used in managerial functions. The use of such automation must not lead to obscuring managerial responsibility. Hence, in order for workers to be able to protect their rights when algorithmic management practices are used, they must be aware that they are subject to this form of management and be able to get sufficient information on the operations of the algorithmic systems to assess whether their rights are infringed. Above, algorithmic opacity as an obstacle to explainability in automated decision-making has been discussed. Furthermore, an account of potential weaknesses of the transparency regime in the GDPR has been provided.[125]

In the pursuit of explainability tools for protecting the rights of workers subject to algorithmic management, this chapter has discussed the potential of Article 22 GDPR, which contains a prohibition against fully automated decision-making. This Article has been assessed to offer only limited transparency in the context of algorithmic management, as it applies only to fully automated decisions.[126] However, SCHUFA Holding (Scoring),[127] discussed above in Sects. 7.3 and 7.4.1, indicates promising developments from the perspective of workers subject to algorithmic management. Given that the assessment of the circumstances in the case resulted in the decision being pinpointed to the automated phase of the decision-making process, Article 22 GDPR should be interpreted as covering also decisions with some human involvement, if that involvement is not qualitatively decisive. Consequently, the transparency regime in the GDPR on automated decisions[128] will encompass cases of managerial decisions where automation is used to the extent that the human in the process cannot be said to have the decisive role. The regulatory gap would then remain only regarding those managerial decisions where automation does not pass the threshold of being decisive and/or where the effects are not significant enough.

---

[124] For example, in relation to the discussion on opacity in algorithmic decision-making, explainability in managerial decisions in a non-automated setting may be obscured by the opacity of the human brain of the manager. Situations may appear when the manager cannot or does not want to provide the grounds for a certain decision taken.

[125] See Sect. 7.4.1 and references therein.

[126] Adams-Prassl et al. 2023, pp. 140–142.

[127] N. 64.

[128] Article 22, Article 13(2)(f), Article 14(2)(g), and Article 15(1)(h) GDPR.

However, in those situations, the general transparency rights enshrined in the GDPR apply.

The SCHUFA Holding (Scoring) judgment[129] and the Opinion of the Advocate General in the case[130] in particular also offer clarity regarding the extent of the explainability potential of Article 15(1)(h) GDPR, and to what degree the right to protection of trade secrets affects the transparency obligations of data controllers. The takeaway from the Opinion of the Advocate General in this regard is that the individual subject to an automated decision has the right to obtain sufficient information to challenge the decision. Applied to the algorithmic management context and the example provided in Sect. 7.3, this could be translated as entailing that a worker placed in group B—the group of workers not deemed as deserving of promotion—has the right to an explanation of the method used to calculate the score leading to the group allocation. In addition, when applying the reasoning of the CJEU on the scope of the prohibition of automated decision-making in Article 22 GDPR, it is questionable whether the decision-making procedure applied by the manager in this case would be permitted, given that the decision of promotion arguably can be considered one of significant effects. Consequently, the SCHUFA Holding (Scoring) judgment and the Opinion of the Advocate General in the case arguably entail tools for workers and their representatives that can be used to contravene algorithmic opacity.

Explainability in algorithmic management requires that managers are able to explain the decisive factors in the decision-making process. Therefore, it is crucial that they understand the automated systems applied. In this regard, the rules in the AIA and in the Platform Directive on requirements that those persons operating the systems must understand their functioning are important. The aim to guarantee high levels of explainability is clearly visible in both the Platform Directive and the AIA, as both legal acts include requirements of human-in-the-loop.[131] However, there is a need for guidance on how the transparency provisions in the AIA are to be implemented in practice. In this respect, clarification is needed on the distribution of responsibility between the provider of the system and the user regarding the fulfilment of obligations related to high-risk systems used in the employment context. Furthermore, it is notable that the provisions on transparency and human oversight are limited to requiring that the *providers* and *users* understand the functioning of the system.[132] To obtain information about algorithmic systems deployed, *workers* will be referred to seeking redress under the right to request an explanation in the AIA.[133] The provision on a right to explanation of individual decision-making in the AIA will have to be interpreted in the light of Article 22 GDPR given that the AIA is

[129] N. 64.

[130] N. 86.

[131] Article 13 on transparency and information to users and Article 14 on human oversight in the AIA, Article 9 on transparency in relation to automated decision-making systems, Article 10 on human oversight of automated systems, Article 11 on human review of significant decisions in the Platform Directive.

[132] In the algorithmic management context, the user will be the manager who implements the automated systems in managerial functions.

[133] In accordance with the amended provision on a right to explanation in Article 86 AIA.

without prejudice to the GDPR. For the protection of workers' rights in algorithmic management to be effective, a systematisation of the different applicable rights to explanation in the algorithmic management context is urgent.[134]

One obvious weakness in the AIA when it comes to the safeguards of explainability in algorithmic management is the self-assessment system regarding the fulfilment of the requirements for such high-risk AI systems. However, as more specific rules regulating the use of algorithmic management are possible at the member state level, legal remedies may be sought in national legislation if the AIA and the Platform Directive proves toothless in achieving explainability.

7.7 Conclusion

Given the subordination of the worker in the employment relationship and the requirement that consent must be withdrawable, it is not suitable as a legal ground for automated decision-making in the context of algorithmic management.

While awaiting further safeguards of explainability in the AIA and the Platform Directive, it is clear that workers subject to algorithmic management can make use of the GDPR. The SCHUFA Holding (Scoring) offers long awaited clarification on how automation as part of a decision-making procedure is to be interpreted in the light of the prohibition of automated decision-making under Article 22 GDPR. Following the ruling, in order to obtain their information rights when subject to algorithmic management, workers and their representatives must focus on two things. First, they must argue that the decision-making at hand is to be considered automated under Article 22 GDPR (even if some human participation has taken place in the decision-making process). Second, they must require information about what factors were decisive for the decision (in this regard trade secrets will not suffice as an argument for the manager not to supply information).

Ultimately, the level of explainability in algorithmic systems used for management will depend on the ability of the person using the systems (the human manager) to understand them. In this regard, it is crucial that the provisions in the AIA and in the Platform Directive aimed at securing that managers using the automated systems understand their functioning become more than just empty phrases.

References

Abraha H (2023) Regulating Algorithmic Employment Decisions through Data Protection Law. European Labour Law Journal 14(2) 172–191. https://doi.org/10.1177/20319525231167317

[134] Rules on a right to explanation exist in Article 22 GDPR, Article 86 AIA, and Article 11 Platform Directive.

Adams-Prassl J (2019) What if Your Boss Was an Algorithm? Economic Incentives, Legal Challenges and the Rise of Artificial Intelligence. Comparative Labor Law and Policy Journal 41(1) 123–146.

Adams-Prassl J (2022) The Challenges of Management by Algorithm: Exploring Individual and Collective Aspects. In: Gyalavári T, Menegatti, E (eds.) Decent Work in the Digital Age. London, Hart Publishing, pp. 231–244.

Adams-Prassl J, Abraha, H, Kelly-Lyth, A, Silberman, M, Rakshita, S (2023). Regulating Algorithmic Management: A Blueprint. European Labour Law Journal 14(2) 124–151. https://doi.org/10.1177/20319525231167299

Ajunwa I (2020) The Paradox of Automation as Anti-Bias Intervention. Cardozo Law Review 41 1696-1707.

Article 29 Working Party (2017) Guidelines on Consent under Regulation 2016/679 (WP259) (28 November 2017).

Article 29 Working Party (2018) Guidelines on Automated Individual Decision-Making and Profiling for the Purposes of Regulation 2016/679 (WP251rev.01) (6 February 2018)

Baiocco S, Fernández-Macías E, Rani U, Pesole A (2022) The Algorithmic Management of Work and its Implications in Different Contexts. Seville, European Commission.

Barros Vale S, Zanfir-Fortuna G (2022) Automated Decision-Making Under the GDPR: Practical Cases from Courts and Data Protection Authorities. The Future of Privacy Forum.

Bathaeea, Y (2018) The Artificial Intelligence Black Box and the Failure of Intent and Causation. Harvard Journal of Law & Technology 31(2):890–938.

Binns R, Veale M (2021) Is That Your Final Decision? Multi-stage Profiling, Selective Effects, and Article 22 of the GDPR. International Privacy Law 11(4):319–332.

Bloodworth J (2018) Hired: Six Months Undercover in Low-Wage Britain. London: Atlantic Books.

Briken K, Taylor P (2018) Fulfilling the 'British Way': Beyond Constrained Choice – Amazon Workers' Lived Experiences of Workfare. Industrial Relations Journal 49(5–6):438-458.

Briône P (2017) Mind over machines: New technology and employment relations. Research Paper 02/17. London: ACAS.

Briône P (2020) My boss the algorithm: An ethical look at algorithms in the workplace. London: ACAS.

Brkan M (2019) Do Algorithms Rule the World: Algorithmic Decision-Making and Data Protection in the Framework of the GDPR and Beyond. International Journal of Law and Information Technology 27(2):91–121.

Budhwar P, Chowdhury S, Wood G, Aguinis H, Bamber G, Beltran J, Varma A (2023) Human Resources Management in the Age of Generative Artificial Intelligence: Perspectives and Research Directions on ChatGPT. Human Resource Management Journal33(3):606–659. https://doi.org/10.1111/1748-8583.12524

Burell J (2016) How the Machine 'Thinks': Understanding Opacity in Machine Learning Algorithms. Big Data & Society 1:1–12. https://doi.org/10.1177/2053951715622512

Bygrave L (2021) Article 22 Automated Individual Decision-Making, Including Profiling. In Kuner C, Bygrave LA, Docksey C, Drechsler L (eds.) The EU General Data Protection Regulation (GDPR): A Commentary 2021 Update (OUP 2021). pp 522–542.

Crootof R, Kaminski M, Nicholson Price W (2022) Humans in the Loop. Vanderbilt Law Review 76:429–510.

Dagnino E, Armaroli L (2019) A Seat at the Table: Negotiating Data Processing in the Workplace: National Case Study and Comparative Insights. Comparative Labor Law & Policy Journal 41 (1):173–196.

de Fine Licht K, de Fine Licht J (2020) Artificial intelligence, transparency, and public decision-making: Why explanations are key when trying to produce perceived legitimacy' 35 *AI & Society* (35) 917–926.

Delfanti, A (2021) Machinic dispossession and augmented despotism: Digital work in an Amazon warehouse. *New Media & Society*, *23*(1), 39–55. https://doi.org/10.1177/1461444819891613

Dignum V (2019) Responsible Artificial Intelligence. How to Develop and Use AI in a Responsible Way. Cham, Springer. https://doi.org/10.1007/978-3-030-30371-6

Enqvist L (2023) 'Human Oversight' in the EU Artificial Intelligence Act: What, When and by Whom? Law, Innovation and Technology 15(2):508–535. https://doi.org/10.1080/17579961.2023.2245683

Fitts M (1951) Human Engineering for an Effective Air Navigation and Traffic Control System, Air Navigation Development Board by the Ohio State University Research Foundation, National Research Council, Division of Anthropology and Psychology, Committee on Aviation Psychology, Washington, D.C., https://apps.dtic.mil/sti/pdfs/ADB815893.pdf (Accessed 31 January 2024).

Frey CB, Osborne MA (2017) The Future of Employment: How Susceptible Are Jobs to Computerisation? Technological Forecasting and Social Change 114:254–280.

Hendrickx F (2019) Privacy 4.0 at Work: Regulating Employment, Technology and Automation. Comparative Labor Law & Policy Journal 41(1):147–172.

High-Level Expert Group on Artificial Intelligence (2019). Ethics Guidelines for Trustworthy AI.

Hui X, Reshef O, Zhou Luofeng (2023) The Short-Term Effects of Generative Artificial Intelligence on Employment: Evidence from an Online Labor Market. Available at https://doi.org/10.2139/ssrn.4527336

Kellogg K, Valentine M, Christin, A (2020) Algorithms at Work: The New Contested Terrain of Control. Academy of Management Annals 14(1):366–410. https://doi.org/10.5465/annals.2018.0174

Lee MK, Kusbit D, Metsky E, Dabbish L (2015) Working with Machines: The Impact of Algorithmic Data-Driven Management on Human Workers. Proceedings of the 33rd Annual ACM SIGCHI Conference 1603–1612.

Mateescu A, Nguyen A (2019) Explainer: Algorithmic Management in the Workplace. Data & Society.1–15. DS_Algorithmic_Management_Explainer.pdf (datasociety.net) (Accessed 31 January 2024).

Mendoza I, Bygrave L.A (2017) The Right Not to Be Subject to Automated Decisions Based on Profiling. In: Synodinou T, Jougleux P, Markou C, Prastitou T (eds) EU Internet LAW: Regulation and Enforcement, Springer, pp. 77–98.

O'Neil C (2016) Weapons of Math Destruction: How Big Data Increases Inequality and Threatens Democracy, Random House, New York, NY.

Pasquale F (2015). The Black Box Society: The Secret Algorithms That Control Money and Information. Harvard University Press, Cambridge.

Pehrsson E (2018) The Meaning of the GDPR Article 22. EU Law Working Papers No.31:1–31. pehrsson_eulawwp31.pdf (stanford.edu) (Accessed 31 January 2024).

Polson N, Scott J (2018). AIQ: How Artificial Intelligence Works and How We can Harness its Power for a Better World. Bantham Press, London.

Rosenblat A, Stark L (2016). Algorithmic Labor and Information Asymmetries: A Case Study of Uber's Drives. International Journal of Communication 10:3758–3775.

Rönnmar M (2006) The Managerial Prerogative and the Employee's Obligation to Work: Comparative Perspectives on Functional Flexibility. Industrial Law Journal 35(1):56–74.

Schweyer A (2018) Predictive Analytics and Artificial Intelligence in People Management. McLean: Incentive Research Foundation.

Tambe P, Cappelli P, Yakubovich V (2019) Artificial Intelligence in Human Resources Management: Challenges and a Parth Forward. California Management Review 61(4):15–42.

Veale M, Edwards L (2018) Clarity, Surprises and Further Questions in the Article 29 Working Party Draft Guidance on Automated Decision-Making and Profiling. Computer Law & Security Review 34(2):398–404.

Wachter S, Mittelstadt B, Floridi L (2017) Why a Right to Explanation of Automated Decision-Making Does Not Exist in the General Data Protection Regulation. International Privacy Law 7(2):76–99.

Wachter S, Mittelstadt B, Russel C (2018) Counterfactual Explanations Without Opening the Black Box: Automated Decisions and the GDPR. Harvard Journal of Law & Technology 31 (2):841–888.

Wood A (2021) Algorithmic Management: Consequences for Work Organisation and Working Conditions. European Commission, Seville.

Table of Cases

Case C-634/21 OQ v. Land Hesse, Joined party: SCHUFA Holding AG (Scoring), proposal for decision by Advocate General Pikamäe 16 March 2023Case C-634/21 OQ v. Land Hesse, Joined party: SCHUFA Holding AG (Scoring) Judgment of the Court (First Chamber) issued 7 December 2023.

Case C-634/21 OQ v. Land Hesse, Joined party: SCHUFA Holding AG (Scoring) Judgment of the Court (First Chamber) issued 7 December 2023.Gerechtshof Amsterdam Appellants v. Uber B.V. 4 April 2023, 200.295.742/01Gerechtshof Amsterdam Appellants v. Uber B.V. 4 April 2023, 200.295.742/01

Gerechtshof Amsterdam Appellants v. Uber B.V. 4 April 2023, 200.295.747/01

Gerechtshof Amsterdam Appellants v. Ola Netherlands B.V. 4 April 2023, 200.295.806/01

Sonia Bastigkeit Ericstam is a Swedish labour law lawyer who works at the Legal Bureau of the Swedish Trade Union Confederation. She studied Law at Lund University (2017) and obtained her Master of Laws (LL.M.) at the Raoul Wallenberg Institute of Human Rights in Lund (2018). She is a Doctoral Candidate at Stockholm University. Her dissertation explores legal aspects of the use of algorithmic management and is part of the Wallenberg AI—Autonomous Systems and Software Program—Humanities and Society (WASP-HS).

Part II
Designing Legal Solutions for Digital Governance

Chapter 8
AI Acts' Ripple Effect on Biometric Data: Harmonising or Fragmenting the Regulation of Biometric Data

Bilgesu Sumer, Natalia Menéndez González, Abdullah Elbi, Catherine Jasserand, Jan Czarnocki, and Els J. Kindt

Contents

Abstract The integration of biometric technologies into a myriad of sectors, from electronic authentication systems like FaceID to border control mechanisms, signifies a leap towards enhancing security and convenience. However, their integration poses a host of legal and ethical risks. The EU has introduced multiple regulations to address the widespread use of biometrics in both public and private domains. To begin with, the General Data Protection Regulation (GDPR) and the Law Enforcement Directive (LED) introduced provisions targeting biometric data processing,

This chapter has received funding from H2020-MSCA-ITN-2019-860315 (PriMa), H2020-MSCA-ITN-2019-860813 (TReSPAsS), H2020-MSCA-IF-2019-895978 (DATAFACE), and H2020-883356 (iMars).

B. Sumer (✉) · E. J. Kindt
KU Leuven (KUL) Centre for IT and IP Law (CiTiP), Biometric Law Lab (BLL), Leuven, Belgium
e-mail: bilgesu.sumer@kuleuven.be

E. J. Kindt
e-mail: els.kindt@kuleuven.be

N. Menéndez González
European University Institute, Centre for a Digital Society, Leuven, Belgium
e-mail: natalia.menendez@eui.eu

A. Elbi · J. Czarnocki
KUL, CiTiP, BLL, Leuven, Belgium
e-mail: abdullah.elbi@kuleuven.be

K. Prifti et al. (eds.), *Digital Governance*, Information Technology and Law Series 39,
https://doi.org/10.1007/978-94-6265-639-0_8

while their definition of biometric data remains ambiguous. The Schengen Information System (SIS), the European Digital Identity (eIDAS) and the Payment Services Directive (PSDII) use other terminology to refer to biometric data. The latest development in biometric regulation is the introduction of the Artificial Intelligence Act (AIA), which establishes new definitions and requirements for processing biometric data. This contribution discusses the potential impact of the AIA on the regulation of biometric data, which is currently regulated by a scattered regulatory framework, causing diverging interpretations and legal uncertainty. Our study initially explains the current legal landscape that governs biometric data. Following this, we delve into the new definitions introduced during the negotiations in the adoption process of the AIA proposal. We eventually discuss the potential of the AIA to overcome the challenges posed by this emerging complex biometric law.

Keywords Biometric data · GDPR · AIA · LED · eIDAS · SIS · PSDII · Regulation

8.1 Introduction

Contemporary biometric applications typically deploy AI that is increasingly becoming omnipresent in a wide array of fields, from e-gates in border control to Face ID for digital identity. On the other hand, these powerful AI tools pose several risks as they can identify individuals based on their bodily information; hence, they can be used to discriminate individuals[1] and control populations.[2]

In recent years, the European Union (EU) legislators have reacted to the proliferation of AI-based biometric applications in public and private sectors with several regulatory instruments and proposals. For example, the GDPR, as the first general legal data protection framework that specifically regulates biometric data, incorporates several provisions governing biometric data processing.

However, the GDPR definition of Article 4(14) and several other GDPR references, such as Article 9(1) and Recital 51, caused diverging interpretations due to their ambiguity, leading to legal uncertainty. While technical definitions, such as those of the International Standards Organization (ISO), broadly define biometric

J. Czarnocki
e-mail: jan.czarnocki@kuleuven.be

C. Jasserand
University of Groningen, Groningen, The Netherlands
e-mail: c.a.jasserand@step-rug.nl

E. J. Kindt
Universiteit Leiden, eLaw, Leiden, The Netherlands

[1] George 2022, p. 3; Rose 2000, p. 321.

[2] Foucault 2008, p. 34; Gates 2011, p. 27.

data, the GDPR's protection seems narrower, possibly excluding biometric images such as photographs.[3] This delta between technical definitions in international standards and the definition of biometric data in the GDPR (and the Law Enforcement Directive (LED)) has been subject to discussions.[4]

More regulatory instruments that are *lex specialis*, refer to biometric data. For example, biometric data has long been used for identity verification and identification in border control and security at the EU borders in the Schengen Information System. Other sectoral regulations such as eIDAS 2.0. and PSDII also include provisions tacitly mentioning biometric data.

Against this background, the Commission also introduced the AIA proposal, which introduced new categories and definitions of biometric data. The importance of definitions in any regulation deserves particular attention as they do not only determine the legal meaning of the concepts but also the ways a term should be used in factual circumstances.[5] The definitions are particularly critical when it comes to AI-related matters, as the possibility of regulatory disconnection is relatively high due to the high pace of technological advances.[6]

The main purpose of this chapter is to discuss whether, by introducing these new categories, the AIA can harmonize the understanding and protection of biometric data, currently regulated by messy and somewhat inadequate provisions in different pieces of legislation.

For this purpose, Sect. 5.2 provides an overview of selected regulatory frameworks that are part of the efforts of the EU legislators in targeting the use of biometric data: the LED, the Payment Service Directive II (PSDII), the Schengen Information System II framework (SISII) and the European Digital Identity Regulation, i.e., eIDAS 2.0—that explicitly or implicitly govern AI-system biometric data. Following this descriptive section, we analyse divergent interpretations, gaps, areas of potential loopholes, and overlaps in these instruments.

Section 5.4 discusses the AIA and evaluates whether it can provide broader protection by harmonizing the current definitions or if it would create more confusion. Finally, we conclude that although the AIA seeks to enhance fundamental rights and data protection by introducing new definitions of biometric data, it may not effectively unify or clarify the concerns discussed below.

---

[3] Sumer 2022, p. 3.

[4] See for example: Kindt 2018; Jasserand 2016.

[5] Roznai 2014.

[6] As put by Brownsword and Goodwin: '*Indeed, one of the great regulatory ironies is that, where regulators (in an attempt to regulate, know where they stand) try their utmost to establish an initial set of standards that are clear, detailed and precise, the more likely it is that the regulation will lose connection with its technological target (leaving the regulation unclear as to their position)*' Brownsword and Goodwin 2012, p. 400.

8.2 Biometric Data in Regulatory Instruments

This section explains the legal concept of biometric data as personal data under several EU legal instruments, starting with the GDPR and LED and subsequently focusing on the sectoral legislations: eIDAS 2.0, PSD II, and SIS II. This preliminary inquiry demonstrates that there is no harmonised understanding of biometric data within the analysed framework.

8.2.1 Biometric Data as Personal Data

8.2.1.1 The General Data Protection Regulation

The GDPR replaced the former Data Protection Directive 95/46/EC, which contained no reference to biometric data; it was the first general EU regulation that included a definition of biometric data.[7] Article 4(14) defines biometric data as *personal data resulting from specific technical processing* relating to a natural *person's physical, physiological, or behavioral characteristics, which allow or confirm the unique identification* of that natural person, such as *facial images or dactyloscopic data.*

At the same time, Recital 51 further states *the processing of photographs* should not systematically be considered to be the processing of *special categories*, as they are covered by the definition of biometric data only when processed through a *special technical means* allowing *the unique identification* of a natural person. Hence, it seems that the GDPR distinguishes between 'mere' photographs (i.e., images for biometric recognition purposes) and photographs that are 'processed through special technical means' for the specific purpose of identification or verification. The GDPR seems to neglect the possibility that biometric images (before transformation) can also be sensitive data if their processing reveals sensitive information, such as ethnicity or health information.[8] The legal definition does not consider images of biometric characteristics, e.g., photographs, as sensitive data under Article 9. Thus, these images can be collected, centralised and processed for various legal reasons, including legitimate interests and marketing under Article 6.

Furthermore, there is uncertainty as to which biometric functionalities are prohibited by Article 9.1 GDPR, which states that (only) biometric data for *the purpose of uniquely identifying a natural person* shall be prohibited. A discrepancy between Art. 4(14) and Recital 51 in describing the functions/purposes should be observed, as the definition of biometric data under GDPR Article 4(14) seems incompatible with Recital 51. The definition makes a distinction between the functions of '*to confirm the unique identification*' (which contains the identity verification (1:1) function) and '*to allow the unique identification*' (which covers the biometric identification

[7] Regulation (EU) 2016/679 (GDPR); Kindt 2013.

[8] For a detailed discussion on this issue see: Sumer 2022, p. 3. See also, ECJ case on sensitive info inferences, August 2022.

(1:N) function). Some argue that both biometric verification and identification may be covered (and hence prohibited).[9] According to this view, biometric data associated with a specific person and utilised for biometric recognition (identification and verification) are considered sensitive.[10] Others interpret 'uniquely identifying' more narrowly as only referring to the identification functionality.[11] It should be noted that Recitals are, in principle, not legally binding. However, the exclusion of biometric verification from more stringent protection of Article 9(1) might pose risks to fundamental rights and freedoms. Recently, the EDBP clarified that both biometric identification and verification process sensitive personal data,[12] influencing some Data Protection Authorities (DPAs), like the AEPD (Agencia Española de Protección de Datos) (Spanish DPA), to treat biometric verification as processing special categories of data under the GDPR.[13]

8.2.1.2 The Law Enforcement Directive (LED)

The LED aims to protect citizens' fundamental right to data protection whenever criminal law enforcement authorities use personal data for law enforcement purposes.[14] It will, in particular, ensure that the personal data of victims, witnesses, and suspects of crime are duly protected, which will facilitate cross-border cooperation in the fight against crime and terrorism.[15]

Article 3(13) LED defines biometric data identically to the GDPR, and is also including a provision on special categories (Article 10), but there is no equivalence of Recital 51.[16] As explained below, some argue this might mean that the LED refers to and governs biometric images that have not been technically processed.[17] It is widely known that automated biometric systems used by police authorities, such as the Automated Fingerprint System (AFS), process images, e.g., photographs (and not templates). Therefore, one could argue that biometric images, such as photographs, may not be *a priori* excluded as falling under the category of biometric data under the LED, which diverges from the definition in the GDPR.

---

[9] Jasserand 2016 views 'allowing' and 'confirming' the unique identification as referring to the umbrella function of biometric recognition'. p. 309.

[10] Jasserand 2016, p. 309.

[11] Kuner et al. 2021, pp. 51–52 and Kindt 2018, p. 527 argue that Article 9(1) does not cover biometric verification. Also see, Clifford 2019, pp. 177–184; Tamas et al. 2021, p. 2.

[12] EDBP 2023, p. 10.

[13] AEPD, 2023, p. 13.

[14] Directive (EU) 2016/680 (Law Enforcement Directive or LED).

[15] https://commission.europa.eu/law/law-topic/data-protection/data-protection-eu_en#legislation [Accessed 3 March 2024].

[16] Also see: Jasserand 2019, p. 157.

[17] Other related legislations in the area of freedom, security and justice can also be considered related to the scope of the, 'LED' Davoli 2023, pp. 2–4.

8.2.2 *Biometric Data in Other Sectoral Regulations*

8.2.2.1 The eIDAS Regulation and the Amending Proposal (eIDAS 2.0)

The eIDAS Regulation (2014) governs trust in the context of online identity verification.[18] The European Commission, on June 3, 2021, proposed to amend the eIDAS Regulation with a view to updating it to a European Digital Identity Regulation.[19] Both the eIDAS Regulation and the Proposal do not explicitly define biometric data.

However, as in practice, biometrics are often used in AI-based authentication layers, e.g., for unlocking a device or securing access to premises. The eIDAS 2.0. proposal referred to authentication based on biometric data as an assurance factor in its Recitals. Recital 11 indicated that the stakeholders should consider the different levels of risk. It stated that processing biometric data to authenticate is one of the identification methods providing a high level of assurance and refers to the risks that the processing may entail for the rights and freedoms of individuals and the GDPR, hence acknowledging biometric data's 'sensitive nature'.[20]

During negotiations, the Committee on Industry, Research, and Energy (ITRE) suggested more stringent obligations for processing biometric data in the eIDAS 2.0 regulation.[21] Amendments to the Proposal clarified that using biometrics to identify and authenticate should not be a must for using the European Digital Identity Wallet[22] and that biometric data used in the context of eIDAS should not be stored without the user's explicit consent.[23] ITRE was explicitly in favour of limiting the use of biometric data to specific scenarios under Article 9 of the GDPR. Moreover, stakeholders that intend to process sensitive personal information, such as health or biometric data, as defined by Article 9 GDPR, would need prior approval from the competent authorities in the Member State in which they intend to provide their services. In addition, these stakeholders were supposed to comply with the legal bases in Article 6(1) GDPR.[24]

However, the text adopted by the Parliament excluded all these biometric data-specific provisions in the adopted position. It only referred to a concept of 'inherence' to regulate biometric data as a *strong user authentication* factor.[25] This broad concept is analysed in the following section under the PSDII.

---

[18] Regulation (EU) 2014/910 of 23 July 2014 on Electronic Identification and Trust Services for Electronic Transactions in the Internal Market.

[19] Eidas 2.0. proposal, 2021.

[20] Eidas 2.0. proposal, 2021, Recital 11.

[21] ITRE 2021/0136, Recital 11, p. 16.

[22] The wallet is a piece of hardware and software that will store different types of personal data, including biometric data. Sumer and Schroers 2021.

[23] ITRE 2021/0136, Recital 11, p. 16.

[24] Eidas 2.0. proposal, 2021 Recital 11.

[25] European Parliament 2024, Article 3 (j) (51).

8.2.2.2 Payment Service Directive II (PSD II)

PSDII applies to payment services provided in the EU and addresses specific aspects of digital identity authentication regarding financial transactions. It allows for processing personal data for payment authentication and fraud prevention.[26] PSDII requires '*strong customer authentication*', which means an authentication based on the use of two or more elements categorised as:

- knowledge (something only the user knows, e.g., passwords);
- possession (something only the user possesses, e.g., devices);
- inherence (something the user is, e.g., biometric data).[27]

Biometric data is not explicitly defined in the PSDII but is indirectly referred to in the context of authentication like eIDAS particularly *strong customer authentication*, which includes the category of *inherence*: something a user is and relates to their physical or behavioural characteristics, as mentioned in the GDPR definition of biometric data.[28] However, the concept here goes beyond what the GDPR covers, as it might refer to any biometric characteristics that can be used for authentication, including such as e.g., keystrokes, walking patterns, or eye movements.

Moreover, PSDII defines sensitive payment data as '... *data, including personalised security credentials which can be used to carry out fraud* ...'.[29] Therefore, sensitive data in the payment context include all data enabling user authentication, including biometric data. Such data processing must comply with the GDPR, as acknowledged in the Guidelines on the interplay of the Second Payment Service Directive and the GDPR by the European Data Protection Board (EDPB).[30]

8.2.2.3 Biometric Data in the Schengen Information System (SIS)

Biometric data processing is also considered a significant means to enhance security in the context of border control. This function can already be found in the first-generation Schengen Information System (SIS), a precursor EU-wide large-scale system established in 1995 to support the free movement within the Schengen Area.

[26] Directive (EU) 2015/2366.

[27] Strong customer authentication "means an authentication based on the use of two or more elements categorised as knowledge (something only the user knows), possession (something only the user possesses) and inherence (something the user is) that are independent, in that the breach of one does not compromise the reliability of the others, and is designed in such a way as to protect the confidentiality of the authentication data." Directive (EU) 2015/2366, Article 4(30).

[28] This interpretation is common in scientific literature and industry practice. Particularly see: Suleski and others, 2023; European Banking Authority 2020, On the requirements for "inherence" in strong customer authentication (SCA), https://www.eba.europa.eu/single-rule-book-qa/qna/view/publicId/2020_5353 Accessed 13 February 2024.

[29] *Sensitive payment data* means data, including personalized security credentials which can be used to carry out fraud.' Directive (EU) 2015/2366, Article 4(32).

[30] EDPB 2020, p. 4.

SIS is Europe's most widely used and largest information-sharing security and border management system.[31] SIS consists of different legal instruments, such as the one that contributes to police[32] cooperation between Member States, the one ensuring security in external border control[33] by enabling competent authorities to enter and consult alerts on specific categories of wanted or missing persons and migrants in an irregular situation.[34] Each of the objectives mentioned above is regulated by different regulations. Following several revisions, the new second-generation SIS framework (SIS II) became fully operational as of March 2023.[35]

Due to the limitations of the first-generation search method based on biographical data (e.g., name, surname), the modernized SIS II heavily relies on biometric data processing by storing dactyloscopic data (i.e., fingerprints and palm prints), photographs, and facial images for person-related alerts. Additionally, DNA profiles can be entered under SIS II as a last resort to identify a person in the context of police and criminal justice cooperation.[36] Furthermore, Article 42 of the SIS II police cooperation lays down specific rules on biometric data processing. It requires complying with minimum quality standards for each biometric identifier before its storage in the SIS II.

In the context of SIS Regulations for police cooperation and border checks, biometric data encompasses *photographs, facial images, dactyloscopic data.* At the same time, DNA information is only referred to as biometric data under SIS II police cooperation.[37]

SIS II Return does not define biometric data and only refers to the personal data definition under the GDPR.[38] Besides, unlike the GDPR, the other two SIS Regulations do not include behavioural characteristics when defining biometric data.

Another point of divergence would be that they treat photographs and DNA information as biometric data. For the former, the SIS regulations distinguish photographs from facial images, specifying both of them as biometric data without addressing the nuances stressed in Recital 51 GDPR. For the latter, it is essential to note that DNA

[31] European Commission 2023, https://home-affairs.ec.europa.eu/policies/schengen-borders-and-visa/schengen-information-system_en Accessed 3 March 2024.

[32] Regulation (EU) 2018/1862 on the establishment, operation and use of the Schengen Information System (SIS) in the field of police cooperation and judicial cooperation in criminal matters, (SIS II police cooperation).

[33] Regulation (EU) 2018/1861 on the establishment, operation and use of the Schengen Information System (SIS) in the field of border checksl (SIS II border checks).

[34] Regulation (EU) 2018/1860 on the use of the Schengen Information System for the return of illegally staying third-country nationals, (SIS II Return).

[35] For more details, see, EULISA 'Large-scale IT systems' available at: https://www.eulisa.europa.eu/Activities/Large-Scale-It-Systems/Sis-Ii Accessed 3 March 2024.

[36] SIS II police cooperation, 2018/1862, Article 42 (3).

[37] SIS II police cooperation, 2018/1862 'biometric data' means personal data resulting from specific technical processing relating to the physical or physiological characteristics of a natural person, which allow or confirm the unique identification of that natural person, namely photographs, facial images, dactyloscopic data and DNA profiles' Article 3(12).

[38] SIS II for return, 2018/1860 Article3(11).

information would be covered within the scope of *genetic data* under the GDPR and LED rather than biometric data.[39] This distinction is crucial because, unlike biometric data, the processing of genetic data under the GDPR and LED does not hinge on the condition of processing '*for the purpose of uniquely identifying*' to be considered as special categories of personal data. Thus, against the diverging classification of DNA information as biometric data under SIS II police cooperation, its processing falls within the special categories of data processing within the scope of LED. Hence, its processing would fall under special categories of data processing regardless of the heated discussions on purpose-based biometric sensitive data processing, as discussed above.

8.3 Critics of Pre-AIA Regulations of Biometric Data

The definition of Article 4(14) GDPR, which is *lex generalis*, seems to deviate from and does not align with the (earlier) concepts and understanding of biometric data in specific legislation for specific domains, such as in SIS II regulations used in the border context. We mention some main points of attention hereunder.

First, the GDPR's definition of biometric data is not without debate and discussion. As mentioned, the definition encompasses four main constitutive elements as follows:

(i) personal data;
(ii) specific technical processing;
(iii) relating to the physical, physiological, or behavioural characteristics of a natural person;
(iv) which allows or confirms the 'unique identification' of that natural person.

In particular, *specific technical processing* and *unique identification* elements have been subject to critical scrutiny in academic literature. First of all, the phrase 'specific technical processing' is not defined. Therefore, it has created confusion about what 'technical processing' entails and under which circumstances biometric data falls in the sensitive data regime.

Scholars have pointed out that the GDPR allows for collecting and storing biometric data as images for other purposes, e.g., a list of employees or contact persons with facial images, without falling under the prohibition of Article 9 GDPR.[40] Such collection could arguably be based on the less strict data processing regime of Article 6 of the GDPR, which allows, for example, processing based on consent or legitimate interest. The option of processing the images of biometric characteristics based on Article 6 opens the door to a weakened level of protection for processing biometric data of people. Moreover, the GDPR's approach, in particular the prohibitions in Article 9(1) GDPR, relying on the criterion of the processing for identification

[39] Recital 34 and Article 4(13) GDPR 2016/697; Recital 23 and Article 3(12) 2016/680.

[40] Kindt 2018, p. 6; Sumer 2022, p. 3.

purposes as the trigger for the need for more protection, offers only partial protection, *i.e.,* against identification, and not against, e.g., function creep (e.g., use by law enforcement) after collection and, e.g., central storage. Considering the discussions in the literature, it is evident that the purpose criterion in the GDPR may not be regarded as ideal.

Secondly, the functional criteria for *uniquely identifying'* is one significant reflection of the GDPR's general risk-based approach. Identification of an individual is indeed a considerable risk. However, considering both technical definitions and the scope of the data protection legislation, delineating biometric data to only the biometric data that can uniquely identify an individual lacks the necessary comprehensiveness of the risks of processing such data. For example, behavioural biometric characteristics may not, in all circumstances, allow unique identification; however, they may reveal critical data, e.g., emotions and sensitive information such as ethnicity, that might be used to profile individuals. For example, facial data points are often used to identify human emotions without necessarily uniquely identifying individuals.

The other legislative frameworks and proposals use different technical terms interchangeably, such as authentication (eIDAS) and identification (GDPR), without further explanations, adding to the confusion. For example, eIDAS and PSDII regulate biometric verification (1:1). However, once collected, these biometric data could also be used for identification purposes. Although eIDAS and PSDII are *lex specialis,* they both refer to the GDPR provisions without providing their own definitions of biometric data. Therefore, the legal debates on how to read the GDPR's definition of biometric data remain relevant here.

Some of such divergences among the definitions of biometric data might be considered reasonable, especially between public/private and law enforcement-related regulations, i.e., LED and GDPR serve different purposes. Furthermore, the differences between the instruments pursuing a general purpose (GDPR/LED) and those that are meant to be adopted for a specific purpose, hence the *lex specialis* (border control, payments, or digital identity management) might be justifiable. In the latter, biometric data might be defined or is to be understood differently due to such specific purposes. For example, what is considered a biometric facial image in SIS II is not necessarily biometric data under the GDPR or LED. In SIS II, facial images are exemplified as biometric data and fall in the category of biometric data based on their quality to perform facial recognition. In the GDPR, facial images must be subject to 'specific technical processing' (to be transformed) to be considered biometric data.

As mentioned, the definition of biometric data varies even within the SIS II legal framework. On the one hand, SIS regulations conceive a broader understanding of biometric data, including photographs. On the other hand, a notable narrower scope excludes behavioural biometric data and limits the scope of biometric data to an exhaustive list mentioned in the definition. One could argue that, under the SIS II framework, the legislator favours and strengthens a context-dependent definition of biometric data by emphasizing the purpose of biometric data processing for police cooperation or border checks rather than adhering to the GDPR's primary definition.

8.4 Post-AIA Understanding of Biometric Data

This section provides an overview of definitions subject to negotiations during the AIA's official adoption process. In addition to the official AIA, we discuss the negotiation process, relying on the official texts available, which are mainly the Commission's Artificial Intelligence Act (AIA) proposal and the following adopted texts, i.e., the EU Parliament's draft report (2021) and amendments adopted by the European Parliament on June 14 2023 on the Proposal.

The EU Commission's AIA proposal[41] is part of its European AI Strategy, which aims to make the EU a world-class hub for AI and attempts to ensure that AI is human-centric and trustworthy.[42] The AIA proposes a risk-based approach to using, developing, and deploying AI systems based on four levels of risk: unacceptable risk, high risk, limited risk, and minimal risk. This framework specifically identifies and regulates '*real-time*' and '*post*' remote biometric identification and categorisation by AI systems as forbidden or high-risk AI systems. Such systems are consequently subjected to the rigorous stipulations outlined in the AIA.

In addition to the Commission's proposition to regulate biometric identification, the discussions of the Proposal by the Council and the EU Parliament led to attempts to extend regulatory measures beyond this specific function. The Council proposed a new definition of biometric data in November 2022, removing the controversial *unique identification* prerequisite from the definition.

During the negotiations, more types of use of biometric data, such as for emotion recognition and biometric categorisation have been discussed, of which some are considered in particular domains at first as high-risk, including the amendment to Article 5(1), which addresses '*the placing on the market, putting into service or use of AI systems to infer emotions of a natural person in the areas of law enforcement, border management, in workplace and education institutions*'.[43] The Proposal in Recital 7 states: '*The notion of biometric data used in this Regulation is in line with and should be interpreted consistently with the notion of biometric data as defined in Article 4(14) of [GDPR*].' In conformity with this, Article 3(33) provided an identical definition of biometric data as in the GDPR.

The European Parliament's compromised text, adopted on June 14, 2023, added the concept of 'biometrics-based' data and distinguished between biometric data as understood in the GDPR and biometrics-based data. According to this text, 'biometrics-based data are additional data *resulting from specific technical processing* relating to physical, physiological or behavioural signals of a natural person, such as facial expressions, movements, pulse frequency, voice, key strikes or gait, which *may or may not* allow or confirm the unique identification of a natural person'.[44] The biometric data is defined in the amended text in article 33a as 'data resulting

[41] European Commission 2021 AIA proposal.

[42] European Commission 2023, https://digital-strategy.ec.europa.eu/en/policies/european-approach-artificial-intelligence, Accessed 28 February 2023.

[43] European Parliament 2023, Amendment 219, Article 5(1).

[44] European Parliament 2023, Amendment 21 (Recital 7).

from specific technical processing relating to physical, physiological or behavioural *signals* of a natural person' (italics added). While this is similar to the GDPR, 'signals' seem broader than 'characteristics', and the purpose of processing is not mentioned. The 'biometric-based data' category encompasses data used by biometrics-based systems, including 'emotion recognition systems' and 'biometric categorisation'. The latter two concepts or terms were also discussed and defined in the earlier versions of the AIA proposal; however, they were not included in the agreed draft, so we will not discuss them in detail here.[45]

Against this background, followed by a draft agreement AIA was adopted following lengthy negotiations. According to the unofficial draft agreement on the basis of the final AIA, the EU seems to have abandoned both the Commission's and Parliaments' view and introduced a different definition of biometric data—according to which the requirement for *allowing or confirming unique identification* is not considered a prerequisite for the qualification of biometric data. By recognising that *unique identification* may not always be the primary purpose of all use of biometric data, the AIA covers all personal data relating to the physical, physiological or behavioural characteristics from the human body if resulting from technical processing, broadening the scope of the protection offered by the GDPR and the LED.[46] The AIA seems to circumvent the problem by using the legal definition of (GDPR) to include new data types within the scope of biometric data. As mentioned, this is a critical development as not all biometric data are processed to identify an individual, yet they are still sensitive. The main reason for this sensitivity is that, in many AI applications, biometric data are processed to infer emotions (emotion recognition) or categorise people, i.e., biometric categorisation systems, according to shared biometric features revealing sensitive aspects, e.g., gender and ethnicity (Table 8.1).

Recital 14 AIA states that biometric data should be interpreted in light of Article 4(14) of the GDPR and such data can a*llow for the authentication, identification and categorisation of natural persons and for the recognition of emotions* of persons. Yet, the AIA introduces a subtle distinction between the notion of biometric data in the data protection instruments and in the AIA. These definitions are similar but different, as the AIA definition does not refer to the functional purpose of the GDPR.

It should be noted that the scope and the regulatory frameworks governing different biometric applications and functions need attention and a comprehensive approach. The AIA's definition of biometric data can be considered logical and more comprehensive for the protection of fundamental rights. Yet, it risks further confusion when

[45] European Parliament 2023, Amendment 23 to Recital 16 in AIA defines biometric categorisation as assigning natural persons to specific categories or inferring their characteristics and attributes such as gender, sex, age, hair colour, eye colour, tattoos, ethnic or social origin, health, mental or physical ability, behavioural or personality, traits language, religion, or membership of a national minority or sexual or political orientation on AIA and Article 3(39) to Article 3(1) 34: 'emotion recognition system' means an AI system for the purpose of identifying or inferring emotions, thoughts, states of mind or intentions of natural persons on the basis of their biometric data.

[46] Regulation (EU) 2024/1689 AIA.

Table 8.1 Transformation of biometric data definitions during the AIA negotiations. *Source*: EU AI Documents. (2024). The Artificial Intelligence Act. Regulation (EU) 2024/1689 of the European Parliament and of the Council of 13 June 2024 laying down harmonised rules on artificial intelligence and amending Regulations (EC) No 300/2008, (EU) No 167/2013, (EU) No 168/2013, (EU) 2018/858, (EU) 2018/1139 and (EU) 2019/2144 and Directives 2014/90/EU, (EU) 2016/797 and (EU) 2020/1828 (Artificial Intelligence Act)

Commission proposal	EP mandate	Council mandate	AIA
(33) 'biometric data' means personal data resulting from specific technical processing relating to the physical, physiological or behavioural characteristics of a natural person, which allow or confirm the unique identification of that natural person, such as facial images or dactyloscopic data	(33) biometric data as defined in Article 4, point (14) of Regulation (EU) 2016/679 (33a) biometric-based data' means data resulting from specific technical processing relating to physical, physiological or behavioural signals of a natural person	(33) 'biometric data' means personal data resulting from specific technical processing relating to the physical, physiological or behavioural characteristics of a natural person, such as facial images or dactyloscopic data	3(34) 'biometric data' means personal data resulting from specific technical processing relating to the physical, physiological or behavioural characteristics of a natural person, such as facial images or dactyloscopic data

read together with the GDPR's definition of biometric data which may also be applicable to e.g., facial images collected by an AI system using these images for emotion recognition to which the AIA definition of biometric data would apply. While the AIA attempts to provide an additional layer of protection, it does not necessarily harmonise or bring more clarity to the issues discussed in the previous sections.

8.5 Conclusion

The GDPR's narrow and functional definition of biometric data has been subject to academic debates for its limited scope in protecting fundamental rights and creating legal uncertainty. At the same time, other legislation introduced above either replicate the GDPR's definition, deploys its own concepts or refer to the GDPR definition without further elaborating on it. Indeed, regulations such as the eIDAS and the PSDII include specific provisions and uses relating to biometric data, which deviate from the general concept and understanding of the GDPR's definition of biometric data. The reliance is precarious as the GDPR provides limited protection in this context. Consequently, this regulatory landscape for biometric data processing has resulted in a diverse environment with potential discrepancies in the level of protection. The precise interplay between the GDPR and these evolving regulations, which are currently undergoing revision, also remains uncertain.

In response to this uncertainty, the AIA Proposal seeks to address some applications and AI systems on a case-by-case basis and for specific domains only. On top of this, it specifies various uses of identification systems by law enforcement by offering a more detailed definition of identification systems ('real-time' as opposed to 'post' identification). As such, the AIA is expected to play a pivotal role in regulating the risks for these specific biometric applications.

On the other hand, instead of bringing clarity, the AIA may create more confusion when read together with the GDPR's definition of biometric data. For policymakers, it is imperative to reassess and consolidate the definition and regulation of biometric data with clear guidance. We argue that enacting specific and designated legislation with a harmonized approach for defining biometric data is necessary.

References

Brownsword R, Goodwin, M (2012). Law and the Technologies of the Twenty-First Century. Cambridge University Press.

Bygrave LA (2010) The Body as Data? Biobank Regulation via the 'Back Door' of Data Protection Law. Law, Innovation and Technology, 2:1: 1–25.

Clifford D (2019) The Legal Limits to the Monetisation of Online Emotions KU Leuven PhD available at https://www.law.kuleuven.be/citip/en/research/phd-research/finalized/phd-damian-clifford Accessed February 13 2024.

Davoli A (2023) Judicial Cooperation in Criminal Matters. Fact Sheets on the European Union, pp 1-7 https://www.europarl.europa.eu/erpl-app-public/factsheets/pdf/en/FTU_4.2.6.pdf Accessed 13 February 2024.

EDPB (2020) Guidelines 06/2020 on the Interplay of the Second Payment Services Directive and the GDPR Version 2.0.

EDPB (2023), Guidelines 05/2022 on the use of facial recognition technology in the area of law enforcement, Version 2.0, April 26 2023, https://edpb.europa.eu/our-work-tools/our-documents/guidelines/guidelines-052022-use-facial-recognition-technology-area_en Accessed February 13 2024.

European Commission (2023) 'Data protection in the EU' (*European Commission website*) https://commission.europa.eu/law/law-topic/data-protection/data-protection-eu_en Accessed February 13 2024.

European Parliament (2022) Draft Report on the Proposal for a regulation of the European Parliament and of the Council amending Regulation (EU) No 910/2014 as regards establishing a framework for a European Digital Identity (Com(2021)0281 – C9-0200/2021- 2021/0136 (COD)) Committee on Industry, Research and Energy.

Foucault M (2008) *The Birth of Biopolitics*, Palgrave Macmillan.

Gates KA (2011) Our Biometric Future: Facial Recognition Technology and the Culture of Surveillance. New York University Press, New York.

George ER (2022) Bias and Biometrics: Regulating Corporate Responsibility and New Technologies to Protect Rights. Notre Dame Journal Int'l & Comp. L. 12(2) Article 3.

Jasserand C (2016) Legal Nature of Biometric Data: From Generic Personal Data to Sensitive Data. Eur. Data Prot. L. Rev. 2 (3):297–311.

Jasserand C (2019) Reprocessing of Biometric Data for Law Enforcement Purposes: Individuals' Safeguards Caught at the Interface between the GDPR and the 'Police' Directive? (PhD Thesis) https://research.rug.nl/en/publications/reprocessing-of-biometric-data-for-law-enforcement-purposes-indiv Accessed February 13 2024.

Kindt EJ (2013) Privacy and Data Protection Issues of Biometric Applications. A Comparative Legal Analysis, Dordrecht, Springer.

Kindt EJ (2018) Having yes, Using no? About the New Legal Regime for Biometric Data. Computer law & security review 34(3):523–538.

Kuner C et al. (2021) "The EU General Data Protection Regulation: A Commentary/Update of Selected Articles." Update of Selected Articles, May 4, 2021 https://doi.org/10.2139/ssrn.3839645 Accessed February 13 2024.

Kindt EJ (2022) 'Chapter 18. "Biometric data processing: Is the legislator keeping up or just keeping up appearances ?' in G. Gonzalez Fuster, R. Van Brakel and P. De Hert (eds.), *Privacy and Data Protection Law: Values, Norms and Global Politics*, Cheltenham U.K. and Massachusetts, U.S.A., Edward Elgar Publishing, Research Handbook.

Prabhakar S, Pankanti, S, Jain, AK (2003) Biometric Recognition: Security and Privacy Concerns. IEEE Security & Privacy, pp.33–42.

Rose N (2000) 'Government and Control' (2000) 40 The British Journal of Criminology 321.

Roznai Y (2014) A Bird is Known by its Feathers'—On the Importance and Complexities of Definitions in Legislation. The Theory and Practice of Legislation, 2.2: 145–167.

Spanish Data Protection Authority (AEDP) AEPD, 'Guía sobre Tratamientos de Control de Presencia Mediante Sistemas Biométricos v. November 2023' (2023) https://www.aepd.es/documento/guia-control-presencia-biometrico.pdf Accessed 13 February 2024.

Suleski T et al. (2023) A review of multi-factor authentication in the Internet of Healthcare Things. Digital Health, 9.

Sumer B (2022) When do the Images of Biometric Characteristics Qualify as Special Categories of Data under the GDPR?: A Systemic Approach to Biometric Data Processing. 2022 International Conference of the Biometrics Special Interest Group (BIOSIG). IEEE.

Sumer B, Schroers J (2021). The new digital identity Regulation proposal and the EU data protection Regime. CiTiP Blog. https://www.law.kuleuven.be/citip/blog/the-new-digital-identity-regulation-proposal/ Accessed February 13 2024.

Tamas B et al. (2021) Emerging Biometric Modalities and their Use: Loopholes in the Terminology of the GDPR and Resulting Privacy Risks. 2021 International Conference of the Biometrics Special Interest Group (BIOSIG). IEEE.

Legislations

Directive (EU) 2015/2366 of the European Parliament and of the Council of November 25 2015 on payment services in the internal market, amending Directives 2002/65/EC, 2009/110/EC and 2013/36/EU and Regulation (EU) No 1093/2010, and repealing Directive 2007/64/EC.

Directive (EU) 2016/680 of the European Parliament and of the Council of April 27 2016 on the protection of natural persons with regard to the processing of personal data by competent authorities for the purposes of the prevention, investigation, detection or prosecution of criminal offences or the execution of criminal penalties, and on the free movement of such data, and repealing Council Framework Decision 2008/977/JHA (hereinafter Law Enforcement Directive or LED).

Regulation (EU) 2014/910 of the European Parliament and of the Council of July 23 2014 on electronic identification and trust services for electronic transactions in the internal market and repealing Directive 1999/93/EC.

Regulation (EU) 2016/679 of the European Parliament and of the Council of April 27 2016 on the protection of natural persons with regard to the processing of personal data and on the free movement of such data, and repealing Directive 95/46/EC (General Data Protection Regulation).
Regulation (EU) 2018/1860 of the European Parliament and of the Council of November 28 2018 on the use of the Schengen Information System for the return of illegally staying third-country nationals (Consolidated version).
Regulation (EU) 2018/1861 of the European Parliament and of the Council of November 28 2018 on the establishment, operation and use of the Schengen Information System (SIS) in the field of border checks, and amending the Convention implementing the Schengen Agreement, and amending and repealing Regulation (EC) No 1987/2006 (Consolidated version).
Regulation (EU) 2018/1862 of the European Parliament and of the Council of November 28 2018 on the establishment, operation and use of the Schengen Information System (SIS) in the field of police cooperation and judicial cooperation in criminal matters, amending and repealing Council Decision 2007/533/JHA, and repealing Regulation (EC) No 1986/2006 of the European Parliament and of the Council and Commission Decision (Consolidated version).
Regulation (EU) 2024/1689 of the European Parliament and of the Council of 13 June 2024 laying down harmonised rules on artificial intelligence and amending Regulations (EC) No 300/2008, (EU) No 167/2013, (EU) No 168/2013, (EU) 2018/858, (EU) 2018/1139 and (EU) 2019/2144 and Directives 2014/90/EU, (EU) 2016/797 and (EU) 2020/1828 (Artificial Intelligence Act)

Draft regulations and proposals

Council of the EU, The Proposal for a Regulation of the European Parliament and of the Council Laying Down Harmonised Rules on Artificial Intelligence (Artificial Intelligence Act) And Amending Certain Union Legislative Acts (hereinafter Draft AIA), 2021/016 (COD) - Analysis of the final compromise text with a view to agreement.
Draft European Parliament Legislative Resolution on the Proposal for a regulation of the European Parliament and of the Council amending Regulation (EU) No 910/2014 as regards establishing a framework for a European Digital Identity (COM(2021)0281 – C9-0200/2021 – 2021/0136(COD)), available at https://www.europarl.europa.eu/doceo/document/A-9-2023-0038_EN.html Accessed February 13 2024.
European Parliament (2023) Amendments adopted by the European Parliament on June 14 2023 on the Proposal for a regulation of the European Parliament and of the Council on laying down harmonised rules on artificial intelligence (Artificial Intelligence Act) and amending certain Union legislative acts (COM(2021)0206 – C9-0146/2021 – 2021/0106(COD)).
Position of the European Parliament adopted at first reading on February 29, 2024, with a view to the adoption of Regulation (EU) 2024 of the European Parliament and of the Council amending Regulation (EU) No 910/2014 as regards establishing the European Digital Identity Framework.
Proposal for a Regulation of the European Parliament and of the Council amending Regulation (EU) No 910/2014 as regards establishing a framework for a European Digital Identity COM/2021/281 final (eIDAS 2.0 proposal).
Proposal for a Regulation of the European Parliament and of the Council Laying Down Harmonised Rules On Artificial Intelligence (Artificial Intelligence Act) And Amending Certain Union Legislative Acts COM/2021/206 final.

Bilgesu Sumer is a doctoral researcher at KU Leuven (CiTiP) and a Biometric Law Lab (BLL) member. Her research focuses on the data protection implications of biometrics, AI, and blockchains.

Natalia Menéndez González is a Ph.D. candidate at the European University Institute, where she researches the proportionality within the use of Facial Recognition Technology. She is also a Research Assistant at the Centre for a Digital Society, a teaching assistant at the School of Transnational Governance, a co-founder of The DigiCon blog, a visiting researcher at the Biometrics Law Lab of the Center for IT and IP Law at the KU Leuven Faculty of Law and Criminology and former vice-chair of the Ph.D. students in AI Ethics research group. Her other research interests include AI Ethics, especially for Natural Language Processing, and the intersection between artificial intelligence and democracy.

Abdullah Elbi is a legal researcher at KU Leuven (CiTiP), and a member of Biometric Law Lab (BLL). His research focuses on fundamental rights implications of emerging technologies with particular interest in trustworthy artificial intelligence, biometrics, and voice assisstances. He has been involved in various EU and national level research Projects such as iMARS, FAITH, and SALT.

Catherine Jasserand is an assistant professor at the University of Groningen (Netherlands) within the STeP research group. She is an expert in law, AI, and biometrics. Between 2020 and 2023, she was part of the Biometric Law Lab (BLL) at KU Leuven as a Marie Skłodowska-Curie postdoctoral fellow. There, she investigated the impact of facial recognition technologies use in public spaces on the rights to privacy and data protection as part of the MSCA-IF project DATAFACE).

Jan Czarnocki is a Doctoral Researcher and Maria Skłodowska-Curie Fellow at the KU Leuven Centre for IT and IP Law in Belgium, and a member of the Biometric Law Lab (BLL). His work intersects the domains of law, philosophy, technology, and policy. Jan was also recognized as a Non-Resident Fellow at the Stanford Law School Transatlantic Technology Law Forum and an Affiliated Fellow at the Jagiellonian University Private Law of Data Project.

Els J. Kindt is an associate professor and senior research fellow with eLaw of Universiteit Leiden, the Netherlands, respectively the Centre for IT and IP Law (CITIP) of KU Leuven, Belgium. She has been an expert in law and biometrics for over 20 years. In 2020, she set up the Biometric Law Lab (BLL) for exchanging legal knowledge in this domain.

Chapter 9
The Rule of Law for Artificial Intelligence in Public Administration: A System Safety Perspective

Sem Nouws and Roel Dobbe

Contents

Abstract This chapter proposes an analytical lens to comprehensively address the role of Artificial Intelligence (AI) applications in mediating arbitrary exercise of power in public administration and the citizen harms that result from such conduct. It provides a timely and urgent account to fill gaps in conventional Rule of Law

---

S. Nouws (✉) · R. Dobbe
Delft University of Technology, Jaffalaan 5, 2628 CN Delft, The Netherlands
e-mail: S.J.J.Nouws@tudelft.nl

R. Dobbe
e-mail: R.I.J.Dobbe@tudelft.nl

K. Prifti et al. (eds.), *Digital Governance*, Information Technology and Law Series 39,
https://doi.org/10.1007/978-94-6265-639-0_9

thought. AI systems are socio-technical by nature and, therefore, differ from the text-driven social constructs that the legal professions dealing with Rule of Law issues concentrate on. Put to work in public administration contexts with consequential decision-making, technical artefacts can contribute to a variety of hazardous situations that provide opportunities for arbitrary conduct. A comprehensive lens to understand and address the role of technology in Rule of Law violations has largely been missing in literature. We propose to combine a socio-legal perspective on the Rule of Law with central insights from system safety—a safety engineering tradition with a strong scientific as well as real-world practice—that considers safety from a technological, systemic, and institutional perspective. The combination results in a lexicon and analytical approach that enables public organisations to identify possibilities for arbitrary conduct in public AI systems. Following on the analysis, interventions can be designed to prevent, mitigate, or correct system hazards and, thereby, protect citizens against arbitrary exercise of power.

Keywords Rule of law · Public algorithmic systems · Arbitrary use of power · Artificial intelligence · System safety · Citizen harms

9.1 Introduction

Governments often fall short in adequately protecting citizens from harm inflicted through their dependency on algorithmic applications for the provision of public services. In the Netherlands, childcare benefit recipients were falsely accused of fraud based on a risk indication model.[1] Similarly, the Robodebt program in Australia falsely assigned debts to citizens based on automatically calculated overpayments.[2] False accusations and the subsequently imposed harsh penalties have resulted in grave harm done to unguilty citizens, often ruining lives and amounting to significant human right violations. Both cases are exemplary for the increased use of algorithmic and data-driven applications in the public sector. Especially the introduction of Artificial Intelligence (AI) applications such as machine learning illustrates a new step in automating processes in public administration by facilitating fraud prediction, risk assessment, and allocation of public resources. The exemplary cases of the childcare benefit scandal and the Robodebt scheme show that public organisations seem to fall short in preventing, mitigating, or correcting citizen harms inflicted by the use of algorithmic applications.

This chapter focuses on the use of AI in a public administration context. First, AI applications are rule- and/or data-driven software-based technologies that predict or generate output. These applications are used to automate or augment processes in public administration, which we refer to as AI practices. Second, it is important to stress that AI applications are one of several different components in a system.

[1] Peeters and Widlak 2023.

[2] Braithwaite 2020.

They are part of a larger bureaucratic environment that aims to provide a public service or execute public policy.[3] This means that AI applications are operated by human agents—e.g., public servants—that interact with or otherwise monitor the technology.[4] Moreover, the AI applications are situated in an institutional context—i.e., a set of formal and informal social rules that structure human behaviour and the technical specification of AI applications.[5] In the rest of this chapter, we will refer to this broader and systemic understanding as *public AI systems*.

Where public organisations use these applications to increase efficiency or address complex policy issues, their institutional and administrative practices are also challenged.[6] For example, practices are changed by creating opaqueness or changing power dynamics. In the already complex web of public services, AI applications can make the impact to households harder to predict and understand, e.g. by automating the determination of repayments. Changing power dynamics can be observed in the shift of discretionary power from the frontline worker to the developer of AI applications.[7] Moreover, these applications intervene in the fundamental relationship between citizen and government by formalising the structuration of citizen behaviour.[8] Consequently, the power imbalance between government and citizens increases;[9] creating possibilities for arbitrary use of power.[10] In cases of automated decision-making, public organisations often offload responsibility for proving eligibility and receiving benefits to citizens.[11] Besides, the necessary knowledge needed to navigate complex benefit systems, often consisting of a multitude of policies and services with various dependencies, can amount to an impossible barrier for citizens.

Disruption of institutional practices following from the use of AI applications also interferes with Rule of Law practices—i.e., efforts to reduce arbitrary use of power. Several authors have argued that AI and other forms of automation are a challenge or threat to the Rule of Law.[12] Others discuss the role of technology or AI applications in arbitrary use of power.[13] Current approaches to the Rule of Law seem to fall short in addressing issues arising from public AI systems as they do not integrate institutional and technical expertise.[14] However, apart from calls for ideas like 'legal protection by design',[15] it is still unclear how such an integration can be achieved in practical terms.

---

[3] Mulligan and Bamberger 2019.

[4] Fountain 2001.

[5] Orlikowski 1992.

[6] Veale and Brass 2019.

[7] Bovens and Zouridis 2002; Alkhatib and Bernstein, 2019.

[8] Janssen and Kuk 2016.

[9] Yeung 2018.

[10] Brownsword 2016; Zalnieriute et al. 2019.

[11] Widlak and Peeters 2020.

[12] Bayamlıoğlu and Leenes 2018; Hildebrandt 2018; Greenstein 2022.

[13] Brownsword 2016; Zalnieriute et al. 2019.

[14] Zalnieriute et al. 2019.

[15] Hildebrandt 2011.

In this chapter, we develop an analytical lens that provides a way to detect and correct arbitrary conduct in contexts where AI applications are deployed to administer public services. We draw a relationship between protecting citizens against the system hazards in public AI systems and reducing arbitrary conduct. For this aim, we employ the socio-legal perspective on the Rule of Law suggested by Krygier and Selznick,[16] situating public service decision-making and its risk of arbitrary conduct in a social context in combination with a system safety approach. The latter leans on decades of insights from safety engineering and (socio-technical) systems theory about dealing with system hazards in software-based automation in complex processes.[17] The resulting conceptualisation opens new avenues to interpret and enrich the socio-legal perspective to account for the causal ways in which AI applications restructure and impact (arbitrary) conduct, as well as for the role of organisational and systemic factors contributing to such causal outcomes.

This chapter starts with discussing the need for a socio-technical perspective in the Rule of Law. In Sect. 9.2, we unravel the role of AI systems in arbitrary use of power by linking these systems to manifestations of arbitrary conduct. Sect. 9.3 examines how Rule of Law perspectives understand the role of technical artefacts in arbitrary conduct and how that understanding disregards the structuring nature of technology. Thereafter, in Sect. 9.4, we show the merits of including a socio-technical perspective in the Rule of Law and argue for the suitability of system safety as a specific socio-technical perspective. The subsequent sections discuss three focus points on which the socio-legal perspective and system safety could be combined: a lexicon, an analytical approach, and safety-guided design. Sect. 9.5 presents a lexicon that rephrases dominant conceptualizations of arbitrary use of power through a system safety lens and adjacent systems engineering concepts. Applying the system safety lens to public sector decision-making and law execution involving AI systems, can then open up various avenues presented in Sect. 9.6 to analyse safety hazards—i.e., possibilities for arbitrary conduct—in such processes. From there we identify readily available methods to address such issues, as well as opportunities to extend system safety approaches to be of value in addressing Rule of Law issues related to public AI systems. In Sect 9.7 we show how known measures from the Rule of Law can be appropriated to system safety control actions. These action either prevent arbitrary conduct from occurring in AI practices or instigate mitigating measures in the operation of AI practices or the surrounding organizational governance.

---

[16] Selznick 1999; Krygier 2009.

[17] Leveson 2012.

9.2 Arbitrary Conduct Mediated by Public AI Systems

To address arbitrary use of power mediated by public AI systems, the role of such systems in arbitrary conduct needs to be clarified. However, arbitrary use of power as a concept itself is under-theorised.[18] Mak and Taekema, and Krygier have provided first attempts to categorise and define arbitrary conduct.[19] We base our discussion of arbitrary conduct in public AI systems on four—non-exclusive and non-exhaustive—manifestations of arbitrariness listed by these authors: (1) reasoning by public servants based on 'own will or pleasure'; (2) inability of citizens to engage in or contest decision-making; (3) unpredictability and incomprehensibility of conduct for those affected; and (4) unfair decision-making in concrete situations. This section exemplifies how these four manifestations may emerge in public AI systems.

9.2.1 Reasoning Based on Own Will or Pleasure

Conduct is arbitrary if it is based on the own will or pleasure of an individual exercising power. This means that a rational basis or good arguments for a decision are missing.[20] Such a rational basis is formed by formal rules and regulations, procedures, or mandates and steers or limits the power exercised by decision-makers.[21]

Public AI systems enable two types of actors to impose their own will or pleasure on others: the operator(s), that is, the public servant deploying the system or using its output, and the designer(s) of the system, that is, the actors responsible for specifying or developing the system. The system's operator can intentionally use the system to 'rationalise' their decision based on own will or pleasure, thereby possibly overriding other rational arguments. AI systems may also be used selectively to confirm one's own biases.[22] Another issue arises when operators blindly follow faulty AI output, not using their own critical reasoning to prevent an undesirable outcome. This phenomenon is sometimes referred to as automation bias, and hints at the risk of deskilling and loss of operational discretion.[23] However, the operational actors are not always to blame.[24] Often, errors are a function of the environment in which an operator is acting.[25] In other words, operators often lack the right information or resources to oversee or work with an AI system. In such cases, discretion of the

[18] Krygier 2016.

[19] Krygier 2016; Mak and Taekema 2016.

[20] Mak and Taekema 2016.

[21] Krygier 2016.

[22] Young et al. 2021.

[23] Green and Chen 2019.

[24] Green 2022.

[25] Leveson 2012.

system's operator at the operational level is effectively reduced or distorted by design choices made earlier in the system's life cycle.[26]

Similarly, AI system's designers can base their design choices on their own will or pleasure.[27] A special situation in this respect is the case that rules are not appropriately translated to the logical innerworkings of an AI system. This can be the result of, for example, vagueness or the urge to simplify inherent complex situations in formalistic models.[28] Thereby, system designers may impose a system's logic that does not align with laws, regulations, and policies related to the processes in which the AI system functions.

9.2.2 No Space or Means to Engage or Contest

Citizens should be able to engage in or contest decision-making through possibilities to question or voice arguments and complaints. An important feature of exercising power is that the interests of individuals affected are considered.[29] Therefore, those affected should also have the means and possibility to control and question those in power, and to be heard by them.[30]

Citizens are unable to engage in design processes of or contest AI systems when the responsibilities for such a system are poorly specified. AI applications are known for the responsibility gaps these create.[31] For example, AI systems are dependent on datasets and information architectures that might be situated in other organisational units.[32] In fact, AI systems often rely on vast and potentially global supply chains,[33] with inherent complexities that contribute to developers or users not experiencing or taking responsibility.[34] In the same vein, AI applications may be put in place to widen the *accountability gap* 'between those who develop and profit from AI—and those most likely to suffer the consequences of its negative effects.'[35]

As argued above, the use of AI systems in public administration is shifting power dynamics in public organisations, for example, by shifting discretion from bureaucrats to system designers,[36] or by strengthening the relative position of executive branches in governments.[37] Hence, assigned responsibilities may not reflect the

[26] Cf. Peeters and Widlak 2018; Zouridis et al. 2020; Leveson 2012.

[27] König and Wenzelburger 2021.

[28] Dobbe et al. 2021; Alkhatib 2021.

[29] Mak and Taekema 2016.

[30] Krygier 2016.

[31] Santoni De Sio and Mecacci 2021.

[32] Sculley et al. 2015.

[33] Cobbe et al. 2023.

[34] Widder and Nafus 2023.

[35] Whittaker et al. 2018.

[36] Zouridis et al. 2020.

[37] Passchier 2020.

real influence of actors on the AI system. A mounting problem in this context is the handover of the development of AI systems—that intimately mediate public services—to external parties. Thereby, shifting both public accountability as well as autonomy over the quality of the public services from public to private actors.[38] Furthermore, normative design choices may be arbitrary if these are not based on adequate deliberation or (political) mandates.[39]

9.2.3 *Unpredictable and Incomprehensible*

For conduct not to be arbitrary, citizens should be able to comprehend rules in order to comply with these rules.[40] This also means that rules and their enforcement should be predictable.[41] The requirements of predictability and comprehensibility also support citizens in challenging arbitrary conduct (see Sect. 9.2.2).

The opaqueness and complexity inherent to AI systems impedes comprehensibility and predictability of power exercised through public AI systems.[42] Citizens often lack the expertise needed to understand the working of AI systems.[43] Similarly, software-based automation systems can become so complex that operators also run into the limits of cognitive capacity to properly understand how the system functions and what behaviours might emerge under particular circumstances.[44] For example, semi-automated systems may look like the only effective and efficient way to compute and administer eligibility to and height of social welfare policies. Similarly, AI applications may also emerge to address the lack of predictability of complex social welfare systems. However, such semi-automated systems may quickly add their own complexity or their behaviour may turn unpredictable.

9.2.4 *Unfair Decision-Making in Concrete Situations*

Finally, Mak and Taekema stress the fact that unfair decisions can also be arbitrary. To prevent or reduce arbitrariness, decision-makers need to make contextual assessments of concrete situations.[45] This is related to considering the voices and interests of citizens in exercising power.[46]

---

[38] Whittaker 2021.

[39] Hildebrandt 2011; Yeung 2014; Grimmelikhuijsen and Meijer 2022.

[40] Krygier 2016.

[41] Mak and Taekema 2016.

[42] Burrell 2016.

[43] De Bruijn et al. 2022.

[44] Leveson 2012.

[45] Mak and Taekema 2016.

[46] Krygier 2016.

AI systems can contribute to unfair decisions in concrete cases.[47] Discrimination and biases—prevalent in data-driven algorithmic systems such as AI—[48] may result in unfair decision-making. For example, when AI systems are used for allocation of benefits, biases may lead to allocation to citizens on basis of irrelevant characteristics. These biases may find their roots in historical conduct, as well as in the design choices made by developers, or in the ways in which the AI application is used.[49] Likewise, errors, flaws and the statistical or correlational nature of decision-making in an AI system can exclude citizens because of its disciplining nature—in which the consequences of such errors arbitrarily affect citizens.[50]

9.3 The Lack of a Socio-Technical Perspective in the Rule of Law

Section 9.2 shows that the role of AI applications in arbitrary conduct may not be the decisive factor, but cannot be ignored. When understanding the Rule of Law as governing people through law instead of by bureaucrats in order to reduce arbitrary use of power, the Rule of Law also applies to public AI systems. We discuss this role of the Rule of Law in this section. We show that conventional and current Rule of Law thinking lacks ways to bring into view and address the roles and implications of AI applications in arbitrary conduct.

The misconception of technologies' role in arbitrary conduct can be identified by considering the Rule of Law from a structuration lens. Structuration is about the duality or co-constitution of the two components institutions (structure) and human agents (agency).[51] These two components shape one another through interaction. Institutions are social rules that structure human behaviour.[52] In discussing institutions, legal literature mostly refers to legal institutions, such as rules, laws, rights, and procedures. This chapter broadens this conception and includes institutions such as culture, norms, and routines. By enacting institutions, human agents also change the form and function of institutions. Orlikowski has applied structuration to socio-technical systems.[53] Her model adds an extra component to the duality of institutions and human agents: technical artefacts. These artefacts are also in a co-constituting relationship with institutions and human agents.

47 Barocas and Selbst 2016; Dobbe et al. 2018.

48 Hildebrandt 2019.

49 Dobbe et al. 2018.

50 Peeters and Widlak 2018.

51 Giddens 1976; Giddens 1979; Giddens 1984.

52 Hodgson 2006

53 The Structurational Model of Technology by Orlikowski 1992.

9.3.1 Rule of Law in Public AI Systems

Unsurprisingly, various scholars have stressed the threats that public AI systems pose to the Rule of Law—which traditionally is considered the main mechanism to reduce arbitrary conduct.[54] Bayamlıoğlu and Leenes identify challenges to law as a normative, a causative as well as a moral enterprise and even caution 'that the 'rule of law' might be exchanged for the 'rule of technology'—accompanied by Kafkaesque, Huxleyan, and Orwellian discourses of dystopia.'[55] Furthermore, Hildebrandt addresses how machine learning applications challenge contestability, a fundamental element of the Rule of Law.[56] Correspondingly, the use of AI systems in the public domain can undermine the Rule of Law.

On the other hand, the Rule of Law provides a framework to address arbitrary conduct mediated by AI systems. As mentioned, measures and institutions based on the Rule of law should be enacted to protect citizens against arbitrariness.[57] Several authors have argued that although public AI systems are of a different order compared to traditional laws and policy execution, they should fall under the Rule of Law regime. Brownsword stresses the 'continuing link between the regulators' normative intentions [represented in rule-based regulatory instruments] and the translation of these intentions into a technologically managed environment'—public AI systems can create such an environment.[58] Similarly, Hildebrandt argues that data-driven applications that execute laws count as mere administration (and not law), but that administration should also adhere to the Rule of Law.[59]

Consequently, AI applications used in the administration of law are subject to the Rule of Law, but their characteristics may simultaneously undermine Rule of Law mechanisms that are put in place to restrain the processes in which these technologies are applied. As such, the Rule of Law as a regime to reduce arbitrary conduct needs to be reassessed and adapted to ensure public AI systems operate under that regime and do not cause new issues to it. The need for broadening Rule of Law thinking also follows from the fact that it was not able to protect the citizens in the cases discussed at the start of this chapter. The toolboxes that perspectives on the Rule of Law provide did not enable governments to prevent, mitigate, or correct harms by arbitrary conduct in public AI systems.

[54] See Krygier 2009.

[55] Bayamlıoğlu and Leenes 2018, p. 305.

[56] Hildebrandt 2016.

[57] Raz 1979; Krygier 2009.

[58] Brownsword 2016, p. 102.

[59] Hildebrandt 2018.

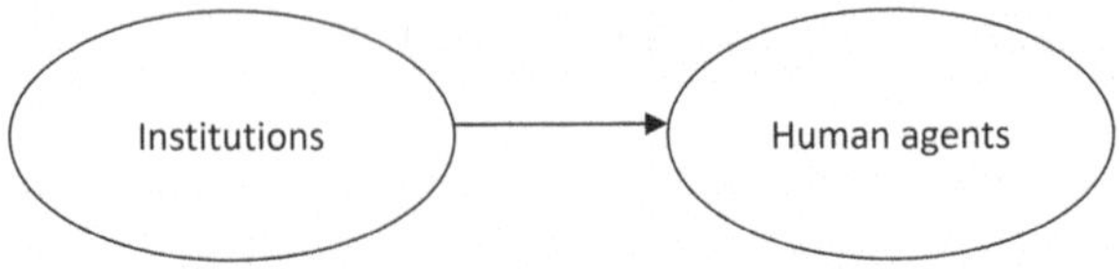

Fig. 9.1 Structuration in 'classic' perspectives on the Rule of Law: institutions structure the behaviour of human agents (Figure by authors)

9.3.2 Gaps in Current Rule of Law Perspectives

The Rule of Law is discussed from different perspectives in legal philosophy. First, we discuss the gaps in the *classic* perspectives in addressing public AI systems. Later, we discuss the socio-legal perspective.

The classic perspectives comprise the three angles—i.e., formal, substantive and procedural—from which scholars traditionally study the Rule of Law.[60] These three perspectives have different views on the nature of the Rule of law; each containing relevant and useful insights for governing public AI systems. The formal perspective provides (lists of) requirements for the form of rules for them to contribute to or comply with the Rule of Law.[61] The substantive perspective perceives the Rule of Law as guiding, demarcating, or constraining the content of rules. It emphasises the connection between rules and the moral and political rights that citizens have. The procedural perspective emphasises the Rule of Law as structuring argumentative practices that achieve objectivity. In other words, the Rule of Law should provide procedures to ensure that such an argumentative practice—e.g., in law-making or in court—runs properly.[62]

Although the three classic perspectives differ in their interpretation of the nature of the Rule of Law, they all focus on the form and function of legal institutions, and how these institutions structure human behaviour. Figure 9.1 visualises this one-way interaction between the institutional component in social systems and human agents. The presupposition in these perspectives seems to be that human agents can engage in arbitrary conduct, but that this can be prevented, mitigated or corrected by establishing the right legal institutions.[63] The effects of human behaviour are thereby overlooked.

The socio-legal perspective considers the same two components but acknowledges that structuration goes in both directions. This perspective developed amongst others by Selznick and Krygier uses insights from sociology to better understand how the Rule of Law can be achieved in practice by acknowledging that institutions are enacted by human agents.[64] It studies the effect that human behaviour has on

[60] Cf. Waldron 2011.

[61] Raz 1979.

[62] Waldron 2011.

[63] Cf. Krygier 2009.

[64] Selznick 2003; Krygier 2014.

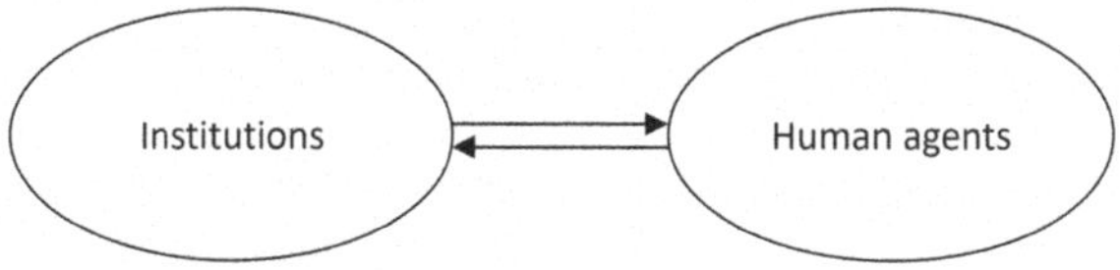

Fig. 9.2 Structuration in the socio-legal perspective on the Rule of Law: human agents also structure the form and function of institutions (Figure by authors)

the realisation of the Rule of Law. Figure 9.2 shows this bidirectional interaction between the institutions and human agents.

Consequently, the perspective not only looks at legal institutions to sustain or materialise the Rule of Law, but has a broader perspective that includes political, administrative, and cultural aspects that organise and determine the functioning of the state. Therefore, a strong institutional context not only consists of legal institutions such as rules, but is backed by informal institutions such as culture, routines, and practices.[65] According to Krygier the 'ability to restrain the ways in which power is exercised needs to be institutionalised.'[66] As such, while the socio-legal perspective takes the role of human behaviour into consideration, it still focuses on institutions as the main point of intervention for upholding the Rule of Law.

We can hence conclude that both the classic as well as the socio-legal perspective on the Rule of Law do not explicitly consider technical artefacts, such as AI applications, as having a structuring function on human behaviour or institutions. Put differently, the perspectives consider institutions—in a narrow or broad sense—as the main point of intervention in establishing the Rule of Law. The importance of the right institutional context for public AI systems is also discussed outside legal literature.[67] Nevertheless, an institutional approach to the Rule of Law in a context mediated, informed or automated by AI applications will fall short in addressing the problems that public AI systems pose if it does not: (1) consider the ways in which AI practices conflict with Rule of Law principles, as well as (2) account for how these practices pose problems by structuring the administration of law and possibilities for arbitrary conduct. Put differently, public organisations need to have a granular understanding of how new technological applications, be they AI or other, structure their core processes and practices.

---

[65] Nonet and Selznick 2001; Krygier 2009; Taekema 2021.

[66] Krygier 2009, p. 12.

[67] E.g., Dobbe 2022; Green 2022; Grimmelikhuijsen and Meijer 2022.

9.3.3 Public AI Systems as Socio-Technical Systems

Mostly, the role of technical artifacts is considered superficially or narrowly in the literature on the Rule of Law.[68] Consequently, the role of AI applications in arbitrary conduct is hard to understand from a purely legal philosophy standpoint. Existing socio-legal interpretations would benefit from a socio-technical structuration perspective, which assumes that an application of technology does not only comprise a technical artefact—i.e., the AI application–, but forms a system with institutions and human agents. System practices and outcomes hence emerge from the interaction between social and technical components when enacted by human agents.[69] Together, the technical, institutional, and agential components create possibilities for arbitrary conduct. Moreover, AI systems are embedded in a broader information architecture—i.e., they are connected to, interdependent with, and interrelated with other technical artefacts or systems.[70]

The three socio-technical components structure each other's form and function, as depicted in Fig. 9.3.[71] The interaction between institutions and technical artefacts is most apparent in the fact that public AI systems are constituted based on formal institutions such as laws, regulations, and policies. Moreover, the form and function of technical artefacts is also influenced by work instructions on how users should use the system. The other way around, the form and function of technology can, for example, institutionalise specific practices.[72] When human agents interact with technical artefacts their behaviour is disciplined by these artefacts. Likewise, human agents assign functions to artefacts by enacting public AI systems within the context of laws and policies by human agents (e.g., civil servant or front worker).[73] In other words, the AI application mediates the tasks or work of human agents and, thereby, can provide the agents with possibilities for arbitrary conduct when using or designing these systems.

Distinguishing the three components of public AI systems and examining their interactions enriches the understanding of the intricate role technical artefacts may play in arbitrary conduct. Furthermore, the three components and various interactions between these provide starting points for interventions in the system that address possibilities for arbitrary conduct.

Regarding arbitrary conduct from a socio-technical perspective provides a systematic appraisal of challenges and opportunities for the Rule of Law in cases of increased automation and augmentation of decision-making. First, there is the general threat to

---

[68] The few authors that write about AI and the Rule of Law do that from a specific focus or consider technology as an external or deterministic factor; e.g., Chiao 2023 has a focus on courts, Yeung 2018 as well as Cuéllar and Huq 2022 focus on regulation, Hildebrandt 2018 focuses on contestability.

[69] Orlikowski 1992.

[70] Nissenbaum 2019.

[71] Orlikowski 1992.

[72] Orlikowski 1992.

[73] Cf. Seaver 2017.

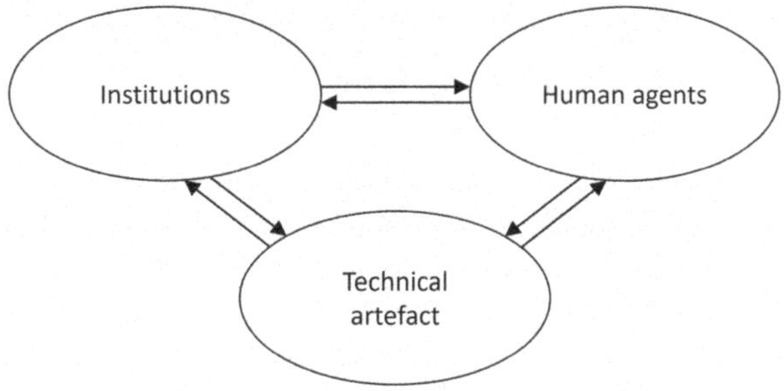

Fig. 9.3 The socio-technical perspective comprises three components that structure each other (Figure by authors, based on Orlikowski 1992.)

Rule of Law discussed by legal scholars.[74] Fig. 9.3 indicates that this threat actually refers to the technical component partly or fully replacing the function of institutions in public administration practices. In this case, the Rule of Law is sidelined by the interplay between the agential and technical component.[75] Second, the figure shows what the Rule of Law as an institutional endeavour can influence: both human behaviour as well as the form and function of the technical component within it. Finally, the figure points out the limitations of the Rule of Law's influence. It is always dependent on the technical artefact and the way in which human agents use both the technical as well as the institutional artefacts. Consequently, actors giving form to the Rule of Law are dependent on actors from other disciplines, e.g., developers of the AI application. Still, the Rule of Law can provide inspiration for the specification that shapes the technical artefact, and, based on the above, one may argue that the development practices of consequential AI applications as well as involved actors should fall under the Rule of Law.

9.4 The Rule of Law and System Safety

This section discusses the starting points for a lexicon, an analysis, and a design practice based on system safety that can operationalise and ensure a socio-technical approach for the Rule of Law in public AI systems. First, the merits of a socio-technical perspective as presented in Sect. 9.3.3 are identified. Thereafter, we examine the elements that are missing in Rule of Law thinking. Finally, system safety is presented as a suitable perspective to enrich the socio-legal perspective on the Rule of Law.

[74] E.g., Bayamlıoğlu and Leenes 2018; Hildebrandt 2018; Greenstein 2022.

[75] E.g., Endicott and Yeung 2022.

9.4.1 Contribution of a Socio-Technical Perspective to the Rule of Law

Bringing a socio-technical perspective to the Rule of Law has at least three contributions, all addressing overlooked systemic issues or flaws that contribute to arbitrary conduct. First, without a socio-technical understanding of failures in AI systems, the Rule of Law will retain its focus on illegitimate decisions in individual cases, arbitrary conduct by individuals or instituting the Rule of Law on the state level. For example, individual citizens can go to court to contest a decision based on a public AI system. In case the decision is deemed erroneous, the individual decision is corrected or its consequences are compensated. However, this does not provide insight on whether this erroneous decision follows from a systemic flaw in the public AI system. König & Wenzelburger show how a design choice that determines the distribution of outcomes of AI systems can lead to arbitrary outcomes: whether a specific citizen is selected by the AI model does not depend on their own characteristics or applicability but on how these factors differ from other citizens in the population or the dataset.[76]

Second, the consequences of systemic interactions can be overlooked without a socio-technical perspective. Public AI systems may interact with other processes and systems, e.g. in how the outputs form inputs to other decisions, either within or outside the organisation it is situated in. These interactions may cause emerging effects in other, but related systems—also called *ripple effects*—that were not anticipated at the level of single processes or organizations, and which may significantly harm citizens.[77] Both sustaining the individual focus and neglecting systemic interactions may obscure responsibilities.

Finally, without acknowledging the socio-technical nature of public AI systems, the separation between Rule of Law practices and AI application design practices will persist and communication will be hindered. Following from the classic Rule of Law perspectives, it is sufficient to have law-makers craft legal institutions. The socio-legal perspective already shows that the behaviour of policymakers and users should be considered. On the other hand, AI applications are generally designed by technical developers who are guided by policies. The socio-technical perspective, therefore, puts emphasis on designing institutions and technology symbiotically.[78] This requires collaboration between actors from different disciplines,[79] and striving for alignment between institutional and technical components.[80]

The DUO case in the Netherlands shows the consequences of missing a socio-technical perspective. Until 2015, Dutch students were paid monthly study grants to cover a.o. costs of living by DUO—an executive agency of the ministry of education.

76 König and Wenzelburger 2021.

77 Peeters and Widlak 2018; Pel 2022.

78 Koppenjan and Groenewegen 2005.

79 De Bruijn and Herder 2009.

80 Kunneke et al. 2021.

Students living with their parents received a lower amount than students that lived on their own. This was determined on basis of address registration of students. A public AI system was implemented to detect fraud with the grants. The algorithm made a first selection of potential fraudsters that was refined by five public servants of DUO. Based on this selection, external bureaus checked the suspicion by paying house visits. The decision that followed could be contested at DUO first and, if denied, students could challenge the decision in court.[81]

In the summer of 2023, the discriminatory working of the public AI systems surfaced. Lawyers were noticing that a high number of students accused of fraud had different ethnic backgrounds. Moreover, in court, most of these accusations were annulled. Although there were several flaws in the institutional design such as the illegitimacy of the house visits by external parties, the case mostly shows that the algorithm was biased and that this bias was not resolved by the human-in-the-loop—i.e., the public servants of DUO. DUO did not evaluate its system on bias.[82] It took quite some time and effort from lawyers and journalists to detect this system flaw. The DUO case shows the lack of system level correction by only detecting and correcting individual cases.

9.4.2 Expanding Perspectives on the Rule of Law

The problems discussed above show that the lexicon in the Rule of Law discipline falls short in examining socio-technical systems. This starts with the lack of a clear definition of what arbitrary conduct is.[83] The role of technical artifacts in arbitrary conduct is overlooked even more in currently available definitions. The lexicon emphasises institutions, mostly legal institutions, and the role of human conduct and social context. In that respect, the socio-legal perspective provides an important contribution by broadening the understanding of institutions. But for a full understanding of arbitrary conduct in public AI systems the role of the technical component also needs to be included in the Rule of Law lexicon.

Following from the deficiencies in the Rule of Law lexicon, the discipline lacks a methodology to detect where and analyse how public AI systems fall short in protecting citizens from harm. Again, in Rule of Law thought, analysis of arbitrary conduct focuses on what human behaviour counts as arbitrary use of power, how institutions are falling short to prevent or reduce such behaviour, and what institutions are needed to achieve that reduction. There is a need for an analytic approach that provides a comprehensive examination of opportunities for arbitrary conduct in public AI systems.

---

[81] Belleman B, Heilbron B, Kootstra A (2023) "Ik wil dat iemand zegt dat ik geen fraudeur ben". De discriminerende fraudecontroles van DUO. https://www.platform-investico.nl/onderzoeken/de-discriminerende-fraudecontroles-van-duo Accessed 16 February 2024.

[82] Ibid.

[83] Krygier 2016.

Similarly, Rule of Law thought provides too little grounding for the governance of public AI systems. Only intervening on the institutional level of public AI systems will fall short in addressing the role of the technical component in arbitrary conduct. As the technical component can play a dominant role in arbitrary conduct, there is a need for aligning technical and institutional design. Our approach will provide a first-of-its kind attempt towards bringing the design and use of public AI systems under the Rule of Law. We do this by complementing a socio-legal perspective on the Rule of Law by system safety.

9.4.3 System Safety

We argue that system safety can play a role addressing the three challenges of current Rule of Law approaches related to AI systems. System safety is a discipline that captures a long history of understanding harms and unsafe outcomes and, therefore, the protection of individuals.[84] The discipline initially arose in the aerospace and aviation domain and has since shaped safety standards and practices in various other sectors. Recently, lessons from system safety were resurfaced for common day AI applications and applied to a systematic study of algorithmic harms in the context of benefit allocation in The Netherlands.[85]

System safety goes beyond a technical perspective on systems. The discipline provides ways to address undesirable outcomes and harms of processes subject to forms of software-based automation. It treats such outcomes and harms as fundamentally 'emergent', which means that you can only understand these through considering social, technical and institutional components of the overall system, including the process of decision-making with its actual technological components, as well as the broader organization and institutional context. Similarly, the tools introduced by system safety address both the socio-technical specification of systems and the systems' working in practice. The discipline argues that technical as well as social and institutional interventions in the system are needed to ensure safety.

System safety does not impose safety as the main or only value that should be pursued. Instead, it provides a vocabulary and toolbox that serves as a system perspective for analysis and design to be used in different disciplines and domains. The lexicon and toolbox equip actors with a framework to map a particular system and to identify points of interventions in order to safeguard a selected value. This value does not necessarily have to be safety. In this chapter, we use the system safety perspective to strengthen values related to the Rule of Law—i.e., protecting citizens against arbitrary conduct. In other words, we are contextualising system safety by applying it to public AI systems and the Rule of Law.

Therefore, we bring the socio-legal perspective in conversation with the socio-technical perspective of system safety. The socio-legal perspective fits best because

[84] Leveson 2012.

[85] Dobbe 2022; Pel 2022.

of its broad understanding of institutions. The combination of these perspectives can enhance the approach towards arbitrary conduct in three ways: a more comprehensive lexicon, an analytical lens that also considers the technical component in arbitrary conduct, and a design approach for operationalizing Rule of Law principles that expands the current practice of institutional design from human conduct to including the form and function of AI applications in conduct. We will discuss these three ways in the next three sections.

9.5 Arbitrary Conduct from a System Perspective

System safety provides a lexicon to examine flaws in socio-technical systems that can lead to harms and other forms of damages or undesirable 'loss'. The lexicon hinges on the distinctive feature of system safety compared to traditional perspectives on safety as it focuses on hazardous system states instead of individual accidents. The lexicon pertains to system safety's socio-technical perspective that considers safety as an emergent property. This lexicon enables actors to investigate and communicate the internal working of systems that can lead to hazards and eventually to individual harms.

The lexicon is the starting point for the analysis and design efforts in system safety discussed in Sects. 9.6 and 9.7. In this section, we show that the lexicon can also provide useful insights for the Rule of Law into systemic issues in AI systems—i.e., we make the connection between system safety and the Rule of Law through the former's lexicon.

9.5.1 System Safety Lexicon

The main concept in system safety—*system hazard*—is defined as a 'system state or set of conditions that, together with a particular set of worst-case environmental conditions, will lead to an accident (loss).'[86] The system state here refers to a process in which a 'controller' makes decisions to arrive at outcomes that accomplish a certain objective and adhere to key (safety) constraints. This controller may be a human decision-maker, a group of human decision-makers, an automated decision-making entity, but can also be human decisions informed by or partly mediated by algorithms or information systems. The safety constraints determine what system behaviour is considered to be a hazard and, therefore, should be avoided through imposing these constraints.[87]

---

[86] Leveson 2012, p. 184.

[87] Leveson 2012.

Safety is considered to be a control problem in system safety. This means that safety constraints are enforced through control mechanisms. These control mechanisms play primarily at the *operational level*, meaning they form a key part of the actions and decisions that are available in the operational process in which the safety constraints need to be enacted. How a controller acts in the operational process is captured in a *process model*, which may be 'both embedded in the control logic of an automated controller or in the mental model maintained by a human controller.'[88]

Beyond the operational process are a variety of *secondary processes*, in which other control mechanisms may be needed to provide the right conditions for the enactment of safety procedures in operation. These processes are largely divided into system operations and system development. System operations includes the primary operational process, but also secondary processes such as operations management, company management, and other processes related to the operations of the main process including standard setting, oversight, insurance, courts, and legislation. System development includes maintenance, manufacturing, design, implementation, project management, innovation management, research, company management, and other processes related to the development of technologies used in the main process. It is thus understood and acknowledged that effective governance for safety requires control mechanisms and contributions from across these many processes and associated actors. The control mechanisms associated vary from audits to standards to work procedures, certification or legal penalties and much more. Each mechanism typically includes some *reference* that it is imposing on a process, which also requires a *measurement* to verify whether the reference is being met. All of the control mechanisms, both in the operational and secondary processes, that contribute to the enactment of safety, as well as the ways in which control mechanisms impose constraints on processes, are captured in a *safety control structure*.[89] Crucially, to ensure that the structural elements in system safety actually function, management and leadership are crucial, including the informal role of safety culture. This culture refers to the need to ensure that people critical in safeguarding a system feel safe themselves to raise possible safety issues, without the fear of being retaliated against or others suffering from it, and that active follow-up of raised issues is organized.[90]

Finally, it is fundamental to define safety as an *emergent system property*. This means that *unsafe situations* can only be understood through the interactions between system components, including technical, human and institutional aspects. The canonical example to explain this is the fact that a valve can never be safe on itself. It is only safe in relation to the plant in which it is used and given that a plant operator knows when and how to open or close it to ensure that the plant runs safely. The emergent nature of systems also means that systems need to adapt to changing conditions and new insights throughout their life cycle. In a system's life cycle things happen such as, changing environmental conditions, and users that assign new functions to institutions and technical artefact. These changes can have an effect on safety in a system

[88] Leveson 2012, p. 87.
[89] Leveson 2012.
[90] Dekker 2012.

that those responsible have to address. A process of feedback to system designers on system hazards and adaptation of control actions is needed to address such changes. In general, achieving safety in socio-technical systems is a learning process.[91]

9.5.2 Connection to Rule of Law

The lexicon of system safety can be used to discuss arbitrary conduct, in which an AI application is involved. The lexicon of system safety has commonalities with that of the Rule of Law. Both start from discussing the protection of individuals from harm. In this, they go back to the causes of such harms in either socio-legal or socio-technical systems. Still, system safety will help to reframe the concept of arbitrary conduct as it is explicitly expanded with the notions of the technical component.

We argue that the arbitrary use of power mediated by AI applications can also be considered an undesired emergent outcome. Part of the opportunities for arbitrary conduct only arise or materialise because of the interaction between system components. Especially over time, this can bring unexpected, unintended, or undesired situations of arbitrary conduct. Hence, we treat possibilities for arbitrary conduct as a subset of hazards with possible citizen harm or undesirable power imbalances as the resulting loss. This means that arbitrary conduct can be conceptualised as a system state, a set of environmental conditions, and control actions. Moreover, as for all socio-technical systems, public AI systems need feedback channels; especially for detecting arbitrary conduct that is ingrained in the system and correcting for it at the appropriate system level (be it technical, social, or institutional).

9.6 System Safety to Analyse Emergence of Arbitrary Conduct

System safety provides tools to analyse system hazards, where they emerge in current systems and what can go wrong in future systems. Considering arbitrary conduct as a system hazard, the analytical techniques of system safety can support in detecting possibilities for arbitrary conduct by tracking and tracing inadequate control mechanisms for arbitrary conduct. After detecting system hazards, system safety focuses on correcting the inadequate control mechanisms. This will be discussed in Sect. 9.7.

---

[91] Leveson 2012.

9.6.1 System Safety Analysis

Leveson suggests an analysis that focuses on two things: the controlled operational process (including process models) and the hierarchical safety control structure,[92] discussed in Sect. 9.5.1. Across these two, system safety analysis centres around the ex ante and ex post identification of *potential for inadequate control.* Inadequate control may happen at the level of actions in the operational process or at the level of institutional mechanisms in the safety control structure. Control mechanisms may either be (1) incorrect/unsafe, (2) not provided when necessary, (3) provided at the wrong time, or (4) applied too long or stopped too soon.[93] Each of such inadequacies may contribute to the system entering some unsafe state, violating a safety constraint. Analysis may start with the identification of inadequate control. It can also focus on a particular form of loss or harm, and try to understand what safety constraints are missing or how existing constraints were violated and what inadequacies in control actions and institutional mechanisms may contribute to it. Here, system safety both addresses direct causal scenarios but also *constitutive factors* (both organizational and systemic) that allow hazards to emerge in the operational process. Based on the analysis, concrete recommendations can be made to inform subsequent policy or system design efforts.[94]

9.6.2 Connection to Rule of Law

Mapping a public AI system through a system safety lens enables public organisations to detect potential for arbitrary conduct. The focus of this analysis is already defined in Rule of Law literature. Taekema suggests a 'focus on [the] locus of power and the opportunities for arbitrary conduct with adverse consequences for the interests of others.'[95]

The approach discussed in Sect. 9.6.1 support in tracing the three focus points suggested by Taekema: the locus of power, adverse consequences, and opportunities for arbitrary conduct. First, the system is mapped to determine the locus of power. The socio-technical specifications and practices in public AI systems are mapped by using the safety control structure, process models, and safety constraints. The safety control structure will also bring into view the design and maintenance processes needed to build and govern the technical artefacts. Analysts should consider at least four dimension in the case of public AI systems: (1) does the system comprise one or more processes?; (2) if there are more processes, what processes include an AI application?; (3) where in the system specification, system instantiation or human behaviour are possibilities for arbitrariness situated?; and (4) if these possibilities

[92] Leveson 2012.

[93] Ibid.

[94] Ibid.

[95] Taekema 2021, p. 90.

are emerging from human behaviour, what is the influence of design choices or the output of the system? Together, these dimensions will help identify the relevant loci of power in arbitrary conduct. Second, adverse consequences and opportunities for arbitrary conduct are identified by examining inadequate control actions and their causes.

9.7 Addressing Arbitrary Conduct Through System Safety

Possibilities for arbitrary conduct in public AI systems need to be prevented, mitigated, or corrected. System safety provides safety-guided design approaches to iteratively design required interventions into AI applications and the processes where these are used in. After detecting possible arbitrariness, the socio-technical specification and AI practices can be (re)designed following insights and methods from system safety. In the spirit of convention, this could inform 'Rule-of-Law'-Guided Design approaches currently emerging. In this section, we discuss the basic steps involved in such efforts.

9.7.1 System Safety as Design Approach

Once key hazards and their constitutive factors are in view through an *ex ante* or *ex post* analysis, these can be addressed through safety-guided design, which considers measures that are either technical, social, or institutional, or determine how these should interact. Once a new design is determined, additional hazard analysis can be done to determine whether the hazard and its constitutive factors have been addressed and no new hazards have emerged, hence the iterative nature.

In addressing hazards, the involved designers should follow a three-staged strategy.[96] First, they should see if the hazard can be fully eliminated, which means that the associated situation cannot happen anymore. Second, if elimination is not feasible or leads to disproportionate trade-offs, a next strategy is to reduce the likelihood of the hazard occurring, through installing new control mechanisms. Control mechanisms can either be *passive or active*. Passive controls provide safety constraints through their presence (e.g. a guard rail between a road and an adjacent abyss) and active controls need to be enacted through a safety mechanism that relies on taking control actions (e.g. a lane-keeping function to steer a car away veering into the abyss). The active control may be more functional, but also brings new vulnerabilities and hazards (e.g. the lane-keeping function may not work in certain weather conditions), which is why passive controls are often preferred (a guard rail works regardless of the weather). Third, if controls are not feasible or foolproof, designers should try to minimize the damage in the event a hazard leads to an accident. Efforts

[96] Leveson 2012.

could include ways to dampen the impact (e.g. crumple zones and airbags) or to provide the operator or surrounding actors ways to minimize damage (e.g. providing an emergency hammer to leave a submerged car).

Once the various measures are designed and tested, one can draw up a *gap analysis*, which provides insight into what is needed to go from the current to the desired situation. Many different aspects may come into view, including the impact on production, use and maintenance of the system, the need for regulatory backing, the economic investments needed, and the desired level of knowledge and capability for those using, otherwise interacting with, or governing the system. Clearly, various trade-offs and political choices may emerge in this process, which allow decision-makers to properly gauge responsibilities and efforts to realize or transition towards the desired system configuration.

9.7.2 Connection to Rule of Law

The above-mentioned insights help to identify and design measures that should support the legal institutions of the Rule of Law, in contexts where AI is used in public administration processes. The socio-legal perspective prescribes two steps in arriving at measures:[97] (1) determine the immanent goal of the Rule of Law—i.e., reducing or addressing arbitrary use of power, and (2) design and implement measures that advance that immanent goal or purpose—adapted to the applicable context.[98] The first step we already covered in Sect. 9.6. The design approach of system safety helps to determine what interventions need to be designed.

In this design step, designers can also get inspiration from the classic perspective on legal institutions to address system hazards. Concerning designing hazards *out* of the system, the formal perspective on the Rule of Law can help. It lists formal requirements for rules that also apply to AI applications.[99] In this way, the formal requirements are grounded quality measurements for AI applications. The procedural perspective on the Rule of Law can provide ideas for institutional mechanisms that comprise the safety control structure. If an AI application is hazardous, its institutional environment needs meaningful recourse procedures and feedback mechanisms that citizens can instigate. A safety-guided approach to designing these necessarily includes ways to validate the efficacy of the control mechanism, both in terms of the *reference* it places as well as on the information or *measurement* that is taken to verify whether the reference is met. Crucially, these procedures and feedback mechanisms should provide the possibility to assign a public AI system back to its design mode. For example, front workers should have the room to question the output of an AI application, and have it be changed if the output or the logic through which it is produced has significant flaws or does not meet the needs of the context. Not being

[97] Krygier 2009.

[98] Selznick 1999.

[99] Brownsword 2016.

able to adjust the technical workings of the AI system often means that the issue persists, and worse, that servants lose discretion and citizens their ability to contest, being more prone to be dependent on post-hoc legal protection, if available at all.

9.8 Conclusions

As they are intervening in the relationship between citizen and state, public AI systems and their design processes fall under the Rule of Law regime. AI systems can mediate arbitrary conduct and their socio-technical nature requires adapted approaches towards translating the Rule of Law to AI practices. We argue that this can be done by combining the socio-legal perspective on the Rule of Law with a system safety perspective on AI systems. This synthesis implies that the analytical lens of system safety can support the detection of possibilities for arbitrariness in public AI systems. Moreover, it can support the translation of Rule of Law principles to the socio-technical specification of public AI systems and their associated design and use practices. Applying this combined perspective will not be straightforward. The influence of AI practices on public administration is still highly uncertain, the capacities of public organisation are premature, and these practices cross conventional boundaries and are highly contextual. Nevertheless, the altering of power dynamics in public administration by AI practices urges for protection of citizens against arbitrary use of power by the state mediated by public AI systems.

References

Alkhatib A (2021) To Live in Their Utopia: Why Algorithmic Systems Create Absurd Outcomes. Proceedings of the 2021 CHI Conference on Human Factors in Computing Systems. CHI '21: CHI Conference on Human Factors in Computing Systems https://doi.org/10.1145/3411764.3445740

Alkhatib A, Bernstein M (2019) Street-Level Algorithms: A Theory at the Gaps Between Policy and Decisions. Proceedings of the 2019 CHI Conference on Human Factors in Computing Systems. CHI '19: CHI Conference on Human Factors in Computing Systems https://doi.org/10.1145/3290605.3300760

Barocas S, Selbst AD (2016) Big Data's Disparate Impact. California Law Review. https://doi.org/10.15779/Z38BG31

Bayamlıoğlu E, Leenes R (2018) 'The "rule of law" implications of data-driven decision-making: a techno-regulatory perspective. Law, Innovation and Technology https://doi.org/10.1080/17579961.2018.1527475

Bovens M, Zouridis S (2002) From Street-Level to System-Level Bureaucracies: How Information and Communication Technology is Transforming Administrative Discretion and Constitutional Control. Public Administration Review https://doi.org/10.1111/0033-3352.00168

Braithwaite V (2020) Beyond the bubble that is Robodebt: How governments that lose integrity threaten democracy. Australian Journal of Social Issues https://doi.org/10.1002/ajs4.122

Brownsword R (2016) Technological management and the Rule of Law. Law, Innovation and Technology https://doi.org/10.1080/17579961.2016.1161891

Burrell J (2016) How the machine "thinks": Understanding opacity in machine learning algorithms. Big Data & Society https://doi.org/10.1177/2053951715622512

Chiao V (2023) Algorithmic Decision-Making, Statistical Evidence and the Rule of Law. Episteme https://doi.org/10.1017/epi.2023.27

Cobbe J, Veale M, Singh J (2023) Understanding accountability in algorithmic supply chains. 2023 ACM Conference on Fairness, Accountability, and Transparency. FAccT '23: the 2023 ACM Conference on Fairness, Accountability, and Transparency https://doi.org/10.1145/3593013.3594073.

Cuéllar M, Huq AZ (2022) Artificially Intelligent Regulation. Daedalus https://doi.org/10.1162/DAED_a_01920

De Bruijn H, Herder PM (2009) System and Actor Perspectives on Sociotechnical Systems. IEEE Transactions on Systems, Man, and Cybernetics - Part A: Systems and Humans https://doi.org/10.1109/TSMCA.2009.2025452

De Bruijn H, Warnier M, Janssen M (2022) The perils and pitfalls of explainable AI: Strategies for explaining algorithmic decision-making. Government Information Quarterly https://doi.org/10.1016/j.giq.2021.101666

Dekker S (2012) Just culture: balancing safety and accountability, 2nd edn. Ashgate, Aldershot

Dobbe R, Dean S, Gilbert T, Kohli N (2018) A Broader View on Bias in Automated Decision-Making: Reflecting on Epistemology and Dynamics. http://arxiv.org/abs/1807.00553. Accessed 16 February 2024

Dobbe R, Krendl Gilbert T, Mintz Y (2021) Hard choices in artificial intelligence. Artificial Intelligence https://doi.org/10.1016/j.artint.2021.103555

Dobbe RIJ (2022) System Safety and Artificial Intelligence. The Oxford Handbook of AI Governance https://doi.org/10.1093/oxfordhb/9780197579329.013.67.

Endicott T, Yeung K (2022) The death of law? Computationally personalized norms and the rule of law. University of Toronto Law Journal https://doi.org/10.3138/utlj-2021-0011.

Fountain JE (2001) Building the virtual state: information technology and institutional change. Brookings Institution Press, Washington D.C.

Giddens A (1976) New Rules of Sociological Method. Basic Books, New York

Giddens A (1979) Central Problems in Social Theory: Action, Structure and Contradiction in Social Analysis. University of California Press, Berkeley

Giddens A (1984) The Constitution of Society: Outline of the Theory of Structure. University of California Press, Berkeley

Green B (2022) The flaws of policies requiring human oversight of government algorithms. Computer Law & Security Review https://doi.org/10.1016/j.clsr.2022.105681

Green B, Chen Y (2019) Disparate Interactions: An Algorithm-in-the-Loop Analysis of Fairness in Risk Assessments. Proceedings of the Conference on Fairness, Accountability, and Transparency. FAT* '19: Conference on Fairness, Accountability, and Transparency https://doi.org/10.1145/3287560.3287563.

Greenstein S (2022) Preserving the rule of law in the era of artificial intelligence (AI). Artificial Intelligence and Law https://doi.org/10.1007/s10506-021-09294-4

Grimmelikhuijsen S, Meijer A (2022) Legitimacy of Algorithmic Decision-Making: Six Threats and the Need for a Calibrated Institutional Response. Perspectives on Public Management and Governance https://doi.org/10.1093/ppmgov/gvac008.

Hildebrandt M (2011) Legal Protection by Design: Objections and Refutations. Legisprudence https://doi.org/10.5235/175214611797885693.

Hildebrandt M (2016) Law as Information in the Era of Data-Driven Agency. The Modern Law Review https://doi.org/10.1111/1468-2230.12165.

Hildebrandt M (2018) Algorithmic regulation and the rule of law. Philosophical Transactions of the Royal Society A: Mathematical, Physical and Engineering Sciences https://doi.org/10.1098/rsta.2017.0355.

Hildebrandt M (2019) Privacy as Protection of the Incomputable Self: From Agnostic to Agonistic Machine Learning. Theoretical Inquiries in Law https://doi.org/10.1515/til-2019-0004.

Hodgson GH (2006) What are institutions? Journal of Economic Issues https://doi.org/10.1080/00213624.2006.11506879
Janssen M, Kuk G (2016) The challenges and limits of big data algorithms in technocratic governance. Government Information Quarterly https://doi.org/10.1016/j.giq.2016.08.011
König PD, Wenzelburger G (2021) The legitimacy gap of algorithmic decision-making in the public sector: Why it arises and how to address it. Technology in Society https://doi.org/10.1016/j.techsoc.2021.101688
Koppenjan J, Groenewegen J (2005) Institutional design for complex technological systems. International Journal of Technology, Policy and Management https://doi.org/10.1504/IJTPM.2005.008406
Krygier M (2009) The Rule of Law: Legality, Teleology, Sociology. Relocating the Rule of Law https://doi.org/10.5040/9781472564634
Krygier M (2014) Rule of Law (and Rechtsstaat). The Legal Doctrines of the Rule of Law and the Legal State (Rechtsstaat) https://doi.org/10.1007/978-3-319-05585-5_4
Krygier M (2016) The Rule of Law: Pasts, Presents, and Two Possible Futures. Annual Review of Law and Social Science https://doi.org/10.1146/annurev-lawsocsci-102612-134103
Kunneke R, Ménard C, Groenewegen J (2021) Network Infrastructures: Technology meets Institutions. Cambridge University Press
Leveson NG (2012) Engineering a Safer World: Systems Thinking Applied to Safety. The MIT Press
Mak E, Taekema S (2016) The European Union's Rule of Law Agenda: Identifying Its Core and Contextualizing Its Application. Hague Journal on the Rule of Law https://doi.org/10.1007/s40803-016-0022-1
Mulligan DK, Bamberger KA (2019) Procurement as Policy: Administrative Process for Machine Learning'. https://doi.org/10.15779/Z38RN30793
Nissenbaum H (2019) Contextual Integrity Up and Down the Data Food Chain. Theoretical Inquiries in Law https://doi.org/10.1515/til-2019-0008
Nonet P, Selznick P (2001) Law & society in transition: toward responsive law. Transaction Publishers, New Brunswick, N.J.
Orlikowski WJ (1992) The Duality of Technology: Rethinking the Concept of Technology in Organizations. Organization Science https://doi.org/10.1287/orsc.3.3.398
Passchier R (2020) Digitalisering en de (dis)balans binnen de trias politica [Digitalisation and the (dis)balance within the trias politica]. Ars Aequi 69(10): 916–927
Peeters R, Widlak A (2018) The digital cage: Administrative exclusion through information architecture – The case of the Dutch civil registry's master data management system. Government Information Quarterly https://doi.org/10.1016/j.giq.2018.02.003
Peeters R, Widlak AC (2023) Administrative exclusion in the infrastructure-level bureaucracy: The case of the Dutch daycare benefit scandal. Public Administration Review https://doi.org/10.1111/puar.13615
Pel L (2022) Ripple Effects of Law Execution Automation in Governmental Systems: The Wajong Case. Delft University http://resolver.tudelft.nl/uuid:64271d5f-b3b3-4951-ba13-4c6c9435d9ec. Accessed 16 February 2024
Raz J (1979) The Rule of Law and its Virtue. The authority of law: Essays on law and morality https://doi.org/10.1093/acprof:oso/9780198253457.003.0011
Santoni De Sio F, Mecacci G (2021) Four Responsibility Gaps with Artificial Intelligence: Why they Matter and How to Address them. Philosophy & Technology https://doi.org/10.1007/s13347-021-00450-x
Sculley D, Holt G, Golovin D, Davydov E, Phillips T, Ebner D, Chaudhary V, Young M, Crespo J, Dennison D (2015) Hidden Technical Debt in Machine Learning Systems. NIPS https://doi.org/10.5555/2969442.2969519
Seaver N (2017) Algorithms as culture: Some tactics for the ethnography of algorithmic systems. Big Data & Society https://doi.org/10.1177/2053951717738104

Selznick P (1999) Legal Cultures and the Rule of Law. The Rule of Law after Communism: Problems and Prospects in East-Central Europe https://doi.org/10.4324/9781315085319

Selznick P (2003) "Law in Context" Revisited. Journal of Law and Society https://doi.org/10.1111/1467-6478.00252

Taekema S (2021) Commitment to the Rule of Law: From a Political to an Organizational Ideal. Ethical Leadership in International Organizations https://doi.org/10.1017/9781108641715.003

Veale M, Brass I (2019) Administration by Algorithm?: Public Management Meets Public Sector Machine Learning. Algorithmic Regulation https://doi.org/10.1093/oso/9780198838494.003.0006

Waldron J (2011) The rule of law and the importance of procedure. Getting to the Rule of Law https://doi.org/10.18574/nyu/9780814728437.003.0001

Whittaker, M. *et al.* (2018) AI Now Report 2018. AI Now Institute.

Whittaker M (2021) The steep cost of capture. Interactions https://doi.org/10.1145/3488666

Widder DG, Nafus D (2023) Dislocated accountabilities in the "AI supply chain": Modularity and developers' notions of responsibility. Big Data & Society https://doi.org/10.1177/20539517231177620

Widlak A, Peeters R (2020) Administrative errors and the burden of correction and consequence: how information technology exacerbates the consequences of bureaucratic mistakes for citizens. International Journal of Electronic Governance https://doi.org/10.1504/IJEG.2020.106998

Yeung K (2014) Design for the Value of Regulation. Handbook of Ethics, Values, and Technological Design https://doi.org/10.1007/978-94-007-6994-6_32-1

Yeung K (2018) Algorithmic regulation: A critical interrogation. Regulation & Governance https://doi.org/10.1111/rego.12158

Young MM, Himmelreich J, Bullock JB, Kim, K (2021) Artificial Intelligence and Administrative Evil. Perspectives on Public Management and Governance https://doi.org/10.1093/ppmgov/gvab006

Zalnieriute M, Moses LB, Williams G (2019) The Rule of Law and Automation of Government Decision-Making. The Modern Law Review https://doi.org/10.1111/1468-2230.12412

Zouridis S, Van Eck M, Bovens M (2020) Automated Discretion. Discretion and the Quest for Controlled Freedom https://doi.org/10.1007/978-3-030-19566-3_20.

Sem Nouws is a PhD candidate at the Faculty of Technology, Policy, and Management of Delft University of Technology. His research focuses on the design process of algorithmic and AI systems used in public administration. Sem holds a master degree in Complex Systems Engineering and Management from the TU Delft, and obtained a Bachelor in Law at the Erasmus University.

Roel Dobbe is an Assistant Professor in Technology, Policy & Management at Delft University of Technology focusing on Sociotechnical AI Systems. He received a MSc in Systems & Control from Delft (2010) and a PhD in Electrical Engineering and Computer Sciences from UC Berkeley (2018), where he received the Demetri Angelakos Memorial Achievement Award. He was an inaugural postdoc at the AI Now Institute and New York University. His research addresses the integration and implications of algorithmic technologies in societal infrastructure and democratic institutions, focusing on issues related to safety, sustainability and justice. His projects are situated in various domains, including energy systems, public administration, and healthcare. Roel's sociotechnical and system-theoretic lens enables addressing the sociotechnical and political nature of algorithmic and artificial intelligence systems across analysis, engineering design and governance, with an aim to empower domain experts and affected communities. His results have informed various policy initiatives, including environmental assessments in the European AI Act as well as the development of the algorithm watchdog in The Netherlands.

Chapter 10
Towards Formalising AI Readiness of Standards

Anna Schmitz, Rebekka Görge, Elena Haedecke, Marion Borowski, Adrian Seeliger, and Maximilian Poretschkin

Contents

Abstract Standards and specifications (henceforth standards) greatly simplify our everyday lives and the economy in many areas. By establishing quality benchmarks and promoting interoperability, they form a key pillar for international trade and

Anna Schmitz, Rebekka Görge and Elena Haedecke: Equal contribution.

A. Schmitz (✉)
Fraunhofer-Institut für Intelligente Analyse- und Informationssysteme IAIS, Schloss Birlinghoven, 53757 Sankt Augustin, Germany
e-mail: anna.schmitz@iais.fraunhofer.de

R. Görge · E. Haedecke · M. Borowski · M. Poretschkin
Fraunhofer-Institut für Intelligente Analyse- und Informationssysteme IAIS, Sankt Augustin, Germany
e-mail: rebekka.goerge@iais.fraunhofer.de

E. Haedecke
e-mail: elena.haedecke@iais.fraunhofer.de

M. Borowski
e-mail: marion.borowski@iais.fraunhofer.de

M. Poretschkin
e-mail: maximilian.poretschkin@iais.fraunhofer.de

A. Seeliger
Deutsches Institut für Normung e. V. (DIN), Berlin, Germany
e-mail: adrian.seeliger@din.de

K. Prifti et al. (eds.), *Digital Governance*, Information Technology and Law Series 39,
https://doi.org/10.1007/978-94-6265-639-0_10

competition. As artificial intelligence (AI) emerges as one of the key technologies of the future, two fundamental questions arise regarding standards: (i) What new standards must be developed specifically for AI? (ii) What modifications to existing standards are necessary to fully leverage the potential of AI? The first question is being addressed actively through a variety of standardisation activities and analyses of the status quo. However, much of the second question remains unanswered. Although the problem is discussed in the literature, there is a lack of both a definition of AI readiness and a systematic analysis of the existing body of standards. This chapter, which originates in the project 'AI Readiness of Standards', aims to close this gap. Due to the complexity of the topic, we shall start by focusing on the German body of standards. Nonetheless, we believe our findings and proposals are extrapolatable to other, related contexts. This chapter represents the findings of the abovementioned project: presenting a conceptual definition of AI readiness and, a validated systematic approach for classifying whether an existing standard is AI ready. The procedure outlined here also serves as the foundation for an automated Natural Language Processing (NLP) analysis of the entire German body of standards regarding AI readiness.

Keywords Artificial Intelligence · Standards · AI readiness · Regulation · Flowchart · Document classification · Expert knowledge

10.1 Introduction

AI is becoming increasingly pervasive, both in areas of daily life and in industrial applications. Well-known examples include predictive maintenance, support for medical diagnoses and highly automated driving.[1] As with any other technology, standards form the basis for the successful integration of AI into existing and new production processes and applications. Especially, standards ensure the interoperability of different systems and their subcomponents. Further, standards formulate quality requirements that serve as a basis for the use of various technologies, such as AI. Against the background of complex and international value chains in the field of AI,[2] standards represent a key success factor for the economically productive implementation of many promising AI use cases.

Over the past few years, there has been significant discussion around standards for AI. In addition to interoperability, trustworthiness is a crucial factor driving the formulation of quality criteria and their verifiability.[3] Given the diverse use cases of AI systems, trustworthiness encompasses a wide range of requirements such as fairness, autonomy and control, transparency, traceability, explainability, accuracy, robustness, safety, security, and data protection, which have varying degrees

[1] See Çınar et al. 2020; Görge et al. 2023; Haedecke et al. 2022.

[2] Cho 2023.

[3] Schmitz et al. 2022. See also Smuha 2021; Thiebes et al. 2021.

of impact depending on the application context.[4] The European Union's AI Act (AIA) is the world's first regulation for AI and refers to the New Legislative Framework.[5] This implies that important details of the regulation are specified by so-called harmonised standards, which need to be developed in addition to the law.[6] The European Commission has issued several standardisation requests to the European Committee for Standardisation (CEN) and the European Committee for Electrotechnical Standardisation (CENELEC) to initiate the development of such standards (e.g. on human oversight, robustness, and risk management for AI systems).[7] The German standardisation roadmap provides a good overview of the current AI standardisation landscape,[8] alongside the recently published update,[9] which uncovers gaps and the further need for AI standardisation.

In addition to standards that are formulated explicitly for AI systems, there is a second important perspective regarding AI and standardisation which has not yet been investigated to such an extent: the interaction of the whole existing body of standards with the use of AI. The existing body of standards refers to all standards adopted by a national or international standardisation organisation.[10] Standards touch upon almost every aspect of daily life and cover a broad range of domains reaching from manufacturing, production, and transportation, covering innovative technologies, to the public sector. Specifically, this perspective asks whether existing standards prevent or hamper the use of AI, for example, because they explicitly exclude the use of AI or because they stipulate conditions that make the use of AI more difficult. Prominent examples include the explicit mentioning of several (manual) testing processes, e.g. in railroad maintenance standards, or unclear requirements for the use of AI in safety standards.[11] At the same time, it is essential that standards do not fail to safeguard the quality of (technical) systems, e.g. by omitting specific risks or requirements of novel technologies and frameworks.

Since it is not possible to tell a priori which existing standards are not yet 'AI ready', this perspective is just as important as the creation of new standards that are currently lacking. In addition, the alignment of standards with each other, as well as with values of trustworthiness, needs to be ensured.[12] For this reason, the German Federal Ministry for Economic Affairs and Climate Action (BMWK) commissioned the project 'AI Readiness of Standards' (German: 'KI-Tauglichkeit von Normen') which deals with the German body of standards (about 30,000 standards).

This chapter takes precisely this second perspective and formalises the term 'AI readiness'. To this end, we conducted a literature review of related work (Sect. 10.2)

---

[4] European Commission 2019. See also Poretschkin et al. 2023.

[5] European Parliament and Council 2024.

[6] European Parliament and Council 2012.

[7] European Commission 2022.

[8] DIN e.V. and DKE 2020.

[9] DIN e.V. and DKE 2022.

[10] DIN EN 45020:2007-03.

[11] DIN e.V. and DKE 2020. See also Tarrisse and Masse 2021.

[12] Kop 2021. See also German Federal Ministry of Education and Research 2018.

and relevant prior work and conceptually evaluated these. Moreover, we iteratively developed and validated our hypotheses and insights on the formalisation of AI readiness using empirical methods. This included analysing samples of standards from different domains, consulting standardisation experts and classifying standards together with them. Based on the structured evaluation of the empirical findings, we firstly defined different AI readiness levels (Sect. 10.3) and secondly developed a systematic approach to classify any existing standard of the German body of standards as AI ready or not (Sect. 10.4). Below, we explain how we validated our approach and present concrete examples. The results of this work set the basis for an automated AI readiness classification of standards using NLP methods, that is currently being developed within the project 'AI Readiness of Standards' (see Sect. 10.5).

10.2 Related Work

In our literature research, we have only identified few works that are related to the classification of standards in terms of their need for adaptation, or on the other hand, their 'fitness' to AI-related requirements. While the question of AI readiness has been discussed in the literature, it was so far investigated only in contexts other than standardisation, as explained below. In addition, there exist contributions on classification schemes of standards with regard to general issues unrelated to AI, as well as analyses concerning the adaptation needs of standards in various contexts. In the following, we review this relevant work which has proven to be beneficial for our own research.

Given the large number of standards published to date, grouping them into distinct classes can be useful both for standardisation stakeholders and researchers (e.g. to investigate the economic effects or innovation-friendliness of standards).[13] There are several scientific works that highlight various characteristics (e.g. subject matter, degree of obligation)[14] and functions of standards (e.g. to define minimum quality requirements, to ensure compatibility)[15] on which such a classification can be based. A description of standard types can also be found within standardisation itself.[16]

We identified two works that analyse the adaptation needs of standards due to certain, AI-independent changes. The first, by Kind et al., analyses existing standards for adaptation needs with regard to the consequences of climate change.[17] The motivation for these adaptation needs is, similarly to the notion of AI readiness, to ensure that standards offer the highest possible quality, safety, and resilience in the long term (even in view of climate change). The study suggests several criteria to identify standards for which adaptations might be of particular interest (e.g. changing

[13] Egyedi and Ortt 2017.

[14] Vries 2006.

[15] Egyedi and Ortt 2017.

[16] DIN 820-3:2021-02. See also DIN EN 45020:2007-03.

[17] Kind et al. 2021.

the standard involves little effort, additional costs incurred in practice are low, the standard affects long-term structures or developments). The analysis is performed in two steps. First, based on a keyword-search and human review of title and abstract of the search results, standards are identified whose subject matter is generally affected by climate change issues. Second, for those standards identified as relevant, experts analyse the full text and evaluate its adaptation need. While this evaluation is not further formalised or reasoned, Kind et al. describe conceptually similar challenges to those we are encountering in assessing AI readiness (e.g. at what point a standard sufficiently takes account of climate change, and to what extent specific reference can or should be made at all, given the uncertainties about the effects of climate change). The second work, by the DIN Standards Committee Ergonomics, evaluates the standardisation landscape of the ergonomics of work and product design in terms of its readiness for industry 4.0.[18] The Committee found shortfalls and contradictions in 75% of the 150 normative documents that were analysed, following a detailed approach which gives insights into the perspective of standardisation experts.

Regarding AI related adaptation needs, Becker et al. analyse the standardisation landscape of industrial automation and human resource management with a focus on AI systems, safety, and testing in the German and European market.[19] They show that standards can be organised in different hierarchies and series to evaluate whether the topic of AI is covered sufficiently, especially regarding the EU proposal for a regulation on machinery.[20] Overall, they conclude that current standards (except for those under development) do not provide sufficient guidance for a safe and non-discriminating use of AI in the targeted use cases. Another project that specifically considers AI related standards is 'AI Standardisation Landscape'.[21] It assesses the suitability of existing standards to implement the requirements for high-risk AI systems proposed in the European Commissions draft AIA. First, a general set of potentially 'AI relevant' ISO/IEC standards is identified which includes 'both standards that directly address AI-specific issues and standards that are more tangentially related to AI, such as [...] standards on Big Data'.[22] Next, NLP techniques are used in combination with human evaluation for a 'less subjective' assessment. In addition, the updated version of the AI Standardisation Landscape presents an analysis of the content of relevant IEEE standards.[23] Here, a questionnaire is used as common protocol for the assessment which addresses the standards coverage of the AIA requirements, for example, and is completed by two experts respectively to account for different judgements.

[18] DIN Standards Committee Ergonomics 2020.

[19] Becker et al. 2021.

[20] European Parliament and Council 2023.

[21] Nativi and De Nigris 2021. See also Soler Garrido et al. 2023.

[22] Nativi and De Nigris 2021.

[23] Soler Garrido et al. 2023.

Lastly, the concept of AI readiness has also been investigated in other contexts, for example, with respect to organisations and education.[24] While research on the formalisation and evaluation of AI readiness is still in an early stage, these works provide valuable input for the assessment of standards. Closely related aspects of organisations AI readiness are, for example, how standards can support successful AI adoption, and at what point AI use cases are of such practical relevance to organisations that they should be addressed by standards.

10.3 Approach of Formalising AI Readiness

As defined in DIN EN 45020:2007-03, standardisation is the 'activity of establishing, with regard to actual or potential problems, provisions for common and repeated use [...]'. In this way, normative documents follow acknowledged rules of technology, reflecting the state of the art and ensuring, among other things, fitness for purpose, compatibility, and safety of products, processes, or services. As AI is a state-of-the art technique for a multitude of tasks, it must be ensured that existing standards, which are likely to have been developed years ago, are 'ready' for the use of AI. This implies that standards across various sectors should not hinder innovation through restricting (unjustifiably or even unintentionally) the use of AI. On the other hand, it is essential that standards do not fail to safeguard the quality of (technical) systems, e.g. by omitting specific risks or requirements of novel technologies and frameworks. While the concept of AI readiness is already in play in various contexts (e.g. organisations and education as mentioned above), a formal definition of the term is still missing. To assess a standard in this regard as effectively, objectively, and automatically as possible, it is essential to establish a more formal conception of AI readiness that applies across a wide range of standards from various sectors.

Our approach follows a three-step process: As the definition of 'AI readiness' depends on a common understanding of AI itself, we started by choosing an appropriate definition of AI. Next, we needed to identify all standards that might be related to the application of AI. We call those standards 'AI relevant' and describe the respective subset of standards by defining the term 'AI relevance'. Finally, we defined the term 'AI readiness' for the set of AI relevant standards. It bears mentioning that this corresponds to the need described in the German AI Strategy for '[s]tandards and specifications that are relevant for the application of AI [...]' to be identified and ultimately supplemented with AI specifics.[25]

Various researchers, governments, and institutions have presented definitions of the term 'Artificial Intelligence', which differ, among other things, in the scope of functionalities and technologies or in the extent to which the association with

---

[24] Alsheibani 2018. See also Joehnk et al. 2021 and Luckin et al. 2022.

[25] DIN e.V. and DKE 2020.

Table 10.1 Adopted AI definitions of ISO/IEC and OECD. (*Source*: Own figure)

Reference	AI definition
ISO/IEC 22989:2022	'Engineered system that generates outputs such as content, forecasts, recommendations or decisions for a given set of human-defined objectives. [...] The engineered system can use various techniques and approaches related to artificial intelligence to develop a model to represent data, knowledge, processes, etc. which can be used to conduct tasks. [...] AI systems are designed to operate with varying levels of automation'.
OECD 2022	'An AI system is a machine-based system that can, for a given set of human defined objectives, make predictions, recommendations, or decisions influencing real or virtual environments. AI systems are designed to operate with varying levels of autonomy'.

human intelligence is established.[26] As it is likely that the AI definition of ISO/IEC 22989:2022 is one of the most widely accepted (among the existing definitions), and numerous updated and upcoming normative documents will refer to this, as the first step we adopted this definition as the foundation to further formalise AI readiness. As proposed in ISO/IEC 22989:2022, we supplemented it using the OECD definition (see Table 10.1). [27]

In the second step, we mapped the results of internal preliminary works of DIN e. V. regarding the understanding of the term 'AI relevance' to existing concepts that further describe the functioning and scope of an AI system (see Table 10.2). By additionally validating our preliminary work on a sample selection of standards from different standardisation categories (e.g. product, terminology and process standards) and by considering an exemplary overview of nearly 40 standards with relevance to AI,[28] we identified four criteria with which to classify a standard as not AI relevant (see Table 10.3).

In the third step, which covers the definition of 'AI readiness' for the set of AI relevant standards, we examined a sample selection of more than 20 standards from different domains to determine whether adaptations are necessary for the standard to be suitable for the use of AI. Furthermore, we attempted to find patterns in how to categorise these adaptations. For comparison, we evaluated the standards of ISO/IEC JTC 1/SC 42 (Committee on Artificial Intelligence), where we can assume AI readiness according to standardisation experts. Based on these evaluations and the different motivations for adapting standards as described above, we found several conditions that ensure, when in combination, the AI readiness of a standard. Based on discussions

[26] See Russell and Norvig 2016. See also European Parliament and Council 2024 and European Commission 2019.

[27] It should be noted that after completion of our approach, the OECD has updated their AI definition in November 2023 to reflect technological developments with respect to generative AI (see also https://oecd.ai/en/wonk/ai-system-definition-update, Accessed 25 February 2024).

[28] DIN e.V. and DKE 2020.

Table 10.2 Preliminary works regarding the term 'AI relevance' —three pertinent aspects. (Existing concepts are mapped from *Sources*: Poretschkin et al. 2023 and DIN e.V. and DKE 2020)

1	2	3
Basic topics (Terminology, data, etc.) Horizontal topics (Quality, certification, etc.) Application areas (Industrial automation, etc.) A document whose content impacts the scope, functioning, or agency of an AI system.	Design Development Data AI Component Embedding Operation A document whose content impacts one or several phases of the AI lifecycle.	Capabilities Perception: Sensor data processing, interpretation... Under-standing: Decisions, predictions... Action: (Software) robotics ... Commu-nication: NLP, Human-machine interaction ... A document that contains at least one process step that can be improved or performed more efficiently with the use of AI.

Table 10.3 Definition, examples, and counterexamples of not AI relevant standards. (*Source*: Own table)

Not AI relevant	
Definition	A standard is not AI relevant, if it meets each of the following conditions:
	1. The standard has no impact on the life cycle of an AI system.
	2. It does not describe horizontal topics affecting the operation or scope of action of an AI system.
	3. The use of AI does not introduce any new requirements or risks that would arise for the content or application areas described in the standard.
	4. It does not describe any task or process step, that can currently be performed (or supported) by an AI system with added value compared to conventional methods.
	If any of the conditions do not apply, the standard is considered AI relevant.
Example	✓ DIN EN ISO 216:2007-12
Counterexamples for each condition	Condition 1. DIN 92419:2020-01
	Condition 2. ISO/IEC TR 29119-11:2020
	Condition 3. DIN 31051:2019-06
	Condition 4. DIN ISO 31000:2018-10

and refinement of these conditions in five iterative workshops with ten standardisation experts from five domains (DIN Standards Committee Ergonomics, DIN Standards Committee Mechanical Engineering, DIN Standards Committee Information Technology and selected IT Applications, DIN Standards Committee Road Vehicle Engineering, DIN Standards Committee Aerospace), we formalised the concept of AI readiness as shown in Table 10.4.

Table 10.4 Definition of AI readiness. (*Source*: Own table)

AI ready	
Definition	A standard is considered AI ready, if it is AI relevant and meets each of the following conditions:
	1. The standard does not advise against the use of AI, and it does not relate to application domains or systems which are subject to AI specific legal regulation restricting the use of AI.
	2. Conformity with the standard ensures that an AI based system is safeguarded in accordance with the purpose of the standard.
	3. If AI is used as technical system to accomplish/support a task or safeguarding process described in the standard, the assurance/safeguard provided by the standard is maintained.
	4. The use of AI or requirements or necessary measures resulting from this are sufficiently specified according to the overall level of detail of the standard (such as through reference to horizontal AI standards, see Sect. 10.4.3). The appropriate level of detail depends on the standard's purpose and how technology-specific it is formulated.
	5. Users can clearly and unambiguously understand the aspects of AI described in the standard.
Example	ISO/IEC 22989:2022

Moreover, when discussing standards that fall short of the abovementioned criteria with standardisation experts, we noticed major differences regarding the perception of the level and urgency of adaptation needed. Due to limited capacities, standardisation experts must prioritise the adaptation of standards, and intermediate levels between AI ready and not AI ready are required. Accordingly, we defined a hierarchical ranking system of AI readiness which includes 'not AI relevant' as an independent class, while all other levels assume AI relevance. As well as having AI relevant but not AI ready standards, we defined the intermediate levels 'almost AI ready' and 'marginally AI ready', as well as the level 'not AI ready' (see Table 10.5).

10.4 Systematic Classification of Existing Standards

10.4.1 Requirements and Design Considerations for a Systematic Approach

A formalised and efficient way of evaluating the vast number of existing standards is needed, using these five hierarchical classes of AI readiness and relevance as a basis. The evaluation task should be performed primarily by humans, which means there are certain requirements for the manual practicability and comprehensibility of the procedure. In addition, we plan to apply NLP methods to support humans to classify standards in the future. Therefore, we will also utilise important elements

Table 10.5 Definition of a hierarchical ranking system with several levels of AI readiness. (*Source*: own table)

AI ready (see Table 10.4)	
Almost AI ready	
Definition	A standard is considered almost AI ready, if it is AI relevant, and
	• the standard remains generally applicable given the increasing use of AI, or
	• the standard is particularly high-level or contains descriptions of 'AI paraphrasing' systems without specifying a technology
	but can still be easily clarified and supplemented with AI specific requirements to be made fully AI ready.
Example	ISO 21448:2022
Marginally AI ready	
Definition	A standard is considered marginally AI ready, if it is AI relevant and refers to tasks for which the use of AI would be feasible and useful in the future, but in which AI is not sufficiently represented. Even if AI is not excluded per se, important AI specific changes and additions are needed to enhance the safeguarding promised by a standard.
Example	ISO/IEC 15408:2022
Not AI ready	
Definition	A standard is considered not AI ready, if it is AI relevant but …
	• the standard advises against or implicitly prohibits the use of AI, or
	• it leaves the user in doubt as to whether conformity with the standard can be achieved when using AI, or
	• it falls into an application area in which the use of AI is restricted by regulation or law.
Example	DIN EN 61508-1:2011
Not AI relevant (See Table 10.3)	

and insights from the formalised approach in the development of NLP models at a later stage.

It is already clear from the definition of the various AI readiness and relevance classes that the evaluation criteria are interconnected and require a certain degree of expert judgement. This becomes particularly apparent when evidence cannot be found directly within the standards for many aspects used to differentiate between individual AI readiness levels. Thus, to support human evaluators in generating as consistent and comparable classifications as possible, an approach that provides step-by-step guidance in the evaluation process is necessary.

Flowcharts are suitable for this purpose, as their visual elements provide a clear structure that can be easily and efficiently grasped by humans and adapted to the individual use case. Since their introduction by Gilbreth and Gilbreth in 1921,[29]

[29] Gilbreth and Gilbreth 1921.

flowcharts have been adopted as standards[30] and have been successfully used in many areas for years, for example, as a decision support system.[31] In addition to their clear comprehensibility, their structured presentation also provides a uniform basis for promoting consistent evaluation of the standards, an objective which the AI Standardisation Landscape also addresses using a questionnaire as well as text-mining techniques.[32]

Supplementary to the above, we included the following design considerations in the development of the flowchart:

- The complexity of the flowchart (including its depth and width and the level of detail of the decision questions) should be as low as possible, but still as high as necessary to enable quick and consistent evaluation.
- The individual decision nodes should:
    - be unambiguous in the sense that humans can evaluate the node as clearly/objectively as possible.
    - be supplemented by further, explanatory guiding questions to support the decision.
    - have unique identifiers to enable them to be referenced.
    - enable, to the greatest extent possible, the creation of labels and the identification of relevant text passages, which can be used as database for the prospective NLP methods.
- There should be certain fallback nodes to support the correct decision in case the human evaluators feel uncertain—even if this results in partial redundancy.

10.4.2 Development of the Flowchart

Based on the various AI readiness levels defined, the criteria for deciding whether a standard is AI ready typically depend on the type and characteristics of the standard (e.g. its purpose/function, its level of detail, how close it is to the domain of AI). To determine which aspects are most relevant for the standard to be classified into one of the AI readiness levels, we developed a sequence of 'pre-classifications'. This approach resembles the top-down induction of a decision-tree where the first decision nodes are selected based on the attributes that best separate the data, resulting in the highest information gain.[33] For instance, one of the first separating criteria in the flowchart is whether an AI term is mentioned within the standard.

---

[30] See American Society of Mechanical Engineers 1947 and ISO 5807:1985.

[31] Yilmaz and Yazgan 2018.

[32] Nativi and De Nigris 2021. See also Soler Garrido et al. 2023.

[33] Quinlan 1986. See also Rokach and Maimon 2005.

We developed our flowchart iteratively by hand, evaluating and improving each version with the aforementioned workshops. Since, to our knowledge, no comparable approaches exist that could be adapted or employed, we began with a simple flowchart version comprising a few general decision nodes. Applying it to sample standards and collecting expert feedback, we iteratively extended and refined the flowchart. We also added detailed guidance for nodes which are considered particularly difficult (e.g. those which are more on a meta-level and must rely on external or expert knowledge).[34]

10.4.3 Summary of the Flowchart and Examples of Decision Nodes

In consultation with the experts, we created two versions of the flowchart: a reduced version allowing for quick classification of standards at a glance (see Fig. 10.1) and a detailed version with comprehensive decision questions and additional guidance per node (which, due to its size, is not included in this chapter).

The first node A1 pre-filters AI ready standards that were directly developed by an AI standardisation committee (see Fig. 10.2).

The second node A2 yields two main decision strands: standards that mention AI specific terms (left), standards without textual reference to AI (right). The reasoning behind this separation is that, for the left strand, we can assume that AI related requirements or risks were considered to some extent during the standard's development. Consequently, there are specific questions applicable to this strand (e.g. E2) that are not relevant for the right strand. Furthermore, the strands differ in terms of the possible classification results (e.g. 'AI ready' can only be reached via the left and 'not AI relevant' only via the right strand).

The initial decision nodes of the right strand are for filtering not AI relevant standards. Typically, evidence for being not AI relevant can only be found when reading between the lines and classification heavily relies on expert judgement and domain knowledge. To have certain fallback options and keep evaluations by different experts as consistent as possible, we decided to split this non-trivial classification into three nodes K1, K2 and K3, each addressing distinct aspects of AI relevance. In

[34] In order to be able to answer the corresponding decision question with yes or no for some decision nodes, additional (= external) knowledge is required, which cannot be found in the text of the standard. In addition, specific domain knowledge (= expert knowledge) from the subject area of the standard is often required in order to understand and correctly interpret the contents of the standard.

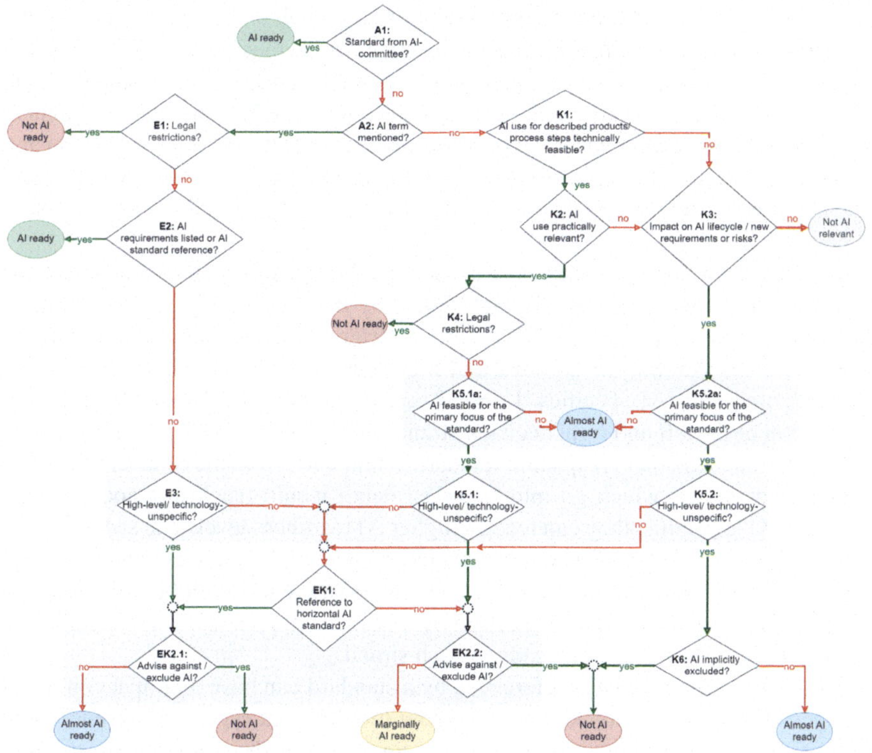

Fig. 10.1 The reduced version of the flowchart. At each decision node, a binary yes/no question is asked with the classification paths ultimately resulting in one of the five classes. (*Source*: Own figure)

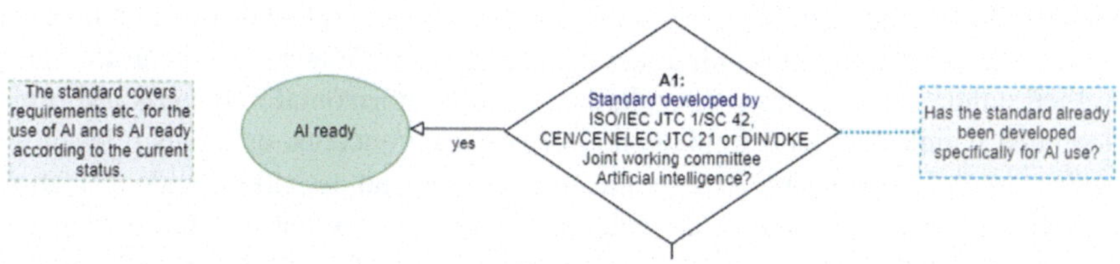

Fig. 10.2 First decision node (with 'A1' as unique identifier) with detailed decision question and guiding question (*Source*: Own figure)

addition, we prepared particularly detailed guidance in the extended version of the flowchart.

After initial application of the flowchart to sample standards, it became apparent that many of the standards identified as AI relevant due to decision nodes K1, K2 and K3 are actually only AI relevant in relation to a small and specific aspect of the standard (e.g. a specification of a manual machine, which requires a visual inspection as part of the quality assurance). Since only minor adaptations of these standards are required, we introduced two supplementary nodes (K5.1a, K5.2a) to filter the extent to which the standard is AI relevant. If only a minor aspect of the standard is AI relevant, it is directly classified as almost AI ready. If the primary focus of the standard is AI relevant, a more detailed evaluation of the level of required modifications needs to be conducted.

Two blocks of general nodes exist in our flowchart, featuring the same questions from each previous path, visually highlighted by the grey bars in the background. The first group of nodes (E3, K5.1 and K5.2) determines the technical detail of the standard, corresponding to the idea that high-level standards are less likely to be supplemented with AI specifics. Located below, the node EK1 provides the only connection of the left and right decision strands and queries as to whether a standard makes reference to other AI specific standards. Standards from the right strand which are AI relevant and which go into technical detail would reach this node. If they reference AI standards, they can reach a higher AI readiness level. The second block (EK2.1 and EK2.2) checks whether the standard potentially advises against AI use. For instance, the standard might include a requirement that cannot be fulfilled by an AI application such as visual inspection by a human. If a standard restricts the use of AI, it is classified as not AI ready in each strand.

Lastly, since the standards referenced by a standard can have an impact on its AI readiness level, as mentioned, understanding the different types of references and their relevance is an important prerequisite for applying the flowchart. In general, references to other standards become necessary if a topic cannot be dealt with comprehensively within a single standard, and relevant content defined externally can be included by means of references (in a purely informative, but also in a mandatory, normative manner). This occurs at different hierarchical levels, whereby references to standards within the same series of standards usually generalise (lower numbers) or concretise (higher numbers) individual detailed aspects. When references are made to other standards or series of standards, so-called horizontal standards are often referenced which deal with fundamental principles, concepts, or topics relevant to a wide range of standards.[35] To provide an overview and assist in the identification of relevant references of standards (e.g. those which are normatively referenced and which lie within the main scope of the standard being evaluated), we have developed an additional flowchart, see Fig. 10.3. This additional flowchart can not only support in the AI readiness classification of an individual standard, but it can also be used for identifying further standards to be adapted. Overarching, horizontal standards in particular have the potential to act as a great lever for the adaptation of the standards referencing them.

[35] https://www.iec.ch/news-resources/horizontal-standards. Accessed 25 February 2024.

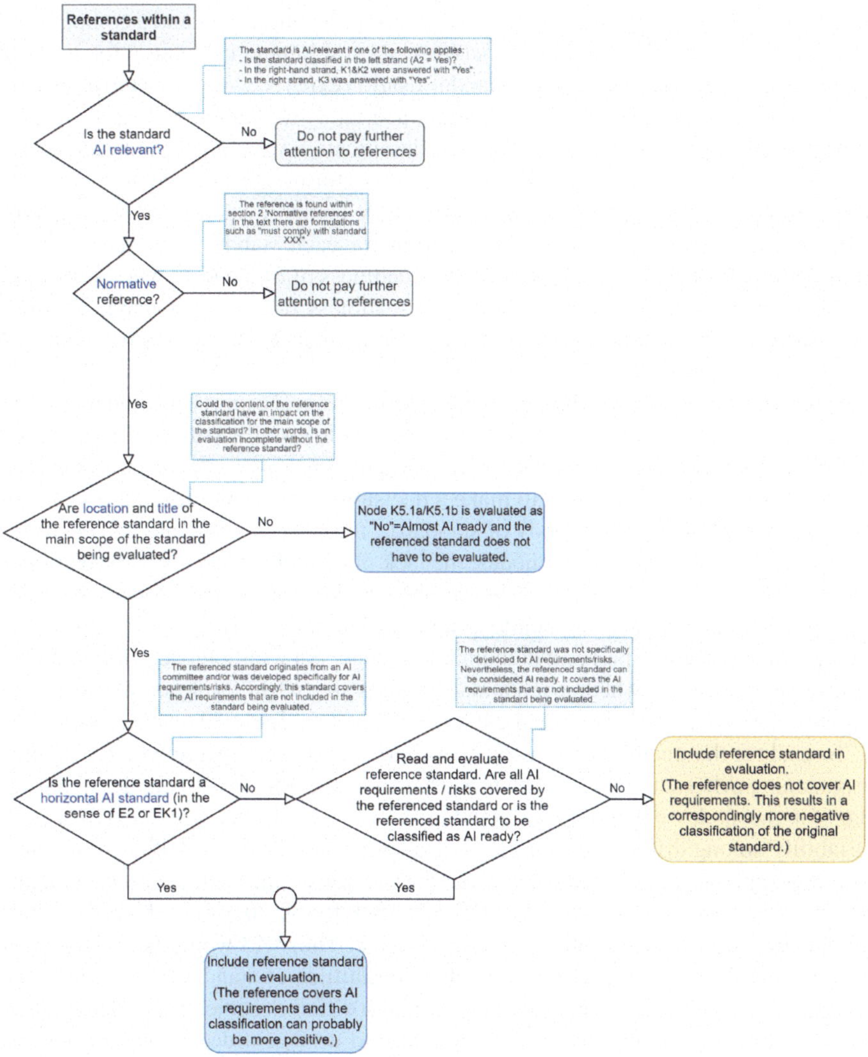

Fig. 10.3 Flowchart to assist in the evaluation process when references to other standards occur (*Source*: Own figure)

10.4.4 Evaluation

We focus on the plausibility and consistency of the flowchart results when evaluating our approach. Since we are not aware of other methods to determine the AI readiness of standards, we cannot benchmark our approach and thus deprioritise the additional requirement of efficiency in the evaluation. The evaluation is based on both the discussions which took place in four additional evaluation workshops with 11 experts from the abovementioned five standardisation committees and a comparative analysis of classification variability between several human evaluators for a set of sample standards. Together with the standardisation experts, we applied the flowchart node by node to sample standards to identify uncertainty for human evaluators, lack of comprehensibility or guidance. To identify classification variability, multiple experts documented for each decision node whether it is affirmed or negated and additionally, if possible, highlighted all decision-relevant textual evidence in the standard. Following the flowchart, a final classification for each standard was assigned. In addition, in a later phase of the project 'AI Readiness of Standards' AI experts used the developed flowchart to evaluate the AI readiness of over 700 standards from three different DIN standards committees, whereby their feedback was incorporated to iteratively improve the flowchart.

When comparing the highlighted evidence from several experts, we find that some decision nodes can be answered easily by referring to specific patterns or keywords generally used within each standard. For example, referring to the responsible DIN Standards Committee is enough to make a decision on node A1 (see Table 10.6). In terms of evaluating the entire body of standards, trivial decision nodes can easily be automated. In contrast, for other nodes, the lack of textual evidence serves to answer the question (e.g. if no AI related term was used in the standard, decision question A2 is answered negatively). More challenging decision nodes rely on standard-specific evidence and require expert and domain knowledge. For example, decision node K3 requires evidence for whether a standard affects the AI lifecycle or whether new requirements are included. Textual evidence is given in Table 10.6 as an example.

To analyse the unambiguity of the flowchart, we also compared which evidence or reasoning different human evaluators used for a specific decision node. In particular, for the nodes depending on standard-specific evidence, we detected a high variability among different evaluators. For example, we face the challenge of determining whether standards that solely describe specific requirements for (components of) an embedded system (such as DIN EN ISO 13850:2016-05 which describes emergency stop functions) affect the AI lifecycle. Thus, K3 would be affirmed for these standards, implying AI relevance for a multitude of standards. Similarly, the comparison between multiple evaluators reveals a different subjective understanding of which terms explicitly describe AI, leading to divergent decisions on node A2

Table 10.6 Exemplary extracts from standards where textual evidence was highlighted by experts for decisions on two nodes. (*Source*: Own table)

Node	Decision	Extract from the standard with highlighted textual evidence
A1: Standard from AI committee?	Negative	'The responsible German body involved in its preparation was the **Normenausschuss Automobiltechnik** (Road Vehicle Engineering Standards Committee)', ISO 15006:2011
K3: Impact on AI lifecycle/new requirements or risks?	Positive	'This International Standard specifies requirements and guidelines for the inherently **safe design, protective measures, and information for use of personal care robots**', DIN EN ISO 13482:2014-11

and, consequently, different final classifications. For instance, opinions differ on whether the term 'robot' can be interpreted as a paraphrasing of AI in terms of the ISO/IEC 22989:2022 AI definition. The evaluation reveals that striving for both domain-independent generality and simplicity leads to some decision nodes that are vague, allowing for different interpretations. Nevertheless, it is questionable as to what extent this can be fully avoided, as even standardisation experts themselves often disagree whether and how to adapt a specific standard.

The feedback from the AI experts applying the flowchart to over 700 documents from three different domains generally confirmed its overall applicability. For some nodes, AI experts found similar evidence in each professional domain respectively. Still, the AI experts reported as a main difficulty that often, AI was restricted or excluded by the standards only implicitly. They found it difficult to identify textual evidence for the respective nodes, as domain knowledge was required to recognize the implicit restrictions of AI. Due to this, the AI experts used the flowchart rather as a guidance than a strict guideline.

10.5 Conclusions

In this chapter, we introduced AI readiness levels that describe the need for adaptation of standards with regard to the new risks and requirements resulting from the use of AI. The levels represent different gradations according to the scope and urgency of adaptation. In addition, we presented a systematic procedure for classifying a standard into one of these levels. We visualized this procedure in a flowchart that supports experts in identifying adaptation needs through a series of decision nodes on the form and content of a standard.

In the academic literature, this work is the first to address systematically the adaptation need of the existing German body of standards due to AI applications. Through its empirical, interdisciplinary approach, it offers relevant links to the legal and economic disciplines. For example, AI readiness is particularly important in the context of harmonized standards that will operationalise the EU AIA. Here it must be ensured that these standards are practicable from the user's point of view on the one hand, and in line with the recitals of the AIA on the other. The classification approach presented and the considerations and trade-offs that have been incorporated into it can be used as a starting point for examining upcoming (also AI-specific) standards from a legal perspective. On the other hand, we showed in this chapter that there is a large number of existing (initially AI-unspecific) standards that are nevertheless relevant to AI in many cases. The possible effects described (e.g. banning or discouraging the use of AI) have an economic dimension. This chapter further contributes to the debate between innovation-friendliness and quality assurance through standards in the face of potentially disruptive technologies such as AI, as the classification scheme incorporates both objectives and is suitable for identifying specific examples in their field of tension.

Furthermore, the results presented contribute to addressing societal needs as well as practical challenges of standardisation. In a broader perspective, standards can promote quality, interoperability, and innovation. To this end, it is essential for standards to reflect the state of the art, especially when it comes to leveraging the specific potential of AI. At an operational level, standards are therefore regularly reviewed (e.g. whether they are to be reaffirmed, changed, or withdrawn) by standardization experts and our classification approach can be used complementarily as a granular and AI-specific check.[36] Especially given limited capacities, our approach supports in prioritizing adaptation needs in a targeted manner, and with a view to potential automation (see below), it offers a unique first step to expedite the review of existing standards and adapt them to the current state of the art. Furthermore, the flowchart can be incorporated into the development of new standards (in areas not specifically focused on AI) to identify, at the earliest stage possible, aspects that should be considered in light of AI.

As standardisation is a consensus-based process, there are clearly limitations to our approach, e.g. how specific the classification guidance can be and how much it can contribute to consistent results. Given the various types and domains of standards, we identified a trade-off between concretising guidance (with the risk of overfitting to a specific set of standards) and maintaining general applicability of the flowchart. For instance, in the field of machinery safety, the classification of type-A, type-B and type-C standards gives (clear) guidance on nodes E3, K5.1, K5.2, but this guidance is not applicable to other standardisation domains such as road vehicles. In addition, our discussions with standardisation stakeholders show that experts might evaluate the adaptation need of a standard differently and there is (aleatoric) uncertainty in several aspects of the classification task even for experts.[37]

The interim results presented in this paper will be iteratively improved during the 'AI Readiness of Standards' project. Based on feedback and domain-specific expert knowledge (from a total of 14 different experts from five domains), we will prepare additional guidance to decrease decision uncertainty and, thus, classification variability (e.g. a descriptive supplemental handout or labelling guidelines). In particular, the weaknesses identified in the evaluation will be addressed. For instance, we already integrated additional information into K3, so that standards on (components of) systems, that can potentially be used for embedding AI systems, are relevant for the AI lifecycle. Following expert judgement, these standards generally do not require any further adaptation, and are therefore usually AI ready. In contrast, we excluded the term 'robot' as AI paraphrasing in K3 with reference to already long-established industrial robots which follow deterministic rules. Another example is the introduction of the additional flowchart to aid in the process of evaluating standards with references to other standards.

In addition, a further workstream of the 'AI Readiness of Standards' project will examine (partial) automation of the AI readiness classification on the basis of the

[36] DIN EN 45020:2007-03.

[37] See also Kind et al. 2021.

presented flowchart. As mentioned, AI experts used the flowchart to label a variety of over 700 standards from three different domains according to the five levels of AI readiness and annotated textual evidence for individual decision nodes. The labelled standards will be used as training data for NLP methods that may support or automate the AI readiness classification of the existing body of standards. Future work should analyse the application of these NLP methods and gather new insights on the concept of AI readiness from their task performance, e.g. given potential classification variability. In addition, one may extend the classification approach to be applicable to international standards. Lastly, future work could also consider transferring the AI readiness classification system to disruptive technological developments other than AI as needed, though this requires further research. This future work may aim at creating a structured collection of standards to be revised.

Acknowledgements The development of this publication was supported by the German Federal Ministry for Economic Affairs and Climate Action (BMWK) as part of the project 'KI-Tauglichkeit von Normen' (AI Readiness of Standards). The authors would like to thank the project partners and standardisation experts for the successful cooperation.

References

Alsheibani S, Cheung Y, Messom C (2018) Artificial Intelligence Adoption: AI-readiness at Firm-Level. PACIS 4: 231–245

ASME standard: Operation and flow process charts. American Society of Mechanical Engineers (ASME) Std., 1947.

Becker N, Junginger P, Martinez L, Krupka D (2021) KI in der Arbeitswelt: Übersicht einschlägiger Normen und Standards [AI in the world of work: Overview of pertinent norms and standards]. Berlin: Gesellschaft für Informatik e.V., https://testing-ai.gi.de/fileadmin/PR/Testing-AI/ExamAINormenuebersicht2021_04.pdf (Accessed 25 February 2024).

Cho E K (2023) US-China Decoupling Patterns in Supply Chains and Ecosystems for Semiconductors and AI technologies. In: KIET Industrial Economic Review 28(23):39–47

Çınar Z M, Abdussalam Nuhu A, Zeeshan Q, Korhan O, Asmael M, Safaei B (2020) Machine learning in predictive maintenance towards sustainable smart manufacturing in industry 4.0. Sustainability, 2020 Oct 5;12(19):8211.

DIN 31051:2019-06—Fundamentals of maintenance. Deutsches Institut für Normung (DIN e.V.) Std., 2019.

DIN 820-3:2021-02—Normungsarbeit—Teil 3: Begriffe [Standardisation work—Part 3: Terminology]. Deutsches Institut für Normung (DIN e.V.) Std., 2021.

DIN 92419:2020-01—Grundsätze der ergonomischen Gestaltung assistiver Systeme [Principles of the ergonomic design of assistive systems]. Deutsches Institut für Normung (DIN e.V.) Std., 2020.

DIN EN 45020:2007-03—Normung und damit zusammenhängende Tätigkeiten—Allgemeine Begriffe [Standardisation and related activities—General terminology] (ISO/IEC Guide 2:2004), Deutsches Institut für Normung (DIN e.V.) Std., 2007.

DIN EN 61508-1:2011/VDE 0803-1:2011-02 Functional safety of electrical/electronic/programmable electronic safety-related systems—Part 1: General requirements. Deutsches Institut für Normung (DIN e.V.) Std., 2011.

DIN EN ISO 216:2007-12—Writing paper and certain classes of printed matter—Trimmed sizes—A and B series, and indication of machine direction; German version EN ISO 216:2007. Deutsches Institut für Normung (DIN e.V.) Std., 2007.

DIN EN ISO 13482:2014-11—Robots and robotic devices—Safety requirements for personal care robots; German version EN ISO 13482:2014. Deutsches Institut für Normung (DIN e.V.) Std., 2014.

DIN EN ISO 13850:2016-05—Safety of machinery—Emergency stop function—Principles for design; German version EN ISO 13850:2015. Deutsches Institut für Normung (DIN e.V.) Std., 2016.

DIN e.V. & DKE (2020) Standardization Roadmap Artificial Intelligence—Recommendations for AI Standardization—A summary. Available at https://www.din.de/resource/blob/772610/e96c34dd6b12900ea75b460538805349/normungsroadmap-en-data.pdf (Accessed 25 February 2024).

DIN e.V. & DKE (2022) Standardization Roadmap Artificial Intelligence, 2nd edition. Available at https://www.din.de/resource/blob/916798/ed09ae58b60f0d3a498fa90fa5085b7c/nrm-ki-engl-2023-final-web-250-neu-data.pdf (Accessed 25 February 2024).

DIN ISO 31000:2018-10—Risk management—Guidelines. Deutsches Institut für Normung (DIN e.V.) Std., 2018.

DIN Standards Committee Ergonomics 2020. Ergebnisdokumentation des NA 023-00-06 AA 'Ergonomie der Arbeits- und Produktgestaltung in der Industrie 4.0' [Documentation of the DIN Standards Committee Ergonomics], document n 108.

Egyedi T M, Ortt J R (2017) Towards a functional classification of standards for innovation research. In: Handbook of innovation and standards. Edward Elgar Publishing, 2017, pp. 105–132.

European Commission, Directorate-General for Communications Networks, Content and Technology (2019) Ethics guidelines for trustworthy AI. Publications Office, 2019.

European Commission (2022) Draft standardisation request to the European Standardisation Organisations in support of safe and trustworthy artificial intelligence. Available at https://ec.europa.eu/docsroom/documents/52376 (Accessed 25 February 2024).

European Parliament and Council (2012) Regulation (EU) No 1025/2012 on European standardisation. Official Journal of the European Union, L 316/12-33.

European Parliament and Council (2023) Regulation (EU) No 2023/1230 on machinery. Official Journal of the European Union, L 165/1.

European Parliament and Council (2024) Regulation (EU) No 2024/1689 laying down harmonised rules on artificial intelligence (Artificial Intelligence Act). Official Journal of the European Union, (Accessed 12 July 2024).

Federal Ministry of Education and Research (2018) German Artificial Intelligence Strategy. Available at https://www.ki-strategie-deutschland.de/home.html?%20file=files/downloads/Nationale%20KI-Strategie%20engl.pdf. (Accessed 25 February 2024).

Gilbreth F B, Gilbreth L M (1921) Process Charts. American Society of Mechanical Engineers.

Görge R, Haedecke E, Mock M (2023) Using ScrutinAI for visual inspection of DNN performance in a medical use case. *AI Ethics*, https://doi.org/10.1007/s43681-023-00399-x (Accessed 25 February 2024).

Haedecke, E, Mock, M, Akila, M (2022) ScrutinAI: A visual analytics tool supporting semantic assessments of object detection models. Computers & Graphics, Volume 114, 2023, Pages 265-275, ISSN 0097-8493, https://doi.org/10.1016/j.cag.2023.06.010 (Accessed 25 February 2024).

ISO 5807:1985—Information processing—Documentation symbols and conventions for data, program and system flowcharts, program network charts and system resources charts. International Standardization Organization (ISO) Std., 1985.

ISO 15006:2011—Road vehicles—Ergonomic aspects of transport information and control systems—Specifications for in-vehicle auditory presentation. International Standardization Organization (ISO/IEC) Std., 2011.

ISO 21448:2022—Road vehicles—Safety of the intended functionality, International Standardization Organization (ISO/IEC) Std., 2022.

ISO/IEC 15408:2022—Information security, cybersecurity and privacy protection—Evaluation criteria for IT security. International Standardization Organization (ISO/IEC) Std., 2020.

ISO/IEC 22989:2022—Information technology—Artificial intelligence—Artificial intelligence concepts and terminology, International Standardization Organization (ISO/IEC) Std., 2022.

ISO/IEC TR 29119-11:2020—Software and systems engineering—Software testing—Part 11: Guidelines on the testing of AI-based systems, International Standardization Organization (ISO/IEC) Std., 2020.

Joehnk J, Weißert M, Wyrtki K (2021) Ready or not, AI comes—an interview study of organizational AI readiness factors. Business & Information Systems Engineering 63:5–20

Kind C, Terenzi A, Hauer M (2021) Adaptation standard. Analysis of existing standards for adaptation needs with regard to the consequences of climate change. Umweltbundesamt (UBA).

Kop M (2021) EU Artificial Intelligence Act: The European Approach to AI. Stanford-Vienna Transatlantic Technology Law Forum, Transatlantic Antitrust and IPR Developments, vol. 2. Stanford University.

Luckin R, Cukurova M, Kent C, du Boulay B (2022) Empowering educators to be AI-ready. Computers and Education: Artificial Intelligence. https://doi.org/10.1016/j.caeai.2022.100076

Nativi S, De Nigris S (2021) AI Watch: AI standardisation landscape state of play and link to the EC proposal for an AI regulatory framework. Publications Office of the EU. https://doi.org/10.2760/376602

OECD (2022) Recommendation of the Council on Artificial Intelligence, OECD/LEGAL/0449. Available at https://legalinstruments.oecd.org/api/print?ids=648&lang=en (Accessed 25 February 2024).

Poretschkin M, Schmitz A, Akila M, Adilova L, Becker D, Cremers A B, Hecker D, Mock M, Rosenzweig J, Sicking J, Schulz E, Voss A, Wrobel S (2023) Guideline for Designing Trustworthy Artificial Intelligence—AI Assessment Catalog. arXiv preprint arXiv:2307.03681.

Quinlan J R (1986) Induction of decision trees. Machine Learning. https://doi.org/10.1007/BF00116251

Rokach L, Maimon O (2005) Top-down induction of decision trees classifiers—a survey. IEEE Transactions on Systems, Man, and Cybernetics, Part C (Applications and Reviews) 35(4):476–487

Russell S, Norvig P (2016) Artificial Intelligence: A Modern Approach. Pearson Education, Limited

Schmitz A, Akila M, Hecker D, Poretschkin M, Wrobel S (2022) The why and how of trustworthy AI: An approach for systematic quality assurance when working with ML components. at—Automatisierungstechnik, vol. 70, no. 9, 2022, pp. 793-804. Available at https://doi.org/10.1515/auto-2022-0012 (Accessed 25 February 2024).

Smuha N A (2021) From a 'race to AI to a 'race to AI regulation: regulatory competition for artificial intelligence. Law, Innovation and Technology 13(1):57–84

Soler Garrido J, Tolan S, Hupont Torres I, Fernandez Llorca D, Charisi V, Gomez Gutierrez E, Junklewitz H, Hamon R, Fano Yela D, Panigutti C (2023) AI Watch: Artificial Intelligence Standardisation Landscape Update. Joint Research Centre (Seville site), Tech. Rep.

Tarrisse A, Masse F (2021) Locks for the use of IEC 61508 to ML Safety-Critical Applications and Possible Solutions. Proceedings of the 31st European Safety and Reliability Conference. https://doi.org/10.3850/978-981-18-2016-8_661-cd

Thiebes S, Lins S, Sunyaev A (2021) Trustworthy artificial intelligence. Electronic Markets 31(2):447–464

Vries H J (2006) IT standards typology. In: Advanced Topics in Information Technology Standards and Standardization Research, Volume 1. IGI Global, 2006, pp. 1–26.

Yilmaz A K, Yazgan E (2018) Corporate performance management: process of organizational-tailored flow chart. Aircraft Engineering and Aerospace Technology 90:1394–1402

Anna Schmitz is a scientific employee and senior data scientist at the Fraunhofer Institute for Intelligent Analysis and Information Systems IAIS. Her research focuses on the topics of trustworthy AI and certification of AI applications and is primarily conducted within the interdisciplinary project ZERTIFIZIERTE KI. Currently, she is developing systematic approaches for risk analysis and evaluation of AI systems, which have contributed to the Fraunhofer-IAIS AI Assessment Catalog, for example, and which are being applied in pilot AI assessments with industry clients. Anna Schmitz studied mathematics at the Universities of Cologne and Cambridge.

Rebekka Görge is a scientific employee and data scientist at the Fraunhofer Institute for Intelligent Analysis and Information Systems IAIS. Her research topic mainly focuses on the trustworthiness of artificial intelligence systems. As part of an interdisciplinary team, she develops approaches for the testing and certification of AI in the project ZERTIFIZIERTE KI. Currently, she is engaged in robustness and vulnerability testing of AI in the medical domain. Rebekka Görge studied computer science with a focus on image processing and computer vison at the University of Koblenz-Landau.

Elena Haedecke is a scientific employee at the University of Bonn and senior data scientist at the Fraunhofer Institute for Intelligent Analysis and Information Systems IAIS. She primarily conducts research regarding the trustworthiness of deep neural networks within the interdisciplinary project ZERTIFIZIERTE KI. In the context of AI assessment and certification, her research focuses on the development of testing tools that uncover and mitigate DNN weaknesses, as well as methods that make DNNs more understandable. Elena Haedecke studied computer science and electrical engineering at the University of Applied Sciences Sankt Augustin.

Marion Borowski is a senior project manager in the Enterprise Information Integration department at Fraunhofer Institute for Intelligent Analysis and Information Systems IAIS. She holds a diploma in Computer Science and has worked 25+ years as a project manager in various national, European, and industrial projects. She acquired extensive experience in data integration, information modelling, semantic technologies, data space technologies, and AI based approaches. She is part of the International Data Spaces team at the IAIS. Currently, she is coordinating the project activities of Fraunhofer IAIS regarding the evaluation of the AI readiness of standards.

Adrian Seeliger is Project Manager Strategic Development AI at the German Institute for Standardization (DIN). In this role, he is responsible for managing the project AI Readiness of Standards, as well as the working group financial services of the German Standardization Roadmap on AI. Furthermore, he manages standardization activities in the DIN Standards Committee Information Technology and Applications (NIA). His interest in the interface between information systems and organization theory is reflected by activities in research, industry, and consulting. Adrian Seeliger studied business administration and materials and process engineering at RWTH Aachen University.

Dr. Maximilian Poretschkin is "Head of Safe AI and AI-Certification" at the Fraunhofer Institute for Intelligent Analysis and Information Systems IAIS. In this role, Dr. Poretschkin has led a broad variety of projects and AI assessments with global partners from industry and government. Particularly noteworthy is the project ZERTIFIZIERTE KI, which develops testing principles, assessment tools and standards for AI systems and has published one of the first assessment catalogs for AI systems. Dr. Maximilian Poretschkin studied physics and mathematics in Bonn and Amsterdam and received the doctoral award for the best dissertation at the University of Bonn in 2015. He is an alumnus of the German National Academic Foundation.

Chapter 11
Appropriating Legal AI Development: The Existential and Political Dynamics of Legal AI-Artifacts

Cees Zweistra

Contents

Abstract The advance of legal AI applications within the legal profession poses questions about the ethics and the politics of this technological development. Some would argue that these developments are inevitable, and that the legal profession can do little more than to adapt to these developments. Others would say that there is and should still be room to question and proactively shape these developments. This chapter explores the different positions towards legal AI. It argues for the adoption of a notion of ethics and politics of technology that does not take the advance of legal AI as inevitable. Rather, the course of legal AI developments should still be open for questioning and proactive shaping. For this purpose, this chapter develops a notion of reflexive techno-politics and existential-ethics that can both help to appropriate legal AI developments.

Keywords Legal AI · Legal transhumanism · Legal humanism · Politics of technology · Ethics of technology · Tech determinism · Technological inevitability

---

C. Zweistra (✉)
Department Law and Markets, Erasmus School of Law, Rotterdam, The Netherlands
e-mail: zweistra@law.eur.nl

K. Prifti et al. (eds.), *Digital Governance*, Information Technology and Law Series 39,
https://doi.org/10.1007/978-94-6265-639-0_11

11.1 Introduction

In 1893, an American newspaper syndicate surveyed seventy-four prominent Americans about their predictions for the coming era. What would the world look like within a century?[1] One senator predicted that in 1993 everyone would have a private balloon for transportation. It would be just as easy to call one's balloon, the senator predicted, as it is to call one's buggy.[2] Another believed that within a century, urgent messages would be delivered through telephone and telegraph. Ordinary messages would still be carried by stagecoach and horseback rider. Most of the predictors had high hopes for the future of the railway which was booming at the time. Railway was believed to become the fasted mean for transportation in the era to come, with railway tracks running from the North Pole to the South Pole, connecting all major cities. None of the predictors in 1893—which included the leading elite of the time—predicted the breakthrough of mass, motorised transportation, even though the first 'horse-less' wheel carriages had already hit the road, and Karl Benz had laid patent on the internal-combustion engine in 1886.[3]

The story is a nice illustration of the fate of futurology in general and technologies-future in particular. Despite claims laid by many futurists in technology[4] and legal innovation,[5] technological developments rarely if ever follow a predictable *unilinear*[6] trajectory. A Whig-historic[7] reading of technological development, according to which the present was inevitable from the start, has been continuously refuted by social-constructivists research into the history of technology-development.[8]

Technological development is neither inevitable nor deterministic, it rather is the outcome of a process of deliberation and negotiation between technologies and preferences of stakeholders.[9] To put it differently: technological development is not the result of an isolated effort of engineers crafting their prototypes and scientists working in their laboratories.[10] In reality, the development of technology takes place within a social context, in an interplay between technological design and relevant groups of stakeholders (i.e. users, regulators, policy-makers, politicians). This interplay between technology and society could be referred to as the *politics*[11] and the

---

[1] Walter 1992.

[2] Tenner 1997, p. 9.

[3] Ibid.

[4] Kelly 2016.

[5] Susskind and Susskind 2017.

[6] Feenberg 1999, p. 81.

[7] Butterfield 1931.

[8] Pinch & Bijker 1987.

[9] Feenberg 1999, p. 76.

[10] Bijker 1987.

[11] Winner 1980.

existential dynamics[12] of technology. The political and existential-ethical dimensions of technology refer to often neglected or underrepresented elements in ethical engagement with technology in general and AI-ethics in particular.[13]

This chapter will show to what extent this is the case and will propose a tentative outline of what doing politics and existential-ethics will amount to in the context of legal AI. This is a sub-branch of legal tech and is about developing AI-driven technologies that are aimed at either *assisting* or *substituting*[14] legal professionals—legal AI used by the public will be left out in this chapter. As will be shown, whether the direction of legal AI is headed towards either assistance or replacement has important political and existential-ethical ramifications. First, I will show that the politics and ethics of legal AI refer to different momentums in our engagement with legal AI.

11.2 The Political and Existential-Ethical Momentum in Ethical Engagement with Legal AI

In its original context, the politics of technology refers to inherent or designed-in properties of technologies.[15] Although contested,[16] this perspective on the societal impact of technological-design could still be made fruitful in the context of AI-research. In this area, research is predominantly focused on a rather narrow and risk-based approach to ethics. This at the neglect of studying the socio-political[17] and existential-ethical[18] dimensions of AI.

The existential dynamics of technology refers to the way in which technologies influence (through authorising, affording, encouraging, suggesting, etc. certain behaviours.[19]) *how* we live. It pays attention to changing practices and connected accounts of meaning instead of merely focusing on the specific risks that are introduced by a certain technology or AI-application.

The political and existential-ethical dynamics of legal AI, refer to complementary *momentums* in possible ethical engagement with advancing legal AI. It is for instance a question of techno-politics whether we want the *legal system* as such to move towards full automation and *substitution* of human legal professionals. It is a matter of doing ethics to question whether, how and to what a degree a law firm should strive to implement lawyer-*assisting* technologies. The former gives way to asking questions of a political nature, such as: 'what kind of society do we want to create?'

[12] Borgmann 1984; Verbeek 2000.

[13] Hagendorff 2020.

[14] Pasquale 2019.

[15] Pasquale 2019.

[16] Pfaffenberg 1992.

[17] Hagendorff 2020.

[18] Borgmann 1984; Waelberg and Swierstra 2014.

[19] Latour 2005, p. 72.

The latter involves asking existential questions such as: 'what kind law-firm do we want to become?'

The politics and existential-ethical dynamics of legal AI refer to different phases or *moments* in possible ethical engagement with legal AI. For instance, AI-powered legal *assistance* technologies are already commonly used[20] and it is a matter of *ethical guidance*[21] how this can be done in a 'good'—not necessarily the same as responsible—manner. Ethical engagement at the level of *assisting* legal AI technologies has reached the ethical moment, whereas AI-powered legal *substituting* technologies have not yet arrived at that stage. Although according to some[22] this will soon be the case, thanks to autonomous technological improvements. At this point however, a politics of technology should step in. As I will argue, this is a prototypical situation in which we should not let the course of societal changes be dictated by the ideology of technological inevitability,[23] but step in through doing a politics of technology. To that end, the notion of techno-politics should be stretched beyond its original connotation, and this will be done in the next paragraph.

11.3 A Reflexive Politics of Artifacts

The development of technology is not autonomous or unilinear. Technologies have the tendency to 'bite back' as historian of technology Edward Tenner has famously noted.[24] That means, as he observes, technologies often introduce more subtle and insidious problems to replace the acute ones. And the acute problems are rarely if ever solved. These are what Tenner calls 'revenge effects.' Revenge effects are not side effects (which could give the false impression that these effects could be curbed) but new behavioural and societal practices and pathways that emerge out of the advance of new technologies.

Revenge effects come within scope of what the philosopher of technology Langdon Winner has described as the 'politics of artifacts.'[25] The politics of technologies refers to the way in which technologies by themselves, through their inherent properties or deliberate design, do have an impact in the organisation of 'the arrangements of power and authority' within society.[26] In his analyses, Winner discerns three ways in which technologies can be political.

First, artifacts can *intentionally* be supplied with political effects. The classic example is about the low-hanging overpasses, designed by architect Robert Moses

---

20 Pasquale 2019.

21 Verbeek 2011, p. 153.

22 Susskind 2019.

23 Zuboff 2019, p. 220.

24 Tenner 1997, p. 9.

25 Winner 1980.

26 Ibid.

in the 1920's, that prevented public buses from entering the beaches of Long Island.[27] This effectively prohibited racial minorities and the poor from reaching the beaches. Secondly, some unintentional but also *unavoidable* political effects can emerge from technologies. Winner's own example is about mechanical tomato harvesters. The introduction of it in the 1940's, raised production but decreased the number of tomato-growers and left thousands without a job. By doing that the machine rearranged power structures, also by *de-skilling* those that still had a job. Meanwhile, the automated harvester changed food-cultures, for only a very specific tomato allowed for mechanical harvesting. Thirdly, some technologies call for a specific politics through intrinsic properties such as nuclear power plants. The introduction and maintenance of these plants require a rigid, hierarchical politics, when compared to for example solar energy which can be implemented in decentralised, democratic structures.[28]

The politics of technology as envisioned by Winner has not escaped controversy.[29] Some have argued that it is overly focused on the inherent properties of artifacts,[30] as if these properties are not interpreted and 'read' within a social context. Technologies, the critique goes, come with a certain hermeneutics, a way of interpreting them within a given context. According to this view, there is not some hidden intrinsic meaning present in the design of an artefact. Technologies are better understood as a kind of *material texts*. Just like texts are interpreted and acquire their proper meaning within a context of different interpretations, so do technologies. And by interpreting technologies, we can also guide them and, so to say, interpret them *otherwise* and *differently*.

Techno-politics in its Winnerian sense appears to be overly one directional and for that matter remains within the deadlock of the techno-determinism it attempted to overcome.[31] It is therefore both needed and possible to develop a notion of techno-politics that pays attention to the dialogical or reflexive[32] relation between technology and society.

A technology might come with a certain politics, it might *afford*[33] the creation of a specific 'world'[34] around it, but it is possible to develop a counter-politics. This counter-politics can be used to project certain values and standards into technology-design and thus influence the kind of world that takes its shape around a technology or set of technologies.

A true politics of technology goes both ways. Technology through its design comes with specific rearrangements of social relations, practices and structures of power in a certain world, such as the world of legal professionals. But this world

[27] Ibid.

[28] Smits 2001, p. 161.

[29] Brey 2005, p. 65.

[30] Pfaffenberg 1992.

[31] Smits 2001.

[32] Feenberg 1999.

[33] Gibson 1979.

[34] Heidegger 2009.

should not take this as a deterministic and *inevitable*[35] process. Within the existing set of practices and relations that make up a particular world, some meaning could be present that might be changed in an undesirable way. This is especially the case within the world of legal professionals as they are bound by professional codes of conduct, the rule of law and their inherent role as mediators in providing access to justice.

The world of legal professionals should therefore try to step up and *reappropriate* the direction of technological development. This might sometimes seem like an unequal struggle and the advance of Big AI does in fact make this the case.[36] That also why a politics of technological reform has been termed unreal or even utopian.[37] But a *politics* of technological reform has the right to be ambitious, although for reasons different from what can be called *legal transhumanism*, the position that currently has considerable influence on the future course of legal AI developments.

11.4 Legal Transhumanism

Inevitability connects to what has been termed technological determinism, a position which stems from the work of the philosopher of technology Jacques Ellul.[38] The deterministic or *autonomous* development of technology means that technology dictates culture, the world we live in, and we have hardly any option but to give in to it. The human world has little or no impact on the technological world—we become gradually absorbed by it.

Next to this more gloomy perspective on tech-determinism, stands a more positive deterministic tradition. This is by no means a novel position.[39] In fact, there is a long-standing tradition that takes technology as some sort of 'exogenous force,'[40] that, through a process of internal and constant development, goes from lesser forms to more advanced forms of technology. Society can little do to influence this autonomous development. We can only adapt and we should adapt. How can we not want the best technologies?

In the context of digital technologies, techno-determinism is often clothed in language about its speed ('Moore's-law')[41], its complexity and enormous volumes of data, to indicate that any attempt to control or influence its development is doomed.[42] It is just too fast, too complex—it is *in fact* an autonomous development guided by mathematicians and engineers, so the story goes. In the legal sector, this language

---

35 Zuboff 2019.

36 Zuboff 2019.

37 Winner 1977.

38 Ellul 1954.

39 Mesthene 1967.

40 Feenberg 1999, p. 77.

41 McGinnis and Pearce 2014.

42 Grunwald 2019.

comes with its own idiom of the 'great disruption'[43] that is already taking place and we could better stop worrying and start preparing for its smooth arrival.[44] The latter comes down to developing successful strategies for its adoption in terms of new business-models,[45] new forms of legal education and different court-procedures.[46]

In the legal sector, this position is advocated by amongst others Richard Susskind,[47] who in turn is inspired by transhumanism.[48] According to Susskind we already are in 'the age of transhumanism.'[49]

Transhumanism is a movement which advocates the adoption of *technological* enhancements,[50] which might help to overcome current human limitations. In the legal context this might lead to the moment that a chip implantation could arrive that will give direct access to 'entire bodies of law and regulation.'[51] This would be an obvious leap beyond an inherent human limitation such as our capabilities to memorise. According to transhumanists, we are now in the phase of 'computing with meat,'[52] but this has never been our destiny, 'chips are destiny.'[53]

In so far as the 'chips are destiny' creed is embraced in the legal sector it can be called *legal transhumanism.* It stands out in the debate on adoption-strategies towards legal AI, for its call to adopt technologies (no other means) that could elevate us from our current human-centred condition and connected limitations. We should strive for legal AI substitution rather than complementation, assistance or augmentation.[54]

Legal transhumanism shares with its transhumanistic origin the assumption that enhancing technologies will provide better futures (faster, easier, cheaper, etc.) without changing the categories of humanity itself: we *remain* what we are, although we live longer and happier than before. It has been argued[55] that this underestimates the transforming power of technologies. These powers are often beyond our control, thus calling for more modest approaches, such as embedded in the notion of *reflexive techno-politics* that will be tentatively developed during this chapter. This notion goes against the grain of the pervasive rhetoric of 'inevitibalism'[56] that is also very present in the debate around legal AI, and which fuels the movement towards legal transhumanism. This movement will be discussed in the next paragraph.

---

43 McGinnis and Pearce 2014.

44 Katz 2013.

45 McGinnis and Pearce 2014.

46 Susskind 2019.

47 Susskind 2019.

48 Kurzweil 1990.

49 Susskind 2019, p. 191.

50 Aydin 2015.

51 Susskind 2019.

52 Kosko 1999, p. 31.

53 Kosko 1999, p. 31.

54 Calo 2017.

55 Aydin 2015.

56 Zuboff 2019, p. 220.

11.5 Riding the Waves of Legal AI

Legal transhumanists argue that we can little do to steer or even question the various 'waves' (a language characteristic of tech-determinism, it is akin to a natural force[57]) of legal tech development. The rather crude course of action that remains open to us is to adapt or perish. This is especially so in the context of the next wave (generative) legal AI. The first wave consisted of legal AI applied in legal search, document generation and models for prediction. But thanks to the relentless efforts within the legal AI community, not seldomly powered by venture-capitalist looking for new fields to disrupt,[58] we are about to undergo the impact of the second wave and this one will really hit. This wave is not only about legal tech assistance but comes with promise of substitution. We *will* be taken over.

The second wave will be about machines with superhuman prediction power, simply because they are in the possession of enormous amounts of data and ever-growing computing powers. This time we will see the advance of 'apparently intelligent' AI-systems that will shake-up the already outdated (advice and hourly billing) business models of law firms. Lastly, Susskind has high disruptive expectations of emotion recognition. Apparently unaware of the ever-growing body of literature that dismisses the notion of emotion-recognition altogether as pseudo-scientific,[59] not to mention the privacy-infringes that are made in training the models,[60] Susskind stresses that 'systems can already differentiate between a fake smile and genuine smiling more reliably than humans'.[61]

At risk of becoming outsmarted by AI we should, according to Susskind, give up 'irrational rejectionism'[62] and give in to the dictate of technological innovation. In fact, disruption *is* already taking place.[63] As his argument goes: the machines are coming for us no matter what *we* do. Doing politics of technology is neither possible nor desirable. Ethics might come in handy, but only in so far as it treats the pace and course of technological development itself as rather unchangeable.

The course of technological development comes with an imperative to embrace it and not fight it. This imperative reaches all the way to the core of the legal system, which after all should be about delivering justice in a time- and cost-efficient manner.[64] And since the legal system gets increasingly clogged-up, there is a call for adoption of innovation that stretches beyond the voices of legal transhumanism.[65]

---

[57] Grunwald 2019.

[58] Pasquale 2019.

[59] Crawford 2021, p. 151, 2021, p. 136.

[60] Crawford 2021.

[61] Susskind p. 187.

[62] Susskind 2019; Salyzyn 2021.

[63] McGinnis and Pearce 2014.

[64] Guillermin et al. 2021.

[65] Van der Put 2021.

This innovation might include for example the legal design movement,[66] but the hopes are most high for the breakthroughs in legal automation.

There is an element of AI-solutionism[67] at work here. As if AI is a one-size fits all solution, ranging from solving the apparent riddle (some would argue that it is not a riddle[68]) of climate-change to ensuring affordable access-to-justice for everyone. It is also questionable whether the hoped-for efficiency gains will be delivered by automation in the legal sector, as examples of the efficiency-paradox[69] indicate that more caution is required. The adoption of legal AI is also advocated because it might deliver better outcomes. In fact, some have already argued that the adoption of legal AI might become ethically imperative[70] because it comes with the promise of less fallibility and better outcomes—in short it is a development that we *ought* to embrace. The latter prediction connects to common perspectives on AI, as one influential definition depicts the study of AI as the endeavour to create 'intelligent agents that take the best possible action in a situation'.[71] Within the law, the calls for adaption of legal AI stem from the believe that AI might indeed give the best (most rational, least biased) option in a given situation, thus contributing to the ideal that the law should be 'a rule of law, not of men'.[72]

The inevitability of legal AI thus comes from a combination of relentless technological development, connected to the fact that it indeed delivers on its high expectations. In order to choose an adoption strategy with regard to legal AI, the question of the degree of inevitability of legal AI development needs to be settled. To what extent is the development of legal AI indeed inevitable? This question determines what kind of possible options for engagement are present. Are these ethical in nature and if so, what kind of ethics? And is there still room for doing politics of legal AI? The latter would imply that legal AI development is not entirely inevitable.

11.6 Degrees of Inevitability in Legal AI Development

Inevitability comes in degrees. There is indeed an inevitability present in legal AI development towards an *assistance* technology.[73] This is a more modest, weak form of inevitability, that has roots in a vision on human-technology relations. Where transhumanists will stress the potential of technology development to elevate human beings to higher, better levels of existence, a less dramatic and less utopian approach

[66] Hagan 2019.

[67] Lindgren 2023.

[68] Klein 2023.

[69] Tenner 2018.

[70] Salyzyn 2021.

[71] Russel and Norvig 2021.

[72] Calo 2017.

[73] Pasquale 2019.

seeks to highlight the existentially *interwoven* character of humans and technologies.[74] Humans create worlds not by themselves, but always in co-creation with their surroundings, which includes things—i.e. artifacts, technologies. We cannot create purely human worlds using solely human means—language, for instance, is one such means that some propose.[75] A more realistic perspective, however, shows that we create the world *with* technologies instead of *despite* them.

The further development and re-creation of the legal world with technologies—including legal AI—is to this extend inevitable. We cannot want otherwise and indeed, if there is such a thing as 'irrational refusal' towards legal AI, it is about a notion which does not foresee a co-creational development between legal professionals and some forms of assisting legal AI. This co-creational development of legal AI and the legal profession is already underway. And so should it be, the human world has never developed in isolation from technology, and so it goes with the legal world. It has for instance been pointed out that law itself has a technological embodiment in so far it is written in text—law is inherently interwoven with a technological architecture.[76]

Law firms tend to struggle with the concept of legal AI,[77] but some form of it is already used for legal research, due diligence, e-discovery and contract analytics.[78] AI is also, albeit modestly, employed in the field of quantitative legal prediction,[79] a field that despite its humble presence continues to be vested with high expectations for future disruptions in the legal sector.[80] There are also a range of legal AI startups active in legal document analysis,[81] document review ('predictive coding'[82]), document structuring,[83] and AI-powered tools for measuring legal performance.[84] Although many lawyers are not aware of it, many of their tools used in their daily practice, already are using some form of AI,[85] whereas lawyers generally tend to think of AI as some form ground-breaking, rocket-science AI that someday might outperform current-day legal professionals. In fact, many AI-solutions remain in the *background* of legal work and already sustain much of legal professional work.

Whenever the language around legal AI is stripped from its transhumanistic overtones present in such notions as a 'relentless change,'[86] a 'great disruption' and even the possibility of legal brain implants, it is not difficult to see that change is happening

[74] Heidegger 2009; Verbeek 2000.

[75] Pasquale 2019.

[76] Hildebrandt 2016.

[77] Weinstein 2022.

[78] Weinstein 2022.

[79] Katz 2013; Custers 2017.

[80] Katz 2013.

[81] Kira Systems (2024).

[82] Salyzyn 2021.

[83] Uncover Legal (2024).

[84] Jiang et al. 2021.

[85] Weinstein 2022.

[86] Kelly 2016.

and will continue to happen. Any other perspective just holds on to a philosophically unsound account of humanism—as if being human means to develop in isolation from technology. The legal sector itself, despite widespread accusations of its persistent traditionalism, has in fact high hopes for technological advances, especially from generative AI, as a means for increasing efficiency, quality and overall performance.[87] However, it becomes again a matter of diverging perspectives, when the question is raised what an ethics of this development towards assistance technology can and should be about.

11.7 The Existential Ethical Momentum in Legal AI

Legal professionals have high hopes for the advances in legal AI, but see some risks in the field of explainability, fairness/bias and consistency.[88] In standard AI-ethics it is attempted to address precisely such issues. For instance, the current flow in AI-ethics is towards accommodating AI, by making it responsible and work for society: state the benefits, reap the benefits, accommodate for the risks.[89] The mushrooming AI-ethical movement is therefore predominantly about creating fair, accountable, confidential and transparent (FACT) AI.[90] The FACT-AI approach has also its offspring in the legal sector where arguments are made for updating existing codes of professional conduct to include matters of privacy, security and even the possible obligation to make use of legal AI whenever available.[91]

The current risk-benefit approach present in the FACT-AI approach misses out on matters of social impact[92] relating to AI implementations. For instance: what future impact will legal AI-usage have on the notion of 'trust' in lawyer-client relations? This is the kind of question a FACT-ethical approach does not address. The FACT-AI approach is also not concerned with ethical questions related to *meaning*.[93] These questions are important when legal AI starts doing parts of the jobs of legal professionals. Although the promise is often that AI will enable doing the more interesting, higher levels of legal practice, this is one such promise that needs to be thoroughly questioned. Is this indeed the case, or could legal AI also lead to a form of de-skilling, rendering the job with less *intrinsic* value? This in turn could further weaken the notion of professionalism, already under siege of so many other factors (commercialisation, specialisation) of current day legal practice.[94]

---

[87] Kluwer (2023).

[88] Ibid.

[89] Russell and Norvig 2021.

[90] Hagendorff 2020; Jobin et al. 2019.

[91] Salyzyn 2021.

[92] Hagendorff 2020.

[93] Waelberg and Swierstra 2014.

[94] Kronman 1995, p. 367.

A FACT-AI approach is also overly focused on the foreground of AI impact (making it work in a FACT-way) whereas much of the ethical concerns are related to its *background*—i.e. adverse labour conditions of crowd workers,[95] depletion of scarce mineral resources and rapidly increasing energy-consumption by AI-models.[96]

The advance of legal AI assistance technology is inevitable, for it connects deeply to what it means to be a human being as well as a (legal) professional. Being skilful[97] implies that one knows 'how' to interact with artefacts, to master them competently in the exercise of a profession. Making the best out of the inevitable development of legal AI assistance, however, requires that ethics moves beyond traditional FACT-AI ethics. What is also needed is what could be called an 'existential-ethics' of legal AI. This ethics does not deal with the more fanciful though contested 'existential risks' (they are mainly important among transhumanists) that are often connected to the advance of AI.

Existential-ethics of legal AI should be about posing the question what being a good legal professional means in the age of advancing legal AI. Its preoccupation with the question of 'good lawyering' makes it existential-ethical in nature, as distinguished from the more technical FACT-AI approach. The *existential-turn* in AI-ethics is called for precisely because legal AI changes what it means to be a good legal professional. This is an existential change that remains yet unaccounted for in predominant AI-ethical approaches.

Legal AI developments require that we try to *think-through* possible scenarios of changes that will be brought about by legal AI and question to what extent these changes are desirable. To the extent that we can ask these questions, the specific influences of legal AI are not inevitable. They are the result of *negotiations* that should take place in any mature relation to technology, and this includes legal AI.

The *weak* form of inevitability can be handled within the ethical momentum of engagement with AI-development, although only insofar the degree of ethical engagement is widened such that it also includes existential elements. The *strong* form of inevitability with its distinctly transhumanistic overtone is by itself political in nature. Here the reflexive politics of legal AI should step in.

11.8 The Politics of Appropriating Technology

Whether legal AI should go in the direction of replacement is not a matter of fact, but one of politics. This question cannot be settled within the narrower confines of for instance professional codes of conduct for legal professionals—this is the area of ethics. It is a question that involves a perspective on the direction which the society at large is headed for. The question is whether the future is transhumanistic or

95 Altenried 2022.

96 Crawford 2021.

97 Dreyfuss 2014.

humanistic. This question is at the root of the debate around possible replacement and substitution of legal professionals. But what does replacement mean? Is it something like the possible arrival of some form of *general* legal AI, that from the one day to next starts taking legal jobs?

As we already saw, much of the rhetoric in legal transhumanism seems to suggest the possibility of some form of general legal AI. Think for example of an advanced, legal application of IBM's Watson, an AI-system that appeared in a 2011 TV quiz, beating two of the best human competitors. Is it unimaginable that we will come to see increasing applications of such systems, taking the jobs of legal professionals? If this possibility is doubted, the legal transhumanist might say: did we also not believe that a computer could *not* play the Chinese strategy game Go? And yet, in 2016 AlphaGo Zero, an AI designed by Google's DeepMind, defeated Lee Se-dol, who was at the time one of the top players of the game. The defeat left him 'speechless.'[98] Before the game started, Lee had been sure of his victory. Are we to a certain extent not like Lee, sure that the legal profession cannot entirely be replaced by legal AI's, while someday we might wake up and find the legal sector disrupted beyond recognition? That is why we should become political about the rhetoric of legal transhumanism itself.

With the advance of generative AI, it will most likely be the case that we have not yet seen the end of breakthroughs in legal AI. But an advance of technological development should not be dictated by what is technologically possible, but by what is humanly desirable. Despite what the legal transhumanists say, our future is not technological, but humane. To that end we need to appropriate[99] legal AI, which means holding it in its right, *appropriate* place. This place is not its being the centre of the legal profession, as some sort of legal *mega machine*[100] which dictates the course of life around it.

This might happen when the politics of legal AI is indeed unilinear, and legal AI comes in society as a dictate that patterns life around it. But a politics of legal AI is not a politics of adaption, but a politics of *pro-active shaping*. This is what a true reflexive politics of legal AI will amount to. It is politics for it entails a vision on what this shaping could be about and based on *what* this shaping could take place. What however is this 'what', this foundation? Is there some sort of *essential* legal professional? From the perspective on human-technology relations that was sketched above, this would be a problematic position. If being human means being related (with technologies), then an openness towards change is at heart of what it means to be human.

---

[98] Crawford 2021, p. 212.

[99] Winner 1977.

[100] Mumford 2010.

11.9 The Essential Legal Professional

If one would argue that there is some 'essence' some unchangeable substance within the legal professional, it is difficult to envision what this could be. Is this something that has remained unchanged over time? This can hardly be the case as other, earlier technologies and broader societal changes have over time already delivered specific types of legal professionals. Just like technologies are not *in-themselves* (as the transhumanists have it), so are legal professionals not *in-themselves*, and never have they been so. The essential legal professional might only exist as ideal.[101] But even if that ideal exists, it is impossible to think of this ideal, essential legal professional, as untouched by technologies. Nobody is ever untouched by technology. We always live in the world, and the world consists of relations between—amongst others—humans and technologies.[102]

Designing the future of the legal profession based on some essentialist picture of technology (it develops according-to-itself towards ever better forms) is what the transhumanists are doing. Believing that the legal profession to some degree will remain itself, no matter what technological development will do, is also essentialist. Neither position accounts for the possibility and desirability of reciprocal influences. And yet that is what a true politics of legal AI should be about: envisioning a desirable future for the legal profession, without lapsing in the trap of some form of unwarranted essentialism.

Envisioning the future requires understanding where technologies come from, what they will do and whether this is desirable. This desirability, however, cannot be constructed based on some notion of the professional as something that remains inherently and essentially untouched by technological development. Professionals *will* change. But it is not change that we want for the sake of change. We want some change for the good. What good could that be?

Although it is true that being a legal professional comes with intrinsic meaning, the profession as such is not there to sustain itself, it does not exist for its own sake, it is there to provide access-to-justice, the administration of justice and the deliverance of justice. Are we then not back within the range of legal transhumanism? Is there indeed not-putting the tech-tough-talk aside—a compelling, intrinsic motivation for the legal professional to overcome itself, to strive for its own abolishment? This is a fundamental question of legal AI politics. A sketch of what this kind of legal AI politics could be about can only be provided tentatively, for its definite construction stretches well beyond the scope of this chapter.

---

[101] Kronmann 1993.

[102] Latour 2005; Heidegger 2009.

11.10 Designing for Legal Humanism

The argument from legal transhumanism is that the future of the legal profession is technological. This could be translated rather sympathetically as a reminder that the system of legal professionals does not exist for its own sake. Legal professionals are only intermediaries between the rule of law and those seeking access to it. And legal professionals should not function as Kafkaesque *guardians,* effectively hindering or blocking access to the law. And the call from legal transhumanism could be interpreted as a call not in favour of legal professionals, but in favour of the rule of law and a smooth access to it.

The counter-argument would be that legal professionals cannot block access to the law so to say 'by their design.' Because the law is a system of rules laid out in language. The mediation of access to a language-system is something that is an inherently human task. One could argue, however, that if the nature of the law resides in language, then this nature can or even should change to make it more compatible with machine-reading capacities.[103] Again, we are back asking the question who decides. Is it technology, is it legal professionals who might have their specific self-centred reason to stick to the status-quo? We also encounter a new problem here. Because is it *inevitable* that human legal professionals should hold centre stage with the process of administering justice? Could this not change?

In fact, this *will* change whenever legal AI development is kept out of politics. Even an incremental adaption to legal AI technologies might eventually lead to a legal system that to large degrees is no longer ruled by human beings. This is not some form of tech-futuristic prediction, it is the consequence of more fundamental assumptions about what it means to be human. The assumption here is that this by no means comes down to being 'purely' human, stripped of a technological context. By contrast: being human means to be interwoven with ones surrounding, and this surrounding *includes* technologies. And here we have a way out of the deadlock. Because, although being human means being connected to technologies, our humanity is not exhausted by this connection, nor is it exclusively determined by this connection.

To be human also means to be connected to other human beings.[104] It could be argued that this connection holds priority over other relations. Being human means being recognised by other human beings, it entails being *judged* as a human being. Being judged as a human being, requires the judgement of another human being. Only human beings can recognise one another or through the same logic ignore one another. It is therefore not so much the question whether emotional recognition is technically possible or not, AI-powered emotional recognition is *inappropriate.* Despite what language suggests, technologies cannot recognise human beings because they are ontologically different, we do not share the same *form of life.*[105]

When the legal sector is no longer a sector in which we can be recognised, when it is in that sense dehumanised, it has become inappropriate. The legal system is not

---

[103] Pasquale 2019.

[104] Levinas 1969.

[105] Wittgenstein 2009.

there to sustain the profession of legal professionals, but legal professionals are there to keep the legal system appropriate, that is humane. From this maxim two important future directions for the politics of legal AI can be derived.

11.11 The Future Direction of Legal AI Politics

The politics of legal AI should articulate the boundaries for any legal AI development towards replacement or substitution. First, it should try to appropriate legal AI, which means steering it away from attempts to remove human legal professionals from the centre of the legal system. Not because this politics seeks to safeguard existing business-models, well-paid jobs or outdated practices in court, but because this attempt is improper. It would render the legal system without its humanistic *raison d'etre* and the intrinsic necessity of human legal professionals to sustain this core. In short: the politics of legal AI is opposed to any attempt to hijack the legal system through radical or incremental movement towards legal transhumanism. Humanism is not some transitory state, it is by all means a state where we have not yet fully arrived at. From this follows the second direction for the future of legal AI politics.

It is not only about keeping legal AI in its proper place, but it should also be about promoting and articulating what it means to be a human legal professional. This is not some given, but something that needs to be developed. It is actually 'an art of existence,'[106] it is something we need to learn and further develop and what this amounts to in the context of the legal profession needs to be worked out. To that extent, the legal AI development also comes with the opportunity to rearticulate and re-design the future of the legal profession.

11.12 Conclusion

It might seem to be a mere matter of definition whether legal AI is about assisting or substituting human legal professionals. A closer inspection however reveals that important matters of techno-ethics and techno-politics are present in the background of this debate. This chapter made an attempt to show that an extended framework of existential-ethics of legal AI might handle the ethical issues that arrive when legal AI is about some form of legal assistance. Matters get complicated with the rather dominant position of legal transhumanism in the debate on the future of legal AI and with that the future of the legal profession. An attempt was made to show that this matter is not yet settled. The role of technology in the future of the legal profession should not be settled through an adoption of the flawed position of tech-determinism. Instead, a politics of legal AI should be developed that strives towards appropriating

[106] Foucault 2018.

legal AI development. At a minimal level, this entails that legal AI developments should be steered away from attempts to develop substituting legal AI technologies. This does not follow from some sort of unwarranted and irrational refusal, but from a notion according to which there is an inherent and interwoven relation between humans and the rule of law. Much of this politics is yet to be developed and the framework in this chapter is merely a first rudimentary attempt to sketch its possible and desirable future.

References

Altenried M (2022) The Digital Factory: the human labour of automation. The University of Chicago Press, Chicago

Aydin C (2015) The Posthuman as Hollow Idol: A Nietzschean Critique of Human Enhancement. *The Journal of medicine and philosophy, 42.* https://doi.org/10.1093/jmp/jhx002

Butterfield H (1931) The Whig Interpretation of History. Penguin Books, New York

Borgmann A (1984) Technology and the Character of Contemporary Life: Philosophical Inquiry. The University of Chicago Press, Chicago

Brey P (2005) Artifacts as Social Agents. In Hans Harbers (eds.) Inside the Politics of Technology. Amsterdam University Press, Amsterdam

Calo R (2017) Artificial Intelligence Policy: a primer and a roadmap. *University of California, Davis Law Review, 49.* https://doi.org/10.2139/ssrn.3015350.

Custers B (2017) Legal Big Data: toepassingen voor de rechtspraktijk. *Nederlands Juristenblad, 34.* 2449 -2456. https://doi.org/10.2139/ssrn.3196084.

Crawford K (2021) Atlas of AI. Yale University Press, Yale

Dreyfuss H (2014) Skilful Coping: Essays on the Phenomenology of everyday perception and action. Oxford University Press, Oxford

Ellul J (1954) The Technological Society. Vintage Books, New York

Feenberg A (1999) Questioning Technology. Routledge, London

Foucault M (2018) Geschiedenis van de Seksualiteit. (J.Holierhoek, trans.) Boom. (Original work published 1984), Amsterdam

Gibson W (1979) The Ecological Approach to Visual Perception. Houghton Mifflin, Boston

Guillermin, et al. (2021) Ethical Digital Lawyering. In Larry DiMatteo (eds.) The Cambridge Handbook of Lawyering in a digital age. Cambridge University Press, Cambridge

Grunwald A (2019) Designing Technology in the age of digitalization: needs for technology assessment and ethics. Mape, 2-1. 612 – 623. https://doi.org/10.2478/mape-2019-0060

Hagan M (2019) Participatory Design for Innovation in access to justice. *Dædalus, the Journal of the American Academy of Arts & Sciences, 148.* 120–127. https://doi.org/10.1162/daed_a_00544

Hagendorff T (2020) The Ethics of AI-ethics: an evaluation of guidelines. *Minds & Machines,* 30. 99–120 https://doi.org/10.1007/s11023-020-09517-8

Heidegger M (2009) Zijn en Tijd. (M. Wildschut, trans.) Sun. (Original work published 1927), Nijmegen

Hildebrandt M (2016) Smart Technologies and the End (s) of Law, Elgar Publishing, Cheltenham

Jiang C et al. (2021) Disruptive Effects of Legal Technology. In Larry DiMatteo (eds.) Cambridge Handbook of lawyering in the digital age. Cambridge University Press, Cambridge

Jobin A. et al. (2019) The Global Landscape of AI Ethics Guidelines. Nature Machine Intelligence, 1. 389 – 399. https://doi.org/10.1038/s42256-019-0088-2

Katz D (2013) Quantitative Legal Prediction - or - How I learned to stop worrying and start preparing for the data driven future of the legal professions. *Emory Law Review, 62.* https://ssrn.com/abstract=2187752
Kelly K (2016) The Inevitable: Understanding the 12 Technological Forces that Will Shape our Future. Penguin Putnam, New York
Klein N (2023) AI machines aren't hallucinating. But their makers are. *The Guardian: US Edition.* https://www.theguardian.com/commentisfree/2023/may/08/ai-machines-hallucinating-naomi-klein
Kurzweil R (1990) The Age of Spiritual Machines. MIT Press, Cambridge Massachusetts
Kronman A (1995) The Lost Lawyer: Failing Ideals of the Legal Profession. Harvard University Press, Harvard
Kosko B (1999) The Fuzzy Future. Harmony, New York
Latour B (2005) Reassembling the Social: an Introduction to Actor-Network Theory. Oxford University Press, Oxford
Lindgren S (2023) Introducing Critical studies of artificial intelligence. In Simon Lindgren (eds.). Handbook of Critical Studies of Artificial Intelligence. Elgar Publishing, Cheltenham
Levinas E (1969) Totality and Infinity: an essay on exteriority. (Alphonso Lingis, trans.). Duquesne University Press.
McGinnis J and Pearce R (2014) The Great Disruption: how machine intelligence will transform the role of lawyers in the delivery of legal services. *Fordham Law Review, 82.* https://ssrn.com/abstract=2436937
Mesthene E (1967) Technology and Social Change. Macmillan Publishing Company, New York
Mumford L (2010) Technics and Civilization. University of Chicago Press. (Original work published 1934), Chicago
Pasquale F (2019) A Rule of Persons, not Machines: the limits of legal automation. Geo. Wash. Law Review, 87-1. https://ssrn.com/abstract=3135549
Pinch T and Bijker W (1987) The Social Construction of Technological Systems. MIT Press, Cambridge Massachusetts
Pfaffenberg B (1992) Technological Dramas. *Science, Technology and Human Values, 17.* 282 – 312. https://doi.org/10.1177/016224399201700
Russel S and Norvig P (2021) Artificial Intelligence: a Modern Approach. (4th edition). Pearson Education, New York
Salyzyn A (2021) AI and Legal Ethics. In Florian Martin-Bariteau & Teresa Scassa (eds.) Artificial Intelligence and the Law in Canada. *LexisNexis Canada.* https://ssrn.com/abstract=3733952
Smits M (2001) Langdon Winner: Technology as a Shadow Constitution. In Hans Achterhuis (Eds.), American Philosophy of Technology: the Empirical Turn (pp. 147 – 169). Indian Series in the Philosophy of Technology, Indiana
Susskind R and Susskind D (2017) The Future of the Professions. Oxford University Press, Oxford
Susskind R (2019) Tomorrow's Lawyers. (2nd edition). Oxford University Press, Oxford
Tenner E (1997) Why Things Bite Back: Technology and the Revenge of Unintended Consequences. Vintage Books, New York
Tenner E (2018) The Efficiency Paradox: what Big Data can't do. Knopf, New York
Verbeek P (2000) What Things Do: Philosophical Reflections on Technology, Agency and Design. Penn State University Press, Philadelphia
Verbeek P (2011) Moralizing Technology: Understanding and Designing the Morality of Things. University of Chicago Press, Chicago
Van der Put M (2021) Kunstmatige Intelligentie bij Rechterlijke Oordeelsvorming: Theoretische Analyse en Praktische Implementatie. Wolters Kluwer, Alphen a/d Rijn
Walter D (1992) Today Then: America's best minds look 100 years in the future on the occasion of the 1893 world's Columbian Exposition. Farcountry, Helena
Waelberg K and Swierstra (2014) The Family of the Future: How technologies can lead to moral change. In Jeroen van den Hoven (eds.). *Responsible Innovation I.* Springer Science, Dordrecht

Weinstein S (2022) Lawyers Perceptions on the use of AI. In B. Custers and E. Fosch-Villaronga (eds.) Law and Artificial Intelligence. Springer Science, Dordrecht
Winner L (1977) Autonomous Technology: technics-out-of-control as a theme in political thought. MIT Press, Cambridge Massachusetts
Winner L (1980) Do Artifacts have politics? *Daedelus MIT Press,* vol. 109 (1) 121-136
Wittgenstein L (2009) Philosophical Investigations. (G.E.M. Anscombe, trans.) Pearson (original work published 1953), Amsterdam
Wolters Kluwer (2023). *Future Ready Lawyer 2023.* Wolters Kluwer. https://www.wolterskluwer.com/en/know/future-ready-lawyer-2023#download.
Zuboff Z (2019) The Age of Surveillance Capitalism: the fight for a human future at the new frontier of power. Profile Books, New York

Cees Zweistra is a Dutch assistant-professor in Law, Ethics and Technology at Erasmus University Rotterdam. He studied both law and philosophy at Utrecht University and obtained a Ph.D. in the philosophy of technology from Delft University of Technology. He also worked as practising legal professional. His academic research is mainly focused on the impact of technology on identity, social relations and the legal profession. He published popular-philosophical books on topics as technology and loneliness, technology and conspiracy theory and identity politics.

Chapter 12
Codes of Conduct in EU Digital Regulation and AI Policy: The Potential and Risks of Soft Law Tools

Rachel Griffin

Contents

Abstract The EU's 2022 Digital Services Act (DSA) is an ambitious piece of legislation. Articles 34–35 DSA establish a risk assessment and mitigation regime for the largest online platforms, which is intended to play a key role in addressing systemic issues like the effects of platform design and recommendations, structural discrimination, and the dissemination of harmful content. However, many open questions remain about how this regime will be implemented in practice. In this context, Articles 45–47 DSA provide for codes of conduct to clarify and supplement these obligations. Codes of conduct could therefore significantly shape the DSA's implementation, and ultimately its effectiveness. They could also serve as a model for codes of conduct under the 2024 Artificial Intelligence Act (AIA). In this chapter, we provide a brief doctrinal analysis of the functions served by codes of conduct in the DSA. We then consider the potential benefits and disadvantages of using soft law codes to supplement the DSA's hard law framework. Finally, using the 2023 contretemps between X (formerly Twitter) and several EU commissioners over X's participation in the Code of Practice on Disinformation as a point of departure, we consider the question of whether participating in such codes is really voluntary. This analysis highlights that codes of conduct are tools that EU politicians can deploy for political purposes—a

R. Griffin (✉)
Sciences Po Law School, 13 rue de l'Université, 75007 Paris, France
e-mail: rachel.griffin@sciencespo.fr

K. Prifti et al. (eds.), *Digital Governance*, Information Technology and Law Series 39,
https://doi.org/10.1007/978-94-6265-639-0_12

dynamic that has once again been illustrated during the negotiations surrounding the AIA.

Keywords Digital services act · Codes of conduct · Disinformation · Illegal content · Soft law · Self-regulation · Co-regulation · European Union · Artificial intelligence act

12.1 Introduction

The EU's Digital Services Act (DSA), which became fully applicable on 17 February 2024, establishes a new consolidated regulatory regime for online user-generated content. As well as promoting internal market harmonisation, it aims to address risks such as the dissemination of illegal or harmful content, and to protect fundamental rights, for example by preventing arbitrary content removal.[1]

The DSA is a complicated piece of legislation, which essentially introduces a tiered regulatory regime. Certain obligations—primarily regarding illegal content removal and user rights—apply to all intermediary services, intermediaries hosting user-generated content, or 'online platforms' which disseminate such content to the public. Others only cover 'very large online platforms' and 'very large online search engines' (hereafter: VLOPs/VLOSEs) with over 45 million EU users, and create 'due diligence' obligations requiring more systemic reforms. For a more comprehensive overview of the DSA, we refer to other literature.[2]

This contribution focuses on Articles 34–35 DSA, which require VLOPs/VLOSEs to regularly assess and mitigate various broadly-defined 'systemic risks' associated with their services. Article 34 specifies four categories of systemic risk: (1) dissemination of illegal content; (2) impacts on fundamental rights; (3) negative effects on democratic processes, civic discourse and electoral processes, as well as public security; and (4) negative effects on public health or protection of minors, serious negative consequences to a person's physical and mental well-being, and gender-based violence (Recitals 80–84 DSA).

As readers will notice, most of these categories are very broad and rather ambiguous (not to mention frequently overlapping: for example, it is unclear whether mentioning gender-based violence adds anything substantive, given that this already clearly falls within risks to fundamental rights and to physical and mental well-being). Many questions remain about how Articles 34–35 DSA will be interpreted, which issues will be prioritised, and how effective this risk assessment and mitigation regime will ultimately be. To address such uncertainty, the DSA provides for

[1] Regulation (EU) 2022/2065 of the European Parliament and of the Council of 19 October 2022 on a Single Market For Digital Services and amending Directive 2000/31/EC (Digital Services Act) (Text with EEA relevance) ('DSA').

[2] G'sell, 2023; Husovec and Roche Laguna 2023.

codes of conduct to 'contribute to the proper application of this Regulation'[3] and in particular the management of systemic risks. Codes of conduct will therefore play an important role in shaping the DSA's implementation in practice.

This aligns with the increasingly common use of codes of conduct in other areas of EU digital policy, such as the 2016 General Data Protection Regulation (GDPR) and the 2018 updated Audiovisual Media Services Directive.[4] Most recently, in the 2024 Artificial Intelligence Act (AIA), European legislators appear to have taken inspiration from the DSA.[5] Not only does it employ a tiered approach reminiscent of the DSA, with progressively stricter obligations for types of AI system deemed to pose different levels of risk;[6] it will also introduce a regime of codes of conduct.

This contribution provides an in-depth analysis of the role of codes of conduct in the DSA, and aims to draw some lessons for their potential role in the AIA. First, Sect. 12.2 provides a brief doctrinal analysis of the key functions and legal status of codes in the DSA's legal framework, arguing that they effectively create mandatory legal obligations for VLOPs/VLOSEs. Sect. 12.3 discusses some potential advantages codes can offer—although Sect. 12.4 warns that realising these benefits may be practically challenging. Finally, Sect. 12.5 aims to draw some lessons from this analysis for what we can expect from codes of conduct in artificial intelligence policy.

12.2 Codes of Conduct in the DSA

Under the heading of the Better Regulation Agenda,[7] the EU has taken inspiration since the 1990s from the 'new governance' movement, whereby various stakeholders such as industry actors, experts and civil servants participate in regulatory processes.[8] This involvement is often referred to as 'self-regulation'[9] or 'co-regulation',[10] depending on how much private or public bodies set the agenda.[11] However, regulatory literature has started to move beyond these labels, in an effort

[3] Article 45(1) DSA.

[4] For a detailed overview see Vander Maelen 2022.

[5] Regulation (EU) 2024/1689 of the European Parliament and of the Council of 13 June 2024 laying down harmonised rules on artificial intelligence and amending Regulations (EC) No 300/2008, (EU) No 167/2013, (EU) No 168/2013, (EU) 2018/858, (EU) 2018/1139 and (EU) 2019/2144 and Directives 2014/90/EU, (EU) 2016/797 and (EU) 2020/1828 (Artificial Intelligence Act) (Text with EEA relevance) ('AIA').

[6] Kaminski 2023.

[7] Garben and Govaere 2018, p. 3.

[8] Curtin 2006, p. 5.

[9] Porter and Ronit 2006, p. 43.

[10] Hans Bredow Institute 2006.

[11] For a detailed analysis and differentiation of these approaches in the digital policy context see Gorwa 2019.

to more precisely capture the near-infinite possible variations and combinations of stakeholder relationships, influence, monitoring and enforcement mechanisms, etc.

This contribution therefore analyses codes of conduct using Abbott et al.'s concepts of 'soft law' and 'hard law'. These authors propose a streamlined yet theoretically-robust model whereby 'hard law' necessarily has three dimensions: obligation (rules or commitments are binding, and regulatees' compliance is scrutinised), precision (there is relatively little ambiguity about the required conduct), and delegation (third parties such as courts or government agencies have authority to implement, interpret, and apply rules; resolve disputes; and possibly also create further rules).[12] Legal instruments which are weakened along one or more of these dimensions are considered 'soft law'.[13] Codes of conduct are traditionally weak in all three dimensions, especially in the EU context, and are therefore a classic example of soft law.

12.2.1 The Purposes of DSA Codes

The EU often employs codes of conduct as either an alternative or a complement to 'hard' legislation.[14] Both these functions can be seen in the DSA. Articles 45–47 on codes of conduct are at the heart of the DSA's 'Section 6: Other provisions concerning due diligence obligations'. As this suggests, the purpose of DSA codes is to simultaneously clarify and supplement the DSA's due diligence framework—most importantly, VLOPs/VLOSEs' obligations under Articles 34–35.

First, Article 46(1) states that codes should 'contribute to further transparency for actors in the online advertising value chain, beyond the requirements of Articles 26 and 39'—which respectively require all platforms to accompany adverts with information about their source and targeting, and require VLOPs/VLOSEs to maintain public ad archives. Second, Article 47(1) mandates a code to promote accessibility for people with disabilities. Other than the brief Article 47(2)(c) (regarding 'user-friendly' forms and disclosures), the DSA does not include any specific obligations regarding accessibility.[15] Thus, these provisions serve subtly different purposes. Article 46 envisages codes building on and aiding enforcement of existing hard law obligations, whereas Article 47 envisages codes addressing an area otherwise not covered by the DSA.

[12] Abbott and others 2000, p. 401.

[13] Abbott and Snidal 2000, p. 422.

[14] European Commission 2007, 'Commission Staff Working Document: Instruments for a Modernised Single Market Policy—Accompanying Document to the Communication from the Commission to the European Parliament, the Council, the European Economic and Social Committee and the Committee of the Regions: A Single Market for 21st Century Europe' p. 10.

[15] Article 34 mentions risks to fundamental rights including non-discrimination, and could encompass systemic discrimination against people with disabilities. However, what fundamental rights require in this context is so ambiguous that this hardly represents a clear obligation to improve accessibility. See: Griffin 2023a, p. 30.

In parallel, Article 45 creates a much broader mandate for the development of codes. Article 45(1) provides that the Commission and European Board for Digital Services ('the Board')[16] should 'encourage and facilitate' development of codes 'to contribute to the proper application of this Regulation, taking into account in particular the specific challenges of tackling different types of illegal content and systemic risks'. This mandate is extremely broad and flexible. Article 3(h) defines 'illegal content' as any information that 'in itself or in relation to an activity' violates EU or national law. As outlined in the introduction, 'systemic risks' under Article 34 include negative effects relating to illegal content, fundamental rights, civic discourse, electoral processes, security, gender-based violence, public health, and people's physical or mental wellbeing. Overall, then, both terms are extraordinarily broad—and 'in particular' suggests these are not the only possible topics for codes. Thus, Article 45(1) could provide a mandate for regulators to promote the development of codes addressing a huge variety of areas. However, Recital 106 names some areas of particular concern: 'specific types of illegal content' (although confusingly, what 'specific types' is unspecified); disinformation and manipulation; and adverse effects on minors.

Article 45(2) further provides that 'where significant systemic risk [sic] within the meaning of Article 34(1) emerge' and concern several VLOPs/VLOSEs, the Commission 'may invite the providers [...] relevant competent authorities, civil society organisations and other relevant stakeholders' to establish codes of conduct including 'specific risk mitigation measures, as well as a regular reporting framework'. Whether this adds anything substantive to Article 45(1)'s general mandate to encourage code development is questionable. Article 45(2) includes some further details on stakeholder consultation, though it is unclear why this would not also be relevant to codes under Article 45(1).

Even before the DSA was passed, two codes of conduct existed within its field of application: the 2016 Code of Conduct on Hate Speech[17] and the 2018 Code of Practice on Disinformation, updated and expanded in 2022.[18] Both can now become official DSA codes under Article 45. The Commission has also started the drafting process for a code on minor protection, by convening an expert group.[19]

---

[16] The Board is described in Recital 131 as 'an independent advisory group at Union level [...] which should support the Commission and help coordinate the actions of Digital Services Coordinators', which are the principal national regulatory agencies responsible for DSA enforcement at member state level.

[17] European Commission 2016, The EU Code of conduct on countering illegal hate speech online. https://commission.europa.eu/strategy-and-policy/policies/justice-and-fundamental-rights/combatting-discrimination/racism-and-xenophobia/eu-code-conduct-countering-illegal-hate-speech-online_en Accessed 25 January 2024.

[18] European Commission 2022, The Strengthened Code of Practice on Disinformation 2022. https://ec.europa.eu/newsroom/dae/redirection/document/87585 Accessed 7 November 2023.

[19] European Commission 2024, Special group on the EU Code of conduct on age-appropriate design. https://digital-strategy.ec.europa.eu/en/policies/group-age-appropriate-design Accessed 25 January 2024.

As it is more recent and far more detailed than the older Code on Hate Speech, and explicitly seeks to build on the DSA systemic risk framework, the Code on Disinformation is particularly interesting for the purposes of this contribution. It includes commitments in diverse areas including transparency, 'safe design practices', and cooperation with civil society. We believe its focus on researching and testing evidence-based design interventions, with input from civil society, offers positive examples for potential codes in other areas—as we discuss further in Sect. 12.4. However, the Code also illustrates some interesting tensions and doctrinal questions around the legal status of DSA codes, and whether these 'soft law' instruments could in practice create *de facto* hard law obligations.

12.2.2 Are DSA Codes Really Voluntary?

In May 2023, the VLOP X—formerly known as Twitter—and its new owner Elon Musk had a public spat with multiple European Commissioners. Twitter/X had neglected to send a complete report on its compliance with the Code of Practice on Disinformation, and European media reported that it planned to officially withdraw the Code.[20] Internal Market Commissioner Thierry Breton responded—ironically through a tweet—with 'You can run but you can't hide.'[21] Commission Vice-President for Values and Transparency Věra Jourová issued an even more interesting, and perhaps somewhat contradictory response: 'I know the code is voluntary but make no mistake, by leaving the code, Twitter has attracted a lot of attention, and its actions and compliance with EU law will be scrutinised vigorously and urgently.'[22]

Such comments, which acknowledge the 'voluntary' nature of codes but unsubtly hint at legal repercussions for failing to respect them, uncover a tension that runs throughout the DSA. The 'voluntary' nature of codes is repeatedly mentioned.[23] Yet given their role in risk mitigation and auditing, for VLOP/VLOSEs, participation is all but inescapable as part of DSA compliance. On the positive side, it offers perhaps the most straightforward way to demonstrate compliance with Article 35.[24] On the negative side, *not* participating brings legal risks. 'Refusal without proper explanations [...] of the Commission's invitation to participate' in a code can be taken into account

[20] Krukowska 2023, Twitter Withdraws From EU Disinformation Code: Commissioner Says. Time. https://time.com/6283183/twitter-withdraws-from-eu-disinformation-code-commissioner-says/ Accessed 9 August 2023.

[21] Hayden 2023, EU's Breton Says Twitter "Can't Hide" after Platform Ditches Disinformation Code. POLITICO. https://www.politico.eu/article/eu-commissioner-thierry-breton-twitter-elon-musk-cant-hide-after-platform-ditches-disinformation-code/ Accessed 9 August 2023.

[22] O'Carroll 2023, Google and Facebook Urged by EU to Label AI-Generated Content. The Guardian. https://www.theguardian.com/technology/2023/jun/05/google-and-facebook-urged-by-eu-to-label-ai-generated-content Accessed 6 June 2023.

[23] See e.g. Recitals 98 and 103 and Articles 45(1) and 46(1) DSA.

[24] Article 45(2) DSA.

when determining whether an infringement of the DSA took place,[25] as could an audit report finding non-compliance with applicable codes.[26] Thus, VLOPs/VLOSEs who do not follow codes of conduct risk significant legal liabilities, giving them a *de facto* binding character—as the aforementioned comments by senior Commissioners underline.

Furthermore, the Commission and Board take leading roles in code development. Even before the DSA was introduced, the self-regulatory codes on hate speech and disinformation were effectively demanded by policymakers threatening harder regulation.[27] Under the DSA, regulators can identify issues that codes should address[28] and invite preferred stakeholders to participate.[29] The Commission will be particularly influential, as it is ultimately responsible under Article 56(2) for determining whether code commitments and platforms' associated compliance measures are sufficient to comply with Article 35. It also chairs the taskforce that oversees compliance with the 2022 Code on Disinformation.[30] However, national regulators also participate in code development via the Board, and are mentioned in Article 45(2) as relevant stakeholders, so national governments and agencies may also exercise significant influence.

Considering Abbott et al.'s three dimensions of hard law—obligation, precision and delegation—we see that DSA codes appear quite 'hard' among all three dimensions. They are envisaged as being detailed and specific, they are effectively mandatory for VLOPs/VLOSEs, and they give public authorities (and private third parties like auditors) substantial powers of interpretation and enforcement. This continues a trend of hardening or 'legalisation' of codes of conduct that has already been observed elsewhere in EU digital regulation.[31]

This is not merely of theoretical interest. If *de facto* regulatory obligations that address highly-politicised and contested issues are developed through informal, opaque negotiations between companies and unelected regulatory agencies, this raises serious questions about their legitimacy and accountability. This has already been raised in relation to the GDPR,[32] but is also very salient in the context of the DSA, which addresses core political issues and values like online speech regulation, media freedom, and public health and security. Similarly, the AIA regulates artificial intelligence—arguably a paradigm-shifting technology, due to its outsized influence across diverse areas of politics, culture and the economy, and one which therefore calls for a broad democratic debate about its regulation.

---

[25] Recital 104 DSA.

[26] Article 75(4) DSA.

[27] Quintel and Ullrich 2020.

[28] Article 45(2) DSA.

[29] Article 45(2) and 63(1)(e) DSA.

[30] European Commission 2022, The Strengthened Code of Practice on Disinformation 2022. https://ec.europa.eu/newsroom/dae/redirection/document/87585 Accessed 7 November 2023.

[31] Vander Maelen 2022.

[32] Vander Maelen 2022.

As the following two sections outline, codes offer potentially very useful tools to regulate these important and fast-developing areas—yet they also raise real legitimacy concerns. The statements by EU Commissioners discussed above, in which 'voluntary' codes are used for political posturing and to informally put pressure on companies, do not help to alleviate such concerns regarding a 'harder' approach to soft law.[33]

12.3 The Advantages of Codes

Codes of conduct could strengthen DSA implementation in three key ways. First, they offer tools to concretise vague regulatory obligations with more specific commitments. Articles 34–35 are not only vague and abstract, but largely delegate interpretation and oversight to platform companies and private auditing firms.[34] This system may be susceptible to 'regulatory bias',[35] where companies only address risks they find convenient. By specifying more detailed risks and mitigation measures, with input from regulators and civil society, codes can reduce platform companies' room for manoeuvre.

Importantly, at the same time, the flexibility of codes means these detailed commitments can be regularly updated. This mitigates one possible drawback of overly-specific regulation, that it rapidly becomes outdated, and could help address emerging or quickly-evolving risks. For example, commentators observed that the DSA did not anticipate the rapid development and deployment of generative AI,[36] yet some Commission representatives have proposed that DSA codes could be used to tackle issues raised by AI, as we detail in Sect. 12.5. Codes can also be tailored to specific types of platform or technical features, as not all companies must sign every commitment.

Second, codes can help develop stronger institutional accountability mechanisms. Establishing concrete commitments, key performance indicators (KPIs) and reporting standards is an important way to facilitate external oversight by regulators, auditors and other stakeholders,[37] but codes can also develop additional oversight institutions. For example, the Code of Practice on Disinformation establishes a permanent taskforce chaired by the Commission.[38] Codes of conduct

[33] Vander Maelen 2022.

[34] Griffin 2023a.

[35] Segal 2001, Institutional Self-Regulation: What Should Be the Role of the Regulator? (Address to the National Institute for Governance Twilight Seminar, Canberra). ASIC. https://asic.gov.au/about-asic/news-centre/speeches/institutional-self-regulation-what-should-be-the-role-of-the-regulator/ Accessed 11 April 2023; Laux and others 2021, p. 105613.

[36] Hacker and others 2023, 'Understanding and Regulating ChatGPT, and Other Large Generative AI Models'. Verfassungsblog. https://verfassungsblog.de/chatgpt/ Accessed 10 March 2023.

[37] Laux and others 2021.

[38] European Commission 2022, The Strengthened Code of Practice on Disinformation 2022. https://ec.europa.eu/newsroom/dae/redirection/document/87585 Accessed 7 November 2023.

can also facilitate data access for researchers, which should significantly enhance accountability.[39]

Relatedly, DSA codes enable diverse stakeholders to participate in shaping and overseeing platforms' obligations. For example, Article 46(1) calls for codes of conduct on advertising to involve a broader array of actors in the 'advertising value chain', as well as civil society. This should be encouraged, as multistakeholder participation can foster more meaningful accountability and transparency,[40] and help translate the information provided by platforms into policy-relevant insights.[41]

Third and finally, codes of conduct offer a way to establish commitments in areas that are otherwise neglected by the DSA—whether due to political compromises, later developments, or other reasons. As mentioned above, the DSA includes few provisions on accessibility, effectively leaving this area to be regulated by soft law. Another particularly significant area in this regard is the design of platform interfaces and recommendation systems. Academic and industry experts widely recognise that design crucially influences a host of pressing policy issues—from the prevalence and impact of harmful content, to mental health, user safety, and political discourse and polarisation.[42] However, the DSA barely addresses platform design; where it is addressed, the legislative text remains vague, as in the systemic risk provisions, or stays on well-trodden ground, making only conservative changes—such as its provisions on deceptive practices[43] and consumer protection,[44] both focused narrowly on individual interests rather than the broader social impacts of platform design.

Codes of conduct offer a promising instrument to emphasise the importance of design in risk mitigation and develop concrete standards in this area. In fact, they have already been used for this purpose: the updated Code on Disinformation includes various commitments about how platforms should research and test 'safe design practices', overseen by its dedicated taskforce. Platforms have previously tested design changes which successfully discouraged abusive behaviour and the virality of harmful content, like 'nudging' users not to post harmful content, or adjusting recommendation algorithms.[45] However, revenue concerns or changing business strategies often led companies to abandon such measures.[46] There is therefore a clear need for regulatory incentives to more consistently and systematically pursue such efforts. By establishing clear commitments and oversight structures, backed up by the legal obligations of Articles 34–35, codes of conduct could provide these incentives.

---

[39] Hendrix 2023, Working Group Publishes New Draft Code for Researcher Access to Platform Data. https://www.techpolicy.press/working-group-publishes-new-draft-code-for-researcher-access-to-platform-data/ Accessed 25 January 2024.

[40] Leerssen 2023; Helberger and others 2018; Griffin 2023a.

[41] Leerssen 2023.

[42] Botero Arcila and Griffin 2023a, b.

[43] Article 25(1) DSA.

[44] Article 31 DSA.

[45] Botero Arcila and Griffin 2023a, b.

[46] Klonick 2023, The End of the Golden Age of Tech Accountability. The Klonickles. https://klonick.substack.com/p/the-end-of-the-golden-age-of-tech Accessed 15 March 2023.

12.4 Risks and Legitimacy Concerns

Regulating platforms through soft law also raises questions about legitimacy—actual and perceived. We evaluate legitimacy using Schmidt's influential framework,[47] which identifies three types of legitimacy—each raising interesting questions relevant to codes of conduct. First, input legitimacy: will DSA codes be shaped by democratic institutions? Second, throughput legitimacy: will the development and oversight of codes be transparent and inclusive? And third, output legitimacy: will they produce outcomes that serve the public?

On the first point, industry-led codes inherently delegate regulatory authority from democratically-legitimated public authorities to private actors. However, this is not inherently negative. As Sect. 12.3 argued, it can enable more detailed, regularly-updated standards. It can also enhance legitimacy by enabling more pluralistic participation, taking advantage of private and civil society stakeholders' knowledge, perspectives and resources.[48] Furthermore, involving the state directly in regulating communications platforms raises concerns regarding freedom of expression and media independence—which, for many authors, speaks in favour of more polycentric regulatory frameworks, involving networks of private actors.[49]

Thus, where the DSA text establishes broad goals and parameters, we suggest that using codes to establish more detailed standards can appropriately balance input legitimacy, flexibility and independence. On the other hand, using codes to fill gaps on issues like accessibility and safe design which are barely addressed in the DSA text at all is more problematic. It suggests that these areas were inadequately considered in the legislative process, and that there will be a lack of democratic input into how they are regulated.

Additionally, we highlight two groups of actors whose roles have particular implications for DSA codes' input legitimacy. First, the European Commission—arguably the least representative EU legislative institution—will exercise significant influence throughout the lifecycle of a DSA code. Under Article 45, it has the power to invite specific actors to take part in drawing up codes on the topics of its choice (see also Recital 104 DSA). Given that it is ultimately responsible for determining whether VLOPs/VLOSEs have complied with their risk mitigation obligations, its views on what these codes should contain are likely to be listened to. The Commission reportedly set out quite prescriptive expectations for previous code negotiations, e.g. on disinformation.[50] However, there is little oversight of how it uses these powers to set priorities and expectations for DSA codes. Arguably, this reflects a more general deficit of accountability mechanisms enabling oversight of the Commission's DSA enforcement strategy by other EU institutions.

---

[47] Schmidt 2013; see also Haggart and Keller 2021.

[48] Marsden and others 2013, p. 20; Salamon 2011, p. 1627.

[49] Gorwa 2019.

[50] Quintel and Ullrich 2020.

Second, the 'big tech' corporations which own most VLOPs/VLOSEs may have an overwhelming influence on code development, creating significant risks of regulatory capture.[51] In the development of soft law frameworks, several practical factors—including technical expertise, financial resources and political connections—often favour larger corporations to the detriment of smaller companies and other stakeholder groups.[52] Indeed, scientific literature observes that dominant corporations often participate in codes of conduct as a way to resist more stringent and costly regulatory interventions.[53] In the worst case, then, the content and priorities of DSA codes may be largely determined by executive authorities on the one hand, and powerful corporations on the other—enabling both to shape platform governance, while bypassing democratic input and accountability.

Turning to throughput legitimacy, codes in principle allow for deliberative processes and multistakeholder participation. However, existing codes have been criticised for failing to include diverse stakeholders.[54] Different stakeholder groups' capacities to participate in negotiation and consultation processes will inevitably reflect existing disparities of power and resources.[55] Moreover, multistakeholder participation offers further potential for corporate capture by 'big tech' platforms. Leading platforms extensively influence activism and academic research through donations, funding programmes and partnerships—shaping the relative resources and power of the very stakeholders meant to provide independent input.[56] Civil society participation can still diversify the interests represented, and ensure that risk mitigation measures reflect external expertise. However, NGOs should not be treated as neutral representatives of the public, and stakeholder participation is not a simple shortcut to legitimacy.[57] To maximise its benefits, the Commission and Board should prioritise diversity and inclusion: for example, by financially supporting NGOs' participation.[58]

Finally, on output legitimacy, how effectively codes will achieve meaningful, socially beneficial changes in business practices is still up for debate. As discussed above, codes *could* promote effective policy interventions: for example, by specifying standards on safer platform design. Creating safer and more inclusive online

[51] Makkai and Braithwaite 1998.

[52] Kampourakis 2021; Griffin 2023b.

[53] Newman and Bach 2004; Wu 2011.

[54] Access Now and others 2022, Joint Statement on Stakeholder Inclusion in the Code of Practice on Disinformation Revision Process. AlgorithmWatch. https://algorithmwatch.org/en/wp-content/uploads/2022/02/Joint_Statement_CoP.pdf Accessed 15 March 2023.

[55] Kampourakis 2021, pp. 119–20; Griffin 2023b.

[56] Griffin 2023b.

[57] Griffin 2023b.

[58] Vergnolle 2023, Putting collective intelligence to the enforcement of the Digital Services Act. DSA Enforcement. https://dsa-enforcement.vergnolle.org/ Accessed 3 May 2023.

spaces would of course be highly desirable from a democratic legitimacy perspective.[59] However, we also see a clear risk that—given the strong possibilities of corporate capture discussed above—codes could end up largely reformulating the limited and low-cost measures platform companies already have in place, like automated moderation, rather than promoting more innovative or far-reaching interventions.

12.5 Codes of Conduct in AI Policy

The increasingly prominent role of codes in EU digital regulation seems set to continue, as they feature prominently in the AIA. Article 95 AIA is dedicated to codes of conduct.

AI systems that are not classified as 'high-risk AI systems'—which comes with stricter regulatory requirements under the Act's tiered approach[60]—are encouraged to nonetheless voluntarily apply the higher standards in Chapter III of the AIA.[61] Responsibility for overseeing code development will rest jointly with member states and the European AI Office, a new department being set up within DG CNECT (the same Commission department responsible for DSA enforcement).[62]

The wording of Article 95 is quite similar to that of Article 45 DSA (e.g. 'key performance indicators') and Article 40 GDPR (e.g. the emphasis on small and medium-sized enterprises). However, one notable addition is Article 95(2), which states that codes of conduct should not only have clear objectives and key performance indicators, but should also include elements such as ethics, energy efficiency, promotion of AI literacy, inclusive and diverse design, and prevention of negative impacts on vulnerable persons or groups. As outlined in Sect. 12.3, providing more specific commitments related to issues like these is one of the main benefits DSA codes can offer. Signalling more explicitly that these should be priority areas for AIA codes is therefore a clear positive point, making it more likely that action will be taken on these important collective issues.

As will be shown, many of the other questions and concerns raised in our analysis of the DSA also appear highly relevant to the AIA. However, we highlight three particularly noteworthy developments. First, codes appear to have become more politicised, playing a controversial role during the fraught final stages of the AIA negotiations. Second, the Commission appears to be trying to 'repurpose' the DSA,

[59] Botero Arcila and Griffin 2023a, b.

[60] Kaminski 2023.

[61] Article 95(1) AIA.

[62] European Commission 2024. Commission Decision Establishing the European AI Office. European Commission. https://digital-strategy.ec.europa.eu/en/library/commission-decision-establishing-european-ai-office-0 Accessed 25 January 2024. One question that could be raised here is whether a new regulatory agency to be built from scratch, with responsibility for overseeing a very lengthy and complex regulation, will have sufficient operational capacities to effectively coordinate the development of AIA codes.

and especially the Code of Practice on Disinformation, to regulate unforeseen developments in generative AI. Third, in the longer term, it seems to be using codes of conduct as a tool to pursue EU policy goals at a global level.

12.5.1 The Politicisation of Codes of Conduct

With rare exceptions like the contretemps over Twitter/X's withdrawal from the Code of Practice on Disinformation, codes of conduct have hitherto been a rather low-profile and technical area of EU technology policy. However, in the final phases of the AIA trilogue negotiations[63]—in which bitter disputes over key areas like the regulation of the most powerful 'foundation models' and of surveillance technologies led to marathon all-night negotiating sessions[64] and even raised the prospect that the AIA would not be passed in the 2017–24 parliamentary term[65]—codes of conduct unexpectedly played a starring role.

In one of the most difficult points of disagreement, the French, German and Italian governments abruptly announced, much to the dismay of other member states and stakeholders, that they wanted 'foundation models'—general-purpose machine learning models trained on very large datasets—to be largely exempted from the AIA's hard law regulatory regime. Instead, they proposed, foundation models should be regulated by codes of conduct.[66] This volte-face was driven by concerns that hard regulation would hold back innovation, ultimately reflecting national concerns about industrial policy and digital sovereignty: advanced AI is for now dominated by US and Chinese companies, but both France and Germany have promising tech start-ups working on foundational models (respectively Mistral AI and Aleph Alpha) and do not want them held back by the AIA.[67] Commentators highlighted Mistral and Aleph Alpha's political connections, suggesting that lobbying and 'revolving door' tactics were being used to undermine the effectiveness of regulation.[68]

---

[63] This refers to the final stages of the EU legislative process, in which—after agreeing internally on their respective negotiating positions—the Council, Commission and Parliament must reach agreement on a final text acceptable to all three institutions.

[64] Volpicelli 2023, EU's AI talks sputter over intrusive security loopholes. https://www.politico.eu/article/ai-act-negotiations-enter-their-19-hour/ Accessed 25 January 2024.

[65] Bertuzzi 2023, EU's AI Act negotiations hit the brakes over foundation models. https://www.euractiv.com/section/artificial-intelligence/news/eus-ai-act-negotiations-hit-the-brakes-over-foundation-models/ Accessed 25 January 2024.

[66] Bertuzzi 2023, France, Germany, Italy push for 'mandatory self-regulation' for foundation models in EU's AI law. Euractiv. https://www.euractiv.com/section/artificial-intelligence/news/france-germany-italy-push-for-mandatory-self-regulation-for-foundation-models-in-eus-ai-law/ Accessed 23 January 2024.

[67] Hartmann T (2023) Behind France's stance against regulating powerful AI models. Euractiv. https://www.euractiv.com/section/artificial-intelligence/news/behind-frances-stance-against-regulating-powerful-ai-models/ Accessed 23 January 2024.

[68] Hartmann 2023, Ibid.

In these debates, codes were portrayed by proponents as balancing flexibility and innovation against safety, justice and other public-interest issues—whereas detractors suggested they would enable regulatory capture and a free hand for corporations.[69] In the final compromise text, it appears that foundation models will be subject to a mixture of soft-law codes and hard-law obligations—though the details of many mandatory obligations are left to be resolved later through technical standards, raising many similar concerns about democratic legitimacy, transparency and accountability, and corporate capture.[70]

12.5.2 *Realpolitik and Repurposing of Codes*

In parallel, key figures within the Commission are also more explicitly politicising codes of conduct and using them to press their own political agendas. The very rapid deployment and commercialisation of generative AI tools such as ChatGPT and DALL-E throughout 2022 and 2023 caught the EU institutions—who had been working on the AIA for several years by that point—by surprise. Already, midway through the AIA negotiations, scholars were raising concerns that aspects of the law were outdated.[71]

EU Commissioners have therefore suggested using soft law tools to implement faster and more flexible AI policies—whether through an entirely new self-regulatory 'AI Pact', advocated by Breton,[72] or by 'repurposing' existing instruments like the Code of Practice on Disinformation. For example, Jourová has suggested that signatories to the Code of Practice should be required to label AI-generated content,[73] since artificial intelligence could significantly facilitate the creation and large-scale

---

[69] Giulia Geneletti and Philipp Hacker 2023, [Interview] On the Ongoing EU AI Act Trilogues and Specific Provisions Covering the Regulation of Foundation Models (FMs): Questions to Professor Hacker. https://www.sciencespo.fr/public/chaire-numerique/en/2023/11/28/interview tthe-ongoing-ai-act-negotiations-questions-to-prof-hacker/ Accessed 25 January 2024

[70] Veale and Borgesius 2021.

[71] For example, the AIA's differentiated obligations for 'users' and 'providers' of AI software do not map well onto complex software supply chains, especially in the case of general-purpose or 'foundation' models which can be adapted for many different uses, and do a poor job of allocating responsibility to those who are actually capable of addressing risks. See: Cobbe, Veale and Singh 2023, Understanding Accountability in Algorithmic Supply Chains'. 2023 ACM Conference on Fairness, Accountability, and Transparency (FAccT '23). https://papers.ssrn.com/sol3/papers.cfm?abs tract_id=4430778 Accessed 18 August 2023; Hacker, Engel and Mauer 2023, Regulating ChatGPT and other Large Generative AI Models. 2023 ACM Conference on Fairness, Accountability, and Transparency (FAccT '23). https://arxiv.org/abs/2302.02337 Accessed 18 August 2023.

[72] Breton 2023, Artificial Intelligence—Statement by Commissioner Breton. European Commission. https://ec.europa.eu/commission/presscorner/detail/en/statement_23_3344 Accessed 10 August 2023.

[73] O'Carroll 2023, Google and Facebook Urged by EU to Label AI-Generated Content. The Guardian. https://www.theguardian.com/technology/2023/jun/05/google-and-facebook-urged-by-eu-to-label-ai-generated-content Accessed 6 June 2023.

dissemination of convincing disinformation.[74] As of January 2024, the signatories have reportedly 'set up a subgroup on generative AI that has quickly become the largest one'.[75]

Even more explicitly than before, EU Commissioners are using codes of conduct as a political tool to steer the agenda in these fast-developing policy debates. In this highly mediatised policy area, it is understandable that policymakers are keen to stake out a position. From this realpolitik perspective, Jourová's 'repurposing' of the Code of Practice serves dual purposes: quickly addressing an unforeseen policy issue using already-existing regulatory standards, while also portraying the Commission as an institution—and herself personally—as staying on top of rapid technological developments.

It is true that AI systems are widely used within online platforms and other intermediary services regulated by the DSA, and today's largest digital platforms are owned and run by the same 'big tech' corporations that are leading AI development.[76] However, given that DSA and AIA codes exhibit important differences—e.g. in their scope of application, signatories and oversight structures—attempting to repurpose DSA codes to regulate issues that are primarily within the scope of the AIA runs the risk of ending up with a confusing or incoherent regulatory landscape.

12.5.3 The Global Dimension of Codes of Conduct

European Commission Executive Vice-President Margrethe Vestager has also proposed applying codes of conduct to regulate AI—not only within the EU, but at the global level. Vestager pushed for the EU-US Trade and Technology Council (TTC) to develop a joint code of conduct on AI.[77] Aligning with the traditional understanding of soft law, the code was presented as containing 'non-binding standards around transparency, risk audits and other technical details for companies'[78]. With the code reportedly drafted 'over an hour-long lunch of cod loin and chocolate praline',[79] questions could also be raised about how substantial or stringent these non-binding standards will be.

---

[74] Bontridder and Poullet 2021.

[75] Bertuzzi and Tar 2024, Tech Brief—Dual-use R&D options, France's influencer law EU alignment. Euractiv. https://mailchi.mp/euractiv/tech-brief-ai-final-act-commissions-dsa-showdown-with-x-494352?e=ac007aa1f9 Accessed 24 January 2024.

[76] This notably includes Microsoft, Amazon, Google and Meta. See Srnicek 2022.

[77] Scott, Chatterjee and Volpicelli 2023, The Struggle to Control AI. POLITICO. https://www.politico.eu/article/washington-eu-trade-and-tech-council-join-forces-to-stop-ai-harms/ Accessed 9 August 2023.

[78] Scott, Chatterjee and Volpicelli 2023. Ibid.

[79] Ibid.

Interestingly, however, Vestager described the code as a joint transatlantic proposal that would ultimately be presented to G7 leaders as the basis for further international negotiations.[80] Lo and behold: a few months later, the G7 leaders unveiled the 'Hiroshima Process International Code of Conduct for Organizations Developing Advanced AI Systems'.[81] The code contains 11 overarching principles, with some concrete recommendations on how these can be implemented in practice. Nonetheless, it is clearly a first version and the code is explicitly labelled as a 'living document'.[82] The first signatories will also be announced later.

This suggests that Vestager is seeking to use EU-led codes to promote the EU's favoured regulatory approach at a global level. Codes of conduct are already well-known tools in public international law, where they often serve as a politically digestible way to achieve policy progress in fields where binding rules are non-existent or insufficiently developed,[83] often because of ideological differences. Over time, such soft law tools can 'establish a common set of principles and raise awareness', favouring globalisation of standards in the long term.[84]

This represents a notable evolution in the role of EU codes of conduct. So far, the EU has used codes to regulate its internal market,[85] either within the framework of EU regulations targeting private actors (like the GDPR and DSA) or through codes aimed at harmonising policy between member states (such as the infamous 'Code of Conduct on Business Taxation'[86]). In contrast, Vestager's push for common standards through the G7 represents, to our knowledge, the first time the EU explicitly uses codes of conduct in its foreign policy agenda—and, notably, in a sensitive policy area with significant geopolitical implications.[87]

[80] Ibid.

[81] European Commission 2023, Commission Welcomes G7 Leaders' Agreement on Guiding Principles and a Code of Conduct on Artificial Intelligence. https://ec.europa.eu/commission/presscorner/detail/en/ip_23_5379 Accessed 24 January 2024.

[82] Group of Seven (G7) 2023, Hiroshima Process International Code of Conduct for Organizations Developing Advanced AI Systems.

[83] Friedrich 2010.

[84] Birnhack 2008, The EU Data Protection Directive: An Engine of a Global Regime. Computer Law & Security Review 24:508–520.

[85] For an overview of the diverse ways the EU has used codes of conduct, see: Vander Maelen 2022.

[86] Gribnau 2010.

[87] Zhang and Levine 2023, Why AI Is Next Flashpoint in US-China Tech Rivalry. Washington Post. https://www.washingtonpost.com/business/2023/06/29/what-is-the-state-of-us-china-competition-in-ai/80b116c2-165d-11ee-9de3-ba1fa29e9bec_story.html Accessed 18 August 2023.

12.6 Conclusion

Codes of conduct are set to play an important role in the implementation of the DSA. In this chapter, we have identified three key advantages they offer: concretising platform obligations; strengthening institutional accountability mechanisms; and establishing commitments in otherwise neglected areas. However, there are important concerns relating to their legitimacy. The influence of the Commission and 'big tech' companies arguably undermines input legitimacy, while lack of meaningful multi-stakeholder participation (especially civil society) could also weaken throughput legitimacy. At this early stage, on output legitimacy, the jury is still out.

This chapter has also discussed tensions around the 'voluntary' nature of DSA codes, pointing not only to their *de facto* legal force, but also the ways they can be leveraged by policymakers to put pressure on companies. In the context of AI policy, these dynamics appear even more pronounced. Codes of conduct were wielded in a politically motivated manner—largely to favour influential corporate interests—during the AIA negotiations, while several European Commissioners are using codes to steer policy debates in accordance with their own political agendas. Finally, the EU is now using codes of conduct to promote its own interests and regulatory standards on the international level.

Analysing existing EU legislation can provide worthwhile insights for developing instruments like the AIA—especially given the iterative approach to lawmaking that has characterised EU digital policy, with the GDPR serving as a 'mimetic' model for future legislation.[88] The DSA's tiered approach and reliance on soft-law codes have clearly influenced the AIA. Reflecting the central role of dominant platform companies in the developing AI industry,[89] EU policy on digital platforms and AI is also increasingly intertwined, including through codes of conduct.

In closing, we can observe that soft law—and law in general—have always been tools to express political priorities. The distinction lies in the fact that traditional legislation must pass through transparent, predefined procedures that should—at least in theory—give voice to voters' policy preferences. Soft law, on the other hand, follows much more fluid, less transparent procedures that often weaken transparency and democratic accountability. What is a code of conduct in EU law exactly? Depending on the political issue *du jour*, a code seems to be whatever the European Commission wants it to be.

References

Abbott K and others (2000) The Concept of Legalization. International Organization 54:401–419

Abbott K and Snidal D (2000) Hard and Soft Law in International Governance. International Organization 54:421–456

---

[88] Papakonstantinou and De Hert 2022.

[89] Rikap 2021; Srnicek 2022.

Birnhack M (2008) The EU Data Protection Directive: An Engine of a Global Regime. Computer Law & Security Review 24:508–520.

Bontridder N and Poullet Y (2021) The Role of Artificial Intelligence in Disinformation. Data & Policy 3:e32

Botero Arcila B and Griffin R (2023) Social media platforms and challenges for democracy, rule of law and fundamental rights. European Parliament Committee on Civil Liberties, Justice and Home Affairs. https://www.europarl.europa.eu/RegData/etudes/STUD/2023/743400/IPOL_STU(2023)743400_EN.pdf Accessed 7 November 2023

Curtin D (2006) European Legal Integration: Paradise Lost? In: Curtin D and others (eds) European Integration and Law: four contributions on the interplay between European integration and European and national law to celebrate the 25th anniversary of Maastricht University's Faculty of Law. Intersentia, Antwerp, pp 1–56

Friedrich F (2010) Codes of Conduct. In: Max Planck Encyclopedias of International Law. Oxford University Press, Oxford, https://opil.ouplaw.com/display/https://doi.org/10.1093/law:epil/9780199231690/law-9780199231690-e1379 Accessed 7 November 2023

G'sell F (2023) The Digital Services Act (DSA): A General Assessment. In: Antje von Ungern-Sternberg (ed) Content Regulation in the European Union—The Digital Services Act. Trier Institute for Digital Law, Trier

Garben S and Govaere I (2018) The Multi-Faceted Nature of Better Regulation. In: Garben S and Govaere I The EU better regulation agenda: a critical assessment. Hart Publishing, Oxford, pp 3–12

Gorwa R (2019) What is platform governance? Information, Communication & Society 22:854–871

Gribnau H (2010) The Code of Conduct for Business Taxation: An Evaluation of an EU Soft-Law Instrument. In: Dennis Weber (ed) Traditional and Alternative Routes to European Tax Integration: Primary Law, Secondary Law, Soft Law, Coordination, Comitology and Their Relationship. IBFD, Amsterdam pp 67–96

Griffin R (2023a) Rethinking Rights in Social Media Governance: Human Rights, Ideology and Inequality. European Law Open 2:30–56

Griffin R (2023b) Public and Private Power in Social Media Governance: Multistakeholderism, the Rule of Law and Democratic Accountability. Transnational Legal Theory 14:46–89

Haggart B and Iglesias Keller C (2021) Democratic legitimacy in global platform governance. Telecommunications Policy 45:102152

Hans Bredow Institute (2006) Final Report—Study on Co-Regulation Measures in the Media Sector (Study for the European Commission). European Commission, Brussels

Helberger N and others (2018) Governing online platforms: From contested to cooperative responsibility. The Information Society 34:1–14

Husovec M & Roche Laguna I (2023) Digital Services Act: A Short Primer. In: Husovec M & Roche Laguna I (eds) Principles of the Digital Services Act. Oxford University Press, Oxford, forthcoming

Kaminski M (2023) Regulating the Risks of AI. Boston University Law Review 103:1347

Kampourakis I (2021) The Postmodern Legal Ordering of the Economy. Indiana Journal of Global Legal Studies 28:101–152

Laux J and others (2023) Taming the few: Platform regulation, independent audits, and the risks of capture created by the DMA and DSA. Computer Law & Security Review 43:105613

Leerssen P (2023) Seeing what others are seeing: Studies in the regulation of transparency for social media recommender systems. University of Amsterdam 2023, Amsterdam

Makkai T and Braithwaite J (1998) In and Out of the Revolving Door: Making Sense of Regulatory Capture. Oxford University Press, Oxford

Marsden C and others (2013) D4.1 Outline Overviews of Tasks R4.1–R4.4: Regulatory and Governance Methodologies. European Commission, Brussels

Newman A and Bach D (2004) Self-Regulatory Trajectories in the Shadow of Public Power: Resolving Digital Dilemmas in Europe and the United States. Governance 17:387–413.

Papakonstantinou V and De Hert P (2022) The Regulation of Digital Technologies in the EU: The Law-Making Phenomena of "Act-Ification", "GDPR Mimesis" and "EU Law Brutality". Technology and Regulation 2022

Porter T and Ronit K (2006) Self-Regulation as Policy Process: The Multiple and Criss-Crossing Stages of Private Rule-Making. Policy Sciences 39:41–72

Quintel T and Ullrich C (2020) Self-Regulation of Fundamental Rights? The EU Code of Conduct on Hate Speech, Related Initiatives and Beyond. In: Petkova B and Ojanen T (eds) Fundamental Rights Protection Online. Edward Elgar, Cheltenham pp 197–229

Rikap C (2021) Capitalism, Power and Innovation: Intellectual Monopoly Capitalism Uncovered. Routledge, Abingdon

Salamon L (2011) The New Governance and the Tools of Public Action: An Introduction. Fordham Urban Law Journal 28:1611–1674

Schmidt V (2013) Democracy and legitimacy in the European Union revisited: Input, output and "throughput"'. Political Studies 61.

Srnicek N (2022) Data, Compute, Labour. In: Graham M and Ferrari F (eds) Digital Work in the Planetary Market. MIT Press, Cambridge pp 241–261.

Vander Maelen C (2022) Hardly Law or Hard Law? Investigating the Dimensions of Functionality and Legalisation of Codes of Conduct in Recent EU Legislation and the Normative Repercussions Thereof. European Law Review 47:752–772.

Veale M and Borgesius FZ (2021). Demystifying the Draft EU Artificial Intelligence Act. Computer Law Review International 22(4):97.

Wu T (2011) Agency Threats. Duke Law Journal 60: 1841–1857.

Rachel Griffin is a Ph.D. candidate and lecturer in law at Sciences Po Law School, where she is researching European social media regulation and its implications for structural social inequalities. She has published in journals including JIPITEC, European Law Open and the International Journal of Communication, and co-authored (with Prof. Botero Arcila) a report on current issues in social media regulation for the European Parliament's LIBE Committee.

Chapter 13
Rethinking Algorithmic Explainability Through the Lenses of Intellectual Property and Competition

Lucas Costa dos Anjos

Contents

Abstract Algorithmic decision-making is integral to digital platforms, influencing user experiences and societal dynamics. This paper chapter scrutinizes algorithmic opacity, highlighting the inherent biases, the anti-competitive strategies that may result from dominant market power and the potential for discrimination within these systems. Despite the promise of objectivity, algorithms often operate under a veil of opacity, shaping content and information access, with significant implications for individual perspectives and societal functioning. The chapter explores the legal challenges posed by the protection of algorithms through the lenses of intellectual property rights and competition law. It calls for a multifaceted regulatory approach to ensure transparency. The analysis emphasises the need to balance innovation with competition and societal well-being, advocating for a right to explanation in the face of automated decisions within the European Union.

Keywords Algorithmic decision-making · Neutrality · Bias · Transparency · Regulation · Digital platforms

---

L. C. dos Anjos (✉)
Postdoctoral researcher at École de Droit Sciences Po, 13 rue de l'Université, 75337 Paris, France
e-mail: lucas.costadosanjos@sciencespo.fr

K. Prifti et al. (eds.), *Digital Governance*, Information Technology and Law Series 39,
https://doi.org/10.1007/978-94-6265-639-0_13

13.1 Introduction

Algorithmic decision-making with the help of machine learning has become pervasive in our society, shaping our online experiences and influencing our daily lives. They allow computers to understand patterns and forecast or make judgments based on data without the need for literal and explicit programming. Such is the case of predictive algorithms for personalized advertising, content moderation and matching. However, concerns about bias, discrimination, and lack of transparency have raised significant regulatory challenges. This chapter examines the evolving landscape of algorithmic neutrality and the increasing need for effective rights to explanation in the face of algorithmic decision-making.

While machine learning algorithms promise efficiency and objectivity, their pervasive nature has ushered in a slew of concerns, particularly surrounding their inherent biases and potential for discrimination. The widespread assumption that platforms like Google, Facebook, and Twitter operate under a veil of neutrality is increasingly being challenged.[1]

In reality, these algorithms, often shrouded in opacity, play a pivotal role in shaping the content we are exposed to in a social network such as Twitter, in the information we retrieve in a Google Search results' page, product recommender systems on Amazon and in the societal dynamics of political debates intermediated by public digital discourse. The consequences of algorithmic choices are not neutral and can have profound impacts on our access to information, our perspectives, and the overall functioning of society.

Moreover, the dominance of certain platforms in the digital market presents additional challenges. Market power abuse, anti-competitive strategies, and the lack of transparency in algorithms hinder fair competition and limit users' freedom of choice. The concentration of power in a few platforms raises even more concerns about the implications for market dynamics and the overall diversity of online content.[2]

The legal inscrutability of algorithms further complicates the regulatory landscape. The protection of algorithmic decision-making through trade secrets and intellectual property rights creates barriers to understanding how decisions are made and whether biases are present. As algorithms increasingly drive critical processes in areas such as finance, employment, and criminal justice, the need for transparency and a right to explanation becomes more pressing.[3]

---

[1] Abiteboul and Stoyanovich 2019, p. 9.

[2] Google is one of the main perpetrators of these abuses of dominant position. In the European Union, the company has been scrutinized by competition authorities under several prisms, most noticeably in the Android, Ads and Search cases. Notably, in 2017, it was fined €2.42 billion for abusing its dominant position in the online search market by favoring its own price comparison service. Again in 2018, Google was penalized for restricting competition in the mobile internet sector through its Android operating system. These actions, considered illegal under EU antitrust rules, hindered innovation and competition, leading to reduced choices and potentially higher prices for consumers. Anjos and Leurquin 2021, p. 121–122. See also: Zuboff 2019, p. 112.

[3] O'Neil 2016, p. 78.

In this context, addressing the challenges of algorithmic decision-making requires a multifaceted approach. Regulatory frameworks need to be developed to ensure transparency and mechanisms should be established to challenge biased outcomes and protect user rights. Collaboration among stakeholders, including policymakers, platform operators, and civil society, is essential to develop effective solutions that balance innovation, competition, and societal well-being.

This paper analyses the increasing prominence of algorithmic decision-making, which requires a careful examination of its implications for fairness, transparency, and accountability. This investigation aims to acknowledge the biases inherent in algorithms, address market power concerns, and promote legal and theoretical grounds in favour of a right to explanation of automated decisions in the European Union. The study diverges from the scope of Article 22 of the GDPR, which centres on data protection law, by concentrating on different legal dimensions, specifically intellectual property and competition law. The objective is to scrutinize issues related to market power and broaden the perspective beyond data protection, encompassing the wider legal and market implications of algorithm-driven decision-making processes.

13.2 Technological Neutrality and Determinism

The presumption of neutrality often held by users of digital platforms increases the possible impacts of algorithmic bias when it comes to search results.[4] Since its users primarily assume that, for example, Google's search engine is synonymous with 'research,' and trust that its results are the best possible outputs that can be generated from their queries' inputs, Google can have a strong influence over users' everyday lives. The same can be said about Twitter, Facebook and Instagram's feed: there is nothing neutral about the choices of content a user is exposed to.

In order to better define neutrality as a legal concept, it is possible to extract its meaning from other areas in which this discussion has been progressing for a longer time. For example, the concept of net neutrality involves non-discrimination by internet service providers toward content providers (message source), users (message destination), or the content itself (message).[5] Thus, neutrality is actually defined by its antonym, discrimination.

---

[4] Newspapers have traditionally relied on outrage and sensationalism, understanding human tendencies that algorithms have also identified. The key distinction is that newspapers can be held legally accountable for their content, and people usually grasp their editorial biases. Algorithms, appearing neutral, escape accountability. Bartlett 2018, p. 80. Janssen 2020, p. 82. Martin 2019, p. 839.

[5] Abiteboul and Stoyanovich 2019, p. 3.

This reasoning can be expanded to other areas where neutrality is key.[6] For example, non-neutral algorithms would be discriminatory algorithms. However, discrimination can be at the core of some algorithmic business models, such as Google's. Discrimination is of the utmost importance to ranking results, determining relevance, and personalizing the outcomes of automated decision-making.

Digital platforms need to exercise some level of discrimination in order to perform well (to curate content in linear timelines, like on Instagram and Twitter, or to match results according to geolocalization, like on Google Search, for example), and it would not be a stretch to affirm that it is precisely its discriminatory abilities, which have been perfected over years, that make it so competitive as business models.[7] Nonetheless, some discriminatory behaviours are unacceptable by law, such as 'discrimination based on any ground such as sex, race, colour, ethnic or social origin, genetic features, language, religion or belief, political or any other opinion, membership of a national minority, property, birth, disability, age or sexual orientation.'[8]

For this reason, this analysis does not aim to impose neutrality as an absolute value on algorithms. By definition, the ranking algorithm of a search engine or a newsfeed algorithm of a social network needs to evaluate, discriminate, and choose which results and posts are more important than others. Rather than striving to be neutral in every way, the real issue with digital platforms lies in identifying when algorithms are not neutral. This includes situations where they discriminate against protected groups, infringe on fundamental rights, or confuse consumers.

There is the risk of bias. A digital platform perceived as neutral has the chance to significantly influence its users through its algorithm, either by omitting certain content or highlighting others (through higher rankings on the recommendations, for example).[9] Also, altering its design layout may cause confusion concerning what is being commercially sponsored and what are the non-sponsored results.

There is also the possibility of constraints on freedom of communication and expression.[10] Application providers might decide to impede certain forms of speech from appearing high in the ranking of results or keep them from appearing in the

[6] '[N]ew forms of neutrality are emerging such as device neutrality (Is my smart phone blocking certain apps and favoring others?), and platform neutrality (Is this particular web service providing neutral recommendation?). For instance, app stores like Google Play and the Apple App Store, tend to refuse to reference certain services, perhaps because they are competing with the company's own services.' Abiteboul and Stoyanovich 2019, p. 7.

[7] Stinson 2021.

[8] Charter of Fundamental Rights of the European Union 2012, art. 21.

[9] Saurwein et al. 2015, p. 37. Regarding bias Joanna Mazur contends that using artificial intelligence to evaluate current discriminatory practices for making automated decisions about the future can create an illusion of impartiality. The absence of human involvement might seem to make the process more equitable. Yet, it's important to remember who supplies the data and analysis tools. Mazur 2018, pp. 179–180.

[10] Saurwein, Just, and Latzer, p. 37.

results at all due to their nature, tone, and other characteristics contrary to the standards of 'appropriateness,' whether they be political or cultural.[11] Also, due to an increasing quest for intermediate liability in online content nowadays, with concerns regarding fake news and hate speech online, platforms might be overzealous in the removal (or moderation) of content in order to avoid liability in the future.

13.3 Dominant Market Power and Anti-Competitive Strategies

The concept of market power is especially relevant for this analysis.[12] It is worth establishing a precise legal definition of this concept, since market power is not illegal per se, but its abuse and anti-competitive practices stemming from the privileges inherent to a dominant position in a relevant market are.[13] Therefore, to analyse the abuse of power and abusive practices, it is important to determine which market is being considered.

The European Commission Notice on the definition of relevant market for the purposes of Community competition law defines a relevant market according to two main dimensions: product and geography. A relevant product market refers to a set of products and services that are interchangeable or substitutable by consumers due to

[11] This matter of ranking prominence was tackled in the European Commission's decision on the Google Shopping Case. 'The Commission's decision refers to the inducement effect of higher rankings or of adding images, prices and merchant information to product search that result in increases of traffic, as confirmed by eye-tracking studies and similar research on the impact on user behavior and click-through rates. As the Commission concludes, citing Google's own submissions, the rationale for higher rankings and inducement to click is to 'dramatically increase traffic' by leveraging 'universal search initiatives' to 'drive the bulk of increase in traffic to Google's comparison-shopping service'. A form of user-inertia similar to the one identified in Microsoft case seems to be particularly at play for the first three to five generic search results and for results displayed with richer graphic features, which seem to have a major impact on the click rates of a link, irrespective of the relevance of the underlying page.'

Iacobucci and Ducci 2019, pp. 29–30.

[12] In EU competition law, market power entails a company's ability to influence market conditions, which is especially relevant under Article 102 of the Treaty on the Functioning of the European Union (TFEU), that prohibits the abuse of a dominant position. This concept is particularly pertinent in the digital sector, where platforms can rapidly gain significant market influence. Transparency for such platforms is crucial to safeguard consumer rights, ensuring users are informed about data use and to prevent anti-competitive practices. Moreover, it aids regulatory bodies in monitoring compliance with competition laws, fostering fair competition and market efficiency. This is essential in digital markets, where the dominance of a few players and the rapid evolution of technology can significantly impact market dynamics.

[13] Treaty on the Functioning of the European Union 2012, arts. 101 and 102.

their characteristics. A relevant geographic market refers to an area in which conditions for supply and demand of certain products or services are relatively homogenous and distinguishable from other areas.[14]

A staff working document from the European Commission, released on July 12, 2021, suggested that a review of the Market Definition Notice, which is part of EU competition law, showed that the importance of defining the market and its fundamental principles have mostly stayed the same since 1997. This consistency has been largely upheld in decisions made by EU Courts.[15]

For example, in the case of Google, there are concerns regarding its abuse of market power.[16] Since Google currently holds almost 90% of the search engine market share worldwide and more than 93% in Europe,[17] it could, fuelled by the possibility of favouring its own affiliate applications in query results,[18] abuse its dominance through monopolistic practices, stifling consumer choice and reducing competitiveness in other sectors.[19]

Additionally, there is an issue regarding business-to-business relations on digital platforms, as well as a lack of possibilities to compete.[20] Due to business models being generally geared toward generating revenue through advertisements, there is little incentive to include content from direct or secondary competitors. In the Google example, it is extremely important to businesses' relevance nowadays to be well ranked in its search query results. If the criteria used by Google to rank one company higher than another is not transparent and in accordance with users' expectations, this may lead to infringements on users' freedom to conduct business online.[21] One example of a possible way such infringements could be committed, would be setting the parameters of the PageRank algorithm to divert users' traffic away from competitors in unfair ways.

If we consider Lawrence Lessig's idea of (computer) code producing 'law' in the sense of shaping and steering societal behaviour, one can assume that algorithms also can shape and steer decision-making processes in the steadily growing online pool of internet users.[22] By influencing consumers' behaviour through the direction of online traffic to specific political content or granting of access to particular information (instead of other information that may be purposefully excluded from its results), search engines, social networks, video streaming and other digital platforms can

[14] Commission Notice on the Definition of Relevant Market for the Purposes of Community Competition Law 1997.

[15] Commission Staff Working Document 2021, p. 67.

[16] Saurwein et al. 2015, p. 37. See also: Iacobucci and Ducci 2019, pp. 20–21.

[17] StatCounter Global Stats 2020.

[18] Case AT.39740, Google Search (Shopping), 2017 E.C.

[19] 'The battle against the accumulation of data operated by PageRank reminds the social struggles against the traditional forms of monopoly and accumulation of capitals. PageRank is to the internet, as primitive accumulation and rent are to early capitalism.' Pasquinelli, 'Google's PageRank,' p. 12.

[20] Saurwein et al. 2015, p. 37.

[21] Strader, 2019, p. 560.

[22] Hildebrandt, 'Code Driven Law,' pp. 67–84.

actually precipitate certain behaviours in the same way social norms, nature, and the market do.[23] Thus, the theory that 'code is law' has its merits.

Lawrence Lessig's 'code is law' theory fundamentally impacts market power and transparency in digital markets by highlighting how algorithms, akin to legal codes, can shape consumer behaviour and decision-making. This perspective emphasizes the control digital platforms have over market dynamics, extending beyond traditional market dominance to influencing market conditions themselves. Consequently, greater transparency of algorithmic processes ensures fairness and further protects consumers. This theory calls for a regulatory approach that considers the influence of algorithmic control on competitive practices and consumer choices, highlighting the need for policies that address both traditional aspects of market power and the newer, more nuanced forms of influence in the digital economy.

The main conclusion to be drawn from all this is that these concerns call attention to a lack of transparency surrounding digital platforms. The various conceptions of transparency can be considered in relation to three actors. First, the end-user of platform provides personal data and is subjected to its content. Second, the business user wishes to see its content (website, blog, service, product, etc.) displayed and well-ranked on the platform. Third, regulators in a broad sense, which encompasses competition and data protection authorities, magistrates, superior courts, and members of legislative branches of government, that have mandates to scrutinize, understand analyse and enforce current legislation with regards to these platforms.

Due to a series of contextual circumstances surrounding the conception of most digital platforms' business model, their algorithm is created and developed in a manner that is highly dependent on users' personal data, less prone to regulation, and extremely fierce toward its competitors.[24] Over the years, this business strategy has continued to be employed and perfected, in addition to being appropriated by other tech startups, establishing surveillance capitalism as a standard practice.[25]

Nonetheless, the issues at hand have led to a growing predicament with regard to the unique convergence of issues surrounding this platform. Users, businesses, and governmental bodies alike have a significant stake in the regulation of the mechanism essential to its operations: the algorithm. Therefore, better transparency standards are essential in order to meet the expectations of its users (both individuals and businesses).

---

[23] Ribeiro et al. 2019.

[24] There are many challenges that regulatory frameworks face in effectively governing the complex, rapidly evolving, and data-centric business models of these platforms. This difficulty stems from the technological complexity of algorithms, the fast pace of digital innovation, the global reach of platforms versus local regulatory powers, the intricacies of data privacy, and the resistance of business models centered on surveillance capitalism. Consequently, there often exists a gap between the development of digital technologies and the ability of regulations to adapt and address emerging concerns effectively.

[25] Zuboff, 2019, p. 369.

13.4 Legal Inscrutability of Algorithms

Broadly speaking, one may contend that there is a tendency for the importance of behavioural data to grow even more over the next years and decades. This overflow of data into the digital economy also feeds the artificial intelligences behind automated systems, most of them proprietary. Companies collect, process, and create value out of data, especially to feed predictive models for advertisers and consumers. In essence, the key to success lies in identifying patterns; by analysing past behaviours, companies can forecast future trends.[26]

The data processor is not always the data collector. Since consent, legitimate interest, and other legal bases are understood as the requirements for the processing of personal data, users may be startled to find out about the cross-referencing of data between original collectors and data brokers or even between different applications of the same company.[27] For example, Alphabet Inc. (Google's parent company) invests its efforts into numerous services, but an important asset is the large number of users (and, therefore, their data) of the services offered by their core businesses, like Google Search, Gmail, and YouTube. Unbeknownst to most users, a combination of different data sources might be what determines the logic behind the profiling activities of certain algorithmic decisions.[28]

Because generating extra behavioural data was crucial for income, and keeping it secret was essential for continuously gathering more of this data, the reasoning that directs this processing of data would also remain, for the most part, protected by black boxes sustained by the justification of safeguarding trade secrets.[29] Unaware of how their data is being processed, as this is obscured by the rationale of trade secrets, users remain oblivious to how decisions are being made for them in crucial areas, such as insurance, finance, employment, credit-scoring, policing, and criminal justice, among other vital fields that can profoundly impact their lives.[30]

These areas connect with platforms through the mechanisms used to collect, process, and exploit user data. Digital platforms, ranging from social media networks

---

[26] Pasquale 2015, p. 20.

[27] Pasquale 2015, p. 32.

[28] The Article 29 Data Protection Working Party highlights the statistical deduction nature of profiling and defines it according to three essential elements: '[I]t has to be an automated form of processing; it has to be carried out on personal data; and the objective of the profiling must be to evaluate personal aspects about a natural person.' Therefore, profiling involves a higher legal threshold rather than a simple classification of data subjects. Article 29 Data Protection Working Party 2017, pp. 6–7. See also: Oostveen and Irion, 'Golden Age of Personal Data,' p. 16; Büchi et al. 2020, p. 2.

[29] O'Neil 2016, p. 173. See also: Schneier 2015, p. 230; Guidotti et al. 2019, p. 36.

[30] An algorithm analyzes various statistics to predict the likelihood of an individual being an unsuitable employee, a high-risk borrower, a terrorist, or a poor teacher. This prediction is then converted into a score that has the potential to drastically alter someone's life. However, if the individual attempts to contest this, merely presenting suggestive counter evidence is insufficient. Their argument must be exceptionally strong. As we'll repeatedly observe, individuals affected by these 'Weapons of Math Destruction' are subjected to much stricter evidence requirements than the algorithms are. O'Neil 2016, p. 10. See also: Smith 2019, pp. 7–15.

to search engines and e-commerce websites, are at the forefront of accumulating behavioural surplus because they are integral to users' online activities. These platforms are the primary sites for the generation and collection of behavioural surpluses. Also, they embody the challenges associated with data privacy, algorithmic decision-making, and the lack of transparency, all of which have significant implications for individual autonomy and societal norms. The concerns extend beyond the mere presence of platforms to encompass the broader implications of how data-centric business models influence crucial aspects of our lives, often without clear accountability or oversight.

The case of Google Street View in Germany and other European countries is remarkable and exemplifies this issue. After an audit by the German data protection authority, Google admitted it had 'been accidentally gathering extracts of personal web activity from domestic Wi-Fi networks through the Street View cars it has used since 2007.'[31] Moreover, the company's automobiles were equipped with antennas that scanned and analysed Wi-Fi networks throughout the routes they travelled, collecting information. There was no consent for such data collection nor any apparent legitimate interest that justified a street mapping service engaging in this activity.

To help address this matter, it is worth inquiring into the purported technical challenges to scrutinizing an algorithm.[32] The rendering of data collected from users into something useful, and not just the data in and of itself, is what comprises the function of the algorithm. These probability calculations,[33] as well as profiling and pattern recognition, inform the decisions of platforms, and are directly related to how efficient, user-friendly, and potent the platforms are perceived to be. According to Cathy O'Neil, this is a feature of digital platforms that steers them both towards secrecy and competitiveness.[34]

---

[31] Kiss 2010.

[32] Bayamlıoğlu 2021, p. 15.

[33] Automated decisions consist of a statistical calculation of probability. Depending on certain criteria previously set by algorithm designers, data subjects can be classified into different categories. The more data there is on a subject, the more likely it is for him or her to be adequately classified.

[34] 'And yet many companies go out of their way to hide results of their models or even their existence. One common justification is that the algorithm constitutes a 'secret sauce' crucial to their business. It's *intellectual property*, and it must be defended, if need be, with legions of lawyers and lobbyists. In the case of web giants like Google, Amazon and Facebook, these precisely tailored algorithms alone are worth hundreds of billions of dollars. WMD [Weapons of Math Destruction] are, by design, inscrutable black boxes. That makes it extra hard to definitively answer the second question: Does the model work against the subject's interest? In short, is it unfair? Does it damage or destroy lives?' Note that Cathy O'Neil, an American data scientist and author, treats trade secrets as equivalent to an intellectual property right, which is a concept in dispute. This also has to do with her American practical background and research, a jurisdiction in which the tradition of intellectual property rights assumes a usually excessively protective stance of the right of owners, encompassing a myriad of IP categories to inhibit infringement and protect service providers. Even from a competition standpoint, American authorities such as the Federal Trade Commission are frequently more lenient to companies that ensure lower prices to consumers. O'Neil 2016, p. 29.

It is important to understand that biases and errors are not just technical problems, or things that can be solely managed by means of simple adjustments to the code. Some of these predictive models rely upon choices about what data is used and what is not.[35] These decisions also imbue algorithms with designers' biases, prejudices, priorities, judgments, and misunderstandings. Often, these human shortcomings are passed onto algorithms, which perpetuate injustices and define individuals' realities significantly. Hence, this issue also happens to be a matter of justice, fairness, and morality. Possible solutions will neither be only technical nor solely regulatory or governance related. They will have to take into consideration a legal balancing of rights, a juxtaposition of values, and a counterweighting of political forces.

13.5 The Clash Between Intellectual Property Rights and Societal Well-Being

To understand the role of intellectual property rights and trade secrets in the transparency of algorithms, it is essential to recognise how these legal tools are used to safeguard computer programs. Trade secrets differ from copyrights and patents in that they are not formal intellectual property rights requiring registration or public disclosure. Instead, they protect confidential business information (such as the algorithms performing automated decision-making) that provides a competitive edge, based on secrecy. Unlike the fixed-term protection offered by copyrights (for original works) and patents (for inventions, including in some cases software algorithms), trade secrets can offer indefinite protection as long as the information remains undisclosed. This contrasts with the public disclosure required for patents and the automatic protection copyrights provide. That is why trade secrets contribute to the opacity of algorithms, as they inherently limit transparency by relying on the information's confidentiality.

According to Article 2(1) of the EU's Directive 2016/943, regarding the protection of undisclosed know-how and business information, trade secrets are defined as follows:

> 'Trade secret' means information which meets all of the following requirements: a) it is secret in the sense that it is not, as a body or in the precise configuration and assembly of its components, generally known among or readily accessible to persons within the circles that normally deal with the kind of information in question; b) it has commercial value because it is secret; c) it has been subject to reasonable steps under the circumstances, by the person lawfully in control of the information, to keep it secret.[36]

Since there is some room for state-by-state interpretation of directives in the European Union, a broad analysis of the practical implementation of the Trade Secrets Directive reveals that it is used to provide legal protection to many types of information: 'technical or non-technical data, patterns, compilations, programs, devices,

---

[35] O'Neil 2016, pp. 3–218. See also: Graef 2018, p. 131.

[36] Directive (EU) 2016/943 2016, art. 2.1.

methods, techniques, financial data, customer lists, or supplies that have economic value.'[37]

Companies typically employ a dual approach: utilizing trade secrets, which are intangible assets rooted in competition law, alongside either copyright or patent protections, both forms of IP rights. The visible aspects of computer programs, like the user interface, are often shielded by copyright or patents. These protections are robust against reverse engineering and facilitate interoperability.[38] Additionally, companies might consider patenting the algorithm itself, especially in jurisdictions like the United States where the scope of patent protection is broader than in the EU.[39] This legal strategy, while protecting proprietary interests, inherently contributes to the opacity of algorithms, as it limits the disclosure and scrutiny of the underlying code and operational logic.

Another type of right involved in business models that are based on computer processing is database rights. According to Directive 96/9/EC, a database consists of 'a collection of independent works, data or other materials arranged in a systematic or methodical way and individually accessible by electronic or other means.'[40] Very similar to the logic of copyrights, database rights encompass the concept of authorship and a limited timeframe for protection of exclusive use.

Although a variety of intellectual assets can overlap in legal strategies of algorithmic business models, including intellectual property and *sui generis* rights such as database rights, the present analysis is focused on the aspects related to the trade secret protection of algorithms performing automated decisions. Therefore, though many layers of legal protection can shield the different processes of a company, the black box surrounding the performance of algorithms is of particular interest in a systemic approach.

[37] Desai 2018, p. 490. It is particularly interesting to observe the actual wording of the Trade Secrets Directive, since it distinctively separates trade secrets from intellectual property. Recitals 1 and 2 of Directive 2016/943 refer to trade secrets as 'intellectual capital' and as an alternative to a list of intellectual property rights. Therefore, a noticeable distinction is drawn between trade secrets and intellectual property rights. Internationally and within the European Union, the matter of trade secrets is treated in a parallel manner as intellectual property rights. Recital 39 of the Trade Secrets Directive makes it clear that there is a legal distinction between them. It should be noted that this directive also establishes that member states of the EU are still allowed to apply rules that require disclosures to either the public or to public authorities, if necessary. Moreover, other limitations are set in Article 9 of the same statute regarding the confidentiality of trade secrets during the course of judicial proceedings. These limitations provide an additional layer of protection for companies when providing documents and testimonies to hearings regarding such competitive assets and even provide for the possibility of a confidential version of the decision to be rendered as an exceptional measure to protect trade secrets. See also: Arcidiacono 2016, pp. 1073–1085.

[38] Lu 2020, p. 117.

[39] According to Article 8 of the Directive 2009/24/EC: 'The provisions of this Directive shall be without prejudice to any other legal provisions such as those concerning patent rights, trademarks, unfair competition, trade secrets, protection of semi-conductor products or the law of contract.' This allows for additional intellectual property protection to computer programs' functionalities, not just copyright, or at least a systematic interpretation of those rights within the intellectual property protection realm of possibilities. Directive 2009/24/EC 2009, art. 8.

[40] Directive 96/9/EC 1996, art. 1.2.

There is also a distinction between algorithms and the source code of computer programs, which is of the utmost importance for our analysis, considering it reveals the reasons why copyright does not provide enough protection in the tech industry.[41] A source code is the tangible support (0's and 1's, or other code forms that a literal programming language may entail) by which an algorithm performs its task. According to Directive 2009/24/CE, Recital 11, algorithms resemble programming languages in the logic through which ideas are expressed (computer codes).[42]

The ideas and logic behind an algorithm are not subject to copyright protection, unlike the actual form by which they are expressed (sequence of codes). Thus, if a creator of an algorithm were to protect its creation only through copyright, competitors would be able to base new creations on the underlying ideas and methods of the original, as long as they expressed it in a different way (original code). It is for this reason that trade secrets then become a more advantageous way of protecting the property of the algorithms' creators. Trade secrets, however, tend to be used to protect 'deeper' parts of the provision of software, where it is possible to maintain control of the rationale behind input to output transformation.

There are also significant procedural differences between cases discussing trade secrets and intellectual property rights. While the European Union provides specific pre-litigation evidence collection provisions under the Intellectual Property Enforcement Directive,[43] such provisions have been purposefully avoided by national legislators when regulating the protection of trade secrets in the Union.[44]

The fact that trade secrets, contrary to patents and copyright, are required to meet minimum bureaucratic standards or none at all (such as administrative registration), makes them an interesting option for companies that follow flexible business models with rapidly adaptable characteristics. For this reason, startups and companies seeking to protect proprietary algorithms often opt to protect them under the banner of trade secrets. However, the very characteristics that define trade secrets could also enable them to continue and intensify 'pre-existing biased social frameworks, especially when these systems are left unmonitored and uncontrolled.[45]

Unlike other intangible intellectual assets, the right to trade secrets does not require public disclosure of the object of protection.[46] Pointing this out may seem like a

---

[41] Marty 2019, p. 222.

[42] For the avoidance of doubt, it has to be made clear that only the expression of a computer program is protected and that ideas and principles which underlie any element of a program, including those which underlie its interfaces, are not protected by copyright under this Directive. In accordance with this principle of copyright, to the extent that logic, algorithms and programming languages comprise ideas and principles, those ideas and principles are not protected under this Directive. In accordance with the legislation and case-law of the Member States and the international copyright conventions, the expression of those ideas and principles is to be protected by copyright. Directive 2009/24/EC 2009, Recital 11.

[43] Corrigendum to Directive 2004/48/EC 2004.

[44] Niebel et al. 2018, p. 447.

[45] Moore 2017, p. 6.

[46] Patents offer exclusive rights to new inventions at the cost of revealing them to the public. Conversely, trade secrets don't grant such exclusive rights, but their protection can last indefinitely

tautology, but it is relevant to grasp the effects it may have on digital innovation. Since the object of trade secret protection will not be eventually available to society after a period of time (most importantly, to competitors, which is the case with patents), this creates greater barriers to entry to newcomers in specific markets and, thus, less competition in the medium to long term.[47] Other intangible intellectual rights, such as intellectual property rights, enjoy somewhat limited protection in terms of time (expiration of patents, for example), scope (jurisdiction), and object (some are specifically excluded from intellectual property protection).[48]

Furthermore, companies that envisage worldwide provision of services, which is the case with GAFA (Google, Apple, Facebook, and Amazon), for instance, do not wish to be bound by local jurisdictional, temporal, or object scope. These legal hurdles increase the cost of doing business, especially opportunity costs, i.e., the costs of losing opportunities to launch new products.[49] Thus, trade secrets become an appealing option in the digital realm.[50]

If we systematically interpret these provisions with Article 23(1)(i) of the GDPR, one can see that restrictions to data controllers and processors' rights apply 'when such a restriction respects the essence of the fundamental rights and freedoms and is a necessary and proportionate measure in a democratic society to safeguard the protection of the data subject or the rights and freedoms of others.'[51] Thus, limitations to intangible intellectual assets such as trade secrets may be not only possible but also necessary in order to safeguard users' fundamental rights.[52]

In the context of the European Union, trade secrets are intimately connected to the principle of competition. Even its definition is relational, since the element of market value, a requirement for its characterization, is extracted precisely from

as long as they are not disclosed against the owner's will. This might be seen as a benefit compared to intellectual property rights that expire after a certain period. Niebel et al. 2018, p. 447.

47 Marty 2019, p. 217.

48 Hrdy and Lemley 2021, pp. 10–11. Also, patent law's demand for public disclosure of inventions aimed to foster transparency by conditioning intellectual property protection on detailed public descriptions of the inventions. Over time, however, this open system was overlooked as savvy, but unethical people figured out how to exploit these transparent systems. The lure of gaining profits through exclusive information proved too tempting to ignore. See: Pasquale 2015, p. 193.

49 Svantesson 2017, pp. 65, 109, 117.

50 Globally, the recommendation system of Amazon, Instagram's algorithm for spreading posts, and Google's search algorithms stand out as famous trade secrets. The specific methods Google uses to assess links between pages, improvements in its search system, and criteria to identify manipulations are kept secret. For instance, it's unclear how Google weighs various factors, like the number of links, page traffic, or the organization of a page's source code. See: Brkan and Bonnet 2020, p. 40.

51 Regulation (EU) 2016/679 2016.

52 Ideally, this is a theoretical and legal framework applied through casuistry, not necessarily a hierarchical structure of data protection rights over algorithmic intellectual assets. According to Brkan and Bonnet: '[I]f GDPR always prevailed over trade secrets, the latter could never be protected when providing an explanation of an algorithmic decision to the data subject.' Brkan and Bonnet 2020, p. 40.

a competitive advantage.[53] Frédéric Marty defines it as 'information known by a restricted number of people, with commercial value, effective or potential, due to its secretive character and that is subject to reasonable measures of protection to maintain its secretive character' (my translation).[54]

If it were the case that competitors obtained the information subject to protection by legitimate methods, such as technological advancements, research and development, or reverse engineering, there would be no issue at hand. However, what is considered illicit are anti-competitive practices, such as unlawful disclosure by former employees or business espionage.[55] Both these situations are foreseen by Articles 3 and 4 of the EU directive on the protection of trade secrets.[56]

Thus, unfair competition is a primary concern with regard to this category of intangible business assets and must be considered as a factor of analysis. Nevertheless, how does one compete and innovate in markets based on algorithmic business models? Intellectual property, such as patents and copyrights, are usually characterized by incremental innovations in their respective markets, whereas a scenario widely based on trade secrets requires that competitors invest a similar number of resources into research and development (which can be quite significant in the tech industry) in order to attempt to compete. Trade-secret law uniquely permits owners to withhold information, in contrast to intellectual property rights.[57]

In markets where digital platforms use algorithms to make decisions, new companies often try not to compete directly with dominant players. Instead, they aim to offer products and services that complement those of the established companies. This approach strengthens the leading position of well-established companies in the main market.[58] Hence, trade secrets tend to stifle competition in primary markets, which may not be ideal, depending on the objectives one considers in regulating competition. Its negative externalities might outweigh its positive ones, strengthening oligopolies, for example.

Once again, focusing on the usual business models of this analysis, digital platforms based on behavioural advertising, it is important to note that its putative neutrality is, in fact, also a product of a business model that relies on secrecy in order to thrive.[59] An erroneous assumption by the public, although widespread among its users, is that timelines, recommendations, rankings and results are objective.[60]

---

[53] Hrdy and Lemley 2021, pp. 31–32. See also: Banterle 2018, p. 420.

[54] Marty 2019, p. 214.

[55] Marty 2019, p. 215.

[56] It defines lawful acquisition as that achieved by means of independent discovery, creation, observation, study, and reverse engineering, among other means. Guidotti et al. 2019, pp. 10–11.

[57] Scotchmer 2004, p. 81.

[58] Marty 2019, p. 220.

[59] '[...] Google is not a neutral tool or a non-distorting lens: it is an actor and a stakeholder in itself. And, more important, as a publicly traded company, it must act in its shareholders' short-term interests, despite its altruistic proclamations.' Vaidhyanathan 2011, p. 9. See also: Martin 2019, p. 839.

[60] For example, the automated decisions of Google Search derive from a combination of the mathematics related to the algorithmic relevance of certain content and of the editorial decisions of the

However, this perception actually stems from a highly effective personalization algorithm, as we have seen, and from companies' savvy strategies to characterize its business model as exempt from scrutiny.[61]

Digital platforms, particularly those using algorithms for automated decision-making, have trade secrets play as a key component that shapes (the lack of) transparency and competition. They offer indefinite protection to the more covert elements, creating opacity around algorithms. This legal framework, while protecting proprietary interests, potentially stifles competition and innovation in the market by creating barriers to entry and perpetuating existing market dominance, as newcomers often find it challenging to compete with or innovate beyond the established players. The EU recognizes the delicate balance between protecting trade secrets and ensuring fair competition, indicating the need for regulation that considers the broader impacts on market dynamics and user rights.

Thus, this analysis on the nature of trade secrets brings forward a correlation between Google's opaque algorithm and the core role of its data extraction imperatives, which have been replicated by Facebook and other emerging data-driven companies.[62] The same predilection of these companies for trade secrets over patents and copyrights justifies the need to make the right to protect trade secrets dependent on the guarantee of an effective explanation of algorithmic decision-making.

---

company itself, which chooses not to show results that violate copyrights, contain pornographic content, encourage violence etc. Therefore, even subjective factors influence the ranking of results provided by the search engine. According to Google's Code of Conduct, which interestingly abandoned its quite literal 'don't be evil' motto in 2018, 'Google's intellectual property rights (our trademarks, logos, copyrights, trade secrets, 'know-how,' and patents) are among our most valuable assets.' 'Alphabet Investor Relations: Google Code of Conduct,' Alphabet Inc., accessed July 31, 2018, https://abc.xyz/investor/other/code-of-conduct.

[61] Many people believe that searching for a term on Google yields the same results for everyone, ranked by the company's well-known Page Rank algorithm according to the authority of links from other pages. However, since December 2009, this assumption has become outdated. Currently, Google's algorithm tailors search results to what it deems most relevant for each individual user, meaning different people may see completely different results. Essentially, there's no longer a one-size-fits-all version of Google. See: Pariser 2011, p. 2.

[62] Today's trade secrets, such as Google's search engine algorithm, are often more secure against being revealed. They are usually difficult to reverse engineer, and there are fewer employees who could potentially leave and share their knowledge with a competing company. Hrdy and Lemley 2021, p. 13. See also: Lu 2020, p. 114.

13.6 Market Power and Algorithms: The Digital Markets Act and the Digital Services Act

The Digital Single Market Strategy launched two significant regulations in this field: The Digital Services Act (DSA)[63] and Digital Markets Act (DMA).[64] The DSA is focused on the fact that online intermediaries share responsibilities in ensuring predictability, safety, and protection of fundamental rights within the European Union's digital environment. Thus, many of the provisions it sets out focus on transparency, liability, and risk mitigation (against fundamental rights violations). It particularly applies to recommender systems, a definition which can be applied to Amazon's or Google's results page, for example.[65]

Article 27 of the DSA (recommender system transparency) is of the utmost relevance, since it encompasses the reasoning behind automated decisions, the need for explanations comprehensible to users regarding such reasoning, and finally, the possibility to provide more autonomy to users through the individual personalization of these platforms. It requires platforms to implement explainability tools for its users, in addition to providing them with the choice to adhere or not to these criteria or personalization.

The DSA foresees the need for 'very large platforms' to execute audits in order to conduct 'risk assessments and design their risk mitigation measures with the involvement of representatives of the recipients of the service, representatives of groups potentially impacted by their services, independent experts and civil society organisations.'[66] The Act mentions specific algorithmic audits which should ensure the confidentiality, security, and integrity of the information gathered, such as trade secrets.[67] Even though the DSA is not a competition mechanism, it does provide transparency tools that might increase scrutiny of online platforms, especially larger platforms with recommender systems.

The DMA focuses on *ex ante* rules to ensure contestable, interoperable, and fairer markets in the digital sector where gatekeepers are present. It defines gatekeepers (providers of core platform services when they have a significant impact on the internal market) to raise core issues related to their opaqueness and complexity. And, again, like the Digital Services Act, this central legal definition in the regulation has the potential to profoundly change and influence the realm of digital platform regulation, because it creates additional obligations for these core platform services, based on contestability mechanisms, transparency, and market monitoring investigations.

---

[63] Regulation (EU) 2022/2065.

[64] Regulation (EU) 2022/1925.

[65] 'A fully or partially automated system used by an online platform to suggest in its online interface specific information to recipients of the service, including as a result of a search initiated by the recipient or otherwise determining the relative order or prominence of information displayed.' Article 2, (o), of the DMA.

[66] Recital 90, Digital Services Act, 2022.

[67] Recital 92, Digital Services Act, 2022.

Furthermore, the concept of transparency with regard to users' data is directly linked to a more fertile and competitive market for newcomers.[68]

Another provision requires gatekeepers to allow business users to offer the same products or services to end users through third party online intermediation services at prices or conditions that are different from those offered through the online intermediation services of the gatekeeper.[69] Also, they must provide to any third party providers of online search engines, upon their request, access on fair, reasonable and non-discriminatory terms to ranking, query, click and view data in relation to free and paid search generated by end users on online search engines of the gatekeeper, subject to anonymisation for the query, click and view data that constitutes personal data.[70] These are provisions that directly respond to issues raised against Google in previous antitrust cases, such as those concerned with Google Android and Google Shopping, and that would foster competition in their markets. There is no question that this is part of the European Union's institutional response to the anticompetitive practices in which Google has engaged in the past.

Reflecting on the provisions of the DSA and the DMA reveals both their strengths and limitations in ensuring platform accountability and transparency. While these regulatory frameworks aim to safeguard fundamental rights within the EU's digital environment and ensure fairer digital markets, their effectiveness hinges on its transparency and liability provisions' effectiveness in practice. What will be the depth of explanations provided and will they truly enhance users' autonomy, or merely serve as superficial compliance measures? The complex nature of algorithms might render explainability insufficient for the average user to grasp, limiting its intended empowerment effect.

Moreover, the requirement for algorithmic audits and risk assessments under the DSA points towards a proactive approach in identifying and mitigating risks associated with digital platforms. Yet, the effectiveness of these measures largely depends on the rigor of the audits, the independence of the auditors, and the transparency of the audit process itself. Without stringent enforcement mechanisms and clear standards for these audits, there's a risk that these processes become tick-box exercises rather than substantive evaluations of platforms' impact on fundamental rights and societal values.

The DMA's focus on contestability and fairness through *ex ante* rules for gatekeepers highlights the EU's commitment to curbing anti-competitive practices in digital markets. While the provisions aimed at ensuring interoperability and preventing unfair conditions are vital steps towards a more competitive digital

---

[68] The data protection and privacy interests of end users are relevant to any assessment of potential negative effects of the observed practice of gatekeepers to collect and accumulate large amounts of data from end users. Ensuring an adequate level of transparency of profiling practices employed by gatekeepers facilitates contestability of core platform services, by putting external pressure on gatekeepers to prevent making deep consumer profiling the industry standard, given that potential entrants or start-up providers cannot access data to the same extent and depth, and at a similar scale. Recital 72, Digital Markets Act, 2022.

[69] Article 5.3, Digital Markets Act, 2022.

[70] Article 6.11, Digital Markets Act, 2022.

economy, the challenge lies in their enforcement. The dynamic nature of digital markets and the sophisticated strategies employed by gatekeepers to maintain their dominance demand agile and robust regulatory responses. The current provisions may not fully account for the evolving tactics of gatekeepers, or the complexities involved in implementing and enforcing interoperability requirements.

Furthermore, both the DSA and DMA could benefit from integrating insights and provisions from the recently approved AI Act, particularly concerning advanced AI systems used by digital platforms. The AI Act's focus on high-risk AI applications provides a framework that could complement the DSA and DMA by offering specific guidelines and standards for the ethical and responsible use of AI in digital platforms. This integration could address potential gaps in dealing with AI-driven practices that impact market dynamics and fundamental rights.

While the DSA and DMA represent significant advancements towards regulating digital platforms, their success in ensuring platform accountability, transparency, and contestability is contingent upon robust enforcement, clear standards for algorithmic transparency and audits, and the integration of comprehensive legal reasoning that includes considerations from the AI Act. Addressing these challenges requires an approach that combines regulatory oversight with stakeholder engagement and continuous evaluation of the regulatory frameworks' effectiveness in the face of rapidly evolving digital technologies.

13.7 Conclusion

As we navigate the intricacies of the digital era, the role and influence of algorithmic decision-making systems have become undeniably central to our societal fabric. These algorithms, once heralded as harbingers of objectivity and efficiency, are now under increased scrutiny for their latent biases and potential to perpetuate discrimination.

The once-held belief in the unerring neutrality of platforms like Google, Facebook, and Twitter is being systematically deconstructed, revealing a landscape where content is not merely presented but is actively shaped, often in ways that serve the platforms' interests. The monopolistic dominance of a few digital behemoths further exacerbates these concerns, raising pressing questions about market dynamics, competition, and the very essence of user choice in the digital realm. Addressing these multifaceted challenges necessitates a comprehensive approach, one that fosters collaboration among diverse stakeholders, from policymakers to platform operators. As we stand at this pivotal juncture, the call for transparency, accountability, and a rights-centric approach to algorithmic decision-making has never been more urgent. Only through such concerted efforts can we hope to strike a balance between technological innovation, market competition, and the broader well-being of society in an age defined by algorithms.

In the rapidly evolving digital landscape, the prominence of algorithmic decision-making has raised significant concerns regarding transparency. This chapter has explored the challenges posed by putative neutrality, market power, and the (supposed) legal inscrutability of algorithms. It has also highlighted the increasing necessity of a right to explanation for automated decisions, particularly in the context of personal data processing.

The analysis underscores the inherent biases embedded in algorithms used by digital platforms, challenging the assumption of neutrality. The concentration of market power among dominant platforms further exacerbates the need for regulatory interventions to ensure fair competition and protect user rights. The legal protection afforded to algorithms through trade secrets and intellectual property rights creates barriers to understanding their functioning and potential biases.

To address these challenges, there is a growing call for transparency and accountability in algorithmic decision-making. The notion of a right to explanation has gained traction, emphasizing the need for individuals to understand the logic and consequences of automated decisions that affect their lives. This right should be complemented by robust regulatory frameworks that promote fairness, protect user data, and mitigate the risks of algorithmic discrimination.

Recent developments in the European Union have led to the adoption of the Digital Services Act and the Digital Markets Act, which aim to address issues of transparency and explainability of very large online platforms and of gatekeepers, respectively. The regulations recognize the need for explainability and set requirements for transparency in the provision of platform services online. What is certain is that the challenges posed by algorithmic decision-making call for a multifaceted approach that prioritizes transparency and the protection of individual rights.

Acknowledgements The author would like to acknowledge the support received from Sciences Po's Law School and the McCourt Institute in facilitating the research and development of this chapter. The author would also like to disclose that the views expressed in this chapter are solely those of the author and do not necessarily reflect the opinions or positions of Sciences Po's Law School, the McCourt Institute, or any funding entities.

References

"Alphabet Investor Relations: Google Code of Conduct," Alphabet Inc., accessed July 31, 2018, https://abc.xyz/investor/other/code-of-conduct.

Article 29 Data Protection Working Party, "Guidelines on Automated Individual Decision-Making and Profiling for the Purposes of Regulation 2016/679" (WP251rev.01, 3 October, 2017), https://ec.europa.eu/newsroom/article29/item-detail.cfm?item_id=612053.

Bilel Benbouzid, "Values and Consequences in Predictive Machine Evaluation. A Sociology of Predictive Policing," Science & Technology Studies 32, no. 4 (2019), https://sciencetechnologystudies.journal.fi/article/view/66156.

Bruce Schneier, Data and Goliath: The Hidden Battles to Collect Your Data and Control Your World (New York: W.W. Norton & Company Inc, 2015).

Camilla A. Hrdy and Mark A. Lemley, "Abandoning Trade Secrets," Stanford Law Review 73, no. 1 (January 2021): 10-11, https://review.law.stanford.edu/wp-content/uploads/sites/3/2021/01/Hrdy-Lemley-73-Stan.-L.-Rev.-1.pdf.

Case AT.39740, Google Search (Shopping), 2017 E.C.
Catherine Stinson, "Algorithms Are Not Neutral: Bias in Collaborative Filtering," arXiv:2105.01031 (May 2021), https://arxiv.org/abs/2105.01031.
Cathy O'Neil, Weapons of Math Destruction: How Big Data Increases Inequality and Threatens Democracy (New York: Crown Publishers, 2016).
Charter of Fundamental Rights of the European Union, 2012, O.J. 2012/C 326/02, https://eur-lex.europa.eu/legal-content/EN/TXT/HTML/?uri=CELEX:12012P/TXT&from=EN#d1e364-393-1.
Commission Notice on the Definition of Relevant Market for the Purposes of Community Competition Law (EU), 1997 O.J. (97/C 372 /03), https://eur-lex.europa.eu/legal-content/EN/TXT/PDF/?uri=CELEX:31997Y1209(01)&from=EN.
Commission Staff Working Document, "Evaluation of the Commission Notice on the Definition of Relevant Market for the Purposes of the Community Competition Law of 9 December 1997," (July 12, 2021), at 67, https://ec.europa.eu/competition-policy/system/files/2021-07/evaluation_market-definition-notice_en.pdf.
Consolidated Versions of the Treaty on the Functioning of the European Union, October 26, 2012, https://eur-lex.europa.eu/legal-content/EN/TXT/HTML/?uri=CELEX:12012E/TXT&from=EN.
Corrigendum to Directive 2004/48/EC of the European Parliament and of the Council of 29 April 2004 on the Enforcement of Intellectual Property Rights, 2004, O.J. (L 157), https://eur-lex.europa.eu/legal-content/EN/TXT/HTML/?uri=CELEX:32004L0048R(01)&from=EN.
Dan Jerker B. Svantesson, Solving the Internet Jurisdiction Puzzle (Oxford: Oxford University Press, 2017), https://doi.org/10.1093/oso/9780198795674.001.0001.
Davide Arcidiacono, "The Trade Secrets Directive in the International Legal Framework," European Papers 1, no. 3 (November 7, 2016): 1073-1085, https://www.europeanpapers.eu/en/europeanforum/trade-secrets-directive-international-legal-framework.
Directive 2009/24/EC of the European Parliament and of the Council of 23 April 2009 on the Legal Protection of Computer Programs (Codified Version) (Text with EEA Relevance), 2009 O.J. (L 111), http://data.europa.eu/eli/dir/2009/24/oj/eng.
Directive 96/9/EC of the European Parliament and of the Council of 11 March 1996 on the legal protection of databases. Available at: https://eur-lex.europa.eu/legal-content/EN/TXT/?uri=celex%3A31996L0009.
Directive (EU) 2016/943 of the European Parliament and of the Council of 8 June 2016 on the Protection of Undisclosed Know-How and Business Information (Trade Secrets) against Their Unlawful Acquisition, Use and Disclosure (Text with EEA Relevance), 2016 O.J. (L 157), http://data.europa.eu/eli/dir/2016/943/oj/eng.
Edward Iacobucci and Francesco Ducci, "The Google Search Case in Europe: Tying and the Single Monopoly Profit Theorem in Two-Sided Markets," European Journal of Law and Economics 47, no 1 (February 2019), https://doi.org/10.1007/s10657-018-9602-y.
Eli Pariser, The Filter Bubble: What the Internet Is Hiding from You (London: Penguin Books, 2011).
Emre Bayamlıoğlu, "The Right to Contest Automated Decisions under the General Data Protection Regulation: Beyond the So-called 'Right to Explanation'," Regulation & Governance (March 14, 2021), https://doi.org/10.1111/rego.12391.
European Commission. Regulation (EU) 2024/1689 of the European Parliament and of the Council of 13 June 2024 laying down harmonised rules on artificial intelligence and amending Regulations (EC) No 300/2008, (EU) No 167/2013, (EU) No 168/2013, (EU) 2018/858, (EU) 2018/1139 and (EU) 2019/2144 and Directives 2014/90/EU, (EU) 2016/797 and (EU) 2020/1828 (Artificial Intelligence Act): https://eur-lex.europa.eu/legal-content/EN/TXT/HTML/?uri=OJ:L_202401689
Florian Saurwein, Natascha Just, and Michael Latzer, "Governance of Algorithms: Options and Limitations," Info 17, n° 6 (September 2015), https://doi.org/10.1108/info-05-2015-0025.

Francesco Banterle, "The Interface Between Data Protection and IP Law: The Case of Trade Secrets and the Database Sui Generis Right in Marketing Operations, and the Ownership of Raw Data in Big Data Analysis," in Personal Data in Competition, Consumer Protection and Intellectual Property Law: Towards a Holistic Approach?, org. Mor Bakhoum et al., MPI Studies on Intellectual Property and Competition Law, vol. 28 (Berlin, Heidelberg: Springer Berlin Heidelberg, 2018), https://doi.org/10.1007/978-3-662-57646-5.

Frank Pasquale, The Black Box Society: The Secret Algorithms That Control Money and Information (Cambridge: Harvard University Press, 2015).

Frédéric Marty, "La protection des algorithmes par le secret des affaires: Entre risques de faux négatifs et risques de faux positifs," Revue internationale de droit économique t.XXXIII, no 2 (2019), https://doi.org/10.3917/ride.332.0211.

Gary Smith, "Be Wary of Black-Box Trading Algorithms," The Journal of Investing 28, no 5 (July 31, 2019): 7–15, https://doi.org/10.3905/joi.2019.1.090.

Hannah Bloch-Wehba, "Access to Algorithms," Fordham Law Review 88, no. 4 (March 2020): 1308, https://ir.lawnet.fordham.edu/flr/vol88/iss4/2/.

Heleen L. Janssen, "An Approach for a Fundamental Rights Impact Assessment to Automated Decision-Making," International Data Privacy Law 10, no 1 (February 1, 2020), https://doi.org/10.1093/idpl/ipz028.

Inge Graef, "Blurring Boundaries of Consumer Welfare: How to Create Synergies Between Competition, Consumer and Data Protection Law in Digital Markets," in Personal Data in Competition, Consumer Protection and Intellectual Property Law: Towards a Holistic Approach?, org. Mor Bakhoum et al., MPI Studies on Intellectual Property and Competition Law, vol. 28 (Berlin, Heidelberg: Springer Berlin Heidelberg, 2018), https://doi.org/10.1007/978-3-662-57646-5.

Jamie Bartlett, The People Vs Tech: How the Internet Is Killing Democracy (and How We Save It) (London: Penguin Random House, 2018).

Jay Matthew Strader, "Google, Monopolization, Refusing to Deal and the Duty to Promote Economic Activity," IIC - International Review of Intellectual Property and Competition Law 50, no. 5 (June, 2019): 559-594, https://doi.org/10.1007/s40319-019-00818-9.

Jemima Kiss, "Google Admits Collecting Wi-Fi Data through Street View Cars," The Guardian, May 15, 2010, http://www.theguardian.com/technology/2010/may/15/google-admits-storing-private-data.

Joanna Mazur, "Right to Access Information as a Collective-Based Approach to the GDPR's Right to Explanation in European Law," Erasmus Law Review 11, no. 3 (December 2018), https://ssrn.com/abstract=3356770.

Jonas Heitto, "The Trade Secret Directive Proposal and the Narrow Path to Improving Trade Secret Protection in Europe," Computer Law Review International 16, no. 5 (2015), https://www.degruyter.com/document/doi/https://doi.org/10.9785/cri-2015-0504/html.

Joshua G. Hazan, "Stop Being Evil: A Proposal for Unbiased Google Search," Michigan Law Review 111, no 5 (March 2013), https://repository.law.umich.edu/mlr/vol111/iss5/5.

Kirsten Martin, "Ethical Implications and Accountability of Algorithms," Journal of Business Ethics 160, no 4 (December 2019), https://doi.org/10.1007/s10551-018-3921-3.

Lucas Anjos and Pablo Leurquin, "Condenações da Google pela Aplicação do Direito da Concorrência da União Europeia," Revista de Defesa da Concorrência, Vol. 9, nº 1 (June 2021): 104-124, https://revista.cade.gov.br/index.php/revistadedefesadaconcorrencia/article/view/903/532.

Maja Brkan and Grégory Bonnet, "Legal and Technical Feasibility of the GDPR's Quest for Explanation of Algorithmic Decisions: Of Black Boxes, White Boxes and Fata Morganas," European Journal of Risk Regulation 11, no 1 (March 2020), https://doi.org/10.1017/err.2020.10.

Manoel Horta Ribeiro et al., "Auditing Radicalization Pathways on YouTube," arXiv, August 22, 2019, http://arxiv.org/abs/1908.08313.

Mireille Hildebrandt, "Code Driven Law: Freezing the Future and Scaling the Past," in Is Law Computable? Critical Perspectives on Law and Artificial Intelligence, ed. Christopher Markou and Simon Deakin (United Kingdom: Hart Publishers, 2020), 67-84.

Oostveen and Irion, "Golden Age of Personal Data," 16; Moritz Büchi et al., "The Chilling Effects of Algorithmic Profiling: Mapping the Issues," Computer Law & Security Review 36 (April 2020), https://doi.org/10.1016/j.clsr.2019.105367.

Protocol to the Convention for the Protection of Human Rights and Fundamental Freedoms https://www.echr.coe.int/Pages/home.aspx?p=basictexts&c=.

Regulation (EU) 2016/679 of the European Parliament and of the Council of 27 April 2016 on the Protection of Natural Persons with Regard to the Processing of Personal Data and on the Free Movement of Such Data, and Repealing Directive 95/46/EC (General Data Protection Regulation) (Text with EEA Relevance), 2016 O.J. (L 119), http://data.europa.eu/eli/reg/2016/679/oj/eng.

Regulation (EU) 2022/2065 of the European Parliament and of the Council of 19 October 2022 on a Single Market For Digital Services and amending Directive 2000/31/EC (Digital Services Act) (Text with EEA relevance), 2022 OJ L 277, https://eur-lex.europa.eu/legal-content/EN/TXT/HTML/?uri=CELEX:32022R2065.

Regulation (EU) 2022/1925 of the European Parliament and of the Council of 14 September 2022 on contestable and fair markets in the digital sector and amending Directives (EU) 2019/1937 and (EU) 2020/1828 (Digital Markets Act) (Text with EEA relevance), 2022, OJ L 265, https://eur-lex.europa.eu/legal-content/EN/TXT/HTML/?uri=CELEX:32022R1925.

Rembert Niebel, Lorenzo de Martinis, and Birgit Clark, "The EU Trade Secrets Directive: All Change for Trade Secret Protection in Europe?" Journal of Intellectual Property Law & Practice 13, no. 6 (June 2018), https://doi.org/10.1093/jiplp/jpx227.

Riccardo Guidotti et al., "A Survey of Methods for Explaining Black Box Models," ACM Computing Surveys 51, no 5 (January 23, 2019), https://doi.org/10.1145/3236009.

"Search Engine Market Share Europe," StatCounter Global Stats, accessed December 1, 2020, https://gs.statcounter.com/search-engine-market-share/all/europe.

Serge Abiteboul and Julia Stoyanovich, "Transparency, Fairness, Data Protection, Neutrality: Data Management Challenges in the Face of New Regulation," Journal of Data and Information Quality, ACM (2019): 3, https://hal.inria.fr/hal-02066516.

Shreya Desai, "Shhh - It's a Secret: A Comparison of the United States Defend Trade Secrets Act and European Union Trade Secrets Directive," Georgia Journal of International and Comparative Law 46, no. 2, (2018): 490, https://digitalcommons.law.uga.edu/gjicl/vol46/iss2/7/.

Siva Vaidhyanathan, The Googlization of Everything (And Why We Should Worry) (Los Angeles: University of California Press, 2011).

Sylvia Lu, "Algorithmic Opacity, Private Accountability, and Corporate Social Disclosure in the Age of Artificial Intelligence," Vanderbilt Journal of Entertainment & Technology Law 23, no. 1 (Fall 2020), https://scholarship.law.vanderbilt.edu/jetlaw/vol23/iss1/3.

Taylor R. Moore, Trade Secrets and Algorithms as Barriers to Social Justice, Center for Democracy & Technology, August 3, 2017, 6, https://cdt.org/wp-content/uploads/2017/08/2017-07-31-Trade-Secret-Algorithms-as-Barriers-to-Social-Justice.pdf.

Zuboff, Shoshana, The Age of Surveillance Capitalism. New York: Profile Books Ltd, 2019.

Lucas Costa dos Anjos is a postdoctoral researcher at the École de Droit of Sciences Po—Paris. His research interests include algorithmic transparency and explainability, trade secrets, tech regulation and the new challenges stemming from artificial intelligence. His research on the subject is currently financed by a Postdoctoral Fellowship from Project Liberty (former McCourt Institute). In addition to being a researcher at the Brazilian Data Protection Authority (ANPD), Lucas is also a Professor at the Law School of Universidade Federal de Juiz de Fora. He holds a Doctor degree in Law and in Sciences Juridiques from Universidade Federal de Minas Gerais and Université libre de Bruxelles, respectively, and a Master degree in Law from Universidade Federal de Minas Gerais. He is also the founder and was a scientific advisor of the Institute for Research on Internet and Society (IRIS).

Chapter 14
The Digital Governance of Artificial Intelligence: Conclusive Remarks and Future Directions

Julia Krämer, Kostina Prifti, Esra Demir, Klaus Heine, and Evert Stamhuis

Contents

Abstract The regulatory challenges posed by Artificial Intelligence (AI) are multifaceted and materialise in various sectors of society. Accounting for the disruptive effects of AI requires a comprehensive approach that is capable of connecting the various regulatory pathways. Digital governance, i.e. the creation of an extensive understanding of the actors and the mechanisms for the governance of the digital, can discharge this function. The previous chapters of this book have analysed what regulatory challenges are posed by AI technologies by focusing on specific regulatory areas and how these can be addressed through digital governance. This chapter presents the main findings discussed throughout the book and a vision for future directions in AI governance.

Keywords Artificial Intelligence · Digital governance · Disruption · Regulatory challenges · Future directions

J. Krämer (✉) · K. Prifti · E. Demir · K. Heine · E. Stamhuis
Erasmus School of Law, Erasmus University Rotterdam, Rotterdam, The Netherlands
e-mail: j.k.kramer@law.eur.nl

K. Prifti
e-mail: prifti@law.eur.nl

E. Demir
e-mail: demir@law.eur.nl

K. Heine
e-mail: heine@law.eur.nl

E. Stamhuis
e-mail: stamhuis@law.eur.nl

K. Prifti et al. (eds.), *Digital Governance*, Information Technology and Law Series 39,
https://doi.org/10.1007/978-94-6265-639-0_14

14.1 Introduction

The preceding chapters in this book leave little room for doubt: Artificial Intelligence (AI) technologies pose a serious challenge to the law and its functions. The contributions in this volume delve deeper into these aspects from a regulatory governance perspective, branching out into two approaches. The contributors in Part I have adopted a reflexive approach, aiming to elucidate the disruptive effects of AI in specific regulatory fields. These include, among other things, liability laws, the deployment of biometric technologies, and the use of AI for emotional detection. Part 2 includes contributions that adopt a consequentialist approach, looking for pragmatic solutions. These chapters keep an eye on the disruptive effects but aim to propose comprehensive frameworks that can be used for the purposes of digital governance. In the following paragraphs, we will elaborate on some overarching findings of these two parts and consider a vision of future directions for AI governance.

14.2 The Disruptive Impact of AI Technologies

In Part 1, contributions highlight the disruptive impact of AI. Although this impact is multifaceted, there are three types of overarching findings that authors have brought to light in this part. These are the effects of AI on incumbent doctrinal mechanisms, the need for new doctrinal concepts, and the tension between regulatory objectives. Let us review them more closely.

AI technologies can have a disruptive effect on the mechanisms of the law. For example, van Staalduinen's analysis, which focuses on clinical decision-making support systems (CDSS), reveals that AI-powered technologies raise significant doctrinal challenges, such as calling into question the dichotomy between products and services, or interrupting the causal link that is required for the well-functioning of liability laws.[1] By disrupting legal mechanisms, AI technologies not only violate the rights and liberties of individuals and groups, but they may hinder possible remedial options that should normally be accessible to victims of harm.

In addition to the challenges posed to existing doctrinal mechanisms, AI technologies often present the need for new doctrinal concepts. For example, Akar's contribution suggests that the regulation of AI-based practices of emotional recognition and prediction necessitate the development of the concept of 'emotional privacy' in order to account for human emotions where privacy risks are at stake.[2] As a result, the disruptive effects of AI elucidate the fact that doctrinal law may benefit from innovation just as much as from a critical examination of the relevance of existing concepts.

The contributions in this volume also showed that AI technologies can often reveal a tension between two or more existing regulatory objectives. As Wong-Toropainen

[1] Chap. 2.

[2] Chap. 4.

argues, for instance, regulatory measures that favour user control can have negative implications for the protection of privacy and personal data.[3] Consequently, the need to calibrate delicate trade-offs is apparent. Regulators must consider how one regulatory intervention influences other regulatory goals. These decisions, albeit technical, must not be left to the discretion of the designers but need to be managed through the frameworks of digital governance.

14.3 Designing Digital Governance Solutions

The second part of contributions focuses on the design of solutions, within the digital governance framework, to confront the disruptive impact of AI. Although they focus on specific, discrete topics, these chapters advance three overarching propositions about the objective of confronting the challenges posed by AI technologies.

First, digital governance solutions call for stronger convergence between research fields and their respective methods. Scholars tend to approach the challenges posed by AI either from a governance, ethics, law, and sociology perspective (i.e., the GELSI approach) or from a computer science and engineering perspective (i.e., the CS approach). These perspectives often remain separated even when they influence and inform one another. However, research problems and governance challenges transcend specific disciplines, necessitating a stronger convergence between these perspectives.

In this regard, interdisciplinarity is crucial. When taken further, interdisciplinary research can turn into cross disciplinary (i.e., convergent) research.[4] The difference between the two is important. Interdisciplinary research provides shared knowledge in order to solve common problems, whereas in cross disciplinary research the disciplines are fully merged, and the focus is on providing innovative solutions that were otherwise not available. Perhaps a different framing may be more appealing. If interdisciplinary research is like a potluck dinner, where guests bring their own dishes (knowledge and techniques) from different traditions (disciplines), which are shared with everyone, convergent research is like fusion cuisine, where certain ingredients (techniques) from various traditions (disciplines) are merged to create a new dish (innovative solution) that could not exist within each tradition. Nouws and Dobbe offer one such example in our book.[5] By combining a socio-legal perspective on the Rule of Law with fundamental principles from system safety, the authors propose a method to effectively govern AI systems used in public administration. Convergent, cross disciplinary research is, therefore, a promising and necessary piece of the digital governance puzzle.

Second, the contributions in this volume reveal the importance of adopting a systematic approach for the purposes of digital governance. Partly because AI is

[3] Chap. 6.

[4] Mainzer 2011.

[5] Chap. 9.

viewed (often, albeit not always correctly) as a state-of-the-art technology, scholars and regulators tend to assume that the governance of AI requires new laws, new standards, and overall new methods of governance. Some of the contributions in this book challenge this tendency. Bastigkeit Ericstam, for instance, reveals that new, disruptive practices like algorithmic management of the workplace can be effectively regulated by existing data protection provisions, which are thus far underutilised in this context.[6] Costa dos Anjos, on the other hand, points out that existing laws, namely intellectual property and competition law, have the potential to both support and hinder the goals behind the governance of AI.[7] In addition, Schmitz and colleagues remind us that digital governance initiatives that focus on standardisation tend to prioritise the development of new standards that regulate AI, consequently neglecting how AI technologies impact existing standards.[8]

Last, it is important to remember that legal solutions, framed within digital governance frameworks, often have extra-legal implications. Griffin, for instance, explores the dual nature of the role of 'code of conducts', which are mechanisms incorporated in several EU laws such as the Digital Services Act (DSA) and the Artificial Intelligence Act (AIA).[9] Codes of conduct, as a form of soft law similar to standards, present an opportunity for enhanced effectiveness of the implementation of laws. However, this increased effectiveness may come at the cost of reduced legitimacy.[10] Private actors have been known to capitalise on their involvement in soft law instruments to pursue their private, industrial interests. Although mechanisms like codes of conducts and standards are designed for the practical implementation of legislation, a great deal of interpretation and re-formulation occurs in these processes, which private actors can utilise to undermine public normative values.[11] Consequently, it is crucial to not lose sight of the political and societal implications that may arise from the implementation of valid legal solutions and to ensure that these remedies serve the common good rather than narrow, private interests.

14.4 Conclusion

The disruptive impact of AI systems is still uncertain: will the risks and harms that the preceding chapters have identified be mitigated or exacerbated? Will the proposed solutions outlined in this book realise their potential? Empirical studies are necessary to address these questions. While the contributions in this book primarily focused on the EU landscape, future research needs to consider empirical insights from other

[6] Chap. 7.

[7] Chap. 13.

[8] Chap. 10.

[9] Chap. 12.

[10] Kamara 2017.

[11] Veale and Borgesius 2021.

regions and their legal solutions to provide a more comprehensive understanding of the global implications of AI.

With the adoption of the AIA, the first law in the world specifically targeting AI systems, it remains to be seen as to whether the risks identified in this book can be sufficiently mitigated by this new legal framework. It will be interesting to see if the AIA will balance the potential and the risks stemming from the applications of AI within the EU. It remains an open question what the implementation and the enforcement of the AIA will achieve, especially considering the extensive lobbying by Big Tech during the drafting process of the AIA.[12] The answer will shed a light on the way in which the disruptive impact of digital technologies will be addressed in the future and the lessons to be learned.

References

Kamara I (2017) Co-regulation in EU personal data protection: the case of technical standards and the privacy by design standardisation 'mandate'. European journal of law and technology 8(1).

Mainzer K (2011) Interdisciplinarity and innovation dynamics. On convergence of research, technology, economy, and society. Poiesis & Praxis *7*, 275-289.

Perrigo B (2023) Big Tech Is Already Lobbying to Water Down Europe's AI Rules. Time. https://time.com/6273694/ai-regulation-europe/ Accessed 6 March 2024

Veale M, Zuiderveen Borgesius F (2021) Demystifying the Draft EU Artificial Intelligence Act—Analysing the good, the bad, and the unclear elements of the proposed approach. Computer Law Review International *22*(4), 97-112.

Julia Krämer is a PhD candidate in Empirical Legal Studies in the Department of Law and Business at the Erasmus School of Law. Her research explores whether and how mobile platforms are able to implement and foster the goals of privacy regulation, with a special focus on the role of app stores.

Kostina Prifti is a PhD candidate at Erasmus School of Law, Erasmus University, and a Junior Fellow at the Centre of Excellence on Digital Governance. His research interests lie on regulation of new technologies, with a special focus on regulation by design and Artificial Intelligence.

Esra Demir is a PhD candidate at the Erasmus School of Law and a junior fellow at the Centre of Excellence on Digital Governance. Her research focuses on the field of law and technology in the context of the co-realisation of technological innovation and data protection, from a regulatory governance perspective.

Klaus Heine is professor of Law and Economics, Jean Monnet Chair and the Director of the Center of Excellence on Digital Governance at Erasmus School of Law. He focuses on the fundamental challenges of law through digitalization, especially AI and Big Data.

[12] See, for instance, Perrigo 2023.

Evert Stamhuis Stamhuis holds a chair for Law and Innovation at Erasmus School of Law. He is Academic Director of the LLM program "Law & Technology, Governance, AI & Legal Tech" and Senior Fellow of the Centre of Excellence on Digital Governance.

SPRINGER NATURE

GPSR Compliance

The European Union's (EU) General Product Safety Regulation (GPSR) is a set of rules that requires consumer products to be safe and our obligations to ensure this.

If you have any concerns about our products, you can contact us on ProductSafety@springernature.com

In case Publisher is established outside the EU, the EU authorized representative is:

Springer Nature Customer Service Center GmbH
Europaplatz 3
69115 Heidelberg, Germany

The manufacturer's authorised representative in the EU is Springer Nature Customer Service Centre GmbH, Europaplatz 3, 69115 Heidelberg, Germany. If you have any concerns regarding our products, please contact ProductSafety@springernature.com

Printed and bound by CPI Group (UK) Ltd, Croydon, CR0 4YY
30/09/2026
02225564-0011